NATURALLY CURIOUS DAY BY DAY

A Photographic Field Guide and Daily Visit to the Forests,
Fields, and Wetlands of Eastern North America

MARY HOLLAND

Winner of the National Outdoor Book Award

Published by Stackpole Books
An imprint of Globe Pequot
Trade Division of The Rowman & Littlefield Publishing Group, Inc.
4501 Forbes Boulevard, Suite 200, Lanham, Maryland 20706
www.rowman.com

Distributed by
NATIONAL BOOK NETWORK
800-462-6420

All photos by Mary Holland except: p. preface, top right (Sharon Fisher); p. 2, middle left (John Holland); pp. 5, bottom left; 133, top left; 152, bottom left; 419, bottom left (Mary Sue Henszey); pp. 24, top right; 27, bottom right; 41, top left; 417, top left inset (Susan Holland); p. 31, top right (Otto Wurzburg); p. 50, bottom left (Virginia Barlow); pp. 73, top right (Heather Jacoby); p. 70, bottom right (Patsy Fortney); p. 90, top left (Chiho Kaneko); pp. 66, bottom left (Jeannie Killam); pp. 121, top left; 194, top right; 234, top right; 283, bottom left (Sadie Brown); p. 281, bottom left (Tom Hodgson); p. 381, middle left (Tony Ickes and Susan Holland); p. 419, top right (Bridie McGreavy).

Library of Congress Cataloging-in-Publication Data Available

ISBN 978-0-8117-1412-9 (paperback)
ISBN 978-0-8117-6559-6 (e-book)

DEDICATION

I dedicate this book and all the love of the natural world that went into it to Otis Sumner Brown, so that he can know that every day of the year there is magic to be found right outside his door.

acknowledgments

Enormous gratitude to my Upper Valley naturalist friends who share my passion and support me in every way possible—Ginny, Joan, Erin, Sandra, Alfred, John, Chris, Charlie, Jeannie, Mary Sue, and Kay.

Gratefulness and appreciation to the many friends and strangers who have picked up the phone to let me know about a sighting they've made that I might like to photograph.

Heartfelt thanks to Ginny Barlow, gratis editor extraordinaire, and fellow literary critics Joan Waltermire and Maria van Beuren. Thank you to those of you who allowed me to use your photographs to enhance this book.

And love to three women who have always understood and accepted me, quirks and all—Titus, my rock; Sadie, my heart; and Anne, my soul supporter.

contents

Let
curiosity
open the
door to the
natural world ~
a connection to
and compassion
for all living
things will follow.

—Mary Holland

preface

"All time stops. All thoughts cease. There is only this. This precious moment—of connection."
—Tom Dodgson

Naturally Curious Day by Day is a collection of short essays about daily observations that can be made year-round in the Northeast. The pages of this book invite you to walk fields, woods, and wetlands frequently in order to see the changes that occur and to make new discoveries. Regardless of where you live, in the city or in a remote location, there are endless places to explore, from cracks in a sidewalk to crevices in a stone wall. *Naturally Curious Day by Day* introduces the reader to amphibians, reptiles, birds, mammals, insects, arachnids, plants, fungi, and slime molds that you may observe through the seasons. Because of their size, lifestyle, or numbers, some of the species mentioned may not be familiar, but most should be. Curiosity, sharp eyes, and anticipation are the essential tools of a naturalist. If you are reading this book, you are already curious. A growing familiarity with the natural world will enhance your eyesight. I hope *Naturally Curious Day by Day* will enable you to know what to anticipate seeing or hearing on any given day of the year.

Mary Holland

JANUARY

Signs of Birds Feeding

Signs of avian feeding are plentiful if you take the time to look, and many of these signs are created by species of sap- and insect-eating woodpeckers. These birds use a number of different strategies to reach their food. Stout beaks and anatomical adaptations allow members of the woodpecker family to drill into hard substrates, such as wood, in order to reach the insects and sap within. These excavations assume a number of forms, depending on the species of woodpecker, the particular source of food, and the technique used to obtain it.

One type of excavation that is used in the spring and the summer when sap is flowing is the drilling of yellow-bellied sapsuckers. The resulting similarly sized holes tend to be made in horizontal lines, perpendicular to the tree trunk, near the base of the crown or on the trunk above the lowest living branches. Sapsuckers consume both the sap and the insects that are attracted to the sap. Even when they have scarred over, old sapsucker holes are very obvious.

Hairy, downy, and pileated woodpeckers are more interested in obtaining insects than sap. The holes they drill to reach these insects are, for the most part, larger than those of sapsuckers. The pattern of hairy and downy woodpecker holes appears to be relatively random, whereas pileated woodpecker holes, in addition to being larger, are often arranged vertically on a tree trunk. The openings of the feeding holes of pileated woodpeckers are somewhat rectangular, whereas their nest cavity openings are more circular.

Woodpeckers also engage in the practice of bark sloughing and bark scaling when searching for insects. Bark sloughing is the practice of removing the entire layer of dead bark from a tree. This leaves large patches of bare tree, often with beak marks perpendicular to the trunk or a branch. Bark scaling, on the other hand, refers to the removal of individual scales of bark, which leaves a patchwork pattern of bark on the tree.

Sometimes you may come upon a seed husk or nut shell wedged into a crevice in the bark of a tree, which serves as a vise for a nuthatch or black-capped chickadee. These birds often choose one spot where they repeatedly take seeds and open them.

It takes a keener eye to find the flaps of bark that a downy woodpecker leaves when it finds a scale insect under the bark of a white or yellow birch. Upon discovering the overwintering insect, the woodpecker pecks and cuts a vertical line in the bark and pries under the cut to expose the insect, tearing the bark above and below the cut. This leaves a tiny flap of bark, still attached on one side to the tree, poking out from the trunk. If you find one flap, you usually will find many more.

In general, hairy woodpeckers tend to drill into trees more frequently than downy woodpeckers. Downies are more apt to work on softer substrates, such as the stems of sumac and phragmites. Goldenrod ball galls, abnormal plant growths where the larvae of a gall fly spend the winter, are a favorite drilling site for downy woodpeckers during colder months. A small, ¼-inch-diameter hole in the side of a goldenrod ball gall indicates that the larva is probably no longer in residence.

Red fox trail in the snow.

Downy woodpecker

Pileated woodpecker feeding holes.

Goldenrod ball gall drilled into by downy woodpecker.

Great gray owl impression in snow.

One of the most beautiful signs of avian feeding has to be the wing impressions left by a hawk or owl diving after prey in the snow. Although it may signal the demise of one animal, it also portrays the grace and beauty of another.

Conifer Survival in Winter

Winter poses challenges for every living thing, two of the most crucial being to obtain enough water and nutrients to stay alive, and to not freeze. Humans have it easy: we build houses, wear layers of clothes, bury our water pipes, and, thanks to freezers and grocery stores, have relatively fresh

produce year round. Other animals and plants, so often considered lower forms of life, have come up with equally, if not more, impressive strategies.

Trees, unlike animals, cannot move to avoid extreme winter conditions, and unlike some plants, they don't have the option to overwinter as seeds or rhizomes. So over the years they have adapted in ways that allow them to survive standing in place. Hardwood (deciduous) trees, due to the shortage of available water in winter, lose their leaves to minimize transpiration of water vapor into the air, as their broad leaves are a major source of water loss. But conifers—all but the larches—survive and keep most of their leaves through the winter. Conifers shed their leaves, too, but they keep them for more than one year, unlike deciduous trees.

The structure of a conifer leaf, or needle, is superbly adapted for retaining moisture. To begin with, the leaves of conifers have less surface area than deciduous leaves, due to their needlelike shape, so less water is lost. They also have a waxy, water-repellent coating, cutin, which prevents excessive loss of water. Leaves have little openings, or pores, called stomata, through which gases such as carbon dioxide, water vapor, and oxygen move rapidly in and out. The stomata of conifer needles close more tightly than those of deciduous leaves, which also reduces water loss.

Interestingly, sunny winter days are more stressful for conifers than cloudy days, as far as water retention. Because most needles are dark colored, they readily absorb heat. The temperature of the needles rises considerably above the temperature of the air, causing greater water loss. On a cloudy, windy day, the clouds block solar energy, and wind removes heat from the needles, reducing water loss.

When it comes to freezing, ice crystals inside plant cells are usually fatal, but ice between cells is not. Conifers exhibit a protective behavior known as extracellular freezing. By altering the lipid concentration within their cells, conifers induce water to migrate out of their cells, which lowers the freezing temperature inside the cells. Water outside cell walls freezes first. As this water changes from liquid to solid, small amounts of heat are released, and this heat helps prevent the cellular water from freezing.

The plumbing of conifers differs considerably from that of broad-leaved trees. Given an adequate amount of snow, soil does not freeze, which means some water is available to trees. Deciduous trees lose most of their ability to move water during the winter, as their capillary action is broken after the first freeze. Conifers, however, transport water in tubes that have valves that allow water movement during the winter, should conditions be just right. Conifer cell walls are also stronger than the cell walls of deciduous trees and can better withstand ice expansion.

Even though the conelike shape of most conifers allows snow to more easily slide off their branches, conifers do have higher leaf densities than hardwoods. This means snow can accumulate enough to break branches. To offset this, the branches of most conifers grow at more obtuse angles to the main stem, allowing branches to shed snow with less bending. The longer wood fibers of conifers also provide more flexibility.

Spruce trees.

There are many factors that contribute to the ability of

conifers to survive in a cold, snowy climate. Not only do they survive, but on sunny days, their leaves may even photosynthesize. Their adaptability allows conifers to walk a fine line between water loss, replenishing leaf moisture, and handling the weight of snow.

White-Breasted and Red-Breasted Nuthatches

A bird feeder serves as a gathering spot for a community of seed-eating birds, and just as a small town's general store attracts an assortment of personalities, you can find all kinds of traits in the feathered visitors at a feeder. There are bullying blue jays, twinkle-eyed tufted titmice, chipper chickadees, and gluttonous grosbeaks, to name a few. Dressed in their "tuxedos" are the natty nuthatches. Their name derives from their habit of taking seeds in the fall and winter and caching them in bark crevices, sapsucker holes, and even in the ground, for later consumption.

One quick glance at a white- or red-breasted nuthatch, and its dapper appearance is unmistakable. With clean lines, compact bodies, and chisel-shaped, slightly upturned bills, nuthatches are one of the more sophisticated-looking birds that grace our feeders. Their appeal doesn't end with their appearance, however. It's their unusual foraging technique which often first captures our attention.

Unlike another insect-eating, tree trunk–climbing bird, the brown creeper, which spirals up tree trunks gleaning insects, nuthatches often do the opposite: they spiral downward. They can be observed moving quickly sideways and upward as well, with little regard for the direction in which they are going, particularly out on branches. When you see one on the trunk of a tree, however, it is often descending head-down. Because of this approach, nuthatches are able to detect insects and insect eggs in bark crevices that would be hidden from view for most birds.

Eastern hemlock leaves.

There are some fairly obvious differences, both physical and behavioral, between the white- and red-breasted nuthatch. The white-breasted is larger than the red-breasted, and its plumage differs significantly, as their respective names denote. Experienced ears can discriminate between the two birds' calls: the nasal *yank yank—yank* of the red-breasted nuthatch, said to resemble the blast of a tiny, tin trumpet, and the white-breasted nuthatch's six to eight notes that end with a slight rising inflection.

The white-breasted nuthatch's personality appears to be more staid than the red-breasted nuthatch's. Arthur C. Bent wrote in his book *Life Histories of North American Nuthatches, Wrens, Thrashers, and Their Allies*:

"The white-breasted nuthatch is a droll, earnest little bird, rather sedate and unemotional. He is no great musician and seems to lack a sense of humor. He has none of the irrepressible fidgetiness of the house wren, none of the charming happiness of the song sparrow; he appears to take life on a matter-of-fact level."

In comparison, red-breasted nuthatches appear to be far more sociable and more active than white-breasted nuthatches. Bent describes them as "so happy, animated and lively . . . their voices have such a range of expression that they almost talk—a playful gathering of talkative, irrepressible, woodland gnomes."

While both of these nuthatches tend to associate with black-capped chickadees and tufted titmice in what are called "foraging flocks" in the winter, their breeding grounds differ. The red-breasted nuthatch has a preference for conifers, while the white-breasted nuthatch is more likely to nest in mature deciduous woods.

Both species of nuthatches build their nests in tree cavities; white-breasted nuthatches generally nest in an existing cavity, such as an old woodpecker hole, and red-breasted nuthatches usually excavate their own cavity in a rotted stub or branch of a dead tree. All nuthatches perform some sort of nest entrance modification, but the nature of this modification differs with these two species. Red-breasted nuthatches smear the perimeter of their nesting hole with globules of fir, spruce, or pine pitch, continually adding fresh pitch until their young are fledged. It is thought that this might prevent insects, small birds, or mammals from entering the cavity. Adult nuthatches have been observed flying directly into their nest cavity without touching the rim of the entrance. White-breasted nuthatches engage in "bill sweeping" at the entrance to their nesting cavity, which consists of prolonged sweeping of the bill in a wide arc in or outside the cavity, often while holding an insect, such as a toxic blister beetle, in their bill. One theory is that the crushed insects may repel squirrels from taking over the cavity for their own nests or perhaps preying on eggs or chicks.

Red-breasted nuthatch.

White-breasted nuthatch.

Every so often, red-breasted nuthatches appear in fairly large numbers at winter feeders due to their southward movement, and this is referred to as an irruption. When the coniferous seed crop is poor in the north, certain seed-eating birds, including red-breasted nuthatches, seek food farther south. Even if there's a good seed crop in Canada, however, both red-breasted and white-breasted nuthatches should be plentiful and easy to watch and admire at feeders in the Northeast.

JANUARY 1

Birds Keeping Warm

Birds that remain in the Northeast year-round must not only be able to find enough food in the winter to produce heat and energy, they must find a way to retain the heat they produce. Various strategies have evolved, but feather structure and function play an important role for the winter survival of all birds.

There are different types of feathers, each designed for a different function. The contour, or visible outer feathers, and down feathers are the primary insulating types of feathers. A contour feather consists of a central, hollow shaft on either side of which are many interlocking rows of barbs. They often have interlocking barbs only at the ends, on the part not covered by an overlapping feather. The bottommost, unconnected barbs on these feathers are similar to those of down feathers—not interlinking, but loose and fluffy.

When the temperature dips, birds puff out their contour feathers, making the bird look huge. This action and the structure of the bottom portion of the contour feathers increase the number and size of air pockets between the bird's feathers and its skin. This space provides excellent insulation, preventing much of the bird's body heat from escaping.

Fisher and Mink Tracks

Like all members of the Mustelidae, the weasel family, fishers and mink have five toes on both front and back feet. Often all five digits do not register, but in prime tracking snow, you can frequently see them. Typically, mink tracks are found near water, and fisher tracks are found under a canopy, not in the open. Where you have both water and trees, it is possible to see signs of both animals. Their relative size helps to distinguish them. In this photograph, the smaller mink tracks are in the middle and are heading toward the top of the photograph, and the fisher tracks (topmost and bottommost) are heading toward the bottom of the photograph.

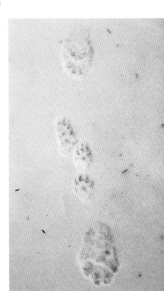

Fisher and mink tracks.

JANUARY 2

Snowshoe Hare Urine

Snowshoe hare scat is distinctive: round, brown, pea-size, fibrous pellets. Equally, if not more, distinct is hare urine, which sometimes is orange,

Male evening grosbeak.

Snowshoe hare
urine and tracks.

red, or pinkish, depending on their diet. Often mistaken for blood, snowshoe hare urine has this color because of chemical compounds called porphyrins which are present in the chlorophyll molecules of green plants that hares consume. These compounds have such vibrant pigments that they were originally extracted from plants and used as dye for clothing.

Sugar Maple Buds and Bark

Maples have what is referred to as opposite branching—the buds, leaves, and branches are positioned opposite one another. If you look at the pointed terminal bud of a sugar maple you will see that the two lateral buds, on either side of the terminal bud, are directly across from each other. This is relatively rare in the woody plant world, and you can narrow down the identity of a tree significantly if you determine that it has opposite branching—maples, ashes, and dogwoods, among others, share this characteristic.

The appearance of a sugar maple's bark depends on the age of the tree. Saplings and younger branches have quite smooth bark, like the branch on the right in the photograph, whereas the bark of an old sugar maple is furrowed with vertical ridges curled outward along one side.

Snow Scorpionflies Active

It always comes as a surprise to see tiny creatures moving nimbly over the surface of the snow. However, there are quite a few insects and spiders that do, thanks to the glycerol that they produce in their body fluids that keeps them from freezing. Snow scorpionflies are tiny insects that are more closely related to fleas than to other scorpionflies. The wings of snow scorpionflies are reduced to bristles or are absent, and they are somewhat compressed, making their resemblance to fleas noticeable. At sub-freezing temperatures, it would be very hard to generate enough energy for maintaining flight muscles, and thus, wings have essentially been eliminated.

Sugar maple bark, old
(left) and young (right).

Sugar maple buds.

Snow scorpionfly.

JANUARY 3

Fisher Beds

As a fisher travels, it leaves many signs in addition to tracks: trampled conifer saplings; a stump or a log where it has marked its territory by depositing urine, scat, or both; and resting spots, often at the base of a tree. Fishers are active day and night—often traveling many miles a day—but even they have to stop now and then to rest. More often than not they defecate before departing.

Fisher bed and scat at base of tree.

JANUARY 4

Black Bear Hibernacula

Black bears den in a range of places, including under logs and stumps, under the branches of a fallen tree, and inside caves and hollow trees. Most adult black bears are not completely protected from the elements while they are hibernating and/or raising cubs, as there is usually a fairly large opening, and the hibernating bear is exposed to the cold. The amount of exposure can vary tremendously, from a relatively protected hollow under a log to complete exposure within a dense thicket or stand of conifers.

Pictured are three different black bear dens: one under a log (top), one under a fallen tree (middle), and the third in the middle of a stand of spruce with a bed of spruce boughs (bottom).

JANUARY 5

How Birds' Feet Stay Warm in Winter

While feathers are excellent insulators, the legs and feet of most birds lack this protective covering. Because of this, legs and feet are a major source of heat loss for birds. Birds' feet are mostly bone and tendons, so, unlike mammals, they have a limited supply of nerves, blood vessels, or muscles to freeze. Their feet are also covered with scales which, like our hair, aren't living tissue and thus are less susceptible to freezing.

Some birds, including waterfowl, gulls, and penguins, have what is called countercurrent heat exchange: arteries and veins in their legs run parallel and in contact with each other. As the warm blood of the arteries enters the legs, the heat is transferred to the returning cold blood of the veins. This allows the cooler blood to get heated up somewhat before reentering the body, which minimizes the heat lost to the cold air. Under very warm conditions, the countercurrent heat exchange mechanism can be bypassed.

Birds exhibit behavioral adaptations as well, such as standing on one leg and tucking the other among breast feathers, reducing by half the amount of unfeathered limb surface area exposed. By sitting down and covering both legs, even on ice, heat loss from limbs is minimized.

Mallards and common merganser on ice.

Gray tree frog.

Gray Tree Frogs in Winter

Gray tree frogs seek out protected underground nooks and crannies, as well as mammal burrows, in which to hibernate. Like the spring peeper and the wood frog, gray tree frogs survive while having much of their body frozen for several days, at up to 20 degrees below zero. The accumulation of glycerol in their blood enables them to be this cold tolerant.

JANUARY 6

Cold Snaps and Hardy Invasive Invertebrates

There is a plus side to the sub-zero temperatures the Northeast experiences in winter: cold weather may decrease the number of invasive pests. An example of this is the hemlock woolly adelgid, the aphid-like introduced insect decimating the eastern hemlock population, which succumbs at 4 or 5 degrees Fahrenheit. However, some insects are not fazed by the cold until it dips way below zero. At -20 degrees, roughly half of the emerald ash borer larvae (an invasive beetle that kills ash trees) overwintering in trees will die. Once the temperature reaches -30 degrees, there's a 90 percent mortality rate. Bed bugs face instant death at -22 degrees, but it takes twenty-four hours to kill them at -11 degrees and seventy-two hours to kill them at 0 degrees.

Emerald ash borer.

Unfortunately, once an invasive insect becomes established, even if its numbers go way down for whatever reason, it usually rebounds in several years' time. Some invertebrates are not affected by cold. The black-legged (deer) ticks that reside on moose, deer, mice, birds, and other hosts can withstand sub-zero temperatures because they are warmed by their hosts' bodies. In order for ticks to succumb to the cold, the frigid air has to last until May, when the fertilized female ticks fall off their hosts to lay their eggs.

Wild Turkeys' Biggest Winter Challenge Is Deep Snow

Wild turkeys do not migrate. During the winter they often separate into three distinct groups—adult males (toms), young males (jakes), and females (hens) of all ages—and spend their days seeking out plant (90 percent of their diet) and animal (10 percent of their diet) matter. In the summer, greens and insects make up much of their diet; in the winter, turkeys rely heavily on acorns, beechnuts, crabapples, and hawthorn fruit, as well as agricultural grains such as corn, buckwheat, soybeans, and oats.

Wild turkey in snow.

The winter survival of wild turkeys depends more on snow conditions that affect the procuring of food than on the temperature. Researchers have found that although turkeys can tolerate very cold temperatures, they need adequate food to keep from losing significant weight and eventually starving to death. Turkeys can't walk on or dig through deep snow in order to reach nutritious nuts. For this reason, they rely heavily on agricultural fields that are windblown and provide relatively easy access to grains.

JANUARY 7

American Crows Roosting

After the breeding season, American crows begin to gather in small, communal roosts. By early to mid-winter the number of crows occupying a roost reaches its maximum. In the morning, shortly before and after daybreak, crows leave their nocturnal roosts in small groups and fly in all directions to feeding grounds. After having spent the day feeding, roughly two to three hours before sunset, small groups of crows gather in pre-roost sites, and from these they fly along regular flight lines to their nocturnal roost. They are often joined by additional crows at pre-roost sites visited along the way. The closer the crows get to their final roost, the larger the group becomes. The same roosting sites may be used for many years, and the number of birds in them varies from a few hundred to many thousands.

American crows roosting.

Eastern Coyotes Marking

The scat of coyotes is typically found in the middle of trails and occasionally on prominent spots such as stones or where trails cross. It is used as a territorial marker for other coyotes. These predators often mark their food sources as well as their territories. The pictured coyote scat contains deer hair and was deposited on top of a deer scapula near the remains of a deer. The deer's rib cage was picked clean, with the ribs gnawed down to nubs, indicating that the deer carcass may have served as the coyote's food supply for several days.

Coyote scat on white-tailed deer scapula.

Meadow Vole Sign

Meadow voles usually deposit their scat along their runs under the snow, in dead-end tunnels that are used as latrines and near their nests. This scat, however, was deposited right next to the entrance to the tiny rodent's subnivean tunnels. Meadow vole scat is tubular with blunt ends and measures ⅛ to ⁵⁄₁₆ inch long.

Meadow vole scat.

JANUARY 8

Snowy Owl Irruption

A change in food supply periodically causes birds that normally remain in northern forests to migrate outside of their normal range in search of food. A shortage of seeds and buds in the north may well cause an influx of redpolls, finches, siskins, and grosbeaks in the Northeast.

Snowy owl.

Some birds of prey may also move south when seed crops are poor and cannot support the rodent populations needed by raptors. Typically, if prey remains abundant, predator populations soar. An abundance of lemmings promotes a highly productive breeding season for snowy owls and results in unusually high numbers of young owls. If there isn't enough prey in the fall and winter to support the increased snowy owl population, some individuals, often the young of the year, are forced to disperse in order to find an adequate food supply. This southward dispersal is referred to as an irruption. Irruptions are somewhat cyclical, with snowy owls appearing south of their Arctic range every four years or so, timed to the lemmings' four-year cycle.

Beaver Breath

It is very subtle, but in winter, especially when it is very cold outside, there is a way to tell if a beaver lodge is occupied. The temperature inside the lodge remains relatively stable at around 34 degrees. When snow falls, it provides added insulation, raising the interior temperature of the

Inhabited beaver lodge on cold winter day.

Horned larks.

lodge slightly. A layer of fat and thick fur keep beavers warmer than the air inside the lodge, plus they raise their body temperatures even more by sleeping piled on top of one another. All the moist, warm air that beavers give off through breathing and evaporation escapes through the vent that goes up through the center of the roof of the lodge. When the warm air inside the lodge rises and hits the cold air outside the lodge, it condenses and forms water vapor that is visible, indicating that there are warm-blooded animals inside.

JANUARY 9

Horned Larks

Although horned larks breed in the Northeast, they are usually seen in the winter, as they are much more common as winter visitors, when they tend to form large flocks mixed with snow buntings and Lapland longspurs. Larks are often in open fields foraging for seeds. When snow is deep and weeds are buried, horned larks frequently seek farmyards where they can obtain grain.

The male's display flight in the spring is as impressive as the American woodcock's. He flies up into the sky as high as 800 feet. Singing, he then circles, closes his wings, and drops headfirst almost to the ground, where he opens his wings at the last second. He then struts around the

female with his wings drooped and "horns" (tufts of black feathers) erect.

Fishers Hunting

Fisher tracks led to a disturbance in the snow that was intentionally made by the fisher. With its feet, the fisher trampled a circular impression in the snow. When a fisher has killed prey and satiated its appetite, it often caches the leftover food in the snow for later consumption, sometimes marking it to discourage other animals from eating it. Initially this appeared to be such a cache. However, close inspection revealed that the center of the circle is not a mound of snow, but that it had been thoroughly packed down by the fisher.

In the center of the circle a hole leads to a mouse or vole tunnel. It would appear that the fisher, detecting the presence of a small rodent,

Fisher sign.

trapped it by methodically scraping snow toward the center of the circle that surrounded the rodent, forcing the escaping mouse or vole to expose itself at the perimeter of the circle. A drop of blood indicates that its hunting strategy was successful.

JANUARY 10

Ruffed Grouse Crop

Some birds, especially those that eat seeds, buds, leaves, and nuts, such as ruffed grouse, eat food very rapidly—faster than it can be passed through the digestive system. These birds usually have a

pouchlike structure called a crop where food is stored to be digested later, when the birds are not out in the open and susceptible to predators. This rapid consumption and storage of food by grouse, often at dawn and dusk, is referred to as "budding."

Ruffed grouse crop contents.

Examining the contents of the crops of road-killed grouse is one way to learn more about this adaptive behavior. The contents of a grouse's crop vary with the season: more herbaceous in the summer and more woody in the winter. The pictured ruffed grouse crop contained 232 male birch flower buds, or catkins.

Ruffed grouse.

Snow Fleas Appear in January Thaw

One rarely even thinks about snow fleas, a species of springtail, until snow falls and then starts to melt. This is when these tiny, wingless arthropods that catapult themselves through the air seem to magically appear out of nowhere. They are present year round, with the great majority living in the soil, feeding on fungi, algae, decaying plant matter, and bacteria. They work their way to the surface of the snow, crawling up the trunks of trees, plant stems, and the sides of rocks where an open channel

Snow fleas.

allows their migration. Thousands can be found on melting snow, especially in tracks or other depressions. No one is sure why they exhibit this behavior, although some scientists feel that these migrations are triggered by overcrowding and lack of food. Eventually those that survive on top of the snow make a return trip into the soil. Formerly classified as insects, snowfleas are now categorized as hexapods, due to features they have which insects do not.

JANUARY 11

Muskrat Lodges in Winter

Muskrats are susceptible to cold and wind and spend a lot of time inside their lodges in the winter. The foot-thick walls of a lodge act as insulation, keeping out the cold. These shelters, constructed with aquatic plants, brush, and mud, are usually situated on a foundation of brush or a stump or occasionally are built from the bottom of a wetland. Inside a muskrat lodge there

Muskrat lodge.

is a snug, dry chamber, slightly above the water level, with one or two plunge holes leading to the water. This inner chamber serves a multitude of purposes, from a place for bearing and raising young to a sheltered spot for eating and sleeping. Even though muskrats are highly territorial and aggressive toward each other, up to ten individuals may share a lodge during winter, huddling together to stay warm. The temperature in the lodge is about 36 degrees higher than the outside temperature.

Great Horned Owls Courting

The intense hooting of great horned owls begins in late December or early January, about a month before actual mating takes place. Males call during most seasons of the year, but the period when they hoot vigorously lasts for a month or six weeks. During the mating season the deep, rich tones of the males are occasionally interspersed with the higher and huskier notes of the females.

Male great horned owl calling.

The answering calls of the females are heard for only a week or two, toward the end of the six-week period.

Eventually, when a male and female approach each other, they do a sort of courtship dance. The male cocks his tail, swells his white bib, and with much bobbing and jerking, utters a series of deep sonorous calls that elicit calling responses by the female. He cautiously approaches the female, continuing much tail-bobbing and posturing. The owls nod, bow, and spread their wings as well as shake their heads. Courting pairs have been observed engaging in high-pitched giggling, screaming, and bill-snapping. Mutual bill rubbing and preening also occurs. Copulation concludes the courtship ritual, with both owls hooting at a rate of four or five hoots per second throughout copulation, which lasts four to seven seconds.

JANUARY 12

Snowshoe Hare Runs

Hares, like cottontails, have runs throughout their territory. These runs are well-maintained escape routes, and the snowshoe hare's life depends on knowing every twist and turn they take.

During the summer, hares keep their runs free of branches by pruning them back. In the winter, they also have to prune as the snow gets higher and the runs encounter more branches. They spend considerable time and energy packing down the snow on these runways so they will have a clear, hard surface on which, if it's necessary, they can make their escape. This runway construction is done by hopping up and down, progressing slowly, inch by inch. It looks like

Snowshoe hare run.

13

many hares have passed by, but it is usually done by one individual and runs through its territory. Snowshoe hares are nocturnal, but during long or heavy snowstorms, they will come out and pack their run during the day.

Bobcats Hunting

The diet of a bobcat varies with the season and the availability of prey. Although known for their preference for snowshoe hares and rabbits, bobcats eat a wide variety of prey, including wild turkeys, deer, small rodents, skunks, raccoons, birds, insects, and even carrion. The manner in which bobcats, as well as most cats, secure their prey differs greatly from that of canids, such as foxes and coyotes. Unlike members of the dog family, which frequently chase down their prey, bobcats move slowly and stealthily through an area, pausing and sitting frequently, hoping to see prey before prey sees them. They generally do not cover large distances while hunting. Bobcats have what are called "hunting lays," spots where they lie with their feet under them, ready to pounce on prey passing by.

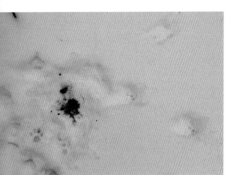

A bobcat caught and killed a red squirrel at this site.

JANUARY 13

White-Tailed Deer Digging for Ferns

White-tailed deer have high energy requirements during the winter and consequently graze and browse on the most nutritious plants they can find. Acorns contain large amounts of fats and carbohydrates, and the fat reserves that result

White-tailed deer digging site.

from a diet of acorns are a source of energy for the deer during periods of winter stress.

As winter progresses, perhaps to have a change from woody browse, deer often turn to ferns. They dig down through the snow with their hooves until they reach the fronds of evergreen species of ferns. How they know where to dig for these delicacies is a mystery. In winter, patches of exposed forest floor and the remnants of fern fronds are a common sight in deciduous or mixed woods where there are white-tailed deer.

Red Fox Beds

Red foxes spend most nights curled up in the open air—winter, summer, fall, and spring. Often they sleep in open fields, in an elevated area where they can keep an eye out for approaching danger. They curl up in a ball and wrap their bushy tail around themselves, covering their faces. When foxes sleep in the open, they usually

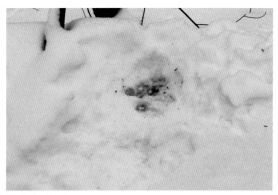

Red fox bed.

doze for fifteen to twenty-five seconds and then wake up, look around carefully, and nap again. Only when a fox sleeps in dense cover does it go into a heavy sleep, waking every hour or so.

JANUARY 14

White Pine Cones

Old (bottom) and new (top) white pine seed cones.

The female, or seed, cones of most pines take two seasons to mature, and the cones of white pines are no exception. While the tiny male cones live only a few months in the spring, until their pollen has been dispersed and they drop to the ground, white pine seed cones develop over two summers. This means that both last year's cones as well as this year's can be seen on a white pine right now. After the seeds in last year's cones have been dispersed, the cones will fall off the tree. In late winter, you will find mostly year-old cones on white pines; new cones will develop this coming summer to replace the ones that fall off the tree this winter.

Great Gray Owl Irruption

Every few winters, great gray owls move—usually en masse—from their boreal breeding grounds in search of food. These mass movements, or irruptions, tend to occur every three or four years; the written record of this phenomenon dates back to the early nineteenth century. Typically, there will be several years of plentiful prey (meadow voles, for the most part), which results in successful great gray owl reproduction. This is often followed by a precipitous crash in the vole population, which leads to an irruption further south. In eastern Canada, when meadow voles become scarce, great gray owls will move rather than feed on an alternative food source such as other small mammals. Those birds that relocate and seek prey elsewhere have a better survival rate than those that remain on their breeding grounds.

Great gray owl.

JANUARY 15

Black-Capped Chickadees Singing Spring Song

Even though there is snow in the air and we still have months of winter ahead of us, a promise of spring can be heard at this time of year. Black-capped chickadees are named for their *chick-a-dee-dee-dee* winter song, but when the days start to lengthen, they begin singing their mating song. Longer days stimulate the production of hormones which initiate breeding behavior. Sounding to some like *fee-bee* and to others like *hey-sweetie*, their delightful song consists of two whistles, each about half a second long, with the second whistle a lower pitch than the first. Although these cavity nesters won't breed

Black-capped chickadee.

until April, we will continue to be serenaded by their courtship song throughout the rest of the winter.

How Beavers Stay Warm in Cold Water

Thick ice has usually formed on ponds by now, and thus beavers are restricted to life beneath it. Because their food supply pile is stashed outside of the lodge, beavers continue to spend time in the water, fetching food. The rationale behind a thick winter coat, waterproofing oil, and a thick layer of fat becomes obvious at this time of year. At 32 degrees a beaver's resistance to heat loss in water is about one-eighth of that in air at the same temperature. This is because its fur is compressed in the water, allowing the insulating air between the hairs to escape—a beaver's pelt accounts for about 24 percent of its total insulation in water and body fat is responsible for the rest. Heat is also retained through a beaver's tail and hind legs, which serve

Beaver.

as heat exchangers. In the summer, a beaver can lose 25 percent of its body heat through its tail, but it only loses 2 percent in winter.

JANUARY 16

Life in a Beaver Lodge

Inside a beaver lodge there are two areas. The main room, where beavers enter and dry off, measures roughly 4 to 5 feet wide and 2 feet high. A second, higher and smaller area serves as the sleeping quarters for the two to twelve beavers that inhabit a lodge in the winter. Wood

Beaver lodge interior.

chips and strips serve as bedding for the beavers. Defecation takes place in the water, and the wood chips are periodically pushed into the water and retrieved after they have been cleansed.

Pileated Woodpecker Droppings Reveal Winter Diet

A pileated woodpecker's diet often shifts with the seasons. One study found that the primary food of these woodpeckers was fruit in fall, carpenter ants in winter, wood-boring beetle larvae in early spring, and a variety of insects in summer. During the winter, with the help of its impressive beak, the woodpecker pries off long slivers of wood from trees containing carpenter ants and exposes

Pileated woodpecker droppings.

Green frog.

the ant galleries. It then uses its long, pointed, barbed tongue and its sticky saliva to catch and extract ants from the ant galleries inside the tree. This winter diet can be confirmed by examining the contents of a pileated woodpecker's droppings. Finding these droppings is simply a matter of locating a tree that has a considerable pile of wood chips at the base, indicating that a pileated woodpecker has spent a lot of time working on the tree—long enough to have deposited droppings on and amongst the chips. The droppings crumble easily and reveal a multitude of tiny, black, shiny carpenter ant exoskeletons along with surprisingly few bits of wood fiber.

Like humans, birds excrete metabolic waste products, mainly nitrogen, which remains after food is broken down. Humans excrete waste nitrogen as urea in urine, which is diluted with water. Birds, needing to be as light as possible for efficient flight, do not have heavy, water-filled bladders. They excrete nitrogen as a chemical called uric acid in a concentrated form, with no dilution necessary. The white outer coating of bird droppings is uric acid, and the insides of the droppings are the actual feces, or the indigestible parts of a bird's diet. Birds simultaneously evacuate uric acid and feces from an opening just under the tail called the cloaca, or vent. The whitewashed end is due to uric acid.

JANUARY 17

Aquatic Frogs Hibernating in Ponds

Most aquatic frogs, such as this green frog, have been deep in hibernation for several months. A common misconception is that frogs spend the winter the way aquatic turtles do, dug into the mud at the bottom of a pond or stream. In fact, hibernating frogs would suffocate if they dug into the mud for an extended period of time. A hibernating turtle's metabolism slows down so drastically that it can get by on the mud's meager oxygen supply. Hibernating aquatic frogs, however, must be near oxygen-rich water, and they spend a good part of the winter just lying on top of the mud or only partially buried. They may even slowly swim around from time to time.

Raccoons Active in Mild Weather

If there is a January thaw and mild weather sets in, raccoons will actively roam the woods and fields, visiting open water and leaving signs of their presence. When cold weather arrives in the

Raccoon tracks.

fall, raccoons search out hollow trees, logs, crevices, and the like, in which to den. They become dormant, but do not hibernate. If the temperature rises above 30 degrees at night they become active, but once the temperature drops back to sub-zero temperatures, they retreat to their dens. During mild winters, raccoons remain active; during colder winters, they are usually dormant between late November and March. A winter with vacillating temperatures has them going in and out of dormancy.

JANUARY 18

Praying Mantis Egg Case

In the fall, after mating, the female praying mantis lays up to four hundred eggs in a frothy substance which she shapes as she deposits it onto vegetation. This 1- to 2-inch-long mass is often found attached to grasses and goldenrod stalks, about 1 to 2 feet off the ground. The frothy structure hardens, providing a protective case for the eggs throughout the winter. The light stripe down the length of the egg case is a series of overlapping scales that cover tiny corridors that lead to a central chamber. The young mantis nymphs emerge all at once through these corridors in the spring.

Praying mantis egg case.

Red Squirrels Tunneling and Feeding on Caches

Red squirrels prepare for the coming months of diminished food supply by caching cones and nuts. Frequently red squirrels will choose wet areas in which to bury their cones and nuts in piles called middens, as here the cones will remain closed (retaining the seeds which the squirrels will later eat) and stay relatively fresh. In winter, red squirrels make tunnels in the snow, which allow them to run from one food source to another in relative safety. The tunnels frequently have a midden at one end. Although most of their food is stored above ground, red squirrels will bury some in underground tunnels. Gray squirrels occasionally will tunnel, but not to the extent red squirrels do.

Red squirrel tunnel.

JANUARY 19

Yellow Warbler Nest

A walk near wetlands in winter often reveals a yellow warbler nest. This nest is quite easy to recognize as it is lined with downy plant fibers and is fairly thick walled. Yellow warblers are often victims of brown-headed cowbirds, which lay their eggs in other birds' nests and therefore avoid the labor of raising their own chicks. Many birds don't recognize a cowbird's egg and incubate it and raise the young cowbird chick as their own. Yellow warblers, however, can distinguish between their eggs and a cowbird's. Upon returning to her nest and finding a cowbird egg (often laid before the host bird begins laying her eggs), the female yellow warbler simply builds another nest right on top of the nest containing the cowbird egg and begins anew. As many as six stories of nests have been found with cowbird egg buried in each layer.

Yellow warbler and nest.

Black Bear Hibernation

Hibernation used to be defined by a certain degree of body temperature reduction, and, because a black bear's temperature remains above 88 degrees, which is within 12 degrees of their normal body temperature of 100 to 101 degrees, bears were not considered hibernators. However, when biologists discovered the many metabolic changes that let black bears hibernate up to six months without eating, drinking, urinating, or defecating, they realized that significant lowering of body temperature was only a small part of hibernation. Mammalian hibernation has been redefined as a specialized, seasonal reduction in metabolism concurrent with scarce food and cold weather.

Bear fur provides excellent insulation, and a bear has a relatively low surface area to mass ratio, so body heat is lost slowly. This enables a bear to cut its metabolic rate by 50 to 60 percent. Respiration in bears decreases from six to ten breaths per minute, to one breath every forty-five seconds during hibernation. They experience a drop in their normal heart rate of forty to fifty beats per minute to eight to nineteen beats per minute during hibernation.

Bears live off a layer of fat built up during the months prior to hibernation, when they may double their body weight. According to the Wildlife Research Institute, bears recycle their

Black bear.

metabolic waste. The urea produced from fat metabolism is broken down and the resulting nitrogen is used by the bear to build protein, which allows it to maintain muscle mass and organ tissues.

JANUARY 20

Autocoprophagy

Beavers, rabbits, and hares engage in autocoprophagy—the ingestion of one's own feces. Autocoprophagy increases protein digestion from 50 percent in one pass through the digestive

Beaver scat.

system to 75 to 80 percent upon a second trip. Cellulose digestion is increased from 14 percent in one pass through the digestive system to two or three times that amount when feces are eaten.

Buds Present in Winter

The buds of trees and shrubs are formed during the summer. If you look at their branches in the winter, they will have buds on them, in the axils of where the leaves used to be. There are two kinds

Red maple terminal buds.

of buds—leaf buds and flower buds—and flower buds are typically fatter than leaf buds. Both are usually covered with scales which help seal in moisture to protect the bud from drying out during the long, dry winters when water is frozen.

Common Redpolls Appearing

The birds most commonly associated with winter irruptions are the winter finches: pine grosbeak, evening grosbeak, red crossbill, white-winged crossbill, purple finch, pine siskin, and common redpoll. Their food supply, or lack thereof, in the Canadian boreal forests where they normally overwinter determines whether or not they will be

Male common redpoll.

seen as far south as the U.S. Key trees affecting finch movements in the boreal forest are spruces, birches, and mountain ash.

Common redpolls feed primarily on the catkins (seed-containing fruit) produced by birch and alder trees. When catkin production is low farther north, common redpolls move to areas where food is more plentiful.

JANUARY 21

Gray Squirrels Breeding

The breeding season of the eastern gray squirrel is stimulated by increasing hours of daylight and occurs in January or February, and again in

Gray squirrel.

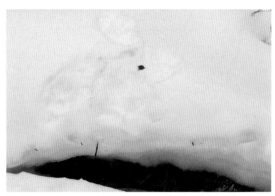

Bobcat urine marking.

May or June. Females are receptive for only eight hours, and there is a scramble among males to be the first to mate with a female. While the female usually mates with several males, the first male to breed with her has an advantage. His sperm is accompanied by material which forms a temporary gelatinous plug in the female's vagina, reducing the success rate of later matings and ensuring that the first mating fertilizes most of her eggs. About forty-four days after breeding, the female typically gives birth to two or three young.

Bobcats Scent Marking

Like most cats, the bobcat is territorial and largely solitary. There is some overlap of males' home ranges, and they use several methods to mark territorial boundaries and to communicate with other bobcats. The signs include claw marks on trees, scrapes (mounds of soil and leaves scraped with the bobcat's hind feet and formed into a pile that is marked with urine or scat), deposits of urine or feces, and secretions from both mouth and anal glands.

Scat is frequently found in the same location, usually in conspicuous places along travel routes, or near a den. (One monitored marking site contained 254 bobcat scats.) Resident bobcats also scent mark with urine, squirting small amounts on rocks, bushes, and snow banks as they travel, from one to five or more scent marks per mile. These scent markings function as biological bulletin boards within and between home ranges. In addition to marking territory, the scent markings are a means by which female bobcats claim a den, transient bobcats avoid resident bobcats, and bobcats find a mate.

When a bobcat encounters the scent mark of another bobcat, it raises its head with its mouth half open, nostrils closed, and upper lip slightly curled back. This behavior is called the "flehmen response." The bobcat inhales the scent into its mouth where its vomeronasal organ (also called Jacobson's organ) detects molecules of the marker's pheromones. This helps identify the marker and indicates if it's a female in estrus and whether or not she is ready to mate.

JANUARY 22

Lapland Longspur Plumage

The Lapland longspur, named for the unusually long claw on its hind foot, breeds in the Arctic tundra and overwinters near fields throughout the northern half of the U.S. in flocks numbering up to four million birds in the West.

21

Male Lapland longspur in winter plumage.

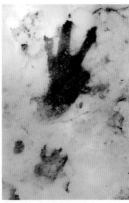

Beaver hind foot track (above), front foot track (below).

Male Lapland longspurs have drastically different plumages in winter and summer. Their winter plumage is somewhat dull. However, in the summer, the back of his neck, or nape, is bright rufous orange, and black feathers form a distinctive facial mask and bib, bordered by a white stripe. The female looks somewhat different than in the winter, but nowhere near as much so as the male.

Unlike most birds with different breeding and non-breeding plumages, longspurs molt only once per year, in the fall, into their non-breeding plumage. How can the males look so different in the breeding season if there isn't a second molt? Much like the European starling's plumage, the outer tips of these feathers wear off to reveal the males' distinctive breeding plumage underneath.

Beavers Take Advantage of January Thaw

If beavers have bank dens on rivers that remain open all winter, they are not confined to a dark, damp lodge for several months. They have access to fresh food year-round and aren't limited to the pile of aging branches under the ice that were stored last fall near their lodge. Beavers living in ponds that freeze over can often find an opening in the ice if there's a big enough January or February thaw. In either case, signs of their activity on land can be found.

While they are locked under the ice, the beavers' entire winter supply of food is a pile of branches they stored in the fall at the bottom of the pond near their lodge. If there is enough of a thaw to allow them to have access to land,

Beaver-cut tree.

they will take advantage of it. While their preferred spring food, herbaceous plants, is not available, the fresh cambium of living trees is most likely a welcome change from their waterlogged winter food.

Winter Crane Flies Mating

If and when temperatures get up into the forties and the sun is out, look for clusters of male winter crane flies hovering 2 or 3 feet above the snow, bobbing up and down as they do their mating dance. Females are on the surface of the snow most of the time, but join a swarm in order to find a mate. Winter crane flies are active throughout the winter and are a source of food for resident songbirds. The larvae feed on decaying vegetation and can be found in leaf litter, shelf fungi, and compost heaps.

Winter crane fly.

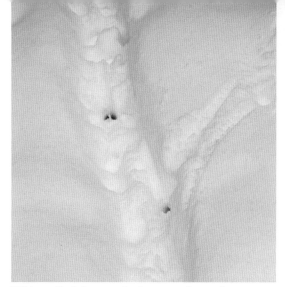

JANUARY 23

White-Tailed Deer Conserving Energy

Animals that remain active in winter expend the least amount of energy possible in order to survive the demanding conditions. It is not uncommon to see one animal taking advantage of another animal's trail, such as the white-tailed deer that chose to walk in the path made by a porcupine in this photograph.

White-tailed deer tracks in porcupine trail.

Winter Shelters

Mammals and birds that overwinter in the Northeast, whether active or hibernating, need some form of protection against the bitter cold temperatures. The shelters made for this purpose are constructed of a variety of materials and are located under, on, or above the ground. Some are constructed by the winter residents; others have served their purpose for the original summer inhabitants and are reclaimed by the new winter inhabitants. Some of these nests and dens are used as is, while others are renovated. Some of the animals use their shelter only during the day or the night, while others reside in them throughout the winter months, and sometimes longer. All of these structures serve as windbreaks and help the animals residing within them to retain body heat and conserve more energy than they would be able to out in the open.

Muskrat lodge.

Gray squirrel drey.

Porcupine den.

Red squirrel tree cavity.

Beaver—lodge
Muskrat—lodge
Squirrel—drey
Bluebirds, chickadees, titmice, nuthatches,
   small woodpeckers—tree cavity
Grouse—snow cave
Voles, mice, shrews—subnivean layer
Mole—tunnels (deeper in winter)
Deer—yard
Mice—hornet nest or bird nest
Woodchuck—burrow
Bear—den

White-breasted nuthatch.

Birds Seeking Shelter in Cavities

Birds that remain in the Northeast year-round use various strategies to withstand cold winter nights. One such strategy involves choosing a site well protected from the wind, such as a thick stand of conifers. Birds that nest in cavities, such as nuthatches and woodpeckers, often roost in holes as well, sometimes in large numbers. As many as twenty-nine white-breasted nuthatches have been found in a large tree cavity.

Red Foxes and the Itch Mite

A tiny, eyeless itch mite is responsible for the loss of fur associated with sarcoptic mange, the scourge of red foxes. After mating on a fox (often near the tail end), the male mite dies, and the female burrows into the fox's skin, laying eggs as she goes. After the eggs hatch, the larvae move to a new patch of skin, burrow in, and after going through a nymphal stage, become adults, ready to mate and continue the cycle. To add insult to injury, red foxes have an intense immune response to the mites' excrement, and the resulting inflammation is extremely itchy. Biting and scratching exacerbate the situation, causing new skin tears where

Female downy woodpecker.

Red fox with mange.

bacteria can enter. Eventually, most foxes with sarcoptic mange die of exhaustion, starvation, and/or infection.

JANUARY 24

Black Walnut Identification

Black walnut is a relatively easy tree to identify in the late summer, as its nearly tennis ball–sized nuts are so evident. In winter, when leaves and fruit no longer are evident, there are other distinctive clues to this tree's identity. The bark of black walnut is dark and deeply furrowed. Its buds are fuzzy, lacking bud scales, and beneath each one is a scar left by a leaf that has fallen off. The vessels that transport food and water throughout the tree, called vascular bundles, are darker than the rest of the leaf scar and are shaped in such a way that the leaf scar somewhat resembles the smiling face of a monkey. (The leaf scars of butternut, a

Black walnut bark.

Black walnut leaf scar.

Pith of black walnut twig.

close relative of black walnut, also look like monkeys, but they have a "furrowed brow" of fuzz on the top edge of the leaf scar.) If you cut a twig of black walnut at an angle, you will see the central portion, or pith, is chambered and brown. The only other tree that has a chambered, not solid, pith is butternut, and butternut's pith is buff colored, not brown.

Staying Warm in Winter

Animals that remain active year-round in the Northeast use different strategies to survive the cold winter temperatures. On cold nights, black-capped chickadees and other species reduce their

Beaver swimming in icy water.

body temperature as much as 22 degrees from their daytime level in a process called regulated hypothermia, or torpidity. Other strategies include shivering, caching food in the fall, growing thick winter coats, puffing out feathers to create insulating pockets of air, excavating tunnels under the snow, huddling, and seeking protection in cavities. These are just a few of the life-saving techniques used by mammals and birds which neither migrate nor hibernate.

JANUARY 25

Tree Seeds Dispersing

Often when tree fruits are developing, they are too high or too small to examine closely. Once they are mature, seeds disperse with the help of wind, mammals, and birds. Many end up on top of the snow, where they are very noticeable. This photograph shows the fruits from five different trees. At the center top is the fruit of the sugar maple, a samara. Each of the two seeds contains a papery wing that aids in dispersal by the wind. Moving clockwise, next is the fruit of the white ash, which has winged seeds borne in clusters. Eastern hophornbeam's fruit is a cluster of papery bladders which usually separate upon dispersal; each bladder contains one seed. Along the bottom is the fruit of American basswood, or linden. Several round seeds are borne on a stalk

Tree seeds dispersed by wind.

Solitary vs. Social Lifestyle

Solitary

Other than mating and when raising young, solitary animals do not interact much with other members of their species.

Advantages: Less competition for breeding and food

- Frog
- Red-tailed hawk
- Fisher
- Red fox
- Porcupine
- Moose
- Mole
- Mink
- Striped skunk
- Bobcat
- Solitary wasps
- Black bear

Social

Social animals spend much of their time with other members of their own species. There is a range of cooperation, with some animals highly organized (ants, bees, wasps) and others much less so.

Advantages: Protection from predators, division of labor, hunting efficiency, ease of finding a mate

- Black-capped chickadee
- American crow
- European starling
- Eastern coyote
- White-tailed deer
- Bats
- Mice
- Rats
- Ants
- Bees
- Social wasps—paper wasps, hornets, yellowjackets

Black bear, a solitary animal.

Eastern coyote, a social animal.

that is attached to a single modified leaf. The last two clusters are the fruit (catkins) of yellow birch. These structures look like little birds' feet, and each contains individual tiny, winged seeds, which you can see scattered throughout the photograph.

Ruffed Grouse Snow Caves

When snow depth is over 10 inches and the temperature is very low, ruffed grouse often dive into the snow at dusk and burrow 3 to 10 feet before hollowing out a small cavity where they seek refuge from the wind and the cold, as well as from predators—a behavior known as "snow roosting." Because the grouse flies into the snow, leaving no tracks and little scent, predators have difficulty detecting them. The major risk is freezing rain, which can form a crust on top of the snow, trapping the grouse.

Ruffed grouse snow cave and wing marks made on exiting. Roof of snow removed when grouse exited.

Coyote tracks and signs of digging at vent of beaver lodge.

Yellow birch bark.

Yellow birch buds.

The ruffed grouse's behavior allows it to conserve a great deal of energy, as the temperature inside this roost rarely falls below 20 degrees. This conservation of energy translates into less time spent up in trees eating buds, exposed to hawks and other predators. When morning comes, the grouse usually bursts out of the snow, leaving a hole, often some scat, and wing marks on the snow.

Coyote Prey

Researchers studying coyote prey in the Adirondack Mountains analyzed coyote stomach contents and found that beavers were second only to white-tailed deer on the coyote's menu. Although beaver lodges are impenetrable, due to 2- to 3-foot walls of frozen mud and stick walls, coyotes are lured to them by the aroma escaping up through the central vent from the living quarters of beavers below. From the thwarted efforts of a digging coyote at the lodge's vent in this photograph, one can see that most coyote predation on beavers must take place during the warmer months of the year, when they are on land.

JANUARY 26

Yellow Birch

Even without its leaves, there are several ways to identify a yellow birch in winter. The thin bark of a mature yellow birch is a very distinctive yellow-bronze color and curls when it separates from the trunk. The bark of saplings is a shiny reddish brown. Yellow birch buds are oval and

pointed, and there are two shades of brown on each of their three to five bud scales. Biting into a twig will tell you immediately if the tree is a yellow birch—it will taste like wintergreen if it is. In the early morning and late afternoon, look for ruffed grouse filling their crops, or "budding," in yellow birch trees—these buds are one of their favorite foods.

Foxes and Winter Hunting

Deep snow presents obvious challenges to predators: for the most part their prey is well hidden, and if they are to survive, they must compensate for not being able to see what they are hunting. Foxes are particularly good at this. A red fox hunting for food is constantly listening for the sound of rodent feet under the snow, and when it hears them—a fox can hear a mouse or vole 3 feet beneath the surface of the snow—it leaps up into the air and pounces on or near the prey with its front feet. Most of the time they are not successful and come up empty-mouthed, but they usually succeed often enough to survive.

Researchers in Czechoslovakia, watching foxes hunt in the wild, determined that a fox's success seems to

Red fox.

correlate with the direction in which it jumps. If the observed foxes jumped to the northeast, they killed on 73 percent of their attacks. If they reversed direction and jumped exactly the opposite way, they killed 60 percent of the time. But in all other directions—east, south, west, or variations thereof—they were successful only 18 percent of the time. Jaroslav Cerveny, the Czech researcher, feels that foxes have a "magnetic sense," and are capable of lining up the rodent sounds that reach their ears with the slope of the earth's magnetic field; when this occurs, dinner is usually caught. This theory has yet to be confirmed, but the likelihood that it is correct is considerable.

JANUARY 27

Snowshoe Hare Succumbs to Avian Predator

One of the most sought-after prey animals in the Northeast is the snowshoe hare. Bobcats, lynxes, coyotes, foxes, and fishers are some of the mammalian predators of this lagomorph. In this particular case, however, the predator had wings (determined by wing imprints in the snow and lack of tracks, other than those of a snowshoe hare). While great horned owls do prey on hares, there was a telltale sign that it was a hawk, not an owl, which produced this pile of fur and bones.

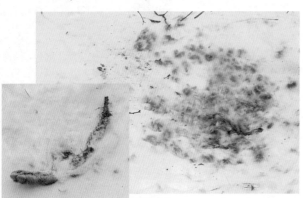

Hind leg of snowshoe hare.

Kill site.

If you look at the upper left and upper right of the photograph, you will see lengthy curved lines of bird droppings, or sprays, that were left by the predator as it plucked its prey. Because it was ejected forcibly and didn't just drop down on the snow where the bird was situated, the scat indicates that it was a hawk, not an owl, which deposited it. A woodland accipiter capable of capturing a snowshoe hare after an extensive chase such as this one is the northern goshawk.

Barred Owls Casting Pellets

Owls swallow small prey, such as mice and voles, whole, while larger prey is torn into smaller pieces before being swallowed. Once eaten, prey goes directly into the owl's stomach. Owls have no crop and thus no ability to store food for later consumption. The indigestible parts of the prey that the owl has eaten are filtered out by the gizzard and then compressed into a pellet, which is coughed up roughly ten hours later.

Barred owl coughing up pellet.

JANUARY 28

Overwintering Red-Tailed Hawks

Red-tailed hawks are "partial migrants"—some individuals are migratory, and others are not. Many red-tails living in the northern portion of the species' range in southern Canada and northern United States migrate to more southerly locations for the winter. A few northern birds, however, remain on their breeding territories even in the most severe winters.

Juvenile red-tailed hawk.

Overwintering red-tailed hawks are generally easy to spot, as they often perch on dead trees overlooking open fields and on telephone poles next to highways, where they watch for prey. Mice, voles, squirrels, snowshoe hares, and an occasional bird make up most of their diet. If you notice the coloration of a red-tailed hawk's tail, it will tell you whether the bird is a juvenile or adult. Adults have rufous tails; juveniles have barred, brownish tails.

Opossums Mating

The mating period of opossums is fairly extensive, stretching from January through July, and sometimes even well into the fall. Twelve to thirteen days after they mate, twenty-one honey bee-size opossums are born. The first thirteen newborns

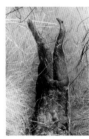

Opossum hemipenis.

to reach their mother's pouch and locate one of her thirteen teats have the potential to reach adulthood. Most unusual is the reproductive anatomy of this marsupial. Males have a forked penis, and females have two uteri and a secondary vagina connected to the primary vagina.

Insects Active in Winter

	Larva	Nymph	Adult
Dragonfly		X	
Mayfly		X	
Stonefly		X	
Honey bee			X
Winter stonefly			X
Snow fly			X
Snow scorpionfly			X
Winter crane fly			X
Winter firefly	X		
Soldier beetle	X		
Sow bug			X
Fly			X
Moth			
Large yellow underwing moth	X		
Bruce spanworm			X
Snow flea			X
Mite	X		
Harvestman	X		

Winter fly.

JANUARY 29

White-Tailed Deer Slipping on Ice

Whether it slips on its own, or is chased out onto the ice by a coyote or some other predator, a fall can be a death sentence for a deer. Because of the manner in which a deer's hip and shoulder joints work, one fall can tear connective tissues in a way that keeps it down. Its legs splay outward

Opossum.

as it falls, and it can't get up. It is then destined to freeze, starve, or be killed by predators.

However, its carcass does not go to waste. It does not take long for predators and scavengers to become aware of this bountiful supply of food. Bald eagles, in particular, often rely on ice-stranded deer for winter survival, but a myriad of other predators and scavengers, including coyotes, red foxes, crows, and ravens reduce deer carcasses to skeletons in short order.

Deer carcass remains on frozen pond.

Carrion a Vital Food Source for Bald Eagles

Eagles obtain food mainly in three ways: by direct capture, scavenging for carrion, and stealing food from other birds and mammals. When securing their own live prey, they hunt from perches or soar over suitable habitat, taking most prey on the wing. Bald eagles' preferred food is live fish, but they are opportunistic foragers that select prey based on availability. Twenty studies from across their range found that bald eagles' diets were composed of, on average, 56 percent fish, 28 percent birds, 14 percent mammals, and 2 percent other.

In addition to capturing live prey, eagles rely heavily on fish, bird, and mammal carrion, especially during the winter. Ice fishermen's leftover bait and/or rejected catches, roadkills, and deer that have slipped and died on ice-covered ponds are three heavily used sources of food at this time of year. If the carrion is small enough, like the opossum in the photograph, it is often carried to a perch where it is inconspicuously consumed. Larger carrion, such as a white-tailed deer, salmon, and waterfowl, that are too big to carry off, are eaten on site and repeatedly visited until consumed.

JANUARY 30

Wood-Drilling Adaptations

While excavating a cavity, a woodpecker's head can strike a tree's surface at speeds up to 13 to 15 miles per hour and continue to do it at over one hundred strokes per minute. To sustain this kind of blow against a tree, woodpeckers have a number of skull adaptations, including strong yet lightweight skulls and bills, a network of bony supports within the skull, extra calcification of the portion of the skull nearest the tip of the bill, flexible (cushioning) cartilage joining the bones between the skull and the beak, shock-absorbing neck muscles, and a brain that is packed very tightly into the brain cavity.

It is not only the brain of a woodpecker that has wood-drilling adaptations. A woodpecker's narrow-slit nostrils are covered with bristly feathers that prevent wood chips and dust from entering. Special cells on the end of its bill are constantly

Bald eagle carrying opossum carcass.

Male hairy woodpecker.

replacing material lost due to drilling. This keeps the chisel-pointed bill strong and resilient, while allowing it to be sharpened with every blow. Less than a second before a woodpecker's bill contacts wood, a thickened nictitating membrane closes over its eyes, protecting them from flying wood chips.

Porcupine Dens Obvious in Winter

Most porcupines den in hollow trees or rocky ledges. These can be relatively easy to find in

Winter porcupine den.

the winter, due to signs that porcupines leave. Scat and urine accumulate in a porcupine den until they flow out of the opening onto the ground. The large pile of pellets at the mouth of a den is not only visible against the snow, but both porcupine scat and urine have a distinctive pungent odor which is easily detected by the human nose. Trails lead from the den to feeding trees, quills often remain stuck in den trees as the porcupine climbs them, and nip twigs often litter the ground, making dens fairly obvious in winter.

JANUARY 31

Bobcats Caching Prey

Rabbits and hares comprise much of a bobcat's diet, but when prey is scarce or hard to capture, adult male or sometimes large adult female bobcats will attack bedded, weak, or injured adult white-tailed deer. Bobcats often cache prey, such as a deer, that is too large to eat in one feeding, returning to feed on it for an extended period of time.

Bobcats scrape up leaves, bark, twigs, soil, and snow—whatever is available—and cover their prey. When feeding on a deer, bobcats bite away

Newly cached white-tailed deer.

the hair to avoid eating it, and this discarded hair may be left windblown around the carcass or is frequently mixed with the debris that the cat drags over the kill to cover it. Characteristic signs of bobcat feeding are this hair that is strewn around the carcass and the lack of broken long bones—bobcats don't have the strength to break them with their teeth. Note deer hair and bobcat scratch marks in the fresh cache photograph.

Typically, a bobcat rests near its cache to protect it, but it doesn't take long for other animals to find such an easy meal. Within three days of this deer being cached, coyotes and common ravens had discovered it, and both they and the bobcat had eaten enough of it to expose the deer's rib cage.

Other predators that occasionally cache and cover their kills include mountain lions, black bears, and fishers. Large caches found in the winter in the Northeast are likely to belong to a bobcat or fisher.

White-tailed deer eaten by bobcat, coyote, and ravens.

Intact white-tailed deer leg bone at bobcat cache.

Bobcat.

FEBRUARY

Subnivean Layer

The thick layer of snow that blankets forests and fields every winter looks at first glance like a vast, empty wasteland, but nothing could be further from the truth. Activity abounds on, in, and under this blanket. Occasionally we get a hint of this—small rodent tracks leading to a tree or a hole in the snow; a ruffed grouse's overnight roosting snow cave; or a pile of pinecone scales, remnants from a red squirrel's meal. These signs indicate that humans aren't the only creatures venturing out on a cold winter's day, but what they don't reveal is the hidden world that exists under the snow—a world known as the subnivean layer or zone.

The word "subnivean" comes from the Latin words for under (*sub*) and snow (*nives*) and refers to the interstice between the snow and the ground. The layer is formed when the snow is warmed by the ground. Solid snow particles transform into water vapor that moves up through the snowpack, changing the lowest snow layer into small particles of ice that act as an insulating roof. Under all that snow is a humid habitat that remains at a relatively stable temperature—around 32 degrees—allowing a range of creatures to remain active through the winter. Many organisms overwinter in this layer, including several species of insects, mammals, plants, and vast mats of fungi and bacteria.

The most common mammals are mice, voles, and shrews which, after 6 to 10 inches of snow have accumulated, are seen much less frequently than when there is open ground. For much of the time, during the winter they get from one place to another in a series of tunnels between the soil and the snow. Their dark-colored coats make them fatally conspicuous on the surface of the snow. These animals' needs are all met in the subnivean layer: they are protected from sub-freezing temperatures and wind; they have access to seeds, plants, bark, and insect eggs; and they are hidden from most predators.

Although protected in many ways from their enemies, the mice, voles, and shrews that inhabit the subnivean layer are still vulnerable to predation. One of their biggest threats under the snow is the ermine, or short-tailed weasel. This predator has a white coat in winter and a brown one in summer, so it is well camouflaged at all times. It is also slim enough to easily fit into the entrances and tunnels of its tiny prey.

Although such predators as foxes, coyotes, and owls cannot see the shrews and rodents running through their subnivean tunnels, they can hear them. A red fox is capable of detecting a mouse by sound alone 2 to 3 feet under the snow. Jumping up into the air and coming down on one of these subnivean tunnels with both front feet, the fox traps the mouse long enough to dive head first into the snow to snatch its next meal.

Occasionally, you see a hole about an inch in diameter in the snow, with no tracks leading in or out of it. These holes are the openings of ventilation shafts that the rodents make from the subnivean layer up to the surface of the snow. The vents allow the carbon dioxide created by animal respiration, as well as that released from the ground, to escape, avoiding a lethal build-up under the snow.

Even though the creatures living in the subnivean layer can be separated from the elements by several feet, they are not totally unaware of

Snow buntings.

Meadow vole hole.

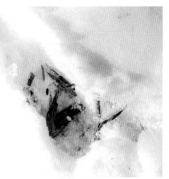

Meadow vole tunnel, scat, and eaten white ash seeds.

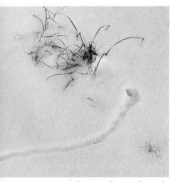

Meadow vole trail and exit/entrance hole.

the passing of time. Scientists have found that voles start to reproduce as much as two to three months before the snowpack has melted. The melting and refreezing that begins with the longer days of spring increases the ability of the snowpack to transmit light. Plants detect this increase in light, begin growing, and are thought to produce chemicals, called phenolics, that stimulate reproductive activity in the animals that eat them.

Come spring, or, if there is a period of time in early winter when there is just 1 or 2 inches of snow on the ground, evidence of this sub-nivean activity becomes visible. A maze of runways is exposed, and the extent to which life has gone on under our snowshoes and skis all winter is quite evident.

Hair

Hair is uniquely mammalian. No other creature possesses true hair, and at least some hair is found on all mammals at some time during their lives. In mammals, the hair, fur, or wool that covers the animal is called a pelage. The pelage provides insulation, concealment on land, buoyancy and streamlining in water, and may be modified for defense or display.

It is not known when hair evolved, as it is usually not preserved in fossils. The small body size of the earliest mammals meant they had a high surface area to mass ratio and, therefore, a propensity to lose heat. This, along with the possibility that they were endothermic (generated their own body heat), suggest that they could not have existed without a good covering of insulation. It is possible that these were the first animals to have hair.

The pelage of most mammals consists of more than one kind of hair. The most conspicuous hairs on most mammals are the guard hairs, which overlay the fur and serve to protect it from abrasion as well as moisture. Guard hairs are sometimes modified to form defensive spines (as in porcupines), bristles (long, firm hairs that grow continuously, such as those that make up the mane of a lion), and awns (hairs that do not grow continuously and that have an expanded tip on a narrower, weaker shaft). Beneath the guard hairs there is usually a layer called the underfur, made up of wool (ever-growing hairs), fur (relatively short hairs with definitive growth), and/or velli (down or fuzz). Mammalian embryos (including humans) are often covered with a pelage called lanugo, a form of velli.

The different animal hairs usually perform various basic functions. Some are sensory, such as whiskers, which provide a tactile sense that is used to locate prey or to navigate in total darkness.

Most hair serves to insulate, to conceal, to signal, and to protect mammals. Thermoregulation is understood to be the main function of hair, with the degree of insulation dependent on its length and density. The color of the pelage of most species is usually cryptic, matching the animal's background. Many mammals have dark-colored backs and relatively pale undersides, a pattern called countershading. This makes sense in the case of aquatic or arboreal species: Predators above look down on a dark coat matching the ground below, while predators beneath the prey see the pale belly against light streaming down from above. The color of hair can provide a means of signaling other members of one's own species, such as the white tail of the white-tailed deer, flashed by a fleeing animal to signal danger, or members of other species, such as the contrasting pattern of a striped skunk, which serves as a warning to predators. The pelage also serves to protect the skin from abrasion and from excessive UV radiation.

Hair is shed periodically in a process called molt. Molt may take place continuously, with a few hairs being replaced at any time, as in humans. More commonly, however, molt is restricted to certain seasons of the year or certain times of an animal's life, at which time all hairs are replaced. A great deal of energy is expended when an animal is molting. As a result, it does not generally take place when other high-energy

demands are made on an animal, such as giving birth or at a time of year when food is scarce.

Two main types of molt, or shedding, occur in most mammals: maturational and seasonal. The maturational molt from juvenile to adult occurs when the pelage of a young animal, usually of fine texture, is shed and replaced with coarser hair.

The seasonal molt is triggered by secretions of the thyroid and pituitary glands in response to the lengthening or shortening periods of daylight, or photoperiod. In temperate parts of the world, many mammals molt twice a year, in spring and in autumn. These molts often involve a change of fur color. As daylight diminishes in autumn, many northern animals will begin to grow thicker and lighter-colored coats, some of which (ermine, snowshoe hare) eventually become completely white. In addition to enhancing an animal's

Northeastern Butterflies That Overwinter as Adults

While some butterflies, like the monarch, migrate south to avoid the Northeast's cold winters, many species of butterflies stay in the Northeast year-round. Butterflies that remain here spend the winter in different stages—some as eggs, many as pupae and larvae, and a few as adults.

Butterflies that overwinter as adults enter winter diapause—a state in which metabolic and respiratory rates are very low. Most reduce the amount of water in their bodies, and as the days shorten during the autumn, they begin secreting natural antifreezes, or glycogens, into their body fluids, which prevent the formation of ice crystals in their cells. These physical changes are triggered by the decreasing amount of daylight. The butterflies then find tree crevices, logs, or cracks in buildings where they are sheltered from the snow and ice. In this state and in these protected spots they can withstand very cold temperatures—mourning cloaks can survive in -80 degrees. These are the earliest butterflies seen in the spring, for they do not

have to metamorphose before emerging. Most butterflies that overwinter as adults have an eight- to ten-month life span, much longer than other species of butterfly.

- Milbert's tortoiseshell
- Compton tortoiseshell
- Mourning cloak
- Question mark
- Eastern comma
- Green comma
- Satyr comma
- Hoary comma

Mourning cloak butterfly.

ability to camouflage itself, the cells of white hairs, lacking pigment, are filled instead with air, an excellent insulator. In some cases, the structure of the hairs also changes with the seasons: white-tailed deer and moose hairs are solid in the summer, and their new winter coat consists of hollow and, therefore, more insulating, hairs. As the days lengthen in spring, the winter coats of mammals are gradually shed and often replaced by a coat with colors or patterns that blend in with the animal's surroundings.

The smaller the animal, the larger the surface area to volume ratio, and the larger this ratio, the more heat loss occurs. Therefore, a small animal like a shrew or vole has a greater potential for losing heat from its body because of its relatively large surface area. A longer, denser coat is one way large mammals retain their body heat in the winter and avoid heat loss, but small mammals don't have the option of growing a thicker, longer coat, as they couldn't support its weight. As a result of their relatively thin winter coats, they rely heavily on the subnivean layer between the snow and the ground to protect them from the winter winds and cold temperatures.

There are keys to help you identify birds, butterflies, ferns, stars—just about everything in the natural world, and hair is no exception. While sensory hairs (whiskers) are not useful in hair identification because their structural pattern is the same in all species, the structure of other hairs varies with species. The outer surface, or cuticle, of a hair is covered with keratinous scales which either encircle the hair shaft or overlap one another. This pattern, combined with characteristics of the scales' edges and the structure of the center of the hair, the medulla, can tell you whether you are examining the hair of a striped skunk, a raccoon, or a woodchuck, although a powerful microscope is needed to see these scales.

The next time you are cold and covered with goose bumps, consider this: Although our body hair is relatively scarce, humans still retain a

Porcupine.

Long-tailed weasel.

Striped skunk.

vestigial trait having to do with it—the involuntary raising of our body hair when we are cold. When this happens, we say we have goose bumps—tiny muscles at the base of hairs contract, causing the hairs to become erect. If our hair were denser, this reflex would trap air next to our body, preventing much of our body heat from escaping into the air.

Cedar Waxwings

One of the delights of winter in the Northeast is the sudden appearance of cedar waxwings as they descend upon a crabapple or mountain ash tree in search of sugary fruits to eat. A sea of gleaming black masks, waxy red feather tips, and lemon-yellow bellies flutter down from the sky to settle on fruit-laden branches where they fill themselves with their favorite food.

Cedar waxwings are named for their fondness for the fruit of red cedar as well as for the wax droplets on the tips of some of their wing feathers. They are among the most frugivorous (fruit-eating) species of bird in North America, especially during the winter months. Research shows that their annual diet consists of 84 percent fruit, 4 percent flower parts, and 12 percent insect prey. Between September and April they eat nothing but fruit. In May the composition of their diet changes, with fruit dropping to about 15 percent of their diet, while flowers comprise 44 percent. In June, fruit intake increases to about 65 percent (as fruits ripen), and their consumption of fruit continues to rise through the summer.

Outside of their breeding season, cedar waxwings are nomadic, sporadically roaming the countryside in large flocks, seeking the sweet fruit of crabapple, hawthorn, and mountain ash, as well as eastern red cedar, winterberry, dogwood, and others. Once one of these trees has been found, the flock swoops down to it en masse, uttering their high-pitched, trilled *bzeee* calls and thin whistles.

Waxwings rarely eat all of the fruit on a given tree in one sitting. They startle easily and fly off but usually return if fruit is plentiful. While perched, each waxwing bends out or down and plucks crabapple after crabapple, swallowing them whole, one at a time; occasionally one will hover briefly in the air while plucking fruit. These social birds are known for their habit of "gifting" fruit to each other.

One liability of this diet is that cedar waxwings are susceptible to alcohol intoxication and even death after eating fermented fruits. When they are really drunk, birds lose their mobility, making them helpless in the presence of predators. To the surprise of many observers, birds that appear lifeless on the ground have been known to eventually sober up and fly away. While birds don't intentionally wish to ingest a lot of alcohol, there are other animals, such as elephants and apes, that will wander for miles to seek the pleasure of fermented fruits.

Many birds that eat a lot of fruit separate out the seeds and then regurgitate them. Cedar waxwings let the seeds pass through, scarifying them and breaking down the outer seed coat in

Avian Territorial/Courtship Communication in February

- SINGING
  - Tufted titmouse
  - Black-capped chickadee
  - Red-winged blackbird
- DRUMMING
  - Woodpecker
- CALLING
  - Great-horned owl
  - Barred owl
  - Screech owl
  - Northern saw-whet owl

Red-winged blackbird.

Hairy woodpecker.

Barred owl.

A cedar waxwing with one of its favorite foods, a crabapple, in its beak.

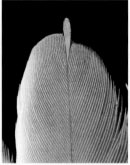

The "wax" on a cedar waxwing's feather.

Cedar waxwing with orange tail tip.

their digestive tracts. After these scarified seeds are deposited, they are more likely to germinate. Because of this, waxwings are considered important seed dispersers for many fruiting plants in North America.

The seeds they spread are not always welcome, however, at least by humans. Waxwings have expanded their summer and fall diet to include the fruit of invasive, non-native honeysuckles in recent years. One interesting effect that these introduced fruits have had on wax-wings is the alteration of their tail band color. In the 1960s, cedar waxwings with orange, not yellow, terminal tail bands started appearing in the Northeast. This color change is caused by a red pigment, rhodoxanthin, which fruits of at least one non-native honeysuckle (Morrow's honeysuckle) contain. If waxwings consume this fruit when they are molting and developing new tail feathers, their tail bands are orange.

Cedar waxwings have many traits that humans admire: they are monogamous (at least within a given breeding season), social, non-territorial, mutual groomers, and generous food-sharers.

FEBRUARY 1

Coyotes Mating

Coyotes mate in January and February, but pre-mating behavior starts two to three months before this. Scent marking increases, as does howling, and males wander far and wide. Large groups may gather together periodically. Female coyotes come into heat only once a year. When this happens, and two coyotes pair up, they

Coyote.

Male coyote urine marking.

Female coyote urine marking with sign of estrus.

Tracks of coyote gathering.

may howl in a duet before mating. If there is an ample food supply, most females will breed, and between 60 percent and 90 percent of adult females will produce a litter. The same pair of coyotes may mate from year to year, but not necessarily for life.

Pileated Woodpecker Feeding Hole Embellishment

Large rectangular excavations in trees, indicating pileated woodpecker feeding activity, are relatively common. These holes give the woodpecker

Unusual pileated woodpecker feeding hole.

access to carpenter ants living in galleries within the tree. What are not common are the horizontal lines radiating out from either side of the top rectangular pileated woodpecker feeding hole on this red pine. It remains a mystery as to why a woodpecker in winter would expend precious energy drilling these lines.

FEBRUARY 2

Woodchucks Fast Asleep

As is true for black bears, if climate conditions are mild and food, such as remnant corn in fields, is available, woodchucks have been known to remain active year-round in parts of their

Woodchuck.

range. However, they typically hibernate during the winter in underground burrows, living off the fat—equaling about a third of their body weight—that they accumulated in late summer and fall. In Pennsylvania, where Groundhog Day is first referenced in North America, male groundhogs, or woodchucks, emerge from their burrows at the end of January or beginning of February. In northern New England, however, we don't usually see signs of this largest member of the eastern squirrel family until the end of February or beginning of March, when males actively start searching for mates. Currently, our woodchucks are curled up in a ball, hibernating beneath the ground, with their heart rate reduced from one hundred beats a minute to fifteen and their body temperature down from about 96 degrees to 47 degrees.

Nature's Recyclers

Each year, Americans waste approximately thirty-three million tons of food—and much of this ends up in landfills where it produces methane, a potent greenhouse gas. This situation is totally

White-tailed deer carcass.

39

alien to other animals in the natural world, which seem to find a use for any and every organic particle. Great crested flycatchers incorporate shed snake skins into their nests, beavers build dams and lodges with branches they have eaten the bark from, and ermines line their nests with the fur and feathers of prey. When it comes to food, there is equally little waste. The carcasses of animals do not linger long, as almost every atom of their bodies is recycled. Fishers, coyotes, foxes, raccoons, opossums, bald eagles, hawks, woodpeckers, ravens, crows, and many other animals make short work of a dead deer in winter. Come spring, if there is anything left, the final clean-up crew consists of legions of turkey vultures, beetles, flies, and bacteria, among others.

Barred Owls Courting

Barred owls call year-round, but their vocalizations expand and increase in February, when

courtship begins. No longer are their calls limited to their year-round *who-cooks-for-you, who-cooks-for-you-all*; males and females engage in duets, as well as many other vocalizations, including cackles, hoots, caws, and gurgles.

Barred owl courtship is not strictly vocal. Male barred owls display by swaying back and forth and raising their wings, while sidling along a branch close to a female. Courtship

Barred owl.

feeding and mutual preening also occur prior to copulation. The nights of February are filled with amorous avian calls and gestures.

FEBRUARY 3

Queen Wasps Hibernating

Fertilized queens are the only wasps in a colony that attempt to live through the winter, and they usually do so in a sheltered spot such as a rotting log or under the loose bark of a tree. In some instances, the queen chews a small chamber for additional shelter. The pictured cavity is roughly 1 inch long and ¼ inch deep. Underneath the wasp are the woody bits of fiber that accumulated from her excavation.

Hibernating queen wasp.

As a rule, hibernating queen wasps protect their wings and antennae by tucking them under their bodies. Some species produce glycerol, which acts as an antifreeze, while others allow ice to form around their cell walls and simply freeze solid. Most queen wasps die over the winter, primarily from predation by other insects and spiders, not the cold. Warm winters tend to affect queens negatively, as they emerge from hibernation too soon and starve due to lack of food.

Vixens Screaming

This is the time of year when you might wake up in the middle of the night and hear a rasping, prolonged scream. It could well be a female red fox, issuing forth a "vixen scream" designed to travel long distances and attract a mate.

Red fox.

This scream is not limited to females in heat—males also can scream, as can females at other times of the year. Once heard, it is never forgotten. Red foxes have a number of vocalizations, among which this scream and a high-pitched bark are the most common.

FEBRUARY 4

Black Bears Giving Birth

Sometime between the end of January (the full moon in January is sometimes called the "bear moon") and the first part of February, black bears give birth to between one and five (usually two) tiny, blind, almost hairless, half-pound cubs, each about the size of a chipmunk. The cubs are totally dependent on their mother for food and warmth. Because the mother's belly has very little fur, her heat is easily transferred to the cub. Most dens are exposed to the cold air, as they are located under fallen logs and brush or are dug into a bank. Occasionally, they are on the ground with little or no cover; in all of these places, the mother acts like a furnace, enveloping her young and breathing on them to keep them warm. The cubs do not hibernate, but nap frequently. Like human mothers, black bear mothers sleep when their young sleep, but awaken quickly to respond to their cries. The black bear cub in the photo is two months old.

Wild Turkeys Making Burdock Balls

If you find clumps of empty common burdock fruits lying on top of the snow, there may well be wild turkeys in the area. During the winter, especially when the snow is deep, wild turkeys feed on vegetation poking up above the surface of the snow, such as burdock seeds. There are telltale signs turkeys have been eating burdock, even if no tracks are evident, because of the way in which they consume the seeds. Turkeys somehow pluck the burdock fruits off and turn them inside out, exposing the seeds, which they then eat. Typically, several of these empty fruits will be stuck together, and small bunches of them will be scattered over the snow.

Black bear mother and cub.

Common burdock ball.

41

FEBRUARY 5

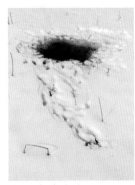

Otter hole in ice.

North American River Otter Sign

River otters are the most aquatic members of the weasel family. They can swim up to 6 or 7 miles per hour on the surface of the water as well as underneath it, and can remain submerged for up to two minutes. Otters spend a great deal of time fishing under the ice and obtain oxygen from open holes such as the one pictured, as well as from air bubbles under the ice. As their tracks indicate, otters come up on the ice to eat their prey, be it fish or crayfish, their two favorite winter meals.

North American river otters.

Snowshoe Hare Hind Feet

It is not hard to see why the individual toe pads in the tracks of a snowshoe hare's feet are rarely very distinct. There is a ¾-inch-thick layer of hair on the bottom of a hare's 5- to 6-inch-long foot.

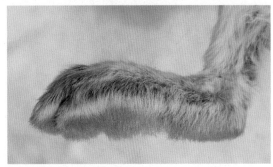

Snowshoe hare's hind foot.

This hair, along with the size of the foot and the ability of the hare to spread its toes to a width of 5 inches, allows it to stay on or near the surface of the snow, and, in the right snow conditions, outrun heavier predators.

FEBRUARY 6

Great Horned Owls Thaw Cached Prey

Great horned owls are among the earliest species of birds to nest in the Northeast—some are already sitting on eggs. Female great horned owls do the lion's share of incubating the eggs, and the male brings her food. While they do eat small rodents, which they swallow whole, the diet of great horned owls also includes rabbits, hares, opossums, squirrels, and skunks, which must be torn into pieces before being swallowed.

Great horned owl.

Great horned owls often kill more than they can eat at one time and cache the extra food for later consumption, when food is scarce. During winter months the cached prey freezes, and if the prey is large, its consumption is challenging. To solve this dilemma, great horned owls sit on their frozen prey until it thaws and then proceed to tear it into bite-size pieces.

Red Foxes Scent Marking and Mating

Animals, including red foxes, communicate in a number of ways, one of which is to scent mark. The amount of marking increases dramatically in February, the peak of their breeding season. Stumps sprayed with urine act as sign posts, and

Red fox.

Researchers have found that when foxes are looking for food, they mark up to seventy times an hour. When just traveling and not hunting, they do not mark as frequently. During the breeding season, male fox urine takes on a strong skunk-like odor, detectable by the human nose.

FEBRUARY 7

Avian Toe Arrangement

along with scat, advertise the fox's presence, its dominance, and sexual status to all other red foxes that pass by. Foxes also mark their cached prey to indicate whether any food remains to

be eaten and to discourage other predators from eating it. Scent marks are also left along the boundary of their territory, as well as within it.

Red fox urine marking.

Often you will find both urine and scat placed strategically on elevated objects, such as rocks, stumps, and vegetation emerging from snow as well as at the intersection of two trails. Both male and female foxes leave scent marks.

Unlike humans, who use the entire bottoms of their feet for support, a bird stands and walks only on the ball of its foot and its toes. When you look at a bird's leg, what appears to be its knee, bending backward instead of forward as it does in humans, is actually its heel.

Most birds have four toes, arranged differently according to the lifestyle of the bird. Songbirds, as well as most other birds, have three toes pointing forward and one pointing back. Most woodpeckers, being active climbers, have two toes pointing in each direction, which enables them to cling to tree trunks. The outer toe (of the three forward toes) of ospreys and owls is reversible, so that they can have two toes in back should they need to get a better grasp on slippery fish or other prey. Some birds that do a lot of running, such as sanderlings and most plovers, have only the three forward toes.

Red fox scent post.

Red-tailed hawk.

43

Flying squirrel.

White-tailed deer tracks and porcupine nip twigs.

Huddling to Stay Warm

One strategy some animals use to keep warm on cold winter nights is to huddle together to conserve warmth. Huddling reduces the animal's surface-area-to-volume ratio, since it turns many small animals into a single big animal. The larger the animal, the smaller the surface-area-to-volume ratio and the less heat is lost.

Bluebirds and flying squirrels are two animals that huddle to keep warm. Eastern bluebirds may huddle together in a tree cavity or hollow log in groups of up to ten. Flying squirrels often huddle together in large communal nests, sometimes with populations numbering over two dozen squirrels. If this doesn't provide enough warmth, the squirrels will enter a state of torpor until temperatures return to normal.

FEBRUARY 8

White-Tailed Deer Opportunists

One of the most obvious signs associated with porcupines is the presence of "nip twigs" on the ground: severed tips of eastern hemlock branches dropped from above by porcupines after they have eaten the buds. These tender hemlock tips that would be out of reach without the assistance of porcupines are quickly consumed by deer. Look for deer tracks and scat beneath trees in which porcupines are feeding. Note the wide porcupine path on the left leading to the den tree. All other trails were made by deer.

White Pine Blister Rust Attracts Rodents

When a white pine has been infected with white pine blister rust, a fungus, a canker appears on a branch and sometimes on the trunk of the tree. A large amount of sap-like ooze flows from the cankered areas. It sometimes dries and forms a sugary crust or film. These areas are, in fact, high in sugar content, and rodents frequently chew them. It is likely that a red squirrel visited and sampled the infected white pine in the photograph, leaving a freshly gnawed patch in the bark.

Red squirrel sign at site of white pine blister rust.

FEBRUARY 9

Meadow Vole Tracks

Meadow voles, white-footed mice, and deer mice leave most of the tiny tracks one sees on the surface of the snow. In deep snow, meadow voles tend to remain beneath the surface in tunnels, but occasionally they travel on top of the snow. Typically, a white-footed or deer mouse leaves a leaping, four-print pattern, often with a tail drag mark running between the sets of prints. A leaping meadow vole may or may not leave a tail mark and usually has paired prints. However, voles leave a variety of tracks patterns, depending on the speed at which they are traveling and the depth of the snow, so it can be confusing.

Although one might think that three different animals made the tracks in this photograph, every tunnel and track was made by a meadow vole. The trail in the lower left was made by a trotting vole, the tunnel on the right was exposed because the layer of crust just under the new snow prevented the vole from going any deeper, and at the top, the vole was quickly bounding into the safety of its deeper tunnel.

Meadow vole tracks.

Cavities Provide Shelter for Birds in Winter

Birds often seek protected places to roost or sleep at night, especially in the winter. Dense vegetation found in thickets or the interior branches of evergreens serves as a windbreak and conceals the birds from predators. A few species of songbirds, especially the ones that nest in tree cavities or birdhouses, roost in cavities in the winter. Research has shown that these shelters, through reduction of wind speed, can cut the windchill factor by 40 degrees. Energy savings in one study ranged from 25 percent to 38 percent for birds roosting in cavities and resulted in an increased fasting endurance of six to seven hours in winter. Sometimes more than a dozen birds will pile into a single box or cavity to conserve heat. This may well have been the case in this pileated woodpecker cavity, given the quantity of bird droppings found in it—or perhaps one lone chickadee took up residence night after night.

Pileated woodpecker cavity containing bird droppings.

FEBRUARY 10

Porcupine Signs

It's fairly obvious when there are active porcupines in the woods, as they leave all kinds of signs. A large pile of scat accumulates beneath a hollow tree den and often outside the entrance to a rock den. The females, who often spend the day in

Porcupine tracks.

Porcupine in den.   Porcupine quills in bark.

Porcupine nip twigs beneath feeding trees and, at right, showing incisor marks.

a hollow tree or rock den, come out at night to eat (males often spend several days up in a tree) and leave very pronounced 6- to 9-inch trails back and forth to their feeding trees. Along this trail, in addition to an occasional quill, there are often pellets of scat as well as urine, which both your eyes and your nose can detect. Only when snow conditions are just right can you discern individual tracks in a trail.

Birds, Water, and Winter

In winter, dehydration can be as much or more of a threat than starvation for birds. At this time of year, birds often drink water from melting icicles and puddles. When it is severely cold and there is no available water, they eat snow. It takes a lot more energy for birds to thaw snow and for their bodies to bring the freezing temperature of the snow to their body temperature (roughly 102 degrees) than it does to take a drink of water. Water is also key to keeping a bird warm in the winter,

Hairy woodpecker eating snow.

as it is used to preen, or clean and realign, their feathers so that they can maintain the pockets of air next to the skin that retain body heat.

Northern Short-Tailed Shrews

Northern short-tailed shrews, with their short legs, minute eyes, and concealed ears, can be found throughout eastern and central U.S. Their eyesight is so poor that all they can do is detect light, but they compensate by using echolocation for navigation and to locate earthworms, slugs,

Short-tailed shrew.

snails, and other invertebrates. The northern short-tailed shrew and the European water shrew are the only mammals that produce a toxic secretion in their salivary glands. This poison is powerful enough to kill small mammals, but is mainly used to immobilize smaller prey. In winter, the short-tailed shrew limits its activity to conserve energy and relies to some degree on food that it stored in its burrow in the fall.

FEBRUARY 11

Moose and White-Tailed Deer Track Comparison

Even though you know that a moose is the largest member of the deer family, the discrepancy between the size of its hoof and that of a white-tailed deer is impressive. A moose's front foot track is somewhere between 4¼ and 7 inches long, whereas a deer's front track is between 1¼ and 4 inches long. Both have hooves that are heart shaped and point in the direction of travel.

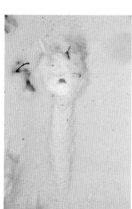

White-tailed deer track in moose track.

Due to their shorter legs, deer are more hindered by snow than moose are. It is not uncommon, where both cervids are found, to find a deer taking advantage of a moose's trail by following the moose's tracks. In the photograph, the moose's foot was dragging as it stepped into the snow, thus causing the groove that leads to the track.

Hairy and Downy Woodpeckers Drumming

Non-vocal communication between birds of the same species becomes apparent at this time of year. Downy woodpeckers have started to hammer out bursts of steady staccato drumbeats on nearby trees. Both male and female woodpeckers drum year-round, but they do so most intensively from January to May, especially during the courtship and early nesting season which begins in March. Woodpeckers drum for a variety of reasons: defending territory, attracting a mate, maintaining contact with a mate, signaling readiness for copulation, and summoning a mate from a distance. Woodpecker pairs do engage in duet drumming, which is thought to play a role in nest site selection and in promoting and maintaining the bond between mates. According to ornithologist David Sibley, the drum of the hairy woodpecker is extremely fast and buzzing, with at least twenty-five taps per second, but has long pauses of twenty seconds or more between drums. The downy woodpecker drums at a slower rate, only about fifteen taps per second, and drums frequently, often with pauses of only a few seconds between each drum.

Downy woodpecker.

Where Do Slugs Go in Winter?

Slugs mate and lay eggs in the spring and fall and can live for twelve to fifteen months. Eggs laid in the fall overwinter in this stage and hatch in the spring. Some members of this generation of slugs may die in the fall, while others hibernate under-

Slug.

ground or beneath loose bark. The survival rate of the hibernators depends upon the harshness of the winter. Look in and under rotting logs to find slug eggs and behind the bark of dying trees to find slug hibernacula.

FEBRUARY 12

American Basswood Buds

American basswood bud.

Bark, silhouettes, and buds are three characteristics that help identify trees in winter. For the most part, buds on different species of trees are distinctly different. American basswood's plump, oval, asymmetrical red buds are unmistakable. Some find basswood buds to be a sweet snack.

White-Footed Mouse and Deer Mouse Tracks

White-footed and deer mice typically move from one place to another by bounding. They have four toes on their front feet and five toes on

their hind feet. Their front feet (¼ inch) are shorter than their back feet (⅝ inch), which are usually placed in front of their front feet. More often than not, the tail leaves a drag mark between each set of tracks. When the snow is soft, the four individual foot tracks often blend into two. Usually white-footed mouse or deer mouse tracks begin and end in cover, often a tree, shrub, or tuft of vegetation. Differentiating the tracks of these two species is usually not possible.

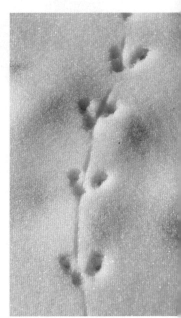

White-footed or deer mouse tracks.

FEBRUARY 13

Snowy Owl Pellets

Snowy owls are the heaviest owls in North America, weighing roughly 4 pounds (a great gray owl is only 2.4 pounds). A lot of fuel is

Snowy owl pellet.

needed to power this magnificent raptor. In the Arctic, where snowy owls live, lemmings are their preferred prey, and one owl may eat more than sixteen hundred of these small rodents in a single year. The indigestible animal parts in this pellet, collected in Massachusetts during an irruption year, consisted of duck feathers, rodent hair, and bones.

Beavers Mating

Reproductive activity begins when a beaver reaches the age of three years. Beavers mate in January and February, with the peak activity taking place in mid-February. Typically, mating takes place in the water, but can occur inside their lodge. Kits, usually three or four, will be born in May or June. Beavers are monogamous and pair for life.

FEBRUARY 14

Happy Valentine's Day

Deer track.

Black raspberry leaves.

Barred owl.

Mating damselflies.

FEBRUARY 15

Northern Saw-Whet Owls Courting

Northern saw-whet owls are rarely seen, in part because they are strictly nocturnal. The males make their presence known this time of year with their far-reaching, distinctive call. Listen for a monotonous series of

Saw-whet owl.

Beaver.

whistled notes, all on the same pitch—a series of "toots" that are heard only during the saw-whet's mating season. Although a saw-whet owl only only weighs about as much as a robin, you would never know it from the volume and carrying power (over 300 yards) of its call.

Snow Doughnuts

"Snow doughnuts," so called because there is a hole in the center of them, or "snow rollers," are a natural phenomenon appearing only when just the right conditions come together. They require a precise balance of air temperature, ice, snow, moisture, and wind in order to form. To begin with, the flat ground surface must have an icy, crusty snow on which new falling snow cannot stick. On top of this, there needs to be about an inch of loose, wet, sticky snow. The air temperature needs to be around 32 degrees. And finally, there must be a strong, gusty wind blowing at 25 miles per hour or more. Snow doughnuts begin to form when the wind scoops chunks out of the top inch or so of snow and these chunks roll, bounce, and tumble, just like tumbleweeds, downwind. They gather additional snow as they roll and become larger and larger until they are too large for the wind to push.

Snow doughnuts can be as small as a tennis ball or as much as 2 feet in diameter, depending on how strong the wind is and how smooth the surface of the snow is. There can be hundreds

Snow doughnut.

of them in a field or patch of woods, usually on level ground. When a snow roller starts to form, there is no hole in the center of it. As it picks up speed and snow, the thin center crumbles, forming the snow doughnut.

FEBRUARY 16

North American River Otter Tracks

North American river otter tracks through a marsh.

Otters have four webbed feet and strong claws that assist them in water as well as on land. Because the pads on the bottoms of their feet lack much hair, the individual toe pads are often well defined in good tracking snow. Each foot leaves a five-toed track, with the inside toe on the front feet being somewhat smaller than the others. In addition to latrine sites, which act as scent markers, otters have four plantar pad glands in the center of each hind foot with which they mark the mounds that they make.

North American river otters.

Foraging Chickadees

If the weather warms up sufficiently in January or February, honey bees use this opportunity to rid their hive of waste that has accumulated since their last flight and to remove the bodies of dead honey bees. Honey bees don't fly very far before dropping either their waste or their dead comrades on the snow. This ritual is quickly noted and taken advantage of by birds, which need constant fuel to survive the cold. Black-capped chickadees help themselves to dead bees at the entrance of the hive body, as well as those littering the surface of the snow close to the hive.

Flock of snow buntings.

Snow Buntings Headed Back to the Arctic

Whirling flocks of snow buntings, a majority of which are males, have begun their migration back to their nesting grounds on the tundra. They breed as far north as the Arctic Ocean—farther north than any other land bird. Male snow buntings are the first migrants to arrive in the Arctic in the spring (in early April), when it can be -20 degrees. Females arrive four to six weeks later, when days are warming and snow is beginning to melt. Scientists believe the males' early return is related to the fact that, unlike most Arctic songbirds, buntings nest in rock cavities, for which there is great competition.

Black-capped chickadee at honey bee hive.

FEBRUARY 17

Deer Mice and the Rigors of Winter

Even though deer mice are active year-round, we don't often see them, as they are active from dusk until dawn. During the winter, when it is very cold, they commonly resort to short periods of torpor (four to nine hours) during the day to conserve energy. While torpid, their body temperature may fall to 55 degrees from a normal temperature of 98 degrees. Sometimes even torpor cannot spare their lives.

Deer mouse.

Snow bunting.

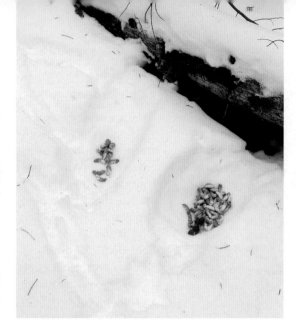

Deep inside narrow cracks, nesting buntings can largely avoid nest predation, but their eggs are susceptible to freezing and require longer incubation than eggs laid in the open. As a result, females remain on the nest throughout much of the incubation period and are fed by the males. This arrangement shortens incubation time and provides the eggs with constant protection from freezing.

Both males' and females' backs and heads are brownish, but by the time their breeding season arrives, the male has a totally white head and belly and a jet-black back. This is not because of a spring molt—snow buntings only molt their feathers once a year, in the late summer. The change in the male's appearance is due to the fact that underneath the colored feather tips, the back feathers are pure black and the body feathers all are white. The male wears off all of the feather tips by actively rubbing them on snow, which reveals his black-and-white breeding plumage.

Ruffed grouse roosts and scat.

FEBRUARY 18

Ruffed Grouse Scat

More often than not, a grouse defecates in its night roost site before leaving in the morning. Grouse scat comes in two forms; one is a dry, fibrous cylindrical pellet with a whitewash of uric acid at one end, and the other a softer, darker brown plop. The vast majority of a grouse's diet (buds, twigs, leaves, catkins) goes directly through its digestive system and forms the dry, coarse scat. Finer (and more nutritious) material such as the cambium layer of woody plants, enters the caeca, two specialized pouches, before passing through the large intestine. The caeca contain bacteria that break down cellulose and produce the more digested, and therefore more liquefied, scat. Sometimes the two kinds of scat are deposited separately and sometimes together, as in the bed on the right in the photograph.

Promethea Moth Cocoon

When the larva of a promethea moth, also called a spicebush silkmoth, is ready to pupate at the end of the summer, it strengthens the stem, or petiole, of a leaf on its host plant (promethea caterpillars favor black cherry, poplar, ash, maple, oak, and willow leaves, among others) with silk and then attaches the silk to a nearby branch, assuring that the leaf will remain attached to the tree. The caterpillar then curls the leaf around itself, spins its cocoon inside the curled leaf, and pupates. The cocoon-bearing leaf remains dangling from the host plant throughout the winter, and in early summer the moth emerges.

Promethea moth cocoon.

FEB

52

FEBRUARY 19

The Eyes of Common Goldeneyes

Common goldeneye.

Common goldeneyes, waterfowl which breed in the boreal forest, overwinter as far north as open water permits, which includes parts of northern New England most years. These birds get their common name from the color of their eyes, but their eyes don't attain this golden color until their first winter. When they hatch, common goldeneye ducklings have gray-brown eyes. Their eyes turn purple-blue, then blue, then green-blue as the ducks age. By the time they are five months old, their eyes are pale green-yellow. They turn bright yellow in males and pale yellow to white in females by mid-winter.

Common goldeneyes.

Winter Identification of White Ash

White ash is relatively easy to identify in winter, between its stout, opposite branches and buds and the corky ridges that form diamond shapes on its bark. There are several species of ash. One feature that distinguishes white ash is the shape of its leaf scars (located

White ash leaf scar.

beneath leaf buds) on well-developed branches. Each leaf scar left by a leaf that fell off the tree is round at the bottom and notched at the top, resembling the letter C on its side. No other ash has c-shaped leaf scars.

FEBRUARY 20

The Perils of Fermented Fruit

In the Northeast, fruit-eating birds are particularly vulnerable in the winter, because they depend so heavily on a food source that ferments, and to get enough protein they need to eat a lot of it.

American robin.

Toxic levels of ethanol can be produced as the natural sugars ferment, causing some consumers to become inebriated. Robins, waxwings, and starlings have been found dead in large flocks after eating fermented berries and diving into the ground or colliding with solid structures. In addition, when they are really drunk, they lose mobility, making them helpless in the presence of predators. To the surprise of many observers, birds that appear lifeless on the ground have been known to sober up and fly away.

FEBRUARY 21

White-Tailed Deer Scraping Trees

White-tailed deer scrapes.

During the winter, white-tailed deer browse on the twigs, buds, and bark of trees. Deer have incisors in the front of their bottom jaw, but none in the front of their top jaw, only a hard palate. They grip the bark with their bottom front incisors and scrape their jaw upward, leaving behind grooves the width of their bottom incisors. Often there are frayed ends of bark at the top end of the groove resulting from the deer having to use its hard palate and incisors, rather than two sets of incisors, to separate the bark from the tree. Favorite trees include red maple, striped maple, oaks, poplar, pines, hemlock, arborvitae, and balsam fir.

Eastern Coyote Beds

Like most carnivores, Eastern coyotes do not have permanent homes, other than the maternal dens in which their young are raised. However, when they rest, usually during the day in the East, they

Eastern coyote bed.

often choose to lie down on a small hummock or boulder so that they can spot both prey and predators (primarily humans) in any direction. When they do so with snow on the ground, they leave a round depression, as they sleep in perfect circles when it is cold out, with their tails covering their noses.

FEBRUARY 22

Icy Crust Effect on Wildlife

Some animals are relatively unaffected by the presence of a crust on the snow. However, many predators and prey are significantly helped or hindered by it. Ruffed grouse cannot seek overnight shelter from the bitter cold and predators by diving into a foot of soft snow and creating a snow cave. On the other hand,

White-tailed deer.

small rodents have a distinct advantage—mice and voles may have several layers of ice between themselves and hungry coyotes, foxes, and owls. Snowshoe hares lose the advantage they have on deep, soft snow—the "snowshoes" that keep them on top of the snow when the bobcat or fisher chasing them has to flounder through it. Turkeys don't have the strength to dig down through crust to reach hidden acorns. If a deer is being chased, its pointed hooves will break through the crust, slowing it down, whereas the crust may well support a lighter predator, allowing it to outrun the deer. Red squirrels have to work much harder to reach their cached winter cones. What is a mere inconvenience to us humans literally costs—as well as saves—the lives of wild animals.

Barred Owl Hunting Story

These beautiful impressions in the snow tell the story of a barred owl diving feet first after prey, most likely a vole or mouse. The fact that there

are no rodent tracks on the surface of the snow indicates that the mouse or vole was hidden in its tunnel under the snow in the subnivean layer at the time. The lack of blood or rodent remnants and the pattern in the snow indicate that the owl's talons did not reach their target on the first dive, and the owl continued to plow through the snow in repeated unsuccessful attempts to capture its prey before taking flight.

Barred owl impressions.

Porcupines Tapping Out

A porcupine eats outer tree bark in order to access the phloem (layer of inner bark cells that transport nutrients) and cambium (produces phloem and xylem cells) layers of a tree, its primary winter diet. In eating these layers, the porcupine unintentionally cuts into the xylem, or sapwood, where the sap, made up of water and dissolved minerals, is transported between the roots and crown of the tree. Thus, inadvertently, porcupines tap the trees whose phloem and cambium they eat. In this case, the weather had warmed up enough to cause pressure in the tree, which in turn caused the sugar maple's sap to flow just as a hungry porcupine happened

Porcupine incisor marks and frozen sap.

along. Soon thereafter, the temperature dropped, causing the sap to freeze and form icicles.

Winter Stoneflies Drumming

Stoneflies spend the larval stage of their life in streams. When the larvae mature, they crawl out of the streams they grew up in, split their larval skins, and emerge as winged adults, ready to mate. Stoneflies are unique among aquatic insects in that there are different species that emerge in all months of the year. Most species mature in warmer months, but some do so during warm spells in winter. There are even two families, referred to as winter stoneflies, that

Stonefly.

emerge only at this time of year, perhaps because of the scarcity of predators.

Warm weather can cause large numbers of winter stoneflies to emerge. In places, the snowy banks of open streams can be littered with half-inch adult stoneflies whose new skins are drying. This entomological exodus from the water typically takes place at night, to avoid being eaten by terrestrial insectivores and birds. After their adult skin dries, winter stoneflies can be seen crawling on top of the snow as they search for a mate.

In many species, males and females locate each other by tapping the tip of their abdomen upon the substrate, a process referred to as drumming. Any stoneflies in contact with that substrate will feel the vibrations of this drumming. Male and female drumming patterns are specific for each species and for each sex. Male stoneflies initiate drumming and females answer. This means of auditory communication is closely related to the "songs" of crickets, grasshoppers and katydids. The difference is that the sound waves of the terrestrial insect songs travel through the air and are loud enough for humans to hear, whereas the sound waves of stonefly drumming travel through a solid medium and are inaudible to us.

Snowshoe Hare Form

Snowshoe hares are elusive, and even though their range extends throughout most of the Northeast, they are rarely seen, as their brown summer coat and white winter coat allow them to be well camouflaged most of the year. In addition, snowshoe hares tend to be active at dusk, dawn, and during the night, when we are not apt to be crossing paths with them.

During the day, hares rest in shallow depressions called

Snowshoe hare form.

forms. Often these sheltered spots are under low conifer branches or other dense cover. When approached, hares frequently remain motionless in their forms before sprinting away. Because they remain in this sheltered area throughout the day, hares often leave a pile of scat in their form. Snowshoe hares may use the same form for rest and shelter throughout the year.

Irruption of Pine Siskins

Flocks of pine siskins and other seed-eating, northern birds may or may not appear at your feeders this winter. Every two years or so, they come south in search of seeds of pines and other conifers, such as cedars, larch, hemlock, and spruce, as well the seeds of deciduous trees including alder, birches, and maples. During winters when these trees have poor crops in Canada, large numbers of birds in the finch family may

Pine siskin.

Mourning doves.

appear in the U.S. This invasion of northern birds is referred to as an irruption.

Pine siskins can temporarily store seeds totaling as much as 20 percent of their body mass in an enlarged part of their esophagus called a crop. They often fill their crop with seeds prior to nightfall, as the energy in this amount of food can sustain them through five to six hours of sub-zero temperatures.

FEBRUARY 25

Mourning Doves Calling

The mournful lament of unmated male mourning doves is one of the first songs heard in the early spring. The frequency of this call builds to a peak from mid-May to mid-June. As in many other pigeons and doves, the mourning dove's main call, or perch coo—*coo-oo, OO, OO, OO*—is an advertising call, sung to attract a mate. Unmated males often establish perches within their territory from which they repeatedly sing.

A shorter nest call is used by a paired male to attract his mate to a potential nest site. The male then gathers nesting material and presents it to the female while standing on her back. While she constructs the nest, he continues to use the nest call to maintain a bond with his mate. Once the nest is built, this call diminishes.

Beavers Grooming

Beavers are constantly grooming and oiling their fur to keep it waterproof. To groom itself, a beaver climbs out of the water onto land or ice. It usually sits upright with its tail between its back legs, which stick out in front, exposing the cloaca—a single opening for all the functions of the scent, reproductive, and excretory organs. The beaver gets oil from its inverted oil glands with its front feet and then rubs it all over its body, using both front and hind feet. It often starts with its head, and then moves to its shoulders and belly. The second toe of each hind foot has a split

Beaver grooming.

nail that the beaver uses to distribute the water-proofing oil and to comb debris out of its coat. Without this coating of oil on their fur, beavers would soon become water soaked and would not be able to tolerate the cold water. During the winter months, grooming takes place inside the lodge unless there's a thaw.

Shrew Defense Mechanism

Coyote tracks end at a hole dug in the snow, with the body of a shrew lying on top of the snow next to the hole. A coyote had succeeded in catching prey it had heard, but upon inspecting it, decided to forego this particular meal. In addition to having poisonous saliva that immobilizes small prey, shrews possess two glands on their sides that emit an unpleasant odor, detectable even by human noses. Very few predators other than owls will consume this insectivore.

Hole dug by a coyote and the shrew it left behind.

Tufted Titmice Singing and Calling

Tufted titmice are declaring the beginning of the end of winter with their fast-repeated, clear whistle song: *Peter—Peter—Peter.* Male titmice repeat this phrase over and over, up to eleven times in succession. Occasionally, females sing a softer version of this song. The call notes (as opposed to song) of tufted titmice, on the other hand, are nasal and mechanical sounding.

Songs are typically more musical and complex than calls and are often sung only by males

Tufted titmouse.

Male red-winged blackbird.

during the breeding season, to attract a mate and claim territory. Calls, on the other hand, have many purposes, including aggression, warning, identification, flocking, hunger, and to announce a food source.

FEBRUARY 27

Returning Red-Winged Blackbirds Survive Cold Temperatures and Few Insects

When the first red-winged blackbirds arrive in the Northeast, it is often still very cold, frequently there is still snow on the ground, and their summer diet of insects has not emerged. A number of factors allow these birds to sustain themselves under these conditions. Red-wings don't limit themselves to one foraging habitat, but seek food in many different places, including marshes, pastures, overgrown fields, shores of lakes and ponds, and windblown, exposed corn fields and crop lands. They look for food on a variety of substrates, including trees and vegetation, and are very adept at gaping—forcing their bill open against the resistance of bark to reach into the crooks and crannies where insects are overwintering. Because their diet adapts to the seasonal availability of food—primarily insects in summer and seeds and grains in fall, winter, and early spring—red-wings can adapt to less-than-ideal conditions.

Red squirrel tapping.

Red Squirrels Eating Buds and Tapping Out

In early spring, when fluctuating temperatures cause the sap to run in trees, red squirrels will bite sugar maple trees down to the sap-bearing

Old red squirrel taps.

xylem, which causes the sap to start flowing from the tree. The squirrels then leave for a period of time, sometimes feeding on the tree's buds, allowing the sap to evaporate (sugar maple sap is 97.5 percent water), and returning later to harvest the sugary sap that remains.

Red squirrel eating bud.

FEBRUARY 28

Tom Turkeys Strutting

When male wild turkeys, or toms, are displaying for one or more females during courtship, their behavior includes something referred to as the "strut." The male turkey fans his tail; lowers his wings, with the middle primary feathers dragging on the ground; raises his back feathers; throws his head back; and inflates his crop as he glides along the ground in view of one or more females. In snow, this performance leaves a relatively straight line of turkey tracks with a line (or several) to either side of the tracks, left by the tom's primary feathers. When the tom turns a corner,

Tom turkeys and hen.

Tracks of tom turkey dragging wings.

several feather tips often leave lines in the snow. Wild turkeys are displaying in and near woodlands, in preparation for mating in March.

Red Fox vs. Coyote Tracks

Red foxes and coyotes, both being canids, have five toes on their front feet (usually only four register) and four toes on their hind feet. Their tracks are similar in shape but very different in size. Red foxes weigh between 7 and 14 pounds. Coyotes weigh between 20 and 50 pounds. The size of their tracks reflects this difference. A red fox's print is roughly 2 inches long, whereas a coyote's is roughly 3 inches. In addition, note that the coyote's toe and metatarsal pads are quite distinct, whereas the furry-footed fox's are not. In the photo, the red fox tracks are on the left, headed down, and the coyote tracks are on the right, headed up.

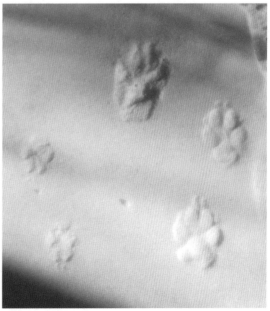

Red fox and coyote tracks.

61

MARCH

Mourning Cloak Butterflies

The mourning cloak butterfly, named because its scales resemble the velvet clothing mourners used to wear, is one of the earliest butterflies to emerge in the Northeast. It can be flying this early in the year because, unlike most butterflies, it overwinters as an adult. Insects that remain in the Northeast year-round overwinter in one of four stages: egg, larva, pupa, or adult. Typically, this far north, all members of a given species (or family) of butterfly overwinter in the same stage. Thus, most swallowtails (Papilionidae) pass the winter as pupae, whereas most members of the family Nymphalidae, or "brush-footed" butterflies (e.g., mourning cloak, question mark, eastern comma, and Compton tortoiseshell) overwinter as adults.

Most butterfly species spend the winter as larvae or pupae, though a few overwinter as eggs. When spring comes, they have one or more stages of metamorphosis to go through before becoming adults and mating. Not so the mourning cloak. As soon as temperatures rise significantly, and occasionally during mid-winter thaws, the mourning cloak butterfly slips out from behind the loose bark or crevice where it spent the winter and takes to the air. Males typically perch in sunny openings during the afternoon and wait for receptive females. After mating, the adult mourning cloak female lays her eggs on one of several species of trees—willow, poplar, elm, hackberry, and birch—whose leaves will have emerged for her larvae to feed on by the time they hatch. The red-spotted black larvae, or caterpillars, live in a communal web and feed together on young leaves. They pupate and

emerge as adult butterflies in June or July. After feeding briefly, the adults become dormant, or estivate, until fall, when they revive to feed and store energy for hibernation.

Overwintering butterflies in any stage enter into a physiological state called hibernal diapause, characterized by a lowered metabolic rate and biochemical changes. The mourning cloak cannot tolerate being frozen, so it reduces the water content of its body and builds up glycerol which acts as antifreeze. This process is called supercooling: lowering the body temperature, without ice formation, to levels below that at which freezing normally occurs.

As you might expect, emerging early in the spring has its disadvantages as well as its advantages. On the downside, there are not many flowers in bloom at this time of year, and therefore little nectar is available. For the most part, emerging adult butterflies make do by feeding on tree sap, especially that of oaks. Mourning cloaks walk down the tree trunk to a spot where a tree has been injured or a branch has broken, and feed head downward. When their wings are closed, they are extremely well camouflaged. Mourning cloaks will occasionally feed on rotting fruit and nectar, if they can find any, and they obtain salts and other minerals from puddles as well as from animal scat. On the plus side of getting an early start in the spring, hatching mourning cloak larvae have first choice of the emerging green leaves of the forest, and many of the migratory birds that feed on them haven't returned yet.

Not only does the mourning cloak have the distinction of being one of the earliest butterflies to emerge in spring, but it is also our

North American river otter slide.

Mourning cloak—wings open.

forming a protective hood that has a narrow opening on one side. Both the color, which varies from yellow green to deep maroon, and the way in which the spathe opens (left to right or right to left) are genetically determined. If you look inside this opening, you will find an inch-long, spherical spadix, consisting of fifty to one hundred tiny flowers packed tightly together.

The flowers of skunk cabbage are sequentially bisexual: the tiny, white, female reproductive parts mature first and later are replaced by the yellow male parts. The first flowers to open (and thus the oldest) are at the top of the flower head and the flowers mature downward, so that when the upper flowers are in the male phase and are releasing pollen, the lower flowers are still in the female phase. Skunk cabbage does not self-pollinate, however, and thus needs an agent to disperse the pollen of one plant to another to produce fruit. Flies, beetles, and other insects become covered with pollen that has fallen to the bottom of the spathe, and they carry this pollen to the next skunk cabbage plant they visit.

longest-lived butterfly. The average life span of the adult mourning cloak is ten months, but some individuals survive for nearly a year. It is not surprising that the mourning cloaks we see in March look a bit worse for wear, with wings often frayed.

Mourning cloak—wings closed.

Pollen is not the only thing that skunk cabbage uses to attract pollinators. In addition to being colorful and smelling much like rotting meat when bruised, this plant also serves as a little warming hut where insects can heat up their flight muscles in the middle of a cold, wet swamp. Skunk cabbage has the unusual ability, through a process called thermogenesis, to absorb oxygen while it grows and produce heat. Not only does it produce heat, it also regulates it. The spadix maintains a temperature of about 68 degrees inside the spathe, regardless of the outside temperature. The temperature inside the spathe may exceed the temperature of the air surrounding it by as much as 77 degrees for a period of two to three weeks, in part thanks to the spongy, insulating tissue of the dark, heat-absorbing spathe. In addition to possibly volatilizing chemicals that produce aromas attractive to insects, the heat generated allows skunk cabbage to grow and flower so early in the spring.

Skunk Cabbage

In the Northeast, animals and plants are showing signs of life. Squirrels, foxes, and fishers are all giving birth and, after a winter of dormancy, the first flowering plants will soon emerge. In swamps and wetlands throughout the Northeast, the flowers of skunk cabbage are poking their heads out of the damp earth, having spent the winter buried beneath it. This member of the jack-in-the-pulpit family derives its name from the skunklike smell given off when its leaves are crushed or bruised.

The structure of skunk cabbage flowers is unusual. The flower consists of a spathe and a spadix. A highly modified leaf referred to as a spathe wraps around the spadix (flower head),

Skunk cabbage flowers.

When skunk cabbage flowers, its leaves are not very apparent. They are usually just barely poking out of the ground, tightly wrapped around each other in a conelike structure next to the flower. When the days get warmer in late April or May, and the flowers have started to wither, the leaves unfurl. They grow to a length of 3 feet and can be a foot wide. Their resemblance to the leaves of another wetland plant, hellebore, is striking. By mid-August, the leaves of skunk cabbage have disappeared and the fruits are evident.

Calcium oxalate crystals are found in all the species in the Araceae family. If you were to eat the leaves of skunk cabbage, these crystals would cause a severe burning sensation in your mouth, throat, and esophagus, and possibly cause your throat to swell. Some animals, however, seem immune to these crystals. Canada geese have been seen eating early leaves, squirrels are known to consume the spadix, and wood ducks eat the seeds. A study of black bears emerging from hibernation found that the bears fed almost exclusively on skunk cabbage unless acorns were plentiful. Even if there was an ample supply of acorns, 52 percent of the bears' diet consisted of skunk cabbage. This is especially surprising when you take into account that acorns are far more nutritious, containing up to 10 percent fat compared to skunk cabbage's 0.2 percent.

Although skunk cabbage is not common in northern New England, its range does extend north into Canada. If you happen to know of a patch, you might want to visit it and carefully kneel down and smell the flower. If you haven't broken or bruised the spathe, it is possible to smell a faintly sweet aroma, particularly if there are female flowers present.

Skunk cabbage leaves.

Idiosyncratic Courtship and Mating Rituals of March Breeders

Most mammals, unlike humans, do not have the luxury of being able to conceive on a regular basis throughout the year. Their reproductive systems are often regulated by lengthening daylight, which triggers hormonal activity that results in mating just once or twice a year. The courtship and breeding behavior of different species of mammals has many similarities, but also includes individualized rituals. During March, many of these rituals take place, revealing different species' idiosyncratic traits.

Eastern Chipmunk

Eastern chipmunks breed twice a year, typically in March and in June. Males emerge from their winter torpor in search of receptive females, engaging in mock battles with any males whose paths they happen to cross. Females, emerging a few weeks after males, are in estrus for a few days or a week, but are receptive for only seven hours. If approached before she is receptive, a female will drive off any male suitors. If a female

Eastern chipmunk.

Non-Vocal Avian Courtship Sounds

The Wilson's snipe and the American wood-cock are both shorebirds in the sandpiper family (Scolopacidae) that breed and nest inland. While both of these species have vocalized calls which play a part in their courtship, they also both have a non-vocal auditory component to their courtship which is produced by their feathers when they are airborne. The feathers utilized by these two species are located on different parts of their bodies.

Air rushing over a snipe's outspread tail feathers creates a winnowing sound. Both male and female produce this sound prior to nesting, usually as they engage in courtship display and are diving in the air toward the ground. It is the outermost tail feathers that generate the sound when the bird is flying at a speed of about 25 miles per hour. This winnowing is used to defend territory when the male makes it, and it is used by both the male and the female to attract a mate.

The male American woodcock's courtship ritual involves both vocal and non-vocal sounds as well. While on the ground, he repeatedly gives a buzzy *peent* call before taking off into the air. Once airborne, he flies in a wide circle, spiraling upward; his wings make a twittering sound as air passes between three outer primaries. When he reaches the apex of the spiral (200–350 feet), the twittering gives way to a vocal chirping call as he zigzags his way back down to the ground, where he resumes his *peent*ing.

Wilson's snipe.

is receptive, the courting male will trill and nudge her affectionately. His intentions are indicated by his up-and-down tail movements. At all other times, chipmunks only move their tails from side-to-side. Occasionally, several males pursue one female, and there is great pandemonium as they vie for her attention and chase her until one male prevails. A female may mate ten to twenty times within about a six- to seven-hour period, not necessarily with the same male.

Virginia Opossum

The peak of opossum breeding takes place in February and March. Both male and female opossums have anatomically unusual reproductive traits. Males have a forked penis, and females have two uteri and two vaginas. The female is receptive for about thirty-six hours every three to five days until she conceives. During this time, if she allows a male to mount her, they soon fall over together onto their right sides. It appears that this fall to the right is an integral part of the process, as no sperm has been found inside a female when the two opossums failed to fall or fell to the left.

North American River Otter

Otters have a prolonged breeding season, from December to April, but may only reproduce every two years in the northern part of their range. When a male and female pair up, they proceed to wrestle, mock fight, and chase each other in and out of the water. When he reaches her, the male, as is common with other members of the weasel family, grabs the back of the female's neck with his teeth, often wounding her, while he proceeds to mate with her, usually in the water. Otters are called "induced ovulators"—if the female is sufficiently stimulated, the act of copulation releases an egg from her ovary.

Eastern Gray Squirrel

Most gray squirrels breed between May and July, but some breed at this time of year. Females are in estrus between eight and twelve hours, and during this time males gather from as far as half a mile away. The males are constantly fighting for dominance as they relentlessly chase the females. The most dominant males are closest to the

Eastern gray squirrel.

female, and when she is ready to mate, the most dominant male approaches and copulation takes place. As an adaptation to assure the male's paternity, his semen forms a gelatinous plug in the female's vagina that reduces the success rate of later matings and ensures that the first male fertilizes most of her eggs. However, following copulation, both male and female squirrels typically clean their genital areas, and in so doing, the female usually removes the plug, occasionally eating it.

Star-nosed mole.

Star-Nosed Mole

Beginning in late February, female star-nosed moles enter estrus repeatedly if they have not bred. Once mated, star-nosed moles share a breeding characteristic with eastern gray squirrels: the males of both species leave a copulatory plug in the females after mating. Secretions from glands in the male moles create this plug, which prohibits other males from mating successfully with the female.

Deer Mouse

Typically, the breeding of deer mice coincides with vegetation growth and insect activity. In the Northeast, mating takes place once each month from March to September. During years when food is scarce, the fertility of both male and female mice is restricted. When food is adequate or ample, courtship takes place, with males and receptive females sniffing each other and often coming nose to nose. As their heads approach each other, they bring their noses and mouths together in a position called "kissing." Gestures we would be tempted to call affectionate often follow, including grooming, nibbling, and licking each other.

Fisher

March is the peak of the fisher breeding season, and this becomes obvious to anyone looking for signs of this animal in the woods. Scent marking and tracks are ubiquitous, as males pursue females for miles. Both males and females engage in scent marking with their urine and scat, and signs where they have rubbed on saplings are usually abundant. A male and female travel and interact for a week or two prior to copulation. The male produces sperm only for about six weeks, and the female is in estrus for six to eight days. After fertilization, implantation of the egg is delayed until February of the following year. Young are born in March and three to nine days later the female is ready to breed again.

While none of these examples is as dramatic as that of the fall-breeding male porcupine, who sprays his mate with urine prior to mating, the courtship and mating behavior of every species of animal reveals individualized rituals and traits. Tail wagging, forked penises, falling to the right, biting, "kissing," vaginal plugs, induced ovulation, delayed implantation, and pheromones all serve to make March a most interesting month for mating.

MARCH 1

Mink Slide

Most mammals that are active in winter hunker down until well after it has stopped snowing, but mink tracks can often be found the morning following a storm. Like other weasels, this bounding carnivore often leaves diagonally paired tracks but, unlike other weasels, its tracks are consistently the same distance (1 to 3 feet) apart. They are most common in or near wetlands.

Mink cover ground in several ways. In addition to bounding on top of the snow, they are known to dive under it and make short tunnels. Although a fierce predator, the mink also has a playful side, much like its cousin, the North American river otter. On top of the snow, especially down inclines, they often slide, saving energy. Look for a groove in the snow about 3 inches in diameter, with paired tracks at either end.

Mink slide and tracks.

Staghorn Sumac Sustains Songbirds

By this time of the year, fruit-eating birds have, for the most part, devoured the choicest fruits available. What remains are the fruits of last resort. While staghorn sumac fruits may not be a preferred food, they provide much-sought-after food for birds in late winter, when most other fruits and seed have either been consumed or are yet to appear. American crows, northern mockingbirds, American robins, eastern bluebirds, and many other species of songbirds incorporate staghorn sumac fruit into their diet. Sumac seeds are important winter forage for game birds such

American robin.

as ruffed grouse, ring-necked pheasant, northern bobwhite, and wild turkey. Staghorn sumac fruits make up in quantity what they lack in nutrition. Although only 5 percent of the fresh weight is protein, it tides many insect- and worm-eating songbirds over until warm weather arrives.

Evening Grosbeak Bills Turning Green

Breeding-season changes in a bird's physical appearance can involve more than a set of new feathers. The colors of birds' feet, legs, and bills also vary in different seasons. The European starling's bill is black in winter and turns yellow as the breeding season approaches. Male and female evening grosbeaks also undergo a change in bill color, from bone-colored in winter, to a greenish hue in spring. Hormones are largely responsible for these pigmentation changes, which often play a role in courtship. Usually a change in the color of the bill is most pronounced among birds that retain the same plumage color and pattern throughout the year, such as starlings and evening grosbeaks.

MARCH 2

Snow Flea Airbags

Warming weather may bring snow fleas out of the leaf litter to the surface of the snow, where they constantly hurl themselves from one spot to another. A close look at them in action reveals that they tuck their heads down just before catapulting through the air. Before launching itself, a snow flea everts three anal sacs from its anus. When it lands, these sticky appendages act like automobile air bags, absorbing the shock of landing as well as preventing the snow flea from bouncing around. There may be another function that they perform, but it is not known what that might be. While there are many genera of snow fleas, only species in the genus *Hypogastrura* possess anal sacs.

Female evening grosbeak.

Snow flea.

Common raven.

Common Ravens Repairing and Building Nests

Common ravens have begun tending their nests. Often ravens will use the same nest for many years, renovating and repairing it every year. They typically nest on or in cliffs and trees—although abandoned cars, a satellite dish, and a barbecue grill have been used—with the female doing the lion's share of the construction. The male assists her by bringing sticks he has found to the nest site. The base of the nest consists of sticks up to 3 feet long, with smaller branches woven into a cup lined with softer material such as sheep's wool, fur, and shredded bark. The finished nest is 2 to 3 feet across and up to 4 feet deep.

Common raven nest.

MARCH 3

Fishers Climbing Trees

Although fishers catch most of their prey and do the vast majority of their traveling on the ground, they are also agile climbers. At this time of year, many are giving birth high up in hollow tree dens. When fishers come down a tree, they often jump to the ground, rather than climb down the tree. If there is snow on the ground, the fisher leaves an impression, the clarity of which is determined by the depth and condition of the snow. In this photograph you can see its four foot tracks as well as a slight depression where its head touched the snow.

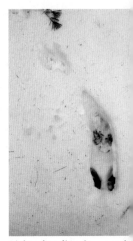

Fisher landing impression snow.

Snowshoe Hares Molting

In most parts of their range, snowshoe hares undergo three molts a year: in early spring, from white to brown; in summer, from brown to brown; and in late fall, from brown to white. Hares seem

Snowshoe hare hair.

Snowshoe hare.

to use the length of the day, rather than temperature or presence of snow, to time their molts. For this reason, climate change has affected their ability to be camouflaged.

MARCH 4

Exposed Bee Hive

In the Northeast, feral honey bees usually choose a protected site such as a hollow tree or rock crevice in which to build their hive, as harsh winters demand this protection. Infrequently, you will see where they've tried to survive the elements

Honey bee comb.

without anything to contain the heat that the honey bees produce by shivering, or to block the wind, snow, or sleet. Inevitably, this far north, the colony will not survive the winter.

Red Foxes Preparing Dens

Red foxes will be giving birth this month or next, so the time for preparing the den has arrived. While it is never hard to see a fox den due to the pile of dirt at its main entrance, the dens are most obvious when there is still snow on the ground and the dirt removed by the foxes is conspicuous against the snow.

Red foxes seldom dig their own dens. More often, they take over a woodchuck's abandoned

Red fox den in snow.

burrow or, in some cases, forcibly drive the woodchuck out. Sometimes they devour the woodchuck. Foxes den in woodlands as well as fields, usually fairly near water and on a sandy knoll where they can observe the surrounding territory and where their den will be well drained. Most dens have one or two entrances. The tunnel usually slants downward about 4 feet beneath the surface and then extends laterally for 20 to 30 feet before resurfacing. An enlarged chamber along the main tunnel serves as a maternity den.

MARCH 5

Bald Eagles Refurbishing or Building Their Nests

Bald eagles in the Northeast are repairing and adding to their nests, even as snow and cold temperatures continue. They may reuse their nests year after year: One nest in Ohio was used for thirty-four years until the tree blew

Bald eagle.

Bald eagle nest.

hemlock, and balsam fir branch tips in order to feed on the cones, leaves, and tender buds. Seeds within the cones are often cached, whereas the buds and leaves are readily consumed, and then the twig is discarded. These nip twigs often litter the surface of the ground.

MARCH 6

Why, When, and What Porcupines Eat

down. Although most don't come close to the record-breaking dimensions of an eagle nest in Florida, which was 9½ feet wide, 20 feet deep, and weighed almost 3 tons, they are impressive structures, averaging 5 feet wide and 3 feet deep.

Typically, eagles will choose one of the biggest trees in an area in which to build their nest. Because their nests will be used for many years, eagles often choose living trees, which will remain standing longer. The nest is usually built in the top quarter of a tree, just below the crown. Both male and female eagles collect sticks for the nest, either finding them on the ground or breaking them off nearby trees. In parts of Alaska and northern Canada, where trees are scarce and short, eagles often nest on the ground.

Red Squirrels Nipping Twigs

Porcupines are not the only rodents that find the tips of conifer branches tasty. Red squirrels nip spruce, pine,

Red squirrel eastern hemlock nip twigs.

The woody plants that a porcupine feeds on change with the season. Sugar maple buds are a rich source of protein in the spring. Because sugar maple leaves contain a lot of tannins, porcupines switch to the cambium of basswood, aspen, and sapling beech trees during the summer. In fall, acorns and beech nuts are highly sought after, and during the winter, porcupines forage on the cambium of eastern hemlocks and, to some extent, sugar maples. Most of this eating is done at night, in part because of changes in plant and leaf chemistry that increase the nutritional value of plants at night.

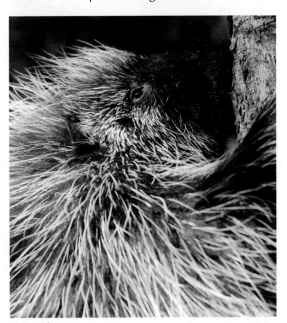

Porcupine.

Active winter spider.

Snow Spiders Active

Although most spiders appear fragile and susceptible to the elements, occasionally you will see one crawling on top of the snow. There are species that remain active in winter, even in the Northeast. Most overwintering spiders live in the leaf litter beneath the snow, but they often emerge when the temperature is between 25 and 35 degrees in late winter and early spring.

MARCH 7

White-Winged Crossbills Nesting

White-winged crossbills inhabit the boreal forests of northern New England. This species, as well as the red crossbill, is named for its bill, which is adapted to extracting seeds from conifer cones. Crossbills use their crossed bills to wedge open cone scales, after which they lift the seeds free with their tongues. Just one bird can eat up to three thousand conifer seeds in a day.

White-winged crossbills are erratic nesters that have been found breeding every month of the year. The birds nest whenever the available food supply is sufficient for egg formation and is likely to remain sufficient for at least the three weeks of the energy-demanding nestling stage. Three nesting periods have been observed, each corresponding to the ripening of cones from different conifer species. The first season occurs when the cones of tamarack, or American larch, and white spruce mature. The second nesting period begins in January and February, when they

White-winged crossbill.

rely mainly on white and red spruce cone crops, and the third season is starting now, as black spruce cones begin to open up.

Woodchucks Emerging and Mating

One of the earliest signs of spring is the emergence of woodchucks, the largest members of the squirrel family in the Northeast, after their winter hibernation comes to an end. Males become active before females, and signs of their arousal are obvious, as one of their first activities is to do some excavating in their tunnel. This endeavor scatters dirt around the entrance, which is easily spotted on any remaining snow. Equally obvious is the muddy trail a woodchuck leaves when he

Woodchuck burrow.

Mating flies.

goes in search of a female, enters her burrow, mates, and then returns to his own burrow for a few more weeks of sleep.

Flies Mating

Some species of flies are not only active this early in the spring, but are mating. Perched on top of coyote scat, surrounded by snow and temperatures still hovering around 32 degrees, these members of the Heleomyzidae family were leisurely copulating. Typically, species in this family of flies are found in dark or cold places and are most likely to be encountered in the spring or late fall. Different species are associated with caves, mammal burrows, carrion, and birds' nests, in addition to scat.

MARCH 8

Eastern screech owl.

Eastern Screech Owls Courting

Screech owls are in the throes of courtship, with males crouching, trilling, and providing food to win the allegiance of a life-long mate. Females sometimes respond by begging and crouching with partly extended wings. Allopreening, the preening of each other, strengthens the pair bond. Mostly monogamous, screech owls generally only seek a new mate following the death of a mate or, in 6 percent of pairs, divorce from a mate, often during or after unsuccessful nests.

Porcupine Digestion

A fisher killed and ate a porcupine, leaving behind a section of the porcupine's digestive tract called a caecum. This is a sac between the large and small intestines where the cellulose in leaves and bark that a porcupine eats is broken down.

During the warmer seasons of the year, porcupines feed on sugar maple buds, leaves of basswood, aspen and beech saplings, grasses and other herbaceous plants, apples, acorns, and beech nuts. In winter, their diet consists mostly of leaves, mainly eastern hemlock in the Northeast, which contain low levels of nutrients and high levels of dietary fiber. Porcupines, along with beavers, hares, rabbits, and ruffed grouse, are also host to bacteria that secrete enzymes capable of digesting cellulose through the process of fermentation. Because these enzymes work slowly, the digestive tract of a porcupine is very long (26 percent of a porcupine's total weight), and fiber passes through it slowly.

Most of the bacterial activity in a porcupine's digestive system takes place in the caecum, which is about the same size as a porcupine's stomach. Here fermentation turns finely ground woody material into molecules small enough to be

Porcupine caecum.

absorbed by the porcupine's body. This process is called "hind gut fermentation" and it supplies 16 percent of a porcupine's energy requirements.

MARCH 9

North American River Otters Sliding

North American river otters' slides.

North American river otter tracks are found at both ends of slide.

Otters will travel long distances from one pond to the next, and, when they do, they frequently alternate between bounding and sliding. They often slide down hills, but they also slide on level ground and sometimes even uphill. While sliding, the otter holds its front feet back along its sides with its hind feet out behind, leaving a trough roughly 6 to 12 inches wide and up to 25 feet long. Two footprints (actually four, but the hind feet land on top of where the front feet landed, so it looks like two) can be found at the end and at the beginning of each slide, where the otter stopped sliding, bounded, and began sliding again. Occasionally, in deep snow on level ground, an otter will use its foot to help push it along, either inside or outside of the trough.

Otters slide at all times of the year, on mud as well as on snow and ice, and they appear to do so to get from one place to another, as well as purely for fun, as when they repeatedly slide down the same slope over and over.

Muskrat Kill Site

Muskrats are active year-round, seeking shelter in two- or three-chambered mounds that they build in the fall. Daily foraging trips are taken under the ice to find vegetation to eat. Often muskrats will take their food to eat inside of small mounds of vegetation called "push-ups" that provide some cover while they eat.

Muskrats have many predators, including hawks, eagles, owls, mink, foxes, coyotes, fishers, raccoons, and otters. One of the most threatening predators at any time of year, but especially winter, is the mink. The mink also resides in wetlands and is agile when it comes to traveling above and below the ice if there are openings.

Low water levels in marshes increase mink predation on muskrats. During the winter, muskrats leave their lodges less frequently, but forage farther away from it. This provides mink, especially large males, with ample opportunity to prey upon muskrats. The rust-colored fur, along with a portion of the upper jaw in this photograph, confirm that it was a muskrat that met its end, and its proximity to water, as well as nearby tracks, indicate that the predator was a mink.

Muskrat kill site.

MARCH 10

Eastern Bluebirds Visiting Nest Boxes

Eastern bluebirds are returning to their nesting areas. Weather affects the timing of their return, in that it determines the availability of the insects required for nesting. Typically, bluebirds return in March, when bare ground is usually beginning to be exposed and insects are emerging.

You may or may not have the same birds nesting in your yard in consecutive years. If bluebirds have a successful nesting season, they are more likely to return to the same area the following year. Year-old bluebirds typically nest close to where they were raised.

Often bluebirds will return, inspect nest boxes, and disappear. In a few days, this may very well happen again. Ornithologists feel this coming-and-going behavior may be food related. On sunny, warm days they may be able to find insects near the nesting area, but on cold, wet days they may have to go farther afield in search of food. Sometimes these birds return to nest, sometimes not. Even if they return and begin nest building, it is not unheard of for early nesting birds to abandon their nest in search of another suitable location.

Winter Fireflies

Most species of fireflies overwinter as larvae, but winter fireflies, after pupating in a rotting log, emerge as winged adults in late summer and are often seen on the trunks of trees. When the temperature starts to drop, they crawl under tree bark and stay there until late winter or early spring, when they reappear. The adults of this species have no light

Winter firefly.

organ, but the larvae and pupae do. Winter fireflies are often abundant on maple trunks at this time of year; it is so common to find them in sap buckets that they're sometimes considered to be pests.

MARCH 11

Migrating Common Grackles Return to Breeding Grounds

Male common grackles have started to arrive on their northeastern breeding grounds, having migrated from the southern U.S. Females will arrive in another week or so. Common grackles typically migrate in flocks of hundreds of birds, not all of them grackles. Red-winged blackbirds,

Common grackles.

Male eastern bluebird.

brown-headed cowbirds, European starlings, and occasionally American robins join common grackles in these migrating flocks. In the early 1990s, magnetic material was found in the heads and necks of common grackles, indicating that the geomagnetic field may play a role in their migratory navigation.

Pitcher Plants Persist through Winter

The pitcher plant flowers that bloomed in bogs last June persist through the winter. Their maroon petals are gone, as is their scent, and they are withered and some-

Pitcher plant.

what drab-colored, but the upside-down flowers are still on display, supported by long, graceful stems protruding above the surface of the snow. Pitcher plants flower for about two weeks at the beginning of summer, during which time their pollen is distributed, primarily by bees. After fertilization, three hundred to six hundred seeds form within each ovary. This is when the carnivorous pitcher leaves develop. In late fall, the "pitchers" begin to wither and the seedpods turn brown and split open, scattering seeds. In three to five years, the plants which these seeds grew into will begin flowering.

MARCH 12

Owls and Humans Share Trait

Birds have three eyelids: an upper eyelid, a lower eyelid, and a third, semitransparent membrane, called a nictitating membrane, that sweeps across the eye much like a windshield wiper. This membrane keeps their eyes moist and protects their corneas from being scratched.

In most birds, including owls, the upper and lower eyelids close the eyes when sleeping,

Barred owl.

and the nictitating membrane is used for blinking. Humans close their eyes mainly by lowering the upper eyelid, but most birds do this by raising the lower lid. Owls, and a few other birds such as parrots, toucans, wrens, and ostriches, are more humanlike in that their upper lids are usually lowered to close their eyes. Owls close their eyes, partly or entirely, when capturing and transferring prey, scratching their faces, preening another owl, or copulating.

MARCH 13

Juvenile Raccoons Dispersing and Adults Mating

When raccoons emerge from their communal winter dens, which they are doing now, the juveniles born last spring disperse. Young males may travel as far as 170 miles, but usually establish their territories no farther than 14 miles from their birthplace. Juvenile females usually remain in their

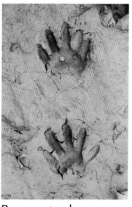

Raccoon tracks.

Raccoon tracks in snow.

birth area, establishing a home range that either overlaps with or is included within the range of their mothers. This time of year is also the peak of the breeding season for adult raccoons. Both males and females have multiple mates.

Male American Goldfinch Seasonal Plumages

Male American goldfinch.

Most songbirds have one complete molt every year, in the late summer. Some, like the American goldfinch, have another partial molt in the spring. Last fall, male goldfinches molted, replacing many of their bright yellow feathers with drab, greenish gray feathers, so that they closely resemble females during the winter. Goldfinches start their partial molt in February, and in the next month or two, males will once again become bright yellow beacons.

MARCH 14

Turkey Vultures Returning to Northern Breeding Grounds

Turkey vultures return to northern New England around the middle of March. Recognizing them is not hard: they are bigger than any other raptor in the Northeast except for eagles. At a distance, turkey vultures look all black, but a closer look reveals that the undersides of the flight feathers, along the trailing edge and wing tips, are lighter in color than the rest of the bird, giving the wing a two-toned appearance. (Black vulture wings are solid black with silvery tips.) The feathers at the wing tips are often separated, which some birders refer to as "fingers". In addition, vultures hold their wings slightly raised, forming a wide open *V* or dihedral shape in the sky as they soar, teeter, and circle while riding the thermals.

Turkey vulture.

Rodents Recycling

Bones, antlers, skulls, turtle shells—all are recycled relatively quickly by rodents seeking minerals, particularly calcium and phosphorus. All rodents have four incisors, two in the front of the upper jaw and two opposite these, on the bottom jaw.

Eastern gray squirrel eating moose skull. Inset: Woodchuck upper mandible with deformed incisor due to missing opposite lower incisor.

78

These incisors, unlike other teeth, never stop growing and are kept in check by wearing against each other or gnawing on hard objects.

If an incisor is broken or lost, the opposing incisor will continue growing in a circle, having nothing to grind against, causing the rodent to die of starvation or from having its brain pierced through the roof of its mouth by the ever-growing incisor.

MARCH 15

Red-Tailed Hawks on Nest

In late February or early March, pairs of red-tailed hawks visit several of their nests from previous years, often choosing two or more nests to repair. Conifer sprigs are sometimes placed on the outside of the structure early in the process, before a nest is chosen, perhaps to advertise ownership. The refurbishing—or the building of a new nest—takes only a few days.

Usually two or three eggs, sometimes four, are laid. Incubation is roughly twenty-eight to thirty-five days. Although both parents have brood patches—a featherless area on the belly of incubating parents that allows direct transfer of body heat—most of the incubating is done by the female, with the male delivering food to her throughout the day.

Porcupines Claiming Dens

At this time of year, if they do not inhabit rocky ledges, porcupines often stake out their den trees by eating patches of inner bark, or cambium, with the exposed fresh inner wood announcing their occupancy. Typically, if a tree den is used year after year, porcupines gnaw off a portion of bark each year, sometimes eating the old, scarred bark, which, due to previous chewing, lacks cambium cells, indicating that this behavior is not for the purpose of obtaining nutrients.

Male and female red-tailed hawks on nest.

Fresh porcupine gnawing at hollow tree den site.

MARCH 16

Ring-Necked Ducks Return

Male ring-necked duck.

Female ring-necked duck.

Although named for the chestnut band, or ring, around its neck, which is barely discernible to the naked eye, this diving duck does have a distinct white ring around its bill. After wintering in the southern U.S., Mexico, and the Caribbean, ring-necked ducks that breed in northern New England arrive on their breeding grounds in mid-March. Before departing, they undertake orientation and exercise flights for a week or so. Flocks of ten to twenty-five ducks migrate north at night, using celestial, landscape, and geomagnetic cues. Extremes in spring weather can temporarily stall or reverse migration and delay arrival on their breeding grounds.

North American Otter Sign

Dead crayfish.

The most prevalent prey item in otter scat is fish, followed closely by crayfish. Otters will take advantage of other prey, such as frogs, salamanders, ducks, muskrats, an occasional young beaver, mice, snakes, insects, and even turtles when readily obtainable, but fish and crayfish are first and second choices.

Black bear cub.

Black Bears Soon to Leave Dens

Two-month-old black bear cubs are weeks away from leaving the shelter of their den and the warmth of their mother. Mother and cubs will

Early Spring Migrants

Bird migration, along with the accumulation of fat, breeding, and molting, are driven by changing photoperiod. Among the first groups of birds to move north in the spring are waterfowl. Ducks, geese, and swans may begin migrating as soon as frozen lakes and marshes start to thaw. The peak of waterfowl migration in the Northeast begins at the end of March and runs through April.

Ponds, flooded fields, and open rivers are frequented by these birds during their migration north.

Female wood duck.

Male hooded merganser.

Male American wigeon.

remain together until next May or June, when the year-and-a-half-old cubs will become independent and their mother will be looking for a mate.

MARCH 17

March Flies Mating

March flies, named for the month in which they typically emerge as winged adults, are often found in large swarms at this time of year. The adults do not live long and are often found with tails connected, copulating. This gave rise to the common name of "love bugs" for one species. After mating, female March flies dig burrows into which they deposit a mass of two hundred to three hundred eggs, after which they die. After hatching, the larvae live underground, emerging usually in the spring, but the adults of some species can be seen in the fall.

The larvae of all members of this fly family, the Bibionidae, feed on dead vegetation or living plant roots. As adults, they feed on the nectar of fruit tree flowers and are considered important pollinators.

Bald eagle.

Bald Eagles Courting and Mating

Bald eagles begin their monogamous, lifelong partnerships with a spectacular courtship, involving vocalizations and acrobatic flight displays. The courting birds, in what is referred to as their cartwheel display, may fly high up in the sky, lock talons, and tumble back toward the earth, separating and lifting up just before reaching the ground.

MARCH 18

Brown Creepers Camouflaged

The brown creeper is an excellent example of cryptic coloration, a form of camouflage in which an animal blends into its environment. A forager of insects and spiders that are tucked away behind and in the crevices of bark, the brown creeper starts its search at the base of a tree. As it climbs upward, it spirals around the trunk until it nears the top. It then flies to the base

Brown creeper.

March flies mating.

of a nearby tree to begin the process again. As W. M. Tyler wrote in 1948 in Bent's *Life Histories of North American Nuthatches, Wrens, Thrashers, and Their Allies*, "The brown creeper, as he hitches along the bole of a tree, looks like a fragment of detached bark that is defying the law of gravitation by moving upward over the trunk, and as he flies off to another tree he resembles a little dry leaf blown about by the wind."

Virginia Opossums Scrounging

Within the last century the Virginia opossum has extended its range northeastward and now is seen sporadically throughout most of the Northeast. Its adaptability to a great variety of habitats and its omnivorous diet have enabled North

Virginia opossum.

America's only marsupial to live in much colder climates than it initially inhabited. As long as food can be found, the opossum's greatest challenge is surviving the Northeast's cold winters. The almost hairless ears and tail of an opossum often suffer from frostbite, and when they do, the edges of its ears and the tip of its tail turn black.

MARCH 19

Great Horned Owls Incubating Eggs

Great horned owls are said to have the widest variety of nest sites of any bird in North or South America. Like other owls and falcons, this raptor does not build its own nest, but rather relies

on abandoned stick nests of other birds. Red-tailed hawk nests are often usurped, as well as those of bald eagles, crows, ravens, and herons. Nests may be lined with shreds of bark, leaves, downy feathers from the owl's breast, fur of prey, and trampled pellets. In addition to bird nests, great horned owls may raise their one to four nestlings (usually two) in tree cavities and snags, on cliffs, in deserted buildings, in squirrel nests, and even on the ground.

Great horned owl in great blue heron nest.

The female great horned owl does all the incubating, and the male delivers prey to her at intervals throughout the night. These early nesters have incubated eggs successfully when outside temperatures have been as low as -27 degrees.

MARCH 20

Song Sparrows Singing

The energetic songs of returning song sparrows announce and celebrate the arrival of spring. The males sing a sequence of notes, including clear whistles and buzzy sounds. Each male has about ten songs in its repertoire and tends to repeat one pattern for several minutes before changing to another. Although other birds may produce more musical songs, you'd have to search far and wide for more enthusiastic outbursts than those of a song sparrow.

Song sparrow.

Eastern Chipmunks Up and Active

Eastern chipmunks typically emerge above ground in mid- to late March, at a time when most mature females are in breeding condition. It takes little time for nearby males to

Eastern chipmunk.

come courting once females appear. During their breeding period, females, for the most part, remain within their territory, whereas males explore much more widely in search of receptive females.

Male suitors congregate at the site of a

female in estrus and work out the hierarchy within the group. The top chipmunk wins the opportunity to breed with the female. During these dominance battles, the males vocalize, wave their upright tails from side to side, chase each other, and fight. The dominant male then breeds with the female. She proceeds to mate several times within about a six- to seven-hour receptive period, not necessarily with the same male. All of this activity takes place within a week of when chipmunks come above ground.

Great blue heron on nest.

MARCH 21

Great Blue Herons Returning

Great blue herons are returning to their breeding grounds in northern New England, where there is usually open water by now. These birds nest in colonies, and, unlike the nests of songbirds, heron nests are used year after year. Although an individual heron does not often choose the same nest every year, they usually do return to the same colony. Some colonies are active for only a few years, but some have been known to house herons for over seventy years.

MARCH 22

Pied-Billed Grebes Returning

In central, northern, and northeastern U.S., where bodies of water freeze and fish, aquatic insects, and crayfish are unavailable, pied-billed grebes migrate south for the winter. In the southern part of their range, they are permanent residents. In spring, their flight north takes place over land and they are one of the first migrating birds to return to the Northeast.

Pied-billed grebe.

Eastern Comma Butterflies Emerging

Commas are a group of butterflies also known as anglewings. Underneath their hindwing there is a

Note the angled wings of this Eastern comma.

83

Owl Calls

Barred owl: *Hoo hoo ho-ho, hoo hoo ho-hooooaw*—"Who cooks for you? Who cooks for you-all?"

Great horned owl: *Hoo-hoo-hoo-hoo-HOO-hoo-hoo*—Soft hoots with a stuttering rhythm.

Eastern screech owl: One or more shrill, descending whinnies followed by even-pitched trill.

Northern saw-whet owl: *Too-too-too-too*—Two whistled notes per second, given on same pitch.

Long-eared owl: From ten to more than two hundred *whoo* notes, evenly spaced about two to four seconds apart.

Short-eared owl: *Poo poo poo*—Muffled, five to six per second in series two seconds long.

Barn owl: Long, hissing shriek.

Eastern screech owl.   Barn owl.

Barred owl.   Great horned owl.

silver mark in the shape of a comma. Like mourning cloaks, these butterflies overwinter as adults in bark crevices, logs, or other protected spots. You often see them in the woods, where they feed on tree sap, mud, scat, and decaying organic matter. When perched with their wings closed, they are well camouflaged and easily mistaken for a dead leaf. Eastern commas are wary and fly exceptionally fast when disturbed.

MARCH 23

Purple Finch Numbers Decreasing in Northeast

The complex warbling and raspberry coloration of purple finches used to be commonplace in the Northeast, but with the introduction of house finches to New York City in the 1950s, their numbers have sharply decreased. Studies show that when these two finch species interact, house finches win out over purple finches 95 percent of the time.

Male purple finch.

Silver Maples Flowering

Silver maple is the first of the maples to bloom in North America. Its reddish buds open to reveal clusters of greenish yellow flowers long before the leaves appear. Separate clusters of female and male flowers may appear on the same tree or on different trees.

Silver maple is often planted as a shade tree along streets, and it grows naturally in swamps, on stream banks, and in seasonally flooded bottomlands. Silver maples are tapped for sugaring, and their sap is considered by some to be equal in sweetness, flavor, and quality to that of sugar maples. However, because their buds break dormancy much earlier than sugar maple buds, the sugaring season for silver maples is much shorter.

Male silver maple flowers.

March most are still in the larval stage and can occasionally be seen feeding on stream or pond bottoms.

Wood Ducks Arriving on Breeding Grounds

Wood ducks are returning to northern New England to breed, having already formed mating pairs. Their courtship displays enable them to maintain this pair bond. Usually the male turns the back of his head toward the female as he swims in front of her while holding his wings and tail high. Chin lifting, feather shaking, wing preening, neck stretching, and bill jerking are just some of the other displays that occur during wood duck courtship.

MARCH 24

Caddisfly Larvae Feeding

Ponds and streams are starting to open up, and it's once again possible to find signs of life in them. The larvae of most species of caddisflies build their portable cases out of available material such as pebbles, sand, leaves, or sticks, and are active through the fall, winter, and into the spring. In late spring they will pupate and emerge, often en masse, as winged adults, but in

Caddisfly larva and stick case.

Wood duck pair with male displaying.

MARCH 25

Ruffed Grouse Drumming

At this time of year, it's not uncommon to hear the incongruous sound of an old tractor or lawn mower starting up in the middle of the woods early in the morning. Chances are great that this is part of the courtship display drumming of a male ruffed grouse as it stands, often on a log or rock, and rotates its wings forward and backward. The air that rushes into the vacuum beneath the wings generates a deep, thumping sound wave, similar to a miniature sonic boom, that carries up to a quarter of a mile. A grouse begins with two or three slow beats, and then gradually increases the speed of its wingbeats, creating a drumlike roll, until the beats blend together. In the eight to eleven seconds that it takes a grouse to complete a sequence, it will have beaten its wings up to fifty times.

Ruffed grouse.

MARCH 26

Pussy Willow Flowers Maturing

The single-scaled buds of pussy willow flowers are starting to open. There are many species of willows—one hundred in North America—and several of the smaller ones are referred to as

Pussy willow.

Female willow catkin.

Male willow catkin.

pussy willows. The species most commonly called pussy willow is the American pussy willow, *Salix discolor*. What we call pussy willows are, in fact, the soft, silvery hairs that insulate the emerging spike of flowers, or catkin, within a willow flower bud. A willow catkin consists of all male or all female flowers, and male and female catkins are borne on separate shrubs.

The first catkins to open in the spring are usually males. The hairs, or "pussies," that emerge when willow buds first open trap heat from the sun, which warms the flowers' reproductive parts in the centers of the catkins. This trapped heat promotes the development of the pollen (or in female flowers, the ovules) of the flowers deep within the hairs. The reproductive parts of the willow flower catkins—the stamens and pistils—emerge later, but until they do, we get to enjoy their silvery fur coats.

Eastern phoebe.

Black bear.

Eastern Phoebes Singing

The eastern phoebe, a member of the flycatcher family, is one of the earliest songbirds to return to the Northeast after spending the winter in the southeastern United States. It is easily identified when perching, because it wags its tail up and down repeatedly while waiting for an insect to fly by. Special feathers, called rictal bristles, which project from many insect-eating birds' beaks, including phoebes, protect the bird's eyes and may assist in catching insects by serving as sensory feelers, much as a cat's whiskers do.

The eastern phoebe is the first bird ever banded in North America: In 1804, John James Audubon tied a small circle of silver thread around the legs of phoebe nestlings and documented their return in successive years.

MARCH 27

Time to Take Feeders Down or Bring Them in at Night

Within the next few weeks, most black bears will be leaving their dens. Although it takes their intestinal systems a bit of time to adjust to a new routine once they are no longer hibernating, they soon will be ravenous. To prevent black bears from visiting backyard bird feeders, Fish & Wildlife departments in the Northeast recommend taking down birdfeeders from April 1 through December 1 and removing anything outdoors that would be of any interest to a hungry bear after it has emerged from hibernation.

Approximately 85 percent of a bear's diet is vegetation. Before green shoots make an appearance in the spring, the flowers of aspen, willow, maple, ash, and hazelnut, along with carrion, make up most of a bear's diet. After losing 23 percent of its body weight during hibernation, a black bear finds protein-packed sunflower seeds very appealing. Make sure your garbage is secured, barbecues clean, and pet food kept indoors. Keeping bears away prevents property damage and keeps bears from becoming nuisance animals that are habituated to food associated with humans—which often leads to the end of a bear's life.

MARCH 28

American Woodcock Displaying on Nesting Grounds

Spring arrives with the familiar series of *peents* uttered by male woodcocks during their courtship ritual at dawn and dusk on early spring days. Even if most of a wet, shrubby field is covered

American woodcock.

which builds up in the subnivean layer from animal respiration as well as CO_2 released from the ground, escapes through ventilation shafts that lead up to the surface of the snow. Voles stay in these tunnels as long as the snow is deep enough not to expose them, finding food in the form of plants, seeds, and bark from bushes and shrubs as they dig through the snow.

with snow, if there's open ground, you may well see two spectacular shows a day for several weeks. After *peenting* repeatedly from the ground to attract a female at dusk, the male woodcock puts on an aerial courtship display for her. He soars into the sky in a wide circle, twittering away with his wings—up, up, up—until he "chips" his way down, zigzagging dramatically as he approaches the ground. Moments later, the *peent*ing resumes and the cycle is repeated until dark— and even well after sunset on moonlit nights. In the early morning, it all begins again.

Meadow Vole Tunnels Exposed

Meadow voles excavate tunnels in the snow next to the ground in what is referred to as the subnivean layer. These tunnels lead from sleeping areas to sources of food, and they provide thermal insulation by protecting the animals from wind and cold—plus, they keep these tasty rodents hidden from predators. Carbon dioxide,

Yellow-Bellied Sapsuckers Back and Establishing Territories

The welcome drumming sound of the yellow-bellied sapsucker is once again reverberating through our woodlands. Although many woodpeckers drum against hard surfaces with their bills, the yellow-bellied sapsucker's pattern is distinctive. These birds usually begin with several rapid strikes in an "introductory roll," followed by a pause, then more strikes in an irregular pattern, which some people liken to Morse code.

Sapsuckers, like most woodpeckers, communicate with each other by drumming on different surfaces—often on dead snags, but also on metal signs and roof tops. The louder the sound, the farther it travels, so the birds try to find the substrate that creates the loudest racket. Males arrive on their breeding grounds and establish territories by drumming before the females arrive. Females return about a week later, at which point drumming will assist male sapsuckers in obtaining a mate. Females also drum, but less frequently, more softly, and for shorter periods of time.

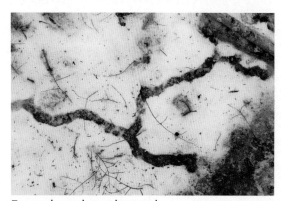

Exposed meadow vole tunnels.

Yellow-bellied sapsucker.

MARCH 29

Waxwings Supplementing Sugary Fruit Diet with High-Protein Insects

During most of the year, the diet of both cedar and bohemian waxwings is primarily sugary fruits, and they can subsist on this diet exclusively for as many as eighteen days. However, in winter, when feeding on fruits they also feed on buds and insects. In warmer months, waxwings fly out over water from exposed perches, much like flycatchers, and snatch emerging aquatic insects such as mosquitoes, midges, mayflies, caddisflies, and dragonflies out of the air. They also glean vegetation-borne prey, such as scale insects. At this time of year, they are taking advantage of winter stonefly hatches over open streams.

Bohemian waxwing.

Stonefly.

Striped Skunks Mating

Striped skunks are on the prowl, as your nose (scent) and your eyes (tracks) may have told you, and males are eagerly seeking out the company of females. During a typical night, a male skunk may cover ¼ to ½ square mile, but during the breeding season, this increases to 4 or 5 square miles. The peak of striped skunk breeding season

Striped skunk.

is the third week in March. Males will mate with several females in succession and they often protect their harem against other males by hitting them with their shoulders or biting their legs. Once a female has been successfully bred, she will not allow further mating and will viciously fight any male that attempts it.

Striped skunk tracks.

MARCH 30

Wild Turkeys Mating

The most prominent courtship behavior of male wild turkeys, or toms, consists of two displays: gobbling and strutting. Both begin in late February in the Northeast, before the females are receptive, but by late March the males begin to reap the fruits of their labor. The males' gobbling attracts hens or competing males over considerable distances, and then they strut to impress

Wild turkeys.

Kit.

one or more females. If a female is receptive, she assumes a "sexual crouch" on the ground, signaling to the male that he may mount her.

Red Foxes Giving Birth

Much is happening below ground at this time of year, including the birthing of red fox kits in a den that is usually dug in a sandy bank. In late March or early April, about seven weeks after mating, female foxes give birth to four to ten young. Each kit weighs about a quarter of a pound, and the white tip of its tail is often already evident. During the first month, the kits grow a dark

Red fox den.

gray coat. They shed this coat and grow a new sandy-colored one about the time they venture out of their den. The mother stays in the den, nursing and curling her body around the kits to keep them warm, for about two weeks, while the father brings her food. She then resumes her normal activity, returning to the den to nurse, clean, and play with her kits.

Sugar Maple Seeds and Sap

The quality of a maple sugaring season is usually associated with the temperature. Warm days and cool nights produce bounteous runs of sap. However, other factors, including the quantity of seed production in the fall, affect the quality of the sap that is produced. A large seed crop in the fall uses more of the carbohydrates stored by the tree, resulting in sap that has relatively low sugar content.

Sap bucket.

MARCH 31

Jelly Fungi Fruiting

The term "jelly fungi" is an informal one applied to species of fungi that have a gelatinous consistency. The reason for this texture is that the structural filaments, or hyphae, of these fungi have walls that are not thin and rigid as they are in most other species, but instead shrink and expand in response to moisture. The hyphae are expanded and gelatinous when moist, but during dry periods they collapse and become rather hard and resistant to bending. Such tissues are able to exist in a dry state for many months and, when exposed to moisture, quickly expand to full size. They may be among the earliest fungi seen in the spring because they have remained dry and inconspicuous all winter, only to revive with the first melting snow or during winter thaws.

Jelly fungi come in several colors. The orange and yellow forms are sometimes referred to as "witch's butter." Jelly fungi can be found on rotting logs and stumps.

Owl Ears

The facial discs of owls consist of feathers in the shape of a funnel around each eye that direct sound waves toward the owl's ears. These discs, plus the different size and asymmetrical placement of its ear openings on the sides of its head, allow an owl to discern the direction a sound is coming from, how far away it is, and its height relative to the owl—even in the dark or under the snow. The exceptional hearing of owls, particularly those in the genus *Strix*, which includes barred and great gray owls, enables them to plunge into the snow and often successfully capture prey, sight unseen.

Jelly fungus.

Barred owl with ear hole showing.

91

Wild Ginger

Skunk cabbage is often the first wildflower to poke its head above the ground in early spring. Right on its heels comes a profusion of spring flowers, including hepatica, bloodroot, spring beauty, wild columbine, Dutchman's breeches, wild ginger, and trout lily. Although small, most of these wildflowers easily catch the eye of a passerby. One, however, wild ginger, is well hidden but well worth searching for. Peer under the two paired leaves and there, next to the ground, you should find a single jug-shaped maroon flower with a white interior and three reflexed, pointed tips—a welcome sign of spring.

The design of wild ginger's flower, like that of all flowering plants, has everything to do with how it is pollinated. The flower is at the junction of the stems of its two broad, heart-shaped leaves. It often lies on the ground or very near it—exactly where carrion flies and beetles that emerge from the ground in spring are likely to find it. These insects are looking for dead animal carcasses to eat or to lay their eggs on. The deep maroon coloring of wild ginger flowers is similar enough to that of rotting meat that it attracts these insects, which, while investigating the flowers, inadvertently acquire pollen on their bodies. As they move from flower to flower, they disperse the pollen to other wild ginger flowers. Not only does wild ginger offer pollinating insects food, but shelter, as well, inside its cup- or bell-shaped blossom.

Wild ginger's seeds are as specialized as its flowers. They are adapted for dispersal by ants. Like the seeds of hepatica, violets, bloodroot, and many other wildflowers, wild ginger seeds have a small, fatty protuberance on them called an elaiosome. Ants are partial to the taste of elaiosomes. They collect wild ginger seeds and haul them into their underground tunnels, where they eat the fatty tidbit and discard the rest of the seed, often on their waste pile—a site very conducive to germination. It is a win-win situation for wild ginger and for ants.

Although not related to the ginger herb we use for flavoring, the root of wild ginger has a similar smell and flavor and has historically been used as a spice. It is harvested, dried, and then ground into a powder. Early settlers cooked pieces of the root in sugar water for several days to obtain a ginger-flavored, candied root. The leftover liquid was then boiled down to syrup that was used on pancakes and other food items. Wild ginger was used by Native Americans to relieve upset stomachs, much as we drink ginger ale today. Consumption of this plant is not advised today, however, as it may contain poisonous compounds.

Wild ginger flower.

Look for wild ginger's evergreen leaves in rich, moist woodlands during April and May. Because they reproduce via their rhizomes, or underground stems, you often find colonies of them. Unlike the

Wild ginger.

Trees Flowering in April

Most tree flowers are pollinated by the wind. This means of pollination is far more effective when there are no leaves on the trees to interfere with the dispersal of pollen. Thus, many trees flower early in the spring, before leaf buds have opened. For the most part, flowers of these wind-pollinated trees (unlike fruit trees, which are insect-pollinated) do not need or have bannerlike petals, strong scent, or nectar. They are often suspended on catkins or have long, thin stems called peduncles that allow wind currents to catch the pollen easily.

- Trembling aspen
- Bigtooth aspen
- Eastern cottonwood
- Red maple
- Silver maple
- Box elder
- American elm
- Speckled alder
- Willows
- Beaked hazelnut
- Shadbush

Box elder.

Willow.

Shadbush.

Red maple.

Eastern cottonwood.

leaves of spring ephemerals, which quickly disappear as the woods become shaded, wild ginger's leaves persist all summer long, producing food which will be stored in its roots and used for next spring's growth.

Cavity Nesters

There are roughly eighty-five species of cavity-nesting birds in North America. Cavities are the safest nest sites for raising young, for they provide protection from predators as well as weather. Because of the added shelter that cavities provide, birds nesting in them are usually among the first species to lay eggs in the spring. Cavity nesters are also under less pressure to raise their young as quickly as possible, and consequently, their young often leave the nest, or fledge, at a comparatively later stage of growth than young birds not raised in cavities. Rather than feeding fewer young the maximum amount of food so that they

will grow as quickly as possible, hole nesters can use the same amount of food to feed more young at a slower rate. Thus, the size of their clutches is often larger than the average songbird's. The cavity-nesting birds we see regularly have other characteristics in common, including the fact that most of them are insectivorous.

Some birds make their own holes and are referred to as primary cavity nesters. Primary cavity nesters include woodpeckers (downy, hairy, pileated, yellow-bellied sapsucker, northern flicker). Many cavity-nesting birds are unequipped to excavate their own holes, and instead use natural cavities or holes that were made by primary cavity nesters. These birds, called secondary cavity nesters, are at a distinct disadvantage compared to birds that can make their own cavities, for there aren't as many holes as there are mated birds, and there is severe competition within and between species for the finite number of cavities that do exist.

94

One adaptive strategy in the competition for these holes by secondary cavity nesters is to be a permanent resident, like the tufted titmouse or white-breasted nuthatch. Such species get the jump on returning migrants in the spring. Most secondary cavity nesters, however, are migratory, and their strategy is to arrive back as early as possible in the spring and claim a cavity before any other bird can do so. Thus, many of our secondary cavity nesters are among the earliest birds to arrive in the spring, including species such as tree swallows, American kestrels, eastern bluebirds, wood ducks, and mergansers.

In response to the secondary cavity nester housing crisis, humans have provided additional cavities for birds in the form of nest boxes. The eastern bluebird population declined drastically in the mid-1900s due to pesticides, nest predation, and loss of habitat. This led to the creation of bluebird trails all over the country that have nest boxes posted at close intervals all along the trails. These boxes have been readily accepted by bluebirds (and swallows), and this strategy has brought the widespread decline in the bluebird population to a halt.

The black-capped chickadee, another secondary cavity nester, is also an opportunist when it comes to nesting. It can excavate its own

Hairy woodpeckers at nest hole.

hole, but will also use an old woodpecker hole, a natural cavity, or even a nest box. Most often, however, a chickadee chooses to create its own cavity. One look at a chickadee's small bill tells you that it is not capable of any serious drilling into healthy, living wood. In fact, it can only make or enlarge a cavity if it is located in soft, rotting, punky wood, which its bill can handle.

For the sake of all primary and secondary nesters, please leave snags standing. Don't harvest them. They are prime habitat for the avian hole nesters that rid forests of thousands of insects, including many forest pests.

Black-capped chickadee removing wood chips.

Tree swallows at nest hole.

Beaver.

Scent mound.

Castoreum

In the spring, just before a mother beaver gives birth, her older offspring—who have been living with her since birth and are now twenty-two months old—leave their lodge. An innate urge tells them that it's time to seek a mate and start a colony of their own. The parents don't discourage this behavior, as it prevents inbreeding and the premature depletion of their food supply. The major challenge facing these young beavers is the fierce territoriality of their species, which can make the search for a new pond or stream to dam challenging.

When they disperse, most young beavers go downstream to look for unoccupied territory. Ideally they come upon an old, abandoned beaver pond that has regrown a good supply of aspens, willows, and birch—a beaver's preferred diet. However, young beavers are rarely that lucky. It is not impossible for these young upstarts to attempt to move in to an inhabited pond site, so resident beavers take measures to alert these youngsters to the fact that the pond is spoken for.

In an attempt to discourage young beavers from lingering, one of the first things adult beavers do in the spring is to mark the perimeter of their territory by making scent mounds. They do so by piling up mud and leaves from the bottom of their pond and depositing castoreum on them. Castoreum is a combination of urine and a thick, yellowish, aromatic secretion of the paired castor sacs that conveys information such as the beaver's age and sex. A beaver deposits the castoreum by straddling a mound, everting its castor sacs, and dragging them across the mound. Scent mounds vary in size, from a height of just a few inches to 3 feet or so, and they are usually located within 2 feet of the water's edge. The pheromones in the castoreum are broadcast far and wide from these mounds. An encroaching two-year-old beaver detects the odor, and if it is smart, continues on its way. If a stray male beaver deposits some of his own scent on a resident's scent mound or stops to feed, the resident male drives him off by hissing loudly, and if that doesn't work, he attacks the interloper.

Both male and female beavers possess castor sacs (technically they are not glands) as well as a pair of anal glands. Castoreum is used for communication, whereas oil from the anal glands is used by the beaver for waterproofing its fur.

Beaver castor sacs.

It is not only beavers that use castoreum to convey information; humans do, as well, but strictly for the purpose of attraction. Beaver castoreum has a distinct fragrance that is appealing to some people and not to others. It is the secret ingredient in some perfumes that supposedly gives them the scent of leather. As one perfumer describes it, "The scent of castoreum is wild and bodily, lustful and passionate, bestowing on the one who wears it a delicate aura of sensuality." Fortunately for beavers, it has been replaced by chemically synthesized castoreum.

Beaver-produced castoreum, however, is still used for some strawberry, raspberry, and vanilla flavoring in alcoholic and non-alcoholic beverages, baked goods, candy, chewing gum, puddings, and frozen dairy products. The next time you indulge in food or drink with one of these flavors, you might want to read the list of ingredients on the bottle or container, though it might not be quite as transparent as you would like—the FDA considers castoreum safe, to the point of allowing companies to refer to it as "natural flavoring."

APRIL 1

Common and Hooded Mergansers Migrating

Common mergansers are seen year-round in northern New England, but , like their relatives, hooded mergansers, their numbers peak at the

Hooded mergansers.

Common mergansers.

end of March and the beginning of April due to the large number of birds that wintered farther south and are migrating to Canadian nesting grounds. These birds are fish eaters, known to consume at least fifty species of fish. Sharp projections along the edges of the bill allow mergansers to grasp and hold their slippery prey. Egg laying is still roughly two months away, but coveted tree cavities where they nest are being investigated.

Raccoon Latrines

Raccoons defecate in communal sites called latrines. Likely spots to look for latrines include the base of good-sized conifers, especially those near water, as well as on top of stone walls and rotting logs or under rock outcroppings. Over time, the scat accumulates. Should you come upon a latrine, it is best not to investigate too closely, as raccoon feces harbor the eggs of parasitic roundworms which can be easily ingested and cause harm—serious eye disease, spinal cord or brain damage, or even death—to humans. One of these roundworms can produce more than one hundred thousand eggs a day, and the eggs remain viable for years in the soil.

Raccoon latrine.

Brown creeper.

APRIL 2

Rusty Tussock Moth Eggs

There are many species of tussock moths, and in their larval (caterpillar) stage, most are covered with tufts of hairlike setae, some impressively long. The female rusty tussock moth is flightless; after emerging from her cocoon, which is usually located on trees whose leaves her larvae will eat, she stays put, releasing

Rusty tussock moth eggs on apple leaf.

alluring pheromones and awaiting the arrival of a male suitor. After mating, she lays up to several hundred eggs on top of her empty cocoon and dies. The flat-topped, cylindrical eggs, which have a dark depression on their top, overwinter, and as soon as leaf buds start opening, the eggs hatch, with ready-made meals inches away. Larvae feed on the leaves of birches, oaks, crabapples, and black cherry, among others.

Brown Creepers Singing

Brown creepers—insect-eating, bark-gleaning, little brown birds—are occasionally spotted as they spiral their way upward around and around a tree trunk, probing under bark with their thin, curved beaks for their next meal. Because they are so well camouflaged, it is easy to miss them. Your chance of becoming aware of their presence is increased if you become familiar with the high, thin, but surprisingly rich song that males sing to establish territories on their breeding grounds at this time of year. Although they continue to sing throughout the nesting period until their young

have fledged, male brown creepers are most vocal early in the season, when they are staking out their territory.

APRIL 3

Red-Shouldered Hawks Courting and Mating

Male red-shouldered hawks put on an impressive courtship display for females. The male enacts a "sky dance," in which he calls while soaring, and then makes a series of steep dives toward the female, climbing back up in wide spirals after each descent before finally diving to perch upon the female's back.

Red-shouldered hawk.

Eastern newt on snow.

Eastern Newts Migrating Back to Ponds

Eastern newt eggs are laid and hatch in ponds, where the larvae spend the summer. As they metamorphose into their red eft stage in late summer, they migrate onto land, where they live for several years before returning to an aquatic life as adult eastern newts. During the winter, some adult newts can be found in the water, and some on land. From mid-March to early April, adult newts that overwintered on land can be found heading back to the pond they grew up in.

APRIL 4

Painted Turtles Basking

Hibernation is coming to an end for painted turtles in the Northeast. Once some of the ice melts on ponds, painted turtles are quick to climb up and bask in the sun on any available floating log or rock, or even on the melting edge of the ice. Having spent the winter in the mud at the bottom of the pond where the temperature is approximately 39 degrees (at this temperature water achieves its greatest density and sinks to the bottom of ponds, which is where the turtles are), ectothermic painted turtles are more than ready to get warm. Like many animals, painted turtles find March and April the most challenging months of the year because of a shortage of food. Warming up in the sun activates a turtle's digestive system, enabling it to utilize the food it does find.

American Robins Foraging for Earthworms

In the spring, only 10 percent of the American robin's diet consists of fruit; invertebrates make up the remaining 90 percent. By contrast, in fall and winter, fruit makes up about 90 percent of the robin's diet, and summer is a fairly even mixture of both.

At this time of year, earthworms are a popular food item with robins, and it can be difficult to tell whether robins use their ears or eyes to locate them. The fact is that most worms are seen, not heard, by robins. Because the sound of worms burrowing in the soil is of low intensity, it usually cannot be heard by robins because of background noise. Using sight, not sound, the robin first aims one eye toward a spot on the ground in front of it, and after holding this position for a few seconds, rotates its head and focuses its other eye on the same spot—an earthworm in its burrow. The robin then quickly thrusts its bill into the burrow in an attempt to extract its next meal.

Painted turtles.

American robin hunting for worms.

Eastern chipmunk with nesting material.

Eastern Chipmunks Preparing Nests and Giving Birth

Eastern chipmunks mate sometime between February and early April. During the next month or so, before the three to five young are born, the

female chipmunk digs a nesting chamber off her underground burrow and creates a bulky nest of leaves inside this 24-inch long by 15-inch wide by 10-inch high room. Usually in April or May the young are born, and within a week, hair and stripes are evident on the young chipmunks. In about a month, when they venture out of the burrow, they look like small adults.

Eastern chipmunk.

APRIL 5

Bald Eagles on Eggs

In the Northeast, bald eagles seek out the tallest trees in which to build their nests. If there are no trees available, as is the case in certain locations in Alaska, coastal California, and northern Canada, they will nest on the ground. When building a tree nest, eagles usually locate it in the

Bald eagles on nest.

top quarter of the tree, on strong limbs just below the crown. The sticks needed for construction are collected from the ground up to a mile away from the nest or are broken off nearby trees.

A bald eagle's clutch consists of one to three eggs. Because incubation begins after the first egg is laid, the young hatch over a period of several days. Both adults have brood patches, but the female's is better developed than the male's, reflecting the fact that she does the majority of incubating for the next thirty-five days.

Beaked Hazelnut Flowering

Like many other shrubs, beaked hazelnut does not have big, flashy flowers, but more subtle and delicate blossoms with beautiful colors and designs. Its flowers bloom before its leaf buds open, enhancing the chance of successful pollination by the wind. Pendant male catkins loaded with

Beaked hazelnut flowers.

pollen and ¼-inch-diameter female flowers adorn the leafless shrubs. The tiny female blossoms should be examined through a hand lens—they are exquisite maroon flowers with magenta highlights and with pistils that curl this way and that in hopes of catching pollen.

APRIL 6

Female Eastern Red-Backed Salamanders Emerging from Hibernation and Laying Eggs

The eastern red-backed salamander is slender, with a whitish salt-and-pepper belly and, usually, a reddish brown stripe down its back. Some red-backs at lower elevations lack the brick red stripe and appear all gray. Eastern red-backed salamanders are terrestrial year-round. They hunt for insects in the leaf litter, only coming to the surface when it is warm and humid enough. Usually in the fall, but occasionally in the spring, red-backed salamanders go through an extensive courtship ritual before the male deposits his sperm on the ground and the female picks it up with her cloaca. In the spring, she lays her three to fifteen eggs in a cluster inside a small cavity in a rotting, often coniferous, log. The entire cluster of eggs is suspended from the roof of the cavity by a single stalk. Unlike most salamanders, whose larval stages live in water, the eastern red-back's larval stage occurs inside the egg, and the young hatch out as miniature adults. The female remains with her eggs until they hatch; she guards and defends them aggressively, biting and lunging at potential predators. In approximately six weeks, after emerging from the egg, a hatchling loses the three gills on each side of its head. Hatchlings remain with their mother in the nesting site for one to three weeks after hatching, and then disperse.

Migrating Dark-Eyed Juncos Passing Through

Dark-eyed juncos are often referred to as "snow birds" due to their presence in much of the United States only during the winter months. Although this member of the sparrow family can be found year-round in the Northeast, over most of the eastern United States, juncos appear as winter sets in and then retreat northward each spring. Many of the juncos that we see now are transitory migrants on the way to their Canadian breeding grounds. They will remain there until next fall, when there will be a similar influx in the Northeast as they head south. Research has found that males migrate earlier than females, and that females tend to migrate farther south than males. The timing of spring migration is regulated primarily by day length.

Eastern red-backed salamander.

Dark-eyed junco.

101

APRIL 7

Beavers See Daylight

Beavers have been locked under the ice, living in a dark, damp lodge with up to nine other beavers, and surviving on water-logged branches for the past four to five months. As the ice thins and more light filters through it, beavers are on the alert for the first hole to open up. Frequently they will help the process along by bumping against thin ice and breaking through. Suddenly there is bright sunlight, heat from the sun, fresh vegetation to eat, and the opportunity to groom thoroughly in the open air.

Beaver.

Coltsfoot Flowering

You'll find coltsfoot, one of the earliest wildflowers to blossom, growing in some of the most barren spots on earth, including nutrient-poor roadsides that are awash with salt from the winter; but if sun and moisture are available, these dandelion look-alikes often thrive. In certain areas, coltsfoot that is invading woodlands and outcompeting native plants is considered invasive. Emerging this early in the spring, when temperatures can still dip down below freezing,

has its challenges. Hairy scales on the flower's stem keep the plant relatively warm. Although the flower head is initially angled downward, when it blooms, it straightens out and greets the sun. During the night and on cloudy or cold days, the flower closes, conserving heat.

Coltsfoot.

Northern Cardinals Singing

Both male and female northern cardinals sing and produce call notes. Their calls are innate, but their songs must be learned. At least sixteen different call notes have been described for this species. Male cardinals sing year-round. Females sing from the nest while incubating and brooding, generally in response to the nearby male's chip calls or songs. The female's songs appear to provide information to her mate about the need for food at the nest.

Northern cardinal.

APRIL 8

Spotted salamander.

Spotted Salamanders Migrating to Breeding Pools

Under the stealth of a rainy late March or April night, when the temperature is in the mid-forties or higher, subterranean-dwelling spotted salamanders migrate to their ancestral breeding pools. At this time of year, the temperature can drop rapidly, and rain can turn to snow, making the trek especially difficult for migrating salamanders. After male spotted salamanders arrive at a pool, they cluster in groups called congresses to await the arrival of females. Once the females slip into the pond, males and females pair up and perform a courtship dance.

Unlike some species of amphibians, the male spotted salamander does not fertilize eggs as the female lays them. Instead, when the female is sufficiently stimulated, the male deposits up to eighty spermatophores—pyramid-shaped plugs of mucus with a sperm capsule at the top—on a submerged branch or leaf. The female then crawls over a spermatophore and positions her vent, or cloaca, so as to allow the lips of her cloaca to detach the sperm capsule and envelope it. Fertilization takes place internally. The male maximizes the chances of insemination by depositing many scattered spermatophores and by covering every spermatophore he encounters,

Wood Frog vs. Spotted Salamander Eggs

In April, both wood frogs and spotted salamanders emerge from hibernation and migrate to their ancestral breeding bodies of water, most often vernal pools, where there are no fish to eat them. After courtship and mating takes place, females of both species lay their eggs in the water. Spotted salamander eggs superficially look like wood frog eggs, but several characteristics distinguish one from the other.

Both the wood frog and the spotted salamander lay their eggs in masses, not individually. A typical wood frog egg mass can have between five hundred and two thousand eggs. Large, soft, and shapeless, wood frog egg masses are usually found clumped together in one area of the pool, as wood frogs are communal egg layers. The egg masses are often near the surface and frequently attached to a branch that has fallen into the pool. The individual eggs in a mass are loosely stuck together, with the eggs on the outside making the mass appear bumpy.

Spotted salamander egg masses resemble those of wood frogs, but they usually contain fewer eggs—typically fifty to two hundred—and the females do not lay their eggs all in one area. The most obvious difference between the two is the protective outer gelatinous layer that spotted salamander egg masses have and that wood frog egg masses lack. The spotted salamander egg mass is relatively firm. The egg masses from both of these amphibian species turn green from the presence of algae.

Wood frog.

Spotted salamander.

Spotted salamander spermatophores, with sperm capsule missing on far left spermatophore.

even his own, with a new spermatophore. In so doing, he increases his spermatophore count, while simultaneously eliminating a rival's spermatophores. Within a short period of time, the salamanders retreat to the woods, where they are rarely glimpsed until next spring.

APRIL 9

Red Fox Kits Venturing Out of Den

For the first four to six weeks of their lives, red fox kits remain in their den. They are born with a coat of dark gray fur, but when they are about a month old, this is replaced by sandy-colored fur.

Red fox kit.

This coincides with their emergence from the den, and the new coat blends in well with the sandy soil surrounding the den entrance, where the kits spend most of their time. By late June they will have acquired the red coat we associate with adult red foxes.

Ospreys Return to Nesting Sites

The osprey is the only North American raptor that eats live fish almost exclusively. When winter comes to the Northeast, ospreys must migrate south to warmer weather and open water in Central and South America, where they can find fish. Satellite transmitters have shown that an osprey may log more than 160,000 migration miles during its fifteen- to twenty-year lifetime.

Osprey.

Once a pair is back on its breeding ground in the spring, the male usually gathers most of the nesting material, including dead branches that he breaks from trees. The female arranges the platform nest. Like most raptors, ospreys return to the same nest each year, adding material to create older nests that measure 10 to 13 feet deep and 2 to 6 feet in diameter.

APRIL 10

Spring Peepers Emerging from Hibernation

Once hibernation has come to an end, spring peepers seek out wetlands, vernal pools, and ponds to breed and lay eggs in before they return to live on the forest floor. In some years, peepers appear so early that they must make their way

Spring peeper.

to open water over the snow. When males reach their breeding ponds, they exercise their voices for the first time in many months.

Like the gray tree frog and wood frog, spring peepers can freeze as solid as a rock for several months during hibernation, and then, on a warm day, thaw out in a few hours and resume a normal, active life. The production of glucose and the formation of ice crystals outside the cells enable this phenomenon to occur.

Common Loons Returning to Breeding Lakes and Ponds

Spring arrival of common loons on nesting lakes and ponds depends largely on the timing of ice-out. During migration, common loons have what are called staging areas—lakes and rivers with open water—where many loons congregate as they proceed northward. Loons make reconnaissance flights to the north from here to see if the ice is on

its way out, but only leave these staging areas for good when there is open water farther north.

APRIL 11

Paper Wasp Queens Emerging from Hibernation

Paper wasps have annual colonies—only the young, fertilized queens overwinter, while the old queen, female workers, and males all perish in the fall. The young queens seek shelter behind tree bark or in rotting logs or stumps and emerge in the spring when temperatures rise and day length is increasing. Last year's nest is not reused; the new queen mixes wood and plant fiber with her saliva and creates several waterproof paper cells into each of which she lays an egg—the start of her future labor force. Because there are so few wildflowers, nectar is scarce, and queens rely instead on the sap from broken tree branches as well as the sap in yellow-bellied sap-sucker wells.

Paper wasp queen.

APRIL 12

Backswimmers Preying on Insects, Tadpoles, and Fish

Backswimmers are small aquatic insects that seek out prey as large as tadpoles and small fish. They row around ponds with their fringed hind legs and grasp prey with their front pair of legs. The piercing mouthparts that they use to kill their prey are also capable of giving humans who

Common loon.

105

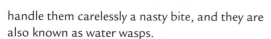
Backswimmer. Inset: Water boatman.

Mating muskrats.

handle them carelessly a nasty bite, and they are also known as water wasps.

Because it spends most of its time on its back, a backswimmer's coloring differs from that of most insects—it typically has a dark belly and a light-colored back, which makes it less conspicuous to predators and prey both from above and from below. This tiny bug can stay submerged for hours thanks to its ability to store air bubbles in two channels on its abdomen which are covered with inward-facing hairs.

Backswimmers are often confused with water boatmen, which are not predaceous, do not bite, and swim right side up. The water boatman's dark color and the parallel lines on its back help distinguish it from a backswimmer.

Muskrats Mating

Muskrats breed year-round in the southern United States, but in the Northeast, ice-out usually determines when they first breed. Prior to mating, these largely monogamous rodent pairs take to the water and engage in a mad chase that often lasts several minutes. Successive breedings take place all summer—by the time one litter is weaned and independent, in about four weeks, the mother is about to give birth again. Several litters of five or six young are produced each year. The mother cares for her young until they are weaned, at which point the father takes over their care.

APRIL 13

Speckled Alder Flowering

The flowers of speckled alder are among the first to open in the spring. This wetland shrub is easy to identify all winter by the presence of last year's fruit, which look like miniature woody cones. Its flowers are also present through the winter, but do not open until now, when the pendulous male flowers open and extend

Speckled alder catkins.

to disperse their pollen. Look above the catkins for the tiny, maroon female flowers, which are exquisite when seen through a hand lens. Even though they flower at the same time on the same shrub, the position of the female flowers above the male flowers discourages self-pollination and encourages cross-pollination in this member of the birch family.

Male yellow-rumped warbler in spring plumage.

Yellow-Rumped Warblers Back

The yellow-rumped warbler—also known as "butterbutt"—has returned to our woodlands. The males' bright yellow, white, gray, and black breeding plumage is hard to miss in April as they migrate to the Northeast and Canada to nest. Some liken the song of this bejeweled songbird—a "slow, soft, sweetly whistled warble" or trill—to the sound of an old-time sewing machine.

APRIL 14

Three Early Emerging Amphibians

These three amphibians share many traits, including being among the earliest amphibians to emerge from hibernation and head for the bodies of water in which they mate and lay eggs.

Wood frog, spotted salamander, and spring peeper.

While their courtship practices are not all the same—wood frogs and spring peepers use their vocal cords, and the silent spotted salamanders dance—all three species return to their woodland habitat to reside inconspicuously for the rest of the year.

APRIL 15

Common Garter Snakes Emerging from Hibernacula and Mating

Common garter snakes have been brumating in groups all winter in their hibernacula. Brumation is a reptilian state of dormancy similar to hibernation in mammals but involving different metabolic processes. When spring weather arrives, a hibernaculum may take two or more weeks to warm up. During this time, the snakes slowly come awake, some making short forays outside the den to warm up by basking in the sun and returning to the hibernaculum at night to avoid the still-cold spring night temperatures above ground. This behavior helps ensure that they will not be caught out during a late frost.

Typically, male garter snakes leave the den first and wait for the females to exit. The males give off pheromones that attract the females, and once the females leave the den, the males surround them, forming what is called a "mating ball" of one female and many males. After

Common garter snake.

the female has chosen her mate and mated, she returns to her summer habitat, while the males stay to mate with other available females. Female garter snakes are able to store the male's sperm for years before fertilization.

Trembling Aspens Flowering

The flower buds of trembling aspen look a lot like pussy willows when they first open up and the tips of the catkins, or flower spikes, emerge. Long before the leaf buds open, the flower buds swell, and their scales open to reveal male or female flowers that mature into pendulous catkins. Male and female catkins are on separate

Male trembling aspen catkins.

trees. A month or so after pollination, the seeds that have developed on the female catkins will be dispersed by the wind, and the air will be filled with cottony fluff.

APRIL 16

Great Egrets Migrating

After overwintering in Central America and the southern United States, great egrets head as far north as the New England coast to breed. The peak of their spring migration occurs in April, and at this time they can be spotted in

Great egret eating crayfish.

wetlands where they stop to rest and refuel en route. Great egrets eat mainly fish, but also crustaceans, amphibians, reptiles, birds, and small mammals.

Hepatica Blooming

Hepatica is opening its hairy buds and greeting the world with its beautiful white, pink, blue, and lavender blossoms. Typically the only wildflowers to appear earlier than this member of the

Hepatica plant.

buttercup family are skunk cabbage and coltsfoot. Like many flowers, hepatica's blossoms open on sunny days and close at night and on cloudy days. This prevents rain from washing out the pollen and nectar which attract pollinating insects, including early flying bees and flies.

Hepatica buds.

Long-Tailed Weasels Completing Spring Molt

Two species of weasels are found throughout the Northeast—the long-tailed weasel and the short-tailed weasel, also known as an ermine. Both are roughly the same size, somewhere between 9 and 16 inches from nose to tail, with

Long-tailed weasel.

Male (left) and female (right) common mergansers.

long thin bodies and short legs. Telling these two species apart can be challenging unless you get a good look at both the tail and the body, and even then, it can be difficult. A short-tailed weasel's tail makes up about 40 percent of the total length, while the long-tailed weasel's tail is more than 45 percent of the head and body length.

By April in the Northeast, both of these carnivores are finishing shedding their white winter coats for summer brown. Beginning in November, they will molt again and start turning white for the winter.

Farther south, in Pennsylvania, fewer than half of the long-tailed weasels turn white, and none south of the Pennsylvania–Maryland border do so.

APRIL 17

Common Mergansers on Eggs

Common mergansers, like other species of mergansers, are cavity nesters. Natural holes in snags, holes made by large woodpeckers, and nest boxes serve as nesting cavities. The female merganser selects the site, which can be up to 100 feet off the ground and is usually within a mile of water. Very little material is added to the

cavity for the actual nest, although the female, after laying eggs, lines the nest with downy feathers she plucks from her breast.

Spring Beauty Flowering

Spring beauty is one of the earliest woodland wildflowers to blossom and is thus an important source of nectar and pollen for the earliest foraging insects. Pink lines called "bee guides" or nectar guides on each of its five petals lead pollinators to the center of the flower, where the nectar is located. The pollinator in this image, *Andrena erigeniae*, is a pollen specialist that collects pollen only from two species of spring beauty and from no other flowers.

Spring beauty and pollinator.

APRIL 18

Frogs Calling

*Peep*s and *quack*s fill the air these days. These calls travel great distances thanks to the action of thin-walled vocal sacs that most frogs have.

Spring peeper calling (single vocal sac).

There are three basic types of vocal sacs: a single throat sac (the most common), paired throat sacs (partially separated by connective tissue), and paired lateral sacs (completely separate chambers on either side of the head). A vocal sac is an outpocketing of the floor of the mouth that amplifies the frog's calls. When calling, a frog closes its mouth and nostrils and expels air from its lungs through the larynx and into the vocal sacs. The vibrations of the vocal cords in the larynx produce a sound that resonates within the vocal sacs. The frog continues calling as muscles within its body wall force the air back and forth between the lungs and vocal sac.

The thickness of the vocal sac wall varies in frogs. Typically, small frogs that call in the air, like

Wood frog calling (paired vocal sacs).

spring peepers, have balloon-like vocal sacs with thin walls, whereas those that call in the water, particularly large species like green frogs and bull frogs, often have thick-walled vocal sacs that appear swollen when filled with air.

APRIL 19

Margined Carrion Beetles Feeding on Winter-Killed Carcasses

The margined carrion beetle is found primarily on and inside carrion, where it arrives shortly after flies arrive. It wastes no time in finding and eating fly larvae, mating, and laying its own eggs. In order to reduce the number of competitors its larvae will have, adult carrion beetles continue eating maggots and the larvae of other insects, as well as the carcass, until the carcass has been consumed. The carrion beetle larvae also feed on the carcass and on other larvae they find. When it is time to pupate, the larvae dig underground to spend the winter and emerge as adult beetles in the spring. This species of beetle is used in forensics for establishing the post-mortem interval—the length of time since a person died.

Green frog calling (single vocal sac).

Carrion beetles.

Blue jay.

Blue Jays Nest Building

Although their eggs won't be laid for several weeks, blue jays have already initiated nest building. A female frequently rubs her breast and belly at the site where her nest will eventually be built, perhaps indicating that she is the one who chooses the nest location.

Both male and female jays contribute to the construction of their nest, which consists of an outer shell of twigs—often taken with considerable struggle from live trees—with added leaves, grasses, lichens, bark, moss, and mud. Blue jays line their nests with rootlets and often fly great distances to obtain them from recently dug ditches, fresh graves in cemeteries, recently tilled land, and newly fallen trees. Bits of paper, cloth, string, wool, and plastic are found in nests built near human habitation.

Spring Azures Flying

The arrival of spring brings the emergence of spring azures, delightful tiny butterflies. Their wings are pale blue on the underside but a much

Spring azure.

brighter sky blue above, as their name implies. There are several forms and/ or species, and they are difficult to tell apart. Until they are further classified, they are collectively referred to as the "spring azure complex."

APRIL 20

Red-Necked False Blister Beetles Pollinating Trout Lily and Mating

Red-necked false blister beetles are commonly found on trout lilies. This group of ardent pollen eaters obtained its common name from the fact that many species cause blisters when pinched or squashed against skin. Pollen attracts the adult beetles, and mating takes place on flower heads during pollen feeding, but not before the female's

False blister beetle on trout lily.

gut is packed full of pollen. She stores pollen in a special intestinal sac, where an enzyme causes the pollen to partially germinate and dissolves the indigestible covering of the pollen grain. She then digests the contents of the pollen grain and uses it to manufacture her eggs.

Marsh Marigold Flower Buds Starting to Open

Although this plant is not a true marigold, part of its common name is accurate—it grows in marshes and other wet areas. The gold sepals of this member of the buttercup family look wet and shiny, like the petals of many buttercups. They reflect ultraviolet light from all parts of the flower except for the very center, thus providing a nectar guide for pollinating insects that can see in the ultraviolet range of the spectrum.

Thoreau observed that marsh marigold has little scent, but "speaks wholly to the eye." It also speaks to the palate of some, who, after boiling

111

Marsh marigold.

Mating snapping turtles.

it several times, consume the young, iron-rich leaves, said to surpass the taste of spinach. The leaves of marsh marigold are toxic when raw.

Green Herons Returning to Open Water

Green heron.

Green herons arrive back on their northeastern U.S. breeding grounds earlier than larger herons. This is perhaps because they feed very early and late in the day, and their crepuscular feeding habits give them a longer feeding day. Mainly fish eaters, green herons are one of few tool-using birds. They fabricate various baits including bread crust, insects, earthworms, twigs, and feathers and drop them on the surface of the water to entice small fish to come within reach.

APRIL 21

Snapping Turtles Mating

Snapping turtles begin to wake up in April, when the water reaches 41 to 50 degrees. They begin to move around and bask, and eggs develop inside the body of the females. When the water reaches about 60 degrees, the turtles begin to eat. Male snapping turtles establish home ranges, and large males usually hold the same home territory year after year. In spring, some fighting can occur when dominance is reestablished for the year.

Mating takes place soon after the turtles come out of hibernation. A male turtle drives off any other competing males and then accompanies a mate into shallow water. Mating in snapping turtles is very aggressive, with the male chasing the female as the female tries to escape and hide. The male grasps the posterior end of the female's carapace, then holds on to the edges of her shell with all four legs as he mounts her. He often bites her head and neck during copulation.

Chimney Swifts Arriving Back

When migrating between the northeastern U.S. and South America every fall and spring, chimney swifts typically stay over land in their northerly spring flight and cross over the Gulf of Mexico on their way south. These fast-flying, aerial insectivores migrate during the day, usually in large flocks of fifty to one thousand birds, and stop at the most convenient roosts— chimneys, hollow trees, caves, or outbuildings— each evening.

Chimney swifts.

APRIL 22

How to Tell If a Beaver Pond is Active

Beaver ponds have started to melt, making it easy to determine whether or not there have been beavers living in any existing lodges over the winter. The telltale sign is the presence of floating debarked sticks and branches. To feed during the winter, beavers leave their lodge, swim to the underwater food supply pile they made the previous fall, and haul branches back to the lodge to consume the bark. When finished with a stick, the beaver discards it into open water through the lodge's entrance hole. These sticks remain hidden under the ice on the surface of the water until warm weather arrives and the ice begins to melt. At this point, the sticks and branches often extend several feet out from the lodge and become visible. They will not go to waste, as the beavers will use them for dam and lodge repairs.

Sign of active beaver pond.

Meadow Vole Damage Revealed

Warming temperatures reveal the signs of meadow vole activity that occurred during the winter under a deep, protective layer of snow. In addition to a multitude of exposed runways, there are ample signs of the voracious appetite of this small rodent. Given that more than 90 percent of a meadow vole's diet consists of vegetable matter, that it can eat more than its own body weight in twenty-four hours, and that it breeds throughout the year, it is no surprise that the bark of many woody plants is consumed every winter, resulting in much girdling—and thus the demise—of many shrubs and saplings.

Meadow vole–girdled shrub.

Wood Frogs Mating

Wood frogs are emerging from hibernation, congregating at woodland pools and ponds, courting, mating, and laying eggs. Unless you see

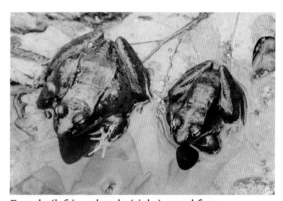

Female (left) and male (right) wood frogs.

Male wood frog clasping female during amplexus.

113

a wood frog in the act of calling (male), laying eggs (female), or mating, it can be hard to distinguish its gender. On average, females are larger and lighter in color than males, and they lack the swollen thumbs of males, which are used for grasping the female during amplexus. The webs between the hind toes are convex in males but concave in females.

APRIL 23

A Gardener's Favorite Beetle

Ground beetles (family Carbidae) are fast moving beetles, many of which are predators with specialized diets. One ground beetle (*Cychrus caraboides*) eats only snails, while another (*Harpalus rufipes*) limits its diet to strawberry seeds. *Loricera pilicornis* uses bristles on its antennae to trap springtails and mites.

Canada goose.

The bronze carabid uses its large curved mandibles to crush and slice through prey--it will eat or try to eat just about any invertebrate, but specializes in capturing and eating slugs. Its hardened forewings, or elytra, have a coppery sheen to them, and parts of its thorax and the edges of its elytra are iridescent purple. This nocturnal, introduced, flightless beetle resides throughout the Northeast and is already actively pursuing slugs.

Bronze carabid.

Canada Geese on Nests

Canada geese are among the earliest nesting birds in the Northeast, arriving at their nesting areas just before the final snowmelt. Most have paired up on their wintering grounds, prior to migrating north. After scraping several nest sites, the female selects one and constructs a nest of vegetation, often grasses, as well as down and other feathers. Two to eight eggs are laid and incubated by the female. In a little over three weeks, the eggs hatch and within twenty-four hours the precocial, down-covered goslings are able to walk, swim, feed, and dive.

Six- and Twelve-Spotted Tiger Beetles Active

Tiger beetles, which are named for their ferocity, can be easily recognized by their quick, jerky movements, huge eyes, and large, multiple mandibles. Look for these voracious hunters in sunny, open spots where they can easily spot prey and potential predators. The six-spotted tiger beetle is hard to miss, thanks to its iridescent green outer wing covers, or elytra. Contrary to what its name implies, this species can have five, two, or even no white spots. It is most likely to be found on exposed rocks, logs, and tree trunks, whereas the twelve-spotted tiger beetle, with twelve or fewer spots, tends to

Twelve-spotted tiger beetle.

Six-spotted tiger beetle.

prefer moist sandy spots. They both run down their prey, masticate it with their formidable mandibles, then squeeze it and swallow the juice. Both of these species of tiger beetles have a two-year life cycle. Females lay eggs in the soil in early summer, and the larvae that develop there live in a vertical tunnel in the soil. The larvae are highly predaceous and catch all kinds of prey from their tunnels. They overwinter in their tunnels and pupate the following July. Adults hatch in August and spend the following winter in their burrows.

Tiger beetles can travel at up to 5.6 miles per hour, which is comparable to a person running 480 mph. If you watch a tiger beetle hunting, you'll see it stop and start frequently. This is because it runs so fast that it goes blind, because its brain can't process the information that zips by, and the beetle must stop to regain its sight.

APRIL 24

Porcupines Giving Birth

This newborn porcupine is about a foot long from the tip of its nose to the tip of its tail, weighs roughly a pound, and has quills about 1 inch long. It was born headfirst in a sac in order to protect its mother from quill damage. Its quills are soft at birth but harden within an hour. The young porcupine will nurse from its mother for the next four months, but within two weeks will be feeding on vegetation as well. Because its one offspring is precocial—capable of traveling and feeding on its own soon after birth—the porcupette's mother is free to leave the young porcupine in a sheltered spot, go off to feed on her own, and return at night to nurse it.

Squirrel Corn and Dutchman's Breeches Flowering

Squirrel corn and Dutchman's breeches are in the same genus, and their leaves and flowers reflect this close relationship. Squirrel corn's flowers are more heart-shaped, and lack the upright, pointed spurs of Dutchman's breeches' flowers. Squirrel corn gets its common name from the clusters of yellow, kernel-like bulblets, or tubers, that form on its roots. Dutchman's breeches resemble pants that used to be worn by men in the Netherlands.

Dutchman's breeches

Young porcupine.

Squirrel corn.

Squirrel corn roots and bulblets.

115

Selected Mammal Breeding and Birthing Dates

Breeding Times

	JAN	FEB	MARCH	APRIL	MAY	JUNE	JULY	AUG	SEPT	OCT	NOV	DEC
Virginia opossum	X	X	X	X	X	X	X	X	X			
Eastern cottontail			X	X	X	X	X	X	X			
New England cottontail			X	X	X	X	X	X	X			
Snowshoe hare	X	X	X	X	X	X						
Eastern chipmunk		X	X	X	X	X	X					
Woodchuck			X	X								
Gray squirrel	X	X	X	X	X	X						
Red squirrel	X	X	X	X	X	X	X	X	X			
Southern flying squirrel		X	X			X	X					
Northern flying squirrel		X	X	X	X		X					
Beaver	X	X	X									
Muskrat		X	X	X	X	X	X	X	X			
Porcupine										X	X	X
Coyote	X	X										
Red fox	X	X										
Gray fox	X	X	X	X	X							
Black bear						X	X					
Raccoon		X	X	X	X	X						
American marten						X	X	X	X			
Fisher		X	X	X								
Ermine					X	X	X	X				
Long-tailed weasel							X	X				
Mink		X	X	X								
Striped skunk		X	X	X								
North American river otter			X	X								
Eastern mountain lion	X Throughout year at 18–24 month intervals	X	X	X	X	X	X	X	X	X	X	X
Canadian lynx			X	X								
Bobcat		X	X									

Birthing Times

	JAN	FEB	MARCH	APRIL	MAY	JUNE	JULY	AUG	SEPT	OCT	NOV	DEC
Virginia opossum		X	X	X	X	X	X					
Eastern cottontail			X	X	X	X	X	X	X			
New England cottontail			X	X	X	X	X					
Snowshoe Hare			X									
Eastern chipmunk				X	X		X	X				
Woodchuck				X	X							
Gray squirrel			X	X			X	X				
Red squirrel			X	X	X			X	X			
Southern flying squirrel				X	X		X	X				
Northern flying squirrel			X	X	X	X	X	X	X			
Beaver					X	X						
Muskrat				X	X	X	X		X	X		
Porcupine				X	X	X						
Coyote			X	X	X							
Red fox			X	X								
Gray fox			X	X								
Black bear	X											X
Raccoon				X	X							
American marten			X	X								
Fisher			X	X								
Ermine				X	X							
Long-tailed weasel				X	X							
Mink				X	X							
Striped skunk				X	X	X						
North American river otter		X		X								
Eastern mountain lion				X	X	X	X	X	X			
Canadian lynx					X	X						
Bobcat					X							

Belted Kingfisher Snags, Stuns, and Swallows Prey

Belted kingfisher with crayfish.

Once there is open water in the Northeast, belted kingfishers return to their breeding grounds, where they now have access to food. They hunt by hovering above the water long enough to focus on prey before diving or by perching on a branch near or overhanging the water and swooping down from there to grab prey near the surface of the water. Once a kingfisher has its prey, which is mostly fish but also crustaceans, frogs, snakes, young birds, and small mammals, in its pincerlike bill, it flies to a nearby perch and pounds the prey against the perch with repeated sideways movements of its head. The kingfisher does this to stun the fish (or other prey) so that it can eventually turn it around and swallow it headfirst.

APRIL 25

Bloodroot Flowering

Bloodroot's contrasting white petals and yellow pollen-bearing stamens attract pollinating insects. The blossoms offer only pollen—no nectar—to visitors. In order to protect the pollen, the petals of this member of the poppy family close on overcast days and nights, a time when most pollinators are inactive. The reopening of the flowers depends on temperature and cloud cover. If it is sunny out, the flowers will open when the temperature reaches 47 degrees. Native bees, which are bloodroot's main pollinators, don't usually fly until it is 55 degrees, so flies, which are capable of flying at slightly lower temperatures,

do most of the cool-weather pollinating.

Bloodroot.

To limit self-pollination, the female stigma becomes receptive before the male anthers of the same flower produce pollen. Furthermore, during the first few days when the flower is open, the anthers bend down toward the outside of the flower, away from the receptive stigma. If insect pollination doesn't take place by the third day of flowering, the anthers bend inward to contact the stigma and allow the flower to self-pollinate.

Big Brown Bats Emerging and Females Forming Maternity Roosts

Big brown bats are emerging from hibernation. In spring, a female big brown bat ovulates and her eggs become fertilized with sperm she has stored in her uterus over the winter. Reproductive females collectively form a maternity roost, and each bat typically gives birth to a single pup in June, after about a sixty-day gestation period.

Big brown bat.

While both little and big brown bats were affected by the fungus causing white-nose syndrome, the big brown bat population has not been decimated like that of the little brown bat. In some locations, big brown bats have even thrived, taking over summer roosting spots formerly occupied by little brown bats.

Common grackle with nesting material.

Common Grackles Nest Building

The common grackle is one of the first bird species to begin nesting in the spring. More often than not, grackles nest in conifers, as deciduous trees normally haven't leafed out this early. Usually the female builds a large, bulky cup nest, incorporating in it all kinds of material in addition to vegetation, sometimes including paper, string, fishing line, cloth, corn husks, bark, moss, feathers, manure, tape, and wire. The nest is lined with mud, and after it dries, grasses or horsehair are added. The female lays one to seven eggs and does all of the incubation. Half of all males desert their mates during this period.

APRIL 26

Eastern screech owl, gray phase.

Eastern Screech Owls on Eggs

As cavity nesters, screech owls seek out hollow trunks, stumps, and limbs as well as holes in trunks or limbs in which to lay their three to six eggs. Woodpecker holes, especially northern flicker nest holes, make up about 30 percent of eastern screech owl nest holes. Apple, cottonwood, oak, and pine trees are commonly used, as well as man-made nest boxes. While the female does all of the incubating and brooding, the male screech owl keeps his mate and their young well fed. There are two color morphs of these owls, rufous and gray, both of which can be found in the same brood. Roughly 30 percent of eastern screech owls are rufous morphs.

Black Bears In "Walking Hibernation"

"Walking hibernation" refers to the two to three weeks following emergence from hibernation when a black bear's metabolic processes adjust to normal summer levels. During walking hibernation, bears voluntarily eat and drink less than

Black bear.

they will later during normal activity. They also excrete less urine, nitrogen, calcium, phosphorus, and magnesium.

Eastern Tent Caterpillars Hatching and Building Tents

The adult eastern tent caterpillar moth lays her eggs in the summer on a tree whose leaves its larvae will eat—black cherry and apple trees are favorites. Two to three hundred eggs are deposited in a mass that encircles a thin branch.

Eastern tent caterpillars hatching.

Within three weeks, fully formed caterpillars develop inside the eggs. The caterpillars remain there until the following spring, when they chew their way out of the eggs just as the buds of the host tree are starting to open. As soon as the caterpillars emerge, they construct a silk tent within which they reside, enlarging it as they grow in size.

Queen tri-colored bumble bee collecting nectar from trailing arbutus.

Queen bumble bee on wild oats.

APRIL 27

Queen Bumble Bees Flying

Most bumble bees, unlike honey bees, die in the fall. Only young, fertilized bumble bee queens overwinter. When they emerge early in the spring, each must start a new colony by herself with no help from worker bees, since there are none. The queen builds a ball of moss, hair, or grass, often in an abandoned rodent nest or small cavity. Within this ball the queen builds a wax honey pot which she provisions with nectar from early-blooming flowers. Next, she collects pollen and forms it into a mound on the floor of her nest. She then lays eggs in the pile of pollen and coats it with wax secreted from her body.

The queen bumble bee keeps her eggs warm by sitting on the pollen mound and by shivering her muscles to raise her body temperature to between 98 and 102 degrees. For nourishment, she consumes honey from her wax pot, which is positioned within her reach. In four days, the eggs, all of which will become female workers, hatch. The bumble bee queen continues her maternal care, foraging for pollen and nectar to feed to her larvae until they pupate. After the

bees from the first brood emerge as adults, the queen concentrates her effort on laying eggs while the new female worker bees raise new batches of larvae. The colony swells in number. At the end of summer, eggs that will develop into new queens and males are laid. These bees will be the way the colony reproduces. The males leave the hive to forage and search for mates. The virgin queens mate with males of the same species, but not necessarily the same colony, and then seek shelter for the winter. Cold temperatures, short lifespans, and no new eggs result in an empty colony by the time winter arrives.

Killdeer Nesting

Killdeer are back on their northeastern breeding grounds, and some are already on eggs. Being a ground nester, the killdeer has many mammalian predators from which it needs to protect its eggs, including weasels, skunks, opossums, and raccoons.

Nesting killdeer have a number of responses to predators, including several different types of distraction displays. These behaviors draw attention to the adult bird and take attention away from its nest. One of the most common displays is that of feigning injury by assuming

Killdeer and nest.

Killdeer displaying.

Wood turtle.

a position that makes the bird appear vulnerable. When a predator approaches, the bird runs away from the nest, crouching with its head low, its wings drooping, and its tail fanned and dragging on the ground as it displays its rufous rump patch. The predator typically follows, seeing an easy meal, and as soon as it gets too close for the killdeer's comfort, the killdeer continues to lead it off with alternate flights and sprints. Notice that the killdeer in the second photo is looking over its shoulder, making sure that its ploy has succeeded.

Wood Turtles Becoming Active and Mating

After spending the winter hibernating in small streams and rivers, wood turtles awaken, become more active, mate, and eventually leave the water to begin foraging for food. In a few weeks, females will deposit between four and twelve

Wood turtle.

eggs in a nest dug in sandy soil. Summer is spent mostly on land, traveling along streams. Rarely do wood turtles stray farther than 1,000 feet from the water.

APRIL 28

Great Blue Herons Mating

Great blue herons have returned to their nesting colonies in the Northeast and their breeding season is underway. Numerous displays lead up to the mating of great blue herons, including neck stretching, bill clacking, wing preening, circling flights, twig shaking, crest raising, and neck fluffing. Great blue herons are monogamous for the duration of any given breeding season, although most choose a new mate every year. After elaborate courtship displays have taken place, the pair copulates, frequently on the nest, and usually in the early morning or evening, as the female is away from the nest in the middle of the day.

Great blue herons mating on nest.

Molting moose.

Moose Molting

A moose's winter coat consists of long (roughly 4 inches on neck and torso and up to 10 inches over the spine near its hump), hollow guard hairs over its entire body and wool hairs, or underfur, everywhere except for on its legs and face. In early spring, the faded and ragged winter hairs are shed and replaced with short, dark, shiny hairs. Adult bulls and barren cows molt first, with lactating cows and juveniles molting soon after.

Wild Leek Leaves Emerging

If you are a fan of wild leeks, or ramps, this is the time to start looking for them. Both leaves and bulbs are delicious. To confirm their identity, make sure that the plant smells like onion. The flower of this wild onion does not appear until after the leaves have died back.

Wild leek leaves.

Spring Peepers Mating

The mating season for spring peepers lasts two months or more. Once a singing male is successful in attracting a female, he mounts and clasps her while depositing his sperm on the eggs she is laying. Up to eight hundred eggs are laid, either singly or in small groups, on plants within the male's territory. The frogs remain joined in a position known as amplexus for up to four hours. After egg-laying and fertilization are completed, the female peeper returns to the woods; the male remains at the pond and resumes singing for some time before returning to the woods.

Mating spring peepers.

Trailing Arbutus Flowering

Trailing arbutus is said to have heralded spring to the winter-weary pilgrims in 1621 and thus is known as "mayflower" by many. Its trailing woody stems bear aromatic, evergreen leaves and creep along the ground where the soil is

Trailing arbutus.

typically quite acidic. In early spring, we are treated to its fragrant pink flowers, which are often nestled under the leathery leaves. Trailing arbutus's indescribably delicate and sweet-smelling scent attracts bumble bee queens that have recently emerged from their winter hiding places at a time when few other plants are flowering.

Red-Shouldered Hawks on Eggs

After copulation, the female red-shouldered hawk lays two to four eggs in a nest that she has most likely used for several years. It is usually located below the canopy but more than halfway up a tree, generally in a crotch of the main trunk. The male and female both build or refurbish the nest, adding fresh evergreen sprigs to it throughout the nesting period. The female, who usually spends nights on the nest, does the majority of the incubating. The eggs hatch five weeks from when they were laid.

Red-shouldered hawk beside nest.

APRIL 30

American Bitterns Courting and Displaying

American bitterns have returned to the Northeast from their southern wintering grounds and are announcing their presence in numerous ways. Even so, it can be difficult to locate one because of its well-camouflaged plumage and stance. Bitterns walk very slowly through the marsh grasses and often stand still and point the bill skyward when trying to avoid notice—a behavior that makes them blend in perfectly with the reeds they inhabit.

American bittern trying to be invisible.

Calls: American bitterns typically nest in tall, standing cattails, rushes, and sedges, where they are well concealed. Like most birds, the male bittern uses its voice to stake out territory and to attract a female. Thick vegetative growth is a problem when it comes to being heard, however. The American bittern overcomes this challenge by having a very low-frequency call, which is audible at great distances in dense marsh vegetation. The call is unmistakable and unforgettable. It is very deep and has three syllables—*oong-ka-choonk*—which are preceded by clicks and gulps. The bittern makes this call over and over by inflating his esophagus while contorting himself quite violently.

American bittern calling.

Courtship Display: Like other members of the heron family, American bitterns possess plumes. These large, white shoulder feathers are visible only at this time of year during territorial and courtship displays and just prior to copulation, when they are erected.

American bittern displaying.

MAY

Bumble Bees

The honey bee's plight gets a great deal of attention, as well it should, for this little insect plays a big part in the U.S. economy and food production, and its population is declining. However, the honey bee is not the only pollinating insect humans depend upon—and not necessarily the most efficient. Bumble bees and solitary bees are responsible for much of the pollination that takes place: bumble bees pollinate about 15 percent of all the crops grown in the nation, which is worth about three billion dollars.

A look at the humble bumble bee reveals several traits that make them better pollinators than honey bees. Most bumble bees are native and have evolved with native flowering plants. They pollinate different varieties of plants than honey bees, which are European natives. Most bumble bees are more active in cooler weather and at lower light levels than honey bees, which extends their working hours, and some species pollinate flowers in ways honey bees have never dreamed of.

Pollination, the process of transferring pollen from a plant's male to female reproductive organs, starts the process of seed and fruit formation. It is estimated that, worldwide, one-third of the human diet can be traced directly or indirectly to animal pollination. Wind disperses a significant amount of pollen, but bees, wasps, ants, moths, flies, beetles, and butterflies are even more crucial to cross-pollination, which is the transfer of pollen from the flower of one plant to another plant of the same species. Each insect has specialized adaptations that allow them to accomplish this task, some more efficiently than others.

What makes bumble bees such effective pollinators? To begin with, like almost all bees, they consume only nectar and pollen, so visiting flowers is a necessity if they are to survive. Bumble bees are generalist foragers, not limited to one or two plant species. That said, both bumble bees and honey bees tend to specialize on one or two species at a time in the interest of efficiency. They learn a given flower's structure, where and how to reach the nectaries and pollen-bearing anthers, and what time of day nectar or pollen is available, and they return repeatedly to the same species. This not only saves the bee time, it also minimizes pollen transfer to the flowers of other, unreceptive plants. (Honey bees are also "flower constant" for the same reason.) Bumble bees mark the flowers they have visited with scent from a gland in their leg, indicating that there is no nectar left. Bees arriving at a flower after the nectar has been taken know not to waste energy trying to collect nectar from that particular flower. Bumble bees are better at learning more complex foraging tasks, such as how to enter and extract nectar or pollen from a bottle gentian or jewelweed flower, than many other insects.

A pollination technique that bumble bees use and honey bees don't is "buzz pollination." In order to release the pollen of certain flowers, bumble bees and some species of solitary bees grab onto the flower and move their thoracic muscles rapidly, causing the anthers to vibrate and dislodge pollen. Some plants are adapted to disperse pollen when vibrated, and some even require it. Only about 8 percent of the world's flowers are primarily pollinated using buzz pollination (also known as sonication), but among them are vegetables that humans are particularly

Red fox kit with wild turkey feather.

fond of, including greenhouse-grown tomatoes, peppers, squash, cucumbers, eggplants, and blueberries. Commercialized bumble bees are primarily used in crops grown in greenhouses.

Bumble bee bodies are well adapted for collecting pollen and nectar. The hair that covers much of the bodies of all bees is branched, but bumble bees are especially hairy, and a lot of pollen inadvertently gets stuck to their bodies.

Bumble bees have a distinct advantage over many other insects in that they can remain active in cool, wet, spring weather. Although, like other insects, bees are cold-blooded, they can maintain a consistent body temperature regardless of the ambient temperature by generating heat. They do this by vibrating their thoracic muscles, and this allows them extended foraging time. The tongues of some bumble bee species are long and feathery, enabling them to reach the nectar in red clover, for instance, that other bumble bees and honey bees can't reach. The legs of bumble bees have hairs and brushes that are used to gather the pollen that has collected in their body hairs and pack it into pollen baskets (one on each hind leg) for transport. When both baskets are full, pollen can make up nearly 50 percent of a bumble bee's weight. Like honey bees, bumble bees possess a "honey stomach" in which they store the nectar they collect. When a pollen basket is full, it can weigh as much as 0.01 gram and contain as much as one million pollen grains.

Bumble bees have a much greater pollen-carrying capacity than honey bees do. On average, they visit twice as many flowers per minute. They will forage for up to two times as long as a honey bee. And 60 to 90 percent of a bumble bee's hive is pollen-foraging bees, compared to 15 to 30 percent of a honey bee hive, depending on the time of year. Even though there are at most only about 250 bumble bees in a colony, compared to a summer population of 50,000 to 60,000 honey bees, some people believe that the potential of bumble bees as commercial pollinators, especially in greenhouses and especially

Tri-colored bumble bee.

for buzz-pollinated crops, should be explored. At the very least, their role as important pollinators should be recognized.

Unfortunately, the population of some bumble bee species has been declining at an alarming rate over the past two or three decades. The cause of this decline is not fully understood, but it appears likely that a number of factors play a role, particularly neonicotinoid pesticides. These pesticides may have a detrimental effect on a wide range of non-target organisms, including bumble bees. Fragmentation of habitat, the importation of parasites and diseases, and the potential effects of climate change also are thought to contribute to the decline of bumble bees. Neonicotinoid exposure interacts with the other threats and exacerbates them, as bees poisoned by neonicotinoids are less able to combat disease and forage for food, and therefore less likely to produce a successful colony.

While humans don't reap the benefit of absconding with pounds of stored honey from bumble bees—even in the largest bumble bee colony, there are usually no more than a few teaspoons of honey, stored for rainy, cold days—their pollinating capabilities link our fate with theirs.

Common Ravens

The raven has long been a part of the folklore of many cultures. Native Americans of the Northwest revere ravens as being the creator of earth, moon, sun, and stars, but they also regard them as tricksters and cheaters. Poets and authors of Western cultures have often used the raven to symbolize death, danger, and wisdom. Even though the raven is regarded in a variety of ways by a variety of cultures, most would agree that it is one of our most intelligent birds: crafty, resourceful, adaptable, and quick to learn and benefit from experience.

The intelligence of common ravens is demonstrated by the ingenious ways in which they find food. Ravens have been seen feeding on tidal flats by flying down and bumping the wet sand to disturb sandworms. It is not uncommon for them to follow cows and other animals (as well as plows) to catch and eat the insects that are stirred up. Ravens wait patiently along roadsides for fresh roadkill. They have been seen flying at an elevation of several hundred feet to drop sea urchins and mollusks, which split open upon landing on the rocks below, ready to be eaten.

A technique the raven uses with turkey vultures demonstrates their canniness. Turkey vultures are gentle and nonaggressive birds. When threatened, they tend to vomit, rather than attack their predator. Ravens take advantage of this by harassing the vulture until it disgorges the food it has recently eaten. The raven proceeds to eat the vomit—instead of the vulture.

Perhaps the most intriguing of common ravens' many skills is their ability to work as a team. Arthur C. Bent, an ornithologist who collected firsthand observations from birders in the 1800s, describes a scene in which a dog eating a bone was discovered by a raven. The raven flew down and proceeded to caw loudly in hopes of scaring the dog away. A second raven appeared, and the two birds harassed the dog as they stood just out of reach, by his head. A third raven then appeared and grabbed the dog's tail in such a manner as to cause the dog to turn to try to snap at the bird, at which point one of the other two ravens rushed in and snatched the bone.

Ravens working together often have amusing interactions with other species. An observer by the name of Ludwig Kumlien witnessed a snowshoe hare being chased by two ravens. He reported that the ravens would spell each other in order to rest. Sometimes the raven would catch the hare by the ears and the hare and raven would roll down the mountain side together 30 or 40 feet, until the raven lost his hold, and then its companion would be on hand to renew the attack.

There are times when this teamwork is essential for catching prey. Ravens have been known to raid seabird colonies, with one bird distracting an incubating adult and the other waiting to grab an egg or chick as soon as it is uncovered. Several times, Kumlien saw ravens capture young seals that lay basking in the sun near their holes.

> The first manoeuvre of the ravens was to sail leisurely over the seal, gradually lowering with each circle, till at last one of them dropped directly into the seal's hole, thus cutting off its retreat from the water. Its mate would then attack the seal, and endeavor to drag or drive it as far away from the hole as possible. The attacking raven seemed to strike the seal on the top of the head with its powerful bill, and thus break the tender skull.*

Even though they are brilliant, ravens are not admired by everyone. They are considered pests by many in the agricultural field due to their appetite for everything from grains to calves. Ravens have been implicated in the decline of several threatened and endangered species,

* "Scientific Results of the Howgate Polar Expedition 1877–78." *Littell's Living Age* 146, no. 1884 (July 24, 1880): 249.

Common raven.

including the California condor, least tern, desert tortoise, and marbled murrelet. Many conflicts arise with humans, but one must give them their due. Whether scavenging or hunting, ravens use their impressive brains to survive. It is small wonder that Wyoming ornithologists discovered that during hunting season, the sound of a gunshot draws ravens in to investigate a possible carcass, whereas they ignore sounds that are just as loud but harmless, such as an air horn or a car door slamming.

Doctrine of Signatures

Before modern medicine, finding cures for ailments was done by trial and error. People turned to plants, and if you ate or inhaled something, you either lived or died. If you lived, and your ailment was cured, the plant became the accepted remedy for this ailment. This hit-or-miss approach had its obvious downside. Eventually, a theory, which came to be known as the Doctrine of Signatures, developed, and it served as an aid to the existing approach to medicine. This theory proposed that the characteristics, or signature, of a plant designated its medicinal value. If a plant's shape or color resembled a human organ, it was used to treat that organ.

Most of the world's cultures have, at one time or other, incorporated this idea in their medical practices. Signature plants are thought to have been first recognized in China. Color and taste were key to this approach: plants that were yellow and sweet were used to treat the spleen; red and bitter plants treated the heart; green and sour plants treated the liver, and black and salty plants were used to treat the lungs. In addition, ailments of the upper half of the body were treated with the upper parts of plants, and ailments of lower parts of the body were treated with below-ground parts.

In Western cultures, signature plants emerged for medical use during the Middle Ages, when they became an important part of the work of traditional healers and herbalists. The man credited with being this theory's most avid advocate was Paracelsus, who named the theory the Doctrine of Signatures. In the early 1500s he traveled throughout Europe, Asia, and Egypt, reputedly curing people with his herbal concoctions. During the late sixteenth and seventeenth centuries, the Doctrine of Signatures adopted a religious slant by endorsing the belief that God provided visual cues to specify which plants were to be used to treat certain human ailments. When botanical physicians learned of this theory, they embraced it, as it justified their practices: the shape, color and growth of plants indicated their divine healing purpose.

Many plants fell under the umbrella of the Doctrine of Signatures. Hepatica, with its three-lobed, liver-shaped leaves, comes from the Greek word for liver. A European species of this family was used as a cure for liver ailments for over two thousand years. In 1883 more than two hundred tons of hepatic leaves were imported from Europe to meet the needs of medicine manufacturers in the United States. The curling stalk of forget-me-not flowers resembled the tail

Bloodroot.

Bloodroot root.

Early saxifrage.

of a scorpion, and for centuries (as far back as 40 to 90 A.D.) this plant was used for treating scorpion bites. Plants with heart-shaped leaves were used in treating heart disease. Members of the genus *Polygonum*, including smartweed and Japanese knotweed, have swollen nodes—the areas on the stem of a plant where leaves and buds occur. This characteristic led herbalists to use species of plants in this genus to treat sore and swollen joints. Boneset, a plant of wet, sunny meadows, bears opposite leaves that clasp and entirely surround the plant's stem. A poultice of this plant was used to help broken bones knit, much like boneset's leaves join together. Saxifrage, which grows on rocks and breaks them apart as it grows, was thought to relieve kidney stones. Plantain, whose seed stalk looks like a snake's head, was used to treat venomous bites as well as to draw infection from the skin. Walnuts,

thought to resemble human brains, were used to cure neurological diseases such as depression. Liverworts, as well as hepatica, relieved liver problems. Toothwort eased toothaches, and maidenhair fern was considered a cure for baldness. Flowers shaped like butterflies became cures for insect bites.

Sometimes characteristics other than the shape and color of a flower were used. Long-lived plants were thought to lengthen a person's life. Plants with rough stems and leaves were used to treat diseases that destroyed the smoothness of the skin. Plants with yellow sap cured jaundice. Red bee balm and bloodroot, with their red sap, were used to purify blood and treat blood-related ailments.

There have been supporters and detractors of this theory since it was first proposed, and there is still controversy

Wild ginger.

Toothwort.

Boneset.

over its efficacy. However, some herbalists continue to endorse this doctrine, and it is hard to refute some of their results. The Chinese have been using ginger for over two thousand years to calm the stomach and cure nausea; the shape of the root somewhat resembles a stomach. Sweet potatoes look like the pancreas and balance the glycemic index of diabetics. The Cherokees' wormlike purslane is truly effective in controlling intestinal parasites. Eyebright has good results when used to treat eye infections.

Although most of today's physicians do not embrace the Doctrine of Signatures, they, as well as herbalists, agree that it was an effective organizing device that facilitated the transmission of medical information through the generations. There were a lot of plants and a lot of cures to keep track of, and these plant and remedy associations were very helpful.

Hepatica.

MAY 1

Tree Swallows Mating

Tree swallows mate about a week before the female lays her eggs. Courtship includes a "flutter-flight" by the male in front of the female as she sits on top of the nesting box or near the nest hole. Mating involves the male making rapid *tick* calls as he flies toward the female, who is perched with her back and tail held horizontally. The male lands on the female's back, and, using his wings

Tree swallows mating.

for balance, grabs her head feathers in his bill. He then pivots his tail under the female's and transfers his sperm as the two birds' cloacas, or vents, touch, referred to as a "cloacal kiss. Blink and you'll miss this brief connection. However, it is not a one-time thing: the male flies off but quickly returns to copulate again, and he repeats this sequence several times.

Eastern Newts Dining on Wood Frog Eggs

Wood frogs, having mated and laid their eggs in ponds and pools, are headed back to their terrestrial, wooded habitat, leaving the eggs to hatch on their own. Amphibian eggs are subject to predation by many aquatic predators, including leeches, fish, insects, and salamanders. Eastern newts, aquatic for much of their lives, are carnivorous and consume insect larvae, fingernail

Wood frog eggs and several eastern newts.

Osprey on nest.

clams, leeches, and amphibian eggs, among other things. At this time of year, wood frog eggs are plentiful and easily accessible. The individual masses, each consisting of one thousand to two thousand eggs, are often deposited adjacent to each other on submerged vegetation. Hungry newts can feed for hours without moving more than an inch, and many do. After discovering an egg mass, a newt plunges its head into the clump of eggs, grabs one in its mouth, shakes its head vigorously to separate the egg from the mass, and quickly swallows it. Seconds later the newt repeats this process and continues until it is satiated.

MAY 2

Ospreys Laying and Incubating Eggs

Ospreys are late-season breeders compared to other raptors of their size and they are just starting to lay and incubate their eggs in the Northeast. This delay allows ice to break up so that fish can move to shallow waters. In years of late ice-out, ospreys may not breed. Both male and female ospreys incubate their one to four eggs, but the female generally does a majority of it, and nearly always is the incubator at night. The male typically brings the incubating female food,

which she takes to a nearby perch to eat while he sits on the eggs. When the eggs hatch, in about five weeks, the young are brooded by the female. The male does the fishing, bringing his prey back to the nest, eating his fill, and then giving it to his mate to tear into small bits before feeding it to their nestlings.

Red Admirals Mating

Red admiral butterflies are hard to mistake: no other butterfly found in this area has such bold, reddish-orange stripes on the surface of its wings, or such fast, erratic flight. In the spring, during

Red admiral.

the late afternoon, males set up territories on hilltops or in clearings and defend them against other males—even darting at people who enter their territory—while they search for females. Eggs are commonly laid on nettle, one of the red admiral larvae's favorite foods.

Spotted Salamander Larvae Feeding

Spotted salamander larva.

A few short weeks ago, spotted salamanders gathered at vernal pools to breed and lay eggs. Since then their eggs have hatched, and gilled spotted salamander larvae can now be found in these pools. The larvae are major predators and feed on many insects and crustaceans, including mosquito larvae and fairy shrimp. During the next two or three months, these larvae will develop lungs, absorb their feathery gills, and begin life as terrestrial amphibians, provided that the temporary pool they are in doesn't dry up prematurely.

MAY 3

Unequal Cellophane Bees Laying Eggs and Provisioning Cells

Ninety percent of bees are solitary: fertile females create their own cells and feed their own young, with no help from a colony of worker bees. They often nest underground, rarely sting, and are excellent pollinators, even though they don't store honey. One species of solitary bee, a plasterer bee, is also known as the polyester bee and unequal cellophane bee. Both of these common

Unequal cellophane bee.

Cell of unequal cellophane bee.

names come from its habit of lining its underground nest cells with a secretion that, when it dries, forms a smooth lining, similar to cellophane or polyester. This cell holds one egg suspended above a collection of pollen and nectar on which the larva will feed. The unequal cellophane bee is crepuscular, which can be deduced by the large size of its eyes. It is one of the earliest species to become active in the spring, sometime between March and May, when the adult bees emerge from underground chambers off a vertical tunnel dug by their mother last spring.

Red Squirrels Preparing Nests

Red squirrels breed once or twice a year, depending on where they live. In the south and east, they breed once in spring and once in late summer; where it is colder, they usually breed once a year. Females often mate with several males. After a gestation period of thirty-six to forty days, the female bears her young in a nest of grass, shredded bark, and leaves, which is often built in the branches of a tree, or in a tree cavity—rarely below the ground. Each individual squirrel has several nests within its territory, and females with

Red squirrel with nesting material.

young move them between nests. Offspring are pink and hairless at birth and first emerge from their natal nests at about six weeks of age.

Broad-Winged Hawks Building Nests

Only a small percentage of broad-winged hawks reuse their nests from year to year. Occasionally, they renovate an old nest of another species but, typically, they build a new nest, which takes them roughly two to four weeks to complete. Broad-winged hawk nests are usually in the first main crotch of a deciduous tree or on a platform of horizontal branches against the trunk of a conifer. Most often it is placed in the lower third of the canopy. Fresh conifer sprigs are broken from the lower half of trees, carried to the nest by the female, and placed on the rim of the nest. These sprigs will be added to an active nest for nearly a month after the eggs have hatched. The nest is constructed of dead twigs that the hawks gather from the ground and carry to the nest in their talons. Bark chips of both deciduous and coniferous trees are used in the lining, and cornhusks, moss, inner tree bark, red cedar, wild grape vine, lichen-covered bark, chicken feathers, and pine needles are occasionally incorporated as well.

MAY 4

Male Rose-Breasted Grosbeaks Return

Many of the rose-breasted grosbeaks that breed in the Northeast spend the winter in Panama and northern South America. When the time comes for their spring nocturnal migration, adult males depart first, flying north at an average of 49 miles per hour, including stopovers. Upon arrival, they establish and maintain their two-acre territories primarily through song. When females arrive and one approaches a singing male, he is initially very aggressive and often attacks the female, but if she persists, he soon comes around and wins her over with courtship displays.

Broad-winged hawk.

Male rose-breasted grosbeak.

Muskrat carrying grass.

Male Muskrats Sharing Family-Rearing Chores

Although muskrats are primarily nocturnal, they occasionally are out in the daytime, especially in spring and fall. They usually reside in ponds or marshes, where they live in the pond bank or build their own houses out of mud, cattails, and other plant materials.

Muskrats are herbivores, favoring cattail roots, arrowhead, bur reed, pickerelweed, and other aquatic vegetation, more often than not eating their food where they find it, especially during the warmer months. The muskrat pictured is not eating but is doing its share of parental care, for this is the time of year when the first of several litters of muskrats are born. While the mother nurses her four or so young, the father gathers bedding material for his offspring. Like their beaver cousins, muskrats tend to keep a tidy house and forage for fresh bedding with some regularity.

MAY 5

American Toad Males Calling

The American toad's breeding call is a familiar sound in spring: a long trill of up to thirty-five seconds that advertises his presence to potential mates. However, American toads have three other calls as well. A shortened version of the courtship trill, which sounds like a chirp, is given by a male

Male American toad calling.

toad with its vocal pouch just slightly inflated. A third, the release call, is heard when a male is clasped by another male. If you want to hear it, pick up a male toad during the breeding season, and it will vibrate as it calls right in your hand. The combination of the call and the vibrations usually causes a clasping male to release his grip. A fourth call, which has been recorded in the lab but not in the field, is a series of quiet clicks given by the male while clasping a female.

Cliff Swallows Beginning to Build a Colony of Mud Nests

From start to finish, a bird's nest represents an enormous amount of work, particularly if the material used is very specific. Cliff swallows are colonial nesters, and their nests are made of nine hundred to twelve hundred pellets of mud packed together into a gourd-shaped nest, often attached to the wall of an outbuilding such as a barn.

The building of a nest requires not only finding a source of mud, but also ferrying lumps of it in their beaks back to the nest site many, many

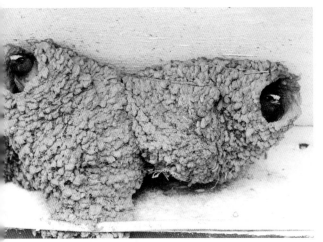

Cliff swallow nests.

times. Once a source of mud has been found, it is used by all the birds in the colony.

Most cliff swallows belonging to the same colony gather mud as a group and return to work on their nests all at the same time. They work together in roughly half-hour shifts, after which they all take a break and forage for insects for ten minutes or so before resuming nest building.

Cliff swallow building nest.

Cliff swallow.

White-tailed deer.

White-Tailed Deer Hearing Ability

With the exception of ultrasonic frequencies that they can hear but humans cannot, the white-tailed deer's hearing ability is very similar to that of humans. However, the size, shape, and maneuverability of their ears allow deer to identify the source of a sound more quickly and better than humans.

MAY 6

Ruffed Grouse Incubating Eggs

A ruffed grouse's nest consists of a simple, shallow bowl on the forest floor. The hen tosses leaves over her shoulders and they fall on her back, slip to the ground, and form a bowl. Ruffed grouse lay anywhere from nine to fourteen eggs at intervals of twenty-five to thirty hours,

135

so it takes about two weeks for a hen to lay an average clutch of eleven eggs. Each of her eggs weighs about 4 percent of her body weight, and the entire clutch will be equal to nearly half of her weight.

When the last egg is laid and incubation starts, the hen's behavior goes from wandering around and feeding voraciously to sitting on the nest and barely moving. Because of this behavior, as well as her cryptic coloration, an incubating ruffed grouse hen is much more likely to see you before you see her. She will stay motionless on her nest, even in the face of danger, hiding her eggs. Only after she is certain that she has been spotted will she fly off the nest, exposing her eggs.

Foxes, crows, ravens, chipmunks, skunks, bobcats, and raccoons are some of the predators responsible for the loss of 25 to 40 percent of grouse nests each year. After the precocial grouse chicks hatch during the first two weeks of June, they will be led away from the nest site by the hen. Within twenty-four hours they will be feeding on insects, and within a week they may double their weight.

Red-tailed hawk nest with nestling.

Ruffed grouse on nest.

Red-Tailed Hawk Eggs Hatching

Nesting red-tailed hawks typically have two or three eggs that hatch after being incubated by both parents for about a month. The nestlings are altricial—born blind and naked, totally dependent upon their parents for food and warmth. Within

Three red-tailed hawk chicks.

days they are covered with downy white feathers. The female parent broods the chicks for the next month or so, while the male provides most of the food for her and their nestlings. Ten to fifteen times a day he arrives at the nest with prey that the female tears into small pieces before feeding it to her young. In about seven weeks, the young will fledge, but the parents continue to provide them with food for the next two months.

Brown creepers at nest.

Whirligig beetle.

MAY 7

Brown Creepers Caring for Young

The brown creeper gets its name from its habit of creeping along tree trunks and spiraling upward, using its sharp, curved bill to probe for insects and spiders hidden in crevices. At this time of year, brown creepers have already made their fibrous nests behind a loose flap of bark on a tree, laid eggs, incubated them, and are now tending to their five or six nestlings. Unlike some species of birds, both adults care for the young.

Whirligig Beetles

Almost as soon as the ice on a pond has melted, you can find whirligig beetles swirling around on top of the water. If alarmed, they swim in circles; hence, their common name. Although these insects are capable of swimming underwater—they carry a bubble of air trapped beneath their elytra, or modified, hardened outer wings—they spend most of their time on the surface. Whirligig beetles have adapted to this by developing binocular vision. Each eye is divided in half, and it looks as if each beetle has two pairs of eyes, one looking up and one looking down. The bottom half of each eye is designed for underwater vision, while the upper half can see in the air.

Hobblebush Flowering

When scouring the forest floor for spring ephemerals, don't forget to look at the shrub layer. One of the most dramatic flowers of spring is found on a woodland shrub called hobblebush. The common name comes from the fact that its branches often bend to the ground and become rooted at the tips, making a walk through the woods somewhat treacherous. Hobblebush's flowers are cleverly designed to attract pollinators: the large, showy, white flowers along the margins are sterile; their sole purpose is to lure insects, such as the tiny, blue spring azure butterfly. The smaller, less conspicuous flowers in the center of the cluster (just starting to open in this photograph) have reproductive parts and are the beneficiaries of visiting pollinators.

Hobblebush flowers.

Painted trillium.

Translucent petals on painted trillium indicate it has been pollinated.

MAY 8

Painted Trillium Flowering

Painted trillium blooms in May, just as the trees are beginning to leaf out. As its name implies, many of painted trillium's parts—leaves, petals, sepals, stamens, and carpels—come in sets of three. Its three leaves are oriented parallel to the ground and face the sun. Painted trillium is found in acidic soil and is often associated with spruce-fir woods and bogs in the eastern third of North America. In the same habitat you often find starflower, sarsaparilla, Canada mayflower, cucumber root, partridgeberry, and goldthread.

Once pollinated, the petals of painted trillium become limp and translucent. The seeds of painted trillium each bear a fatty deposit, or elaiosome, which attracts ants that disperse the seeds.

Pickerel Frogs Snoring

Next to the green frog, the pickerel frog is the most abundant frog in the Northeast. It is often confused with the northern leopard frog, which it closely resembles. The spots on a pickerel frog's back are squarish and aligned in rows, whereas the leopard frog's spots are rounded and randomly scattered over its back. In addition, the male pickerel frog has bright orange on the inner surface of his hind legs, which the leopard frog lacks.

Pickerel frog.

Male pickerel frogs have started calling to attract mates. Each species of frog, just like birds, has its own distinctive call. Spring peepers peep, wood frogs clack, and pickerel frogs snore. Their snore isn't long—it only lasts a second or two—but it is unmistakable. Pickerel frogs call from under water, as well as on top of mounds of vegetation, so if you hear one and then search for it, you may not find it.

Male House Sparrows Building Nests

The house sparrow's reputation leaves a bit to be desired. Also known as the English sparrow, it is an introduced species that has thrived in North America, where it is considered a nuisance species and an agricultural pest. Its tendency to

Male house sparrow with nesting material.

displace native birds such as eastern bluebirds and tree swallows from nest boxes does not endear it to many bird lovers. However, male house sparrows are the exception rather than the rule when it comes to parenting. Males help choose the nest site, build the nest, incubate the eggs, brood and feed the nestlings, and keep the nest clean by removing the nestlings' fecal sacs. This is more than can be said for some of our fondest species of birds, such as male ruby-throated hummingbirds, which disappear shortly after copulation.

MAY 9

Hairy woodpecker nestling.

Hairy Woodpeckers Fledging

For the past month or so, this young hairy woodpecker has been tended to by its parents, who take turns bringing food and providing warmth to their nestlings. As the time for fledging approaches, the young birds spend more and more time at the cavity entrance,

reaching out to receive food from their parents. Once the young birds fledge, they will depend upon their parents for food for the next three or four weeks.

Buckbean

Between April and June, buckbean, also known as bogbean, produces spikes of showy pink or white tubular flowers with distinctively fringed petals. A member of the gentian family, buckbean flourishes in the shallow acidic waters of bogs or in freshwater lakes. The flowers' beauty belies their rank smell, which attracts flies and beetles, as well as bees, for pollination. Buckbean has been used as both food and medicine. In Europe, the leaves were sometimes used as a substitute for hops in beer brewing and were boiled in honey to make mead. Jaundice, indigestion, skin diseases, scurvy, intestinal worms, and rheumatism have been treated with buckbean.

Buckbean.

Woodland Jumping Mouse

It is fairly unusual to set eyes on a jumping mouse, dead or alive, as they are quite secretive. This 1-ounce rodent has long hind feet and a very long tail, which makes up more than half of its total length of 8 to 10 inches. Using its hind limbs for propulsion and its tail for balance, the woodland jumping mouse is able to make leaps of up to 8 feet to escape danger. More often it walks on all fours, or uses short hops for greater speed. Another survival strategy that jumping mice use is to remain motionless for up to several hours, relying on their coloration and cover for

Woodland jumping mouse.

protection. Unfortunately, these adaptations did not save the life of the pictured young woodland jumping mouse.

MAY 10

Fringed Polygala Flowering

Fringed polygala looks a bit like a miniature orchid, but it is in the milkwort family. Also known as "bird on the wing," its ¾-inch bright magenta-pink blossoms are well suited for its bumble bee pollinators. The bee lands on the pink fringe at the front of the flower, and its weight triggers a white "keel" to drop down. A slit at the keel's top opens, exposing the reproductive parts of the flower. Pollen from the stamens

is rubbed onto the bee's hairs while it probes deeply into the base of the flower for nectar, while pollen from a previously visited fringed polygala is scraped off onto the stigma, cross-pollinating the flower.

Fringed polygala.

Question Mark Butterflies Flying

The butterfly known as the question mark is in a group of butterflies known as commas (a silvery comma can be seen on the underside of the hind wings) or anglewings (for their sharply angled forewing margins). The question mark has a silver dot adjacent to the comma, turning it into a question mark. When its wings are open, the question mark is bright orange and quite noticeable, but when it closes its wings, the butterfly transforms into a dead leaf, for the undersides of its wings are dull brown and gray. This question mark was drinking sap from a wound in the trunk of a tree. These woodland butterflies prefer rotting fruit, mud, scat, carrion, and tree sap over the nectar of flowers.

Question mark.

Belted Kingfishers Laying and Incubating Eggs

Belted kingfishers are cavity nesters, typically choosing to excavate their nests in a bank with little vegetation growing on it. A burrow is dug in the bank by both kingfishers in the early morning. One bird digs for up to four minutes, shuffling dirt from the burrow out of the entrance with its

Belted kingfisher nest.

Juvenile belted kingfisher.

feet, while its mate perches nearby and gives its rattle call. The entrance is usually within a foot or two of the top of the bank, and the burrow, sloped upward to prevent flooding, measures roughly 3 to 6 feet long and ends in an unlined chamber. After incubation begins, the adults' regurgitated pellets, consisting of undigested fish bones and scales and the exoskeletons of arthropods, may accumulate, forming a somewhat insulating layer between the eggs and the soil.

MAY 11

Red Fox Kits Still Nursing

Red fox kits continue to nurse during their first weeks above ground. Their parents have introduced solid food to the kits in the form of prey; weaning will soon begin.

Red fox vixen nursing kits.

Warbler Waves Coming Through

Birders wait with great anticipation for the waves of warblers that pass through New England in May. Flocks, or waves, of warblers often consist of several species. The males' plumages are never more brilliant, making the search for these fast-moving, tiny birds well worth the effort. Returning from their wintering grounds in Central and South America, some warblers make non-stop flights covering more than a thousand miles. When they stop to refuel, there is constant movement as warblers forage for insects among

Male yellow-rumped warbler.

Male common yellowthroat.

Male chestnut-sided warbler.

Male american redstart.

Male prairie warbler.

Male black-and-white warbler.

141

Warbler Breeding Ground Foraging Levels

Warblers tend to forage at certain levels of the forest—high in the canopy, in thickets, or on the ground. Sometimes, within a species, males forage at a different level than females. The level where a given species forages may differ from season to season. The spring migration foraging level of a warbler species may differ from that of fall migration. Some species are specialists, found feeding only at one level, while others are generalists and can be found foraging high and low. Some generalizations can be made for some species during their breeding season.

Blackburnian warbler.

Black-throated green warbler.

High In Canopy

- Blackburnian warbler
- Pine warbler
- Cape May warbler

Middle Level

- American redstart
- Black-throated green warbler
- Magnolia warbler

Low Level/Ground

- Ovenbird
- Black-throated blue warbler
- Common yellowthroat

Common yellowthroat.

tree flowers in the canopy. As leaves emerge, it becomes more and more helpful if one is familiar with their songs, as warblers are easily obscured by the foliage.

MAY 12

Dwarf Ginseng Flowering

Dwarf ginseng is a woodland perennial that flowers from April to June throughout the Northeast. Only 4 to 8 inches high, it is smaller than its relative, American ginseng. Not only is there a size difference between these two plants, but each of the leaves of dwarf ginseng has three stalkless leaflets versus the five stalked leaflets of American ginseng. Dwarf ginseng has yellow rather than red

Dwarf ginseng.

berries. Although not used nowadays in herbal medicine, dwarf ginseng was used by Native Americans for ailments as varied as headaches and hives.

Northern Waterthrushes Singing

If it is not singing, the northern waterthrush—actually a large wood warbler and not a thrush—can be recognized by its bobbing body and wagging tail. However, its loud, ringing song is the most diagnostic characteristic of this species and allows one to distinguish it from its look-alike relative, the Louisiana waterthrush. The primary song of the northern waterthrush has three parts: a vigorous, rapid *sweet sweet swee wee wee chew chew chew chew*.

Northern waterthrush.

The northern waterthrush also has a flight song, which is given on its breeding ground, typically in the evening. This song usually starts with loud, sharp, *chip*s of increasing frequency, delivered from the ground or a low perch. The bird then flies upward through and above the canopy, singing snatches of its primary song—but more quickly and for a longer time—framed in a hurried jumble of *chip*s and song notes.

MAY 13

Black Bears Feasting on Jack-in-the-Pulpit Corms

When black bears first emerge from hibernation, they survive mainly on any remaining acorns and beechnuts, as well as emerging green vegetation in wetlands. As the season progresses, there are more and more options to choose from, including a favorite: the corm, or underground bulblike

Jack-in-the-pulpit.

storage structure, of Jack-in-the-pulpit. Even though they are large, somewhat lumbering creatures, black bears dig up and remove these corms as if they had a tiny tool designed just for this job. They barely disturb the earth, leaving only very small holes as evidence of their activity. Apparently the calcium oxalate crystals in Jack-in-the-pulpit that cause the burning sensation in human mouths don't affect bears, at least not enough to protect the plant from this omnivore.

Shorebirds Migrating through the Northeast

Many of the shorebirds that overwinter in Central and South America, as well as southern North America, migrate through the Northeast during the month of May on their way north to their Canadian breeding grounds. Although greater yellowlegs are more solitary than most

Black bear.

Greater yellowlegs.

shorebirds, they tend to migrate in small flocks as they head for the bogs and coniferous forests of northern Canada and southern Alaska. They are recognizable by their upright stance, bright yellow legs, and piercing alarm calls. Their nicknames include "telltale," "tattler," and "yelper."

MAY 14

Northern Mockingbirds Singing

Paired male and female mockingbirds sing during the day, and unmated males are often heard singing at night. As members of the Mimidae family, along with gray catbirds and brown thrashers, northern mockingbirds are excellent mimics. A male's repertoire, which often contains more

Northern mockingbird.

than 150 songs, changes and may increase as the bird ages. In the spring and fall, if you hear a bird singing at night, especially during a full moon, it is often an unmated male mockingbird.

Wild Strawberry Flowering

Wild strawberry, a member of the rose family, grows throughout the Northeast and is one of the parent plants of the cultivated hybrid

Wild strawberry.

strawberry. (The other parent is native to Chile.) Its fruits are a staple food for many animals, but the leaves and flowers of this plant are also an important source of sustenance for a variety of creatures. Cottontail rabbits, snowshoe hares, eastern chipmunks, white-footed mice, white-tailed deer, ruffed grouse, slugs, and a variety of invertebrates, including aphids, weevils, and mites feed on the leaves of wild strawberry. The flowers attract honey bees, bumble bees, butterflies, and other insects that collect its pollen and nectar. Caterpillars of several species of moths feed on the foliage and flowers of wild strawberry.

Painted Turtle Nests Being Raided

A month or two after mating, female painted turtles are leaving their ponds in search of a spot to lay their eggs. Several holes are dug, into one of which is deposited four to eight eggs, which are then covered. Often within just

Raided painted turtle nest.

Painted turtle.

144

Painted Turtle Gender Differences

If you see a painted turtle on land at this time of year, chances are great that it is a female on her way to or from laying her eggs, as that is about the only reason painted turtles ever leave the water. If you see one on the bank of a pond or basking on a log, and can get close enough to it to see its body parts, it is possible to determine its sex. It helps to have both sexes in front of you, as this whole process is all relative, but in general, males have much longer nails on their front feet than females, which are good for gripping females during mating. Males also have longer and thicker tails. The cloaca (the passageway into which the intestinal, urinary, and genital tracts open) of a male painted turtle is close to the tip of the tail, whereas the female's cloaca is near the base of the tail. An extremely large painted turtle, with an 8-inch to 10-inch shell, is more likely to be a female, as the shells of females can grow to larger dimensions than males'.

Male (left) and female painted turtles.

Male	Female
Long, thick tails	Shorter, thinner tails
Cloaca close to tip of tail	Cloaca close to base of tail
Long nails on front feet	Shorter nails on front feet
Stays close to water year-round	

hours of having been laid, these eggs are dug up and eaten by raccoons, striped skunks, or foxes. Painted turtle eggs that survive will hatch in late August or early September.

MAY 15

Ruby-Throated Hummingbirds and Wild Columbine in Sync

Wild columbine is in full flower, and its design and color beckon to a recently returned migrant that is attracted to red as well as to tubular flowers: the ruby-throated hummingbird. Not only does the flowering of wild columbine coincide with the arrival of hummingbirds in May, but the ranges of these two species are nearly the same.

Wild columbine's five petals are in the shape of spurs, the tips of which contain nectar. Only

Wild columbine.

Ruby-throated hummingbird.

hummingbirds and long-tongued bees can reach the nectar, and thus are its primary pollinators. There is also a short-tongued bumble bee that tears open the tip of the spur in order to reach the nectar. While the hummingbird hovers

145

Fertile (left) and vegetative (right) field horsetail.

White admiral caterpillar.

beneath the flower and drinks nectar, its head rubs against columbine's long anthers, and the pollen on the bird's head is brushed off onto the stigmas of the next flower it visits, thereby pollinating it.

Field Horsetail Dispersing Spores

Field horsetail is the most common species of the genus *Equisetum*. The popular and widely used name "horsetail" comes from the Latin words *equus* (horse) and *seta* (bristle), from the peculiar bristly appearance of the jointed stems of the plants. Its ancient relatives, some of which were 100 feet tall, dominated the understory of the late Paleozoic forests nearly three hundred million years ago. This group of non-flowering plants reproduces from spores, not seeds, and is related to ferns. Field horsetail has both fertile and vegetative stems. The fertile, tan, short-lived stem terminates in a spore-bearing cone. The vegetative stem bears whorls of green leaves.

White Admiral Caterpillars Emerging from Hibernation

Butterflies in the family Nymphalidae are referred to as brush-footed butterflies because their front legs are much-reduced, brushlike and nonfunctional. Several species of admiral butterflies belong to this family, and one of the most common in the Northeast is the white admiral. White admirals overwinter as larvae and emerge in mid- to late April to feed for several weeks on the young leaves of cherries, willows, poplars, and birches, as well as other trees, before forming chrysalises and transforming into butterflies. White admiral and red-spotted purple butterfly larvae are our only horned caterpillars that resemble bird-droppings—an effective ploy for avoiding predators.

MAY 16

Bald Eagle Nestlings Growing

When bald eagle chicks hatch they are covered with light gray down and have brown eyes and pink legs. One parent, usually the female, spends most of the day in the nest with her young for the first three weeks, keeping them warm. The male provides most of the food during this time. After he delivers prey, she tears off small pieces and feeds them to the nestlings. The chicks gain

One-week-old eaglet and its mother.

weight rapidly—roughly a quarter pound a day—and in three or four short weeks the young are nearly the size of the adults. Eaglets are roughly six weeks old before they are capable of tearing off food and feeding themselves, and at least eight weeks old before they leave the nest.

Mites Making Galls on Sugar Maple Leaves

Within a week of unfurling, sugar maple leaves are eaten by all kinds of creatures, some of which are mites that cause the leaves to develop abnormal growths called galls. Certain species of eriophyid mites form felt, or erineum, galls,

Erineum galls on sugar maple leaf.

often on silver and sugar maple leaves. After spending the winter months under the scales of buds, these mites emerge in the spring when leaves appear, move to the surface of the leaves, and begin to feed. Their feeding induces the growth of thousands of tightly packed leaf hairs, which provide shelter for the mites on the leaf surface. These hairs appear as bright pink or red patches that resemble felt. The mites, too small to be seen with a hand lens, move to the inside of these structures for the rest of the growing season.

Wild Grapes Developing

Wild grapes won't ripen until late summer, but you can find the tiny clusters of fruit in May if you examine grape vines closely. Animals that will eat the ripened fruits of this vine include wild turkeys, northern cardinals, ruffed grouse, eastern bluebirds, gray catbirds, wood ducks, common crows, great crested flycatchers, northern mocking-birds, American robins, fox sparrows, yellow-bellied sapsuck-ers, European starlings, brown thrashers, tufted titmice, pileated woodpeckers, red-bellied woodpeckers, cedar waxwings, purple finches, blue jays, dark-eyed juncos, eastern kingbirds, Baltimore orioles, white-throated sparrows, red foxes, eastern cottontails, raccoons, Virginia opossums, and striped skunks.

Wild grape.

MAY 17

Parasitoids Controlling Insect Pests

There is a family of parasitic flies (Tachinidae) that includes a large, hairy fly, *Epalpus signifier*. If you look at enough dandelions this time of year, you are likely to spot one: its white rump is a distinctive identifying feature. This fly is a parasitoid of noctuid moth caterpillars, and as such, spends most of its life attached to or within a host organism, getting nourishment from it. Unlike a parasite, which spares its host's life, a parasitoid eventually kills its host. Parasitoids are common in natural environments and can be important in controlling insect pests.

Tachinid fly.

Hermit thrush nest.

White baneberry flower.

White baneberry fruit.

Hermit Thrushes Nesting

Hermit thrushes are typically ground nesters east of the Rocky Mountains. West of the Rockies, they tend to nest off the ground. Often, as in this case, they choose a patch of clubmoss, or ground pine, as a nest site. Usually a branch from a nearby tree, a fern, or some other taller vegetation provides cover and conceals the nest. The female hermit thrush builds the nest and begins incubation after the last of her three or four eggs is laid. Twelve days later the eggs hatch, and twelve or thirteen days after that the young fledge.

Red and White Baneberry

The baneberries are most easily identified in mid-summer, when their flowers have developed into either bright red or white fruits. At this time of year, the delicate white flowers of red baneberry look very much like those of its close relative, white baneberry. The easiest way to differentiate the two species before the fruits develop is to notice the shape of the flower cluster. Red baneberry's cluster is more or less spherical, whereas white baneberry's is more cylindrical.

Red baneberry flower.

Red baneberry fruit.

MAY 18

Chipping Sparrow Eggs Hatching

The female chipping sparrow builds her nest in three or four days. It is usually made of rootlets and dried grasses and lined with horse or other animal hair and fine plant fibers. It is so insubstantial that you can often see light through it. The two to seven pale blue to white eggs hatch in about two weeks, and the young fledge in nine to twelve days. The colorful, open gaping beaks of the nestlings make easy targets for food-bearing adults.

Beaver.

Chipping sparrow eggs and nestlings.

Beavers Eating Woody and Herbaceous Plants

A beaver eats between 1½ and 4½ pounds of bark, twigs, tree leaves, and herbaceous vegetation on average every day. Their favorite tree by far is poplar, or aspen, an acre of which can produce enough energy for ten beavers for over a year.

The manner in which a beaver consumes the bark of a branch is reminiscent of how some humans eat corn on the cob. The beaver holds the branch in both hands and rotates the branch as it eats a small section of the bark, and then moves down the branch bit by bit. Smaller twigs are stuffed into its mouth and eaten whole. A beaver can digest only about 33 percent of the

cellulose taken up; hence, the fibrous, wood chip-filled appearance of their scat, which is typically deposited in water.

Beaver scat.

Dragonflies Eclosing

Aquatic dragonfly larvae go through a process called eclosure as they metamorphose into winged adults. At the end of its larval stage,

Dragonfly in varying states of eclosure.

149

a dragonfly larva crawls out of the water and climbs onto emergent vegetation or a nearby rock, where it clings as its skin splits along its back and head. The adult winged dragonfly pulls itself out of its larval skin through this split and then pumps its body full of air and sends fluid into its wing veins. This fluid causes the wings to enlarge—the wing expansion that is evident in these photographs took place in less than ten minutes. The wings and exoskeleton must dry before the dragonfly can take flight.

When it first emerges from its skin, a dragonfly is pale and soft, and the wings have a pearlescent sheen. Within a day or so the wings lose this sheen, the body hardens, and colors start to develop.

MAY 19

Black-Capped Chickadees Busy Feeding Young

Young black-capped chickadees are fed from the day they hatch until two to four weeks after they leave the nest. Both parents feed the young, carrying food to the nest in their beaks. Most of a nestling's diet consists of animal matter, the majority of which is caterpillars. As the young chickadees get older and bigger, the parents feed them more often. Just before their young fledge, black-capped chickadee parents, like many other birds, feed them less frequently to encourage them to leave the nest.

Black-capped chickadee at nest hole with food.

Miterwort Flowering

Miterwort, also known as bishop's cap, is named for the resemblance of its fruits to the hats, known as miters, worn by bishops of the Roman Catholic Church. Each flower is in the shape of a tiny cup, with five deeply dissected petals arising from the rim. A glandular ring of nectar-producing tissue inside the cup attracts small bees, flies, and ants. Once pollinated, the flowers produce open seed capsules. Water, not animals, disperses miterwort's seeds. The capsules orient themselves so that their opening faces upward. When it rains, the drops splash the seeds out of the capsules, sending them up to 3 feet away from the parent plant. The distance traveled by the seeds depends on the size of the raindrop.

Miterwort.

MAY 20

Blue-Eyed Grass Flowering

There are eight species of blue-eyed grasses in the Northeast—all of which have stiff, grass-like leaves and wiry stems—but they all are irises, not grasses. Each flower has six blue-violet petals, each tipped with a bristle-like point. Dark lines,

Blue-eyed grass.

possibly nectar guides, on the petals lead pollinating insects, mostly bees, to the golden center of the flower. Individual flowers stay open for a day or less and never open at night.

Common Yellowthroats Nesting

Parental care varies according to species, but often only one sex is responsible for the care of offspring. The exception to this rule is birds, where in at least 81 percent of species both parents chip in. The work may not be shared equally, but both contribute in some way. The female common yellowthroat, a warbler, chooses the nesting site, builds the nest, incubates the eggs, and broods the young. The male assists her in gathering food for their nestlings and helps keep the nest clean by removing the nestlings' fecal sacs.

Male common yellowthroat.

American Toads Mating and Laying Eggs

Male American toads are not territorial and they trill for only one reason: to attract a mate. When this has been accomplished, the smaller male toad climbs on top of the larger, reddish female toad, clasps her behind her front legs, locks his thumbs together, and secretes his sperm on her eggs as she

American toads mating.

lays them. This mating position is referred to as amplexus. The female's eggs (there are usually several thousand) are laid in two strings, one from each of her ovaries. Within a week the eggs will hatch, releasing tiny, black tadpoles.

American toad eggs.

MAY 21

Young Otters Just Beginning to Explore Outside Their Den

Between February and April, female North American river otters give birth to an average of two or three young inside their dens, which tend to be near water, usually in an excavated cavity under tree roots, logs, or thickets. Occasionally

Adult North American river otter.

they have been known to give birth in abandoned beaver and muskrat lodges as well as woodchuck dens. The mother doesn't allow her young to exit their den until they are three or four months old, which, for the oldest litters, is just about now. At this point, after their waterproof adult coats have grown in, she begins to teach them how to swim, a skill that is, surprisingly, not innate. The mother continues to be very protective and secretive, hiding and shielding the young (even from their father) until they are about six month old. Thus, although they are out and about, most young otters will escape detection for another two or three months.

Woodchucks Giving Birth

Roughly a month ago, woodchucks were at the peak of their mating season. The Northeast's largest member of the squirrel family will soon give birth to from two to six young. Dead grasses are now being gathered and carried by mouth to the underground nest chamber, which is about 15 inches in diameter. Woodchucks are tidy rodents: the female covers her young's waste with new bedding, and when the nest becomes too bulky or unsanitary, the matted material is removed and fresh bedding is added.

Poplar Fruit Falling

The tiny white bits of fluff that are floating in the air are attached to the seeds of aspens, also known as poplars. The seeds are borne in capsules that develop along a 3- to 6-inch dangling stem. These former flower clusters are called catkins. The capsules on the catkins split apart when the seeds are mature, releasing the cotton-tufted seeds that are designed for dispersal by the wind. A single bigtooth aspen tree can produce over a million seeds.

Female poplar catkin.

MAY 22

Young Barred Owls See the World for the First Time

Barred owl eggs, usually two or three, are often laid in a tree cavity, where the adult female incubates them for roughly a month. Fuzzy, white,

Woodchuck with nesting material.

Barred owl chicks.

downy chicks hatch and remain inside the tree for four or five weeks while being fed by both parents. When the young owls are two or three weeks old, their white down is replaced with gray/buff secondary down, and they gain the strength needed to climb up the inside of the tree and peer out at the world. In and out they go, perching on the rim of the nest hole for several minutes as they await the arrival of their next meal and then retreating back to the safety and warmth of their nest.

MAY 23

Indigo Buntings Singing

An indigo bunting sings its paired notes as many as two hundred times per hour at dawn, and an average of roughly once a minute for the rest of the day. About 80 percent of first-year male indigo buntings copy the song of a neighboring territorial male indigo bunting in their first spring season. When a year-old male returns to its nesting area, its early song is different from the song of its father and from neighboring buntings from the previous year. The first-year bunting then changes this early song to a different song, which usually matches the song of a neighboring

Male indigo bunting.

territorial male. He will keep this later song for years, as long as he continues to return to the same area.

Morels Fruiting

This is the time of year to visit old apple orchards, burned areas, dying elms, cotton-woods, and ash trees in hopes of finding delectable yellow morels, also known as honeycomb morels. Morels produce spores from tiny sacs along the insides of their pits or wrinkles instead of the more common gills, pores, or teeth of other fungi. There are several types of morels, some edible and others inedible or poisonous, so if you're unsure, consult an expert before putting butter in the frying pan.

Common morel.

MAY 24

Showy Orchis Blooming

Several species of orchids flower at this time of year, one of which, the showy orchis, has a stalk of several flowers which typically bear lavender hoods. Potential pollinators, most of which are long-tongued bumble bees, butterflies, moths, and bees, land on a white petal below the hood which acts as a landing pad. The insect then heads for the tip of the nectar-filled spur at the back of the flower. In the process

Showy orchis.

of getting there it brushes against packets of pollen (pollinia) before moving on to the next blossom, where cross-pollination may well take place.

Red Fox Kits Being Cleaned and Groomed

After providing food for their kits for several weeks, red foxes begin to teach their young what to eat, where to find it and, in the case of living prey, how to catch it. When they're not doing this, they can often be found grooming and cleaning their kits. Burs, sticks, and other material that collects in the kits' coats is carefully removed by the parent as it grips the object with its teeth and pulls it out of the kit's fur. Ears are routinely licked clean as well.

Red fox vixen grooming kit.

Red fox vixen cleaning kit's ear.

MAY 25

Baltimore Orioles Building Nests

Once the female Baltimore oriole has selected her mate, she chooses a nest site within his territory, often at the tip of a slender outer tree branch, where it's relatively inaccessible to predators. She usually builds the nest by herself over four to fifteen days. The first few fibers are wrapped loosely around branches. With apparently random poking, knots and tangles are created in these fibers. The female than adds more fibers, one at a time, to extend, close and line the nest. After days of laborious work, the nest takes on its gourd-like shape. Initially, fibers from plants such as grasses, milkweed stems, or grapevine bark are woven in. Horse hair, twine, and synthetic fibers are also used. Toward the end, when the nest lining is added, the bird is hidden inside the nest and all that's visible is periodic bulges where she is applying softer material, often cottonwood, willow seed fluff, or feathers, to cushion her eggs and nestlings.

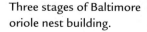

Three stages of Baltimore oriole nest building.

Mayflies Hatching

A mayfly's life cycle starts with males forming a swarm above the water and the females flying into the swarm to mate. The male grabs a passing female with its elongated front legs, and the pair mate in flight. After copulation, the male releases the female and she descends to the surface of the water where she lays her eggs and collapses, soon to be eaten by a fish. The male mayfly rarely returns to the water but instead goes off to die on land.

The eggs fall to the bottom where they stick to plants and stones. Nymphs take anywhere from a few days to a number of weeks to hatch, depending on the species, and then live an aquatic life for up to two years, foraging on the bottom before emerging as an adult mayfly.

Mayflies have two adult stages. The nymph leaves the water, sheds its skin, and emerges as a dull-colored, winged sub-imago (dun), which seeks shelter in bankside vegetation. After a couple of hours or more, the sub-imago sheds its skin again and transforms into the brightly colored, sexually mature imago (spinner). Mayflies are unique among insects in that they molt a second time after acquiring functional wings. The imago has only vestigial mouthparts and doesn't eat. It lives only a very short time—one species less than five minutes—just long enough to mate and produce eggs.

Adult mayfly.

Foamflower Flowering

At this time of year, parts of the forest floor may be carpeted with 6- to 12-inch-tall plants with foamlike clusters of white flowers borne on slender stalks. Commonly known as foamflower, this perennial member of the saxifrage family is found in rich woods throughout the Northeast. Each individual white flower has yellow stamens and five petals in the shape of a star. Its genus name, *Tiarella*, is from the Greek word "tiara," a word for a turban worn by ancient Persians which bears some resemblance to the shape of this flower's pistil.

Foamflower.

MAY 26

Eastern Tiger Swallowtail Butterflies Emerging

Having spent the winter pupating inside a chrysalis, eastern tiger swallowtails are now emerging, just as lilacs and other purple and reddish flowers bloom and provide them with nectar. The male eastern tiger swallowtail butterfly is

Eastern tiger swallowtail.

Eastern tiger swallowtail chrysalis.

155

yellow with four "tiger stripes" on each of its fore-wings. The female can be yellow or black and has more blue on the hind wings than the male.

Eastern tiger swallowtails are now mating and laying green eggs on the leaves of plants that their larvae eat, including black cherry, red maple, American hornbeam, ash, and poplar. When the caterpillars first hatch, they resemble bird droppings—an effective way of decreasing predation. As they get older, the larvae turn green and have a large head and bright eyespots.

Beaverpond Baskettail Dragonflies Flying, Mating, and Laying Eggs

Beaverpond baskettail dragonflies have an early flight season, first taking wing in May in the Northeast. The males cruise over wetlands in a sexual patrol flight, flying back and forth over the same small area. After finding a female, they mate, and the female then produces a long string of eggs which form a ball at the tip of her abdomen. As she flies, she taps the tip of her abdomen on the surface of the water, releasing the eggs.

Male beaverpond baskettail.

Wilson's Snipe Feeding

Wilson's snipe, one of the most abundant and widespread shorebirds in North America, is adept at catching prey. It finds its food by touch, using sensory pits near the tip of its beak as it probes the soil. Another useful adaptation is the ability

Wilson's snipe catching earthworm.

of the tip of its long, flexible beak to open and close with no movement at the base.

The diet of Wilson's snipe is largely larval insects, but it also eats crustaceans, earthworms, and mollusks. When eating something as large as an earthworm, a snipe may beat it several times before swallowing it. Occasionally, snipe feed by stamping their feet or bouncing up and down, apparently to startle prey into moving.

MAY 27

Gray Tree Frogs Calling

The birdlike trill of courting male gray tree frogs is heard in May and builds to a crescendo in June. Warm, humid weather seems to elicit calls from these well-camouflaged amphibians. The chorus ramps up at night, but the songsters can be hard to find during the day. Their large toe pads produce mucus that allows them to adhere to smooth bark, and they often hide high up in the canopy.

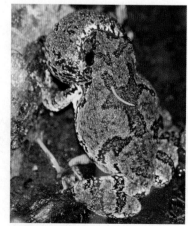

Gray tree frog.

Sequence of Frog Calls

Anurans—frogs and toads—emerge from hibernation and head to ponds and pools to court, breed, and lay eggs in the spring and early summer. Climatic conditions, such as temperature and humidity, dictate the onset of this series of events. Significant changes in the climate can affect the timing of the appearance and the initiation of the vocalizations of frogs and toads; however, there is a rough order in which common Northeastern anuran species are often seen and heard.

- Wood frog
- Northern leopard frog
- Spring peeper
- Pickerel frog
- American toad
- Gray tree frog
- Green frog
- American bullfrog

Spring peeper.

Green frog.

American bullfrog.

Wood frog.

The colors of a gray tree frog vary with the colors of its background and environmental factors such as season and humidity, but shades of gray are most common, with black blotches on the back. Brown, green, and pearl gray tree frogs have been noted, with green being more prominent during the breeding season.

Avian Parents Hard at Work

To appreciate the parental demands on birds, consider the feeding habits of a pair of American robins with a nest full of young. Both parents feed their three to four nestlings, delivering six to seven feedings an hour, each one to a single nestling. Parents tend to arrive with food at a particular location on the nest rim, so there is much jockeying for a position near this spot on the part of the nestlings. Each nestling gets thirty-five to forty feedings a day. This adds up to almost half a pound of food delivered to the nest every day for the thirteen days that young are in the nest. Even then, the parents' work is not done, as they continue to feed their fledglings for up to three weeks after the young leave the nest.

American robin.

American Toad Eggs Hatching

American toad eggs are hatching, and as they do, the thousands of tiny, black tadpoles attach themselves to underwater vegetation and hang vertically, with their heads up. In a week or so, they will crowd the edges of ponds in dense aggregations. Tadpoles from the same egg mass tend to stay together as a school during this stage. In three to six weeks, they will begin to transform into tiny toadlets.

American toad tadpoles along shore.

American toad tadpoles.

MAY 28

Solitary Sandpipers Migrating

Solitary sandpipers—although not truly solitary, they do migrate in smaller flocks than most shorebirds, and sometimes even alone—are passing through the Northeast as they migrate from the tropics to the boreal forests of far northern

Solitary sandpiper.

Canada and Alaska, just south of the tundra, to nest. One of the more unusual behaviors of this shorebird is its tendency to lay its eggs in the tree nests of several different songbirds, including the American robin, rusty blackbird, eastern kingbird, gray jay, and cedar waxwing. Of the eighty-five sandpipers worldwide, only two routinely lay eggs in tree nests instead of on the ground. Unlike most tree-nesting birds, solitary sandpiper young are precocial; they leave the nest and feed themselves as soon as their down dries.

White-Tailed Deer Giving Birth

In late May or early June white-tailed deer give birth. A young doe usually has a single fawn; twins are common in a mature female, and occasionally there are triplets. Predators often

White-tailed deer fawn.

Great horned owl nestlings in a great blue heron nest.

overlook newborn fawns because they have almost no body odor and their reddish-brown coat dappled with white spots provides excellent camouflage. Wisely, a fawn's tendency is to freeze if approached by another animal. The mother leaves her fawns, spread out up to 200 feet from each other, in a secluded habitat within her home range while she goes off to forage, returning periodically to nurse them and to take them to a new location. If you find a newborn fawn, it is best to stay away—its mother is likely to be nearby.

Month-Old Great Horned Owl Nestlings

Great horned owls are said to have a wider range of nest sites than any other bird in the Americas. Most commonly they use tree nests of other species, particularly red-tailed hawks, as well as other hawks, crows, ravens, herons, and squirrels. The young owls grow rapidly, adding nearly a quarter of a pound per day. In six weeks, young owls are climbing out of the nest and perching on nearby branches, and by seven weeks they are taking short flights.

MAY 29

Yellow Lady's Slippers Flowering

There are only about three weeks in the late spring when the blossoms of yellow lady's slippers grace our woodlands and wetlands. The production of an orchid is a complicated process. If pollination and fertilization are successful, hundreds of thousands of some of the smallest seeds of any flower are scattered by the wind. The seeds of yellow lady's slippers and other orchids, unlike most flowering plants, contain no food for the seedling plant. In addition, the coating surrounding the seed is extremely tough, so much

Yellow lady's slipper.

so that the seed can't germinate until *Rhizoctonia* fungi digest the outer coating, which allows the seed to access soil nutrients. This can take two years or more, and then it may take another few years for the plant to produce a flower.

American Bitterns Feeding

American bitterns, creatures of freshwater wetlands, tend to spend much of their time at the fringe of vegetation and on shorelines hunting

for prey in the early morning and late in the day. Their diet consists of insects (23 percent), frogs and salamanders (21 percent), fish (21 percent), crayfish (19 percent), small mammals (10 percent), snakes (5 percent), and small quantities of crabs, spiders, and other invertebrates. This cryptically colored member of the heron family often stands motionless, very slowly stretching its neck and aiming its bill downward, until, with a sudden dart, it seizes its prey with its bill, bites and shakes it, and then swallows it headfirst.

Sawfly Larvae Feeding

Although it looks like a caterpillar, this larva is not going to metamorphose into a butterfly or moth. This is because it is a sawfly larva and is closely related to bees and wasps. It gets its name from the adult female's sawlike, egg-laying ovipositor, which opens like a jackknife from the tip of her abdomen.

There are several ways to distinguish between the larvae of sawflies and those of butterflies or moths. While both have three pairs of true legs on the thorax, caterpillars (larvae of moths and butterflies) have up to five pairs of prolegs, fleshy structures that resemble legs, located on the abdomen behind their true legs, while sawfly larvae have six or more pairs. A closer look at the tips of the prolegs on caterpillars will reveal tiny hooks called crochets, which are lacking on

American bittern with tadpole.

Sawfly larva.

sawfly larvae prolegs. If you see something that looks like a caterpillar feeding along the margin of a leaf, and it rears up its hind end when disturbed (perhaps to frighten predators), it is most likely a sawfly larva.

MAY 30

Common Ravens About to Fledge

Looking as if it were glued to the vertical cliff wall, a raven's nest is often used for several years in a row. The nestlings stay in the nest for five to seven weeks, during which time they go from being an orange pink color, sparsely covered with gray down, to the black plumage of an adult. The pictured nestlings are approximately five weeks old and have just started to exercise their wing muscles in preparation for their first flight. They are panting with open beaks in an attempt to dissipate the heat of an unrelenting May sun. Within a week or two they will leave the nest but will stay nearby for a few days. Raven nests can have an unbelievably unpleasant odor due to the remains of leftover food, carrion, and feces.

Wood Turtles Laying Eggs

Female wood turtles are leaving ponds and streams and heading to soft, sandy soil to dig 6-inch holes in which they lay an average of eight or nine eggs. Their travels are easy to detect, as wood turtles leave footprints, a tail drag, and a 7-inch flattened shell path wherever they go.

Common raven nest and nestlings.

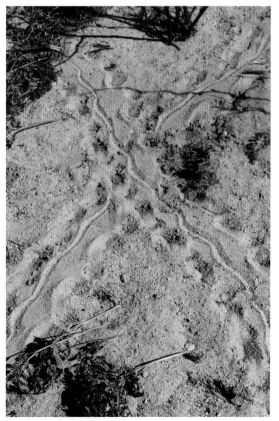

Wood turtle tracks.

Wood turtle after laying eggs and smoothing nest site with plastron.

Young eastern chipmunks.

After the eggs are laid, and the holes are filled and smoothed over with the turtle's bottom shell, or plastron, the nest site can only be seen by humans because of the female's tracks. Predators with a good sense of smell, such as foxes, raccoons, and skunks, however, have very little trouble finding turtle nests. About 85 percent of wood turtle eggs and hatchlings are lost to predation.

Wood turtles are in decline in the Northeast in part due to human development, which not only decreases wood turtle habitat and increases the number of people collecting these turtles, but also increases the number of predators.

Young Eastern Chipmunks Above Ground

Eastern chipmunks mate in late February to early April, usually within a week of when they emerge from their nests. A month later the females give birth to three to five young, each a mere 2½ inches long, pink, blind, and almost hairless. When the young are five to seven weeks old, they are fully weaned and begin to venture from their nest, looking very much like adult chipmunks, just a bit smaller. The young chipmunks will live in their mother's burrow for the next two or three months until they reach adult size.

MAY 31

Birds Keeping Nests Clean

A smelly nest is a dead giveaway to would-be predators, so most birds make an effort to keep their nest fairly clean. In addition, if the nestlings' down feathers get matted, they cannot help keep the young birds warm. While the young of some birds, such as raptors and herons, defecate

Adult black-capped chickadee with fecal sac.

over the edge of the nest as they age, the waste of many young songbirds is excreted in what is called a fecal sac—a nice, tidy bundle which the parents carry off and drop at some distance from the nest. Some species of birds eat their nestlings' fecal sacs when the nestlings are very young, as the sacs contain some nourishment.

Wolf Spiders and Nursery Web Spiders Carrying Egg Sacs

Two common spiders that are often seen carrying egg sacs are the wolf spider and the nursery web spider. Wolf spiders attach their egg sacs to their spinnerets, located on the tip of their abdomen, whereas nursery web spiders carry them with their mouthparts. When nursery web spiders are about to hatch, the mother puts her egg sac into a silk tent she has spun, and they live there for a week or so. When a wolf spider's spiderlings emerge from their egg sac, they climb up onto their mother's abdomen and cling to it while she continues to hunt for food. After about a week, when partially grown,

Nursery web spider and egg sac.

the spiderlings disperse, either by ballooning through the air on silk strands or simply by scurrying off along the ground.

Warbling Vireos Singing on Nests

As a rule, when male birds approach their nest, whether to take their turn incubating eggs, brooding nestlings, or delivering food, they are apt to be silent, or sing much more softly than usual, so as to avoid bringing attention to the nest. However, there are exceptions to this rule: male chipping sparrows, warbling vireos, house wrens, common yellowthroats, hermit thrushes, black-billed cuckoos, scarlet tanagers, orchard orioles, and American goldfinches have been heard singing not just near their nest, but while sitting on it. Warbling vireos are by far the most persistent nest singers. When the male warbling vireo is incubating, he sings at all times of the day, as many as twenty bursts of song during one spell on the nest. Listening for the warbling vireo's song and finding the songster will often lead you to its nest.

Male warbling vireo singing on nest.

Wolf spider and egg sac.

JUNE

Giant Silk Moths

Giant silk moths of the family Saturniidae are among the largest moths in North America, measuring up to 6 inches from wing tip to wing tip. They emerge from their cocoons in June and have only a week or two, at most, to mate and lay eggs before dying. The lives of giant silk moth adults are so short that they have greatly reduced mouthparts and no digestive tract. Eating is strictly a larval occupation—adulthood is for reproduction.

You may be familiar with giant silk moths without realizing that they are part of this group—they include the beautiful green luna moth, the hairy-scaled cecropia moth, the eye-spot-winged polyphemus, and the promethea and Columbia silk moths. These moths share several characteristics in addition to large size: heavy bodies covered in hairlike scales, reduced mouthparts, and small heads. It is fairly easy to determine the sex of a giant silk moth by looking at its antennae—generally males have large, broad, feathery antennae (with which they detect pheromones released by females) while the females' are more modest in size.

Female moths, including giant silk moths, produce chemicals called pheromones that can signal alarm, breeding opportunity, and a number of other messages to moths of the same species. The pheromones that a cecropia moth female releases attract males from miles around. Male cecropia moths detect these pheromones with sensitive receptors located on the tips of their antennae. One millionth of a gram of the pheromones released by a female moth is, in theory, enough to attract one billion male moths.

Bolas spiders are able to mimic the pheromones produced by insects like the cecropia moth, with the result that male moths follow the pheromones and end up becoming the spider's next meal!

There is usually one period of several days to a week, in late spring or early summer, when most adults emerge from their cocoons. This synchrony is important, as it ensures that males and females can find each other for mating. Emergence often takes place during the first real warm spell of the year, when daytime temperatures reach into the 60s and nights stay warm for several days. The adult silk moths emerge from their cocoons in daytime, usually around mid-morning, when the warmth of the day allows them inflate and dry their wings in preparation for the evening's flight.

After mating, female silk moths lay up to two hundred round, slightly flattened eggs on a host tree or shrub on whose leaves their larvae can feed. Some species of larvae are quite well camouflaged, but others are as stunningly colored as the adults and often bear spines or barbed horns. The cecropia caterpillar, for example, is a pale greenish blue and has two rows of red, yellow, and blue spiny tubercles on its body.

For the next two or three months, the larvae do little but eat. Over its short life as a caterpillar the body weight of a silk moth increases by a factor of more than ten thousand. To accommodate this prodigious growth a caterpillar sheds its skin four times, thus passing through five larval stages, which are known as instars. A caterpillar that has shed its skin twice since hatching from the egg is in its third instar. Not only are the caterpillars colorful, but they are, in general,

Showy lady's slipper.

Polyphemus cocoon.

Luna moth.

Cecropia moth.

huge in their later instars, when they can be 2 to 4½ inches long and as big around as a nickel. Although harmless to humans, luna and polyphemus larvae will produce clicking sounds with their mandibles when disturbed.

At the end of the summer, a silk moth caterpillar spins a cocoon as protection for the pupal stage in its life cycle. Giant silk moths draw their collective name from the fine silk they use to spin these cocoons. The moths overwinter as pupae in cocoons that are proportionately as large as the caterpillars, reaching a good 3 inches in length.

Cecropia mouth parts

Cecropia moth antennae.

Gray Tree Frogs

Melodic, birdlike trills lasting up to several seconds emanate from the woodlands at this time of year. They are produced not by birds, but by gray tree frogs, resident amphibians often heard but seldom seen. Singing begins while the males are still in the forests, near where they spent the winter hibernating under leaf litter and rocks. Within a week or two, the frogs begin to move to the perimeter of breeding ponds, where their singing becomes very concentrated and extremely loud, especially at night. The females' preference for males with the most prolonged and frequent calls contributes to the noise level.

The reason this very vocal frog isn't seen more often is a combination of the type of habitat it seeks out while vocalizing and its camouflaged appearance. Unlike many other frogs, male tree frogs tend to stay in and on shrubs and trees close to water while they court potential mates, not out in open water or on the banks of ponds. In addition to being hidden in the shrubbery, gray tree frogs are extremely well camouflaged. Their skin is so mottled that you can get very close and still not see them. As their species name, *versicolor*, implies, gray tree frogs can change the color of their skin, from grayish to greenish, depending upon environmental factors such as the humidity, temperature, and color of their surroundings.

There are two species of true tree frogs in the Northeast—the gray tree frog and the much smaller spring peeper. These two frogs share several universal traits of tree frogs: well-developed discs at the tips of their toes; relatively long limbs and horizontal pupils; and extra cartilage between the last two bones of each toe, allowing them to swivel their

Gray tree frog.

toes and keep them flat against any surface, to name a few. In addition to being larger than the spring peeper, the gray tree frog has a little white spot under each eye and yellow-orange pigmentation on the underside of its hind legs.

The ability of all tree frogs to adhere to smooth vertical surfaces sets them apart from other frogs. They can stick to a surface even when it is tilted way beyond the vertical, to the point where the frogs are upside down. This is possible because each toe pad is coated with a thin layer of mucus that adheres to a surface,

Adult gray tree frog.

Juvenile gray tree frog.

much as wet tissue paper sticks to glass. When they are walking or jumping, they can detach their toe pads easily by peeling themselves off the surface. Researchers at the University of Glasgow wondered how these two apparently contradictory skills were possible and discovered that the change from adhesion to peeling is a gradual process, with adhesive force weakening at angles above 90 degrees. Thus, a gray tree frog sticks to a surface by keeping the angle of its toes with respect to the surface at an angle of 90 degrees or less. Tree frogs that want to cling to the substrate actually spread their legs out sideways to minimize this angle

A mated female gray tree frog produces approximately two thousand eggs, which hatch less than a week after being laid. In a month or two, the green tadpoles, which have orange-red tails, will metamorphose into four-legged frogs and leave the water. At this stage of life, young gray tree frogs are usually a fairly brilliant shade of green, but this color only lasts a day or two before they turn a mottled gray or green.

Black-Legged Ticks

No longer can we roam the woods and fields with careless abandon, as we did just a few years ago, for many small but potentially harmful creatures are waiting to hitch a ride and get a meal from any warm-blooded animal that passes by. The black-legged tick, also known as a deer tick, has become alarmingly common in the Northeast and along with it, the illness it often carries—Lyme disease.

We can't solely blame the ticks, as they are just the middlemen. Ticks aren't born (hatched, really) with Lyme disease, but acquire it from warm-blooded animals—mammals and birds. And not every species of tick carries this disease; of the twelve species of ticks in the Northeast, only the black-legged tick can give you Lyme disease.

It is helpful to be familiar with the black-legged tick's life cycle in order to understand what we, as warm-blooded mammals, are up against. The deer tick's life cycle includes four stages: egg, larva, nymph, and adult, and usually takes at least two years to complete. To transform from stage to stage, the tick needs to feed on the blood of a host. During late spring or early summer, tick eggs hatch into larvae. Throughout summer and early autumn, larvae search for the blood meal that will allow them to molt into eight-legged nymphs. The nymphs lie dormant during the winter and reemerge the following spring. Again they look for a host, and after feeding successfully, they metamorphose into adults. The adult ticks feed and mate on white-tailed deer, birds, mice, and other small mammals, then lay their eggs and die. Black-legged ticks can transmit Lyme disease to humans in the larval, nymphal, and adult stages.

From a human's viewpoint, the larva's first meal is the key to its potential for causing us harm. If it feeds on an animal that has Lyme disease, from then on the tick carries the bacterium that causes Lyme disease, *Borrelia burgdorferi*, in its gut. From here *Borrelia* will eventually be transmitted into the blood of any warm-blooded animal the tick feeds on.

For years, white-tailed deer were blamed for being the primary host of Lyme disease, but

White-footed mouse.

Engorged black-legged tick.

according to a study by the University of Pennsylvania, deer actually play a rather minor role in transmitting the bacterium to feeding ticks, although they are a major cause of the increasing tick density that influences the spread of the disease to humans. Research reveals that larval ticks are more likely to feed on smaller animals, and chief among these are white-footed mice (host of 25 percent of infected ticks), short-tailed shrews (25 percent), masked shrews (25 percent), and eastern chipmunks (13 percent).

Dr. Richard Ostfeld, of the Cary Institute of Ecosystem Studies, is of the opinion that white-footed mice play a key role in perpetuating Lyme disease, due in part to the fact that they don't groom off or kill larval ticks at the rate that shrews and chipmunks do. Ostfeld correlates a spring population explosion of larval black-legged ticks with the white-footed mouse population, which, in turn, he correlates with the acorn crop of the previous fall. A bumper crop of acorns, a favorite food of white-footed mice, results in a bumper crop of white-footed mice and plenty of warm little bodies for black-legged ticks to feed from. Oaks don't produce massive amounts of acorns every year, so in years with little or no mast, the white-footed mouse population crashes. When this happens, a large number of tick nymphs and larvae are looking for another meal source. If white-footed mice are in short supply, it means humans have an even greater chance of finding tiny, black hitchhikers on them at the end of a spring or summer day.

Up to three hundred thousand Americans are diagnosed with Lyme disease every year, according to the Centers for Disease Control and Prevention. Efforts are being made to come up with a preventive, as well as something safe and effective with which to treat people who have found embedded ticks. There is a promising gel, which, if applied shortly after a tick bites you, can destroy the Lyme disease bacteria at the bite site. However, it is not available yet. Until it, or something equally effective, can be purchased, rolling your socks up over your pant cuffs is one harmless precaution easily taken. A second recommended practice is a daily tick check. It reputedly takes twenty-four to forty-eight hours of feeding before a black-legged tick can pass Lyme disease on to a human.

JUNE 1

Blinded Sphinx Moths Emerging

Blinded sphinx moth.

The blinded sphinx moth is a member of the Sphingidae, or hawk moth, family. Most larvae of this family possess a horn at the tip of the abdomen. The adult blinded sphinx moth has strongly scalloped margins on its forewings and a single blue eyespot on each hind wing that is hidden if the moth's wings are folded. Its common name derives from the fact that these "eyes" have no pupils. In its larval stage, the green caterpillar eats the leaves of many deciduous trees, including willow, birch, poplar, and cherry; the adult moth does not feed. After pupating underground, adult moths emerge and mate in June. Males rest with the abdomen curved upward.

Male blinded sphinx moth.

Vixen with turkey foot.

Red Fox Mothers Weaning Kits

The weaning of red fox kits begins when the kits are about five weeks old and they begin eating solid food. In the next few weeks, the mother gradually rebuffs their attempts to nurse, fending off the kits by rolling on her stomach or by barking gruffly at them. Both parents bring food to the kits throughout the day. By the age of eight weeks, red fox kits are usually completely weaned.

Vixen with snake.

Vixen barking at kits.

JUNE 2

Fishing Spiders Catching Prey

The six-spotted fishing spider is an arachnid in the nursery web spider family Pisauridae. As its name implies, the six-spotted fishing spider does occasionally eat small fish, but also consumes other invertebrates and tadpoles. The hunting techniques of fishing spiders are varied. Often they sit patiently with their legs outstretched for hours during the day, waiting out for an unsuspecting insect like the pictured dot-tailed whiteface dragonfly to land within reach. They can and do walk on water and can dive up to 7 inches deep in order to catch aquatic prey. The six-spotted fishing spider in this photograph has removed the head of its prey and is drinking its liquefied innards.

Six-spotted fishing spider consuming dragonfly.

Pink Lady's Slippers Blooming

The pink lady's slipper differs from the yellow and showy lady's slippers in two fairly obvious ways. One is its leafless flowering stalk. The other is the shape of the pouch, or labellum, which has a vertical slit running its length, rather than an oval opening on the top. Bumble bees are the only insects strong enough to push their way through this slit and are the pink lady's slipper's main pollinators.

Given the complexity of the germination process for an orchid, it is amazing that there are as many lady's slippers as there are. The seed of a lady's slipper is extremely small and has no food supply to fuel the growth of the germinating seedling. However, a certain fungus (*Rhizoctonia sp.*) can digest the outer cells of a seed. If this fungus and a lady's slipper seed come in contact with each other, and if the fungus digests the outer cells of the seed but not the inner cells, and if the inner cells absorb some of the nutrients that the fungus obtained from the soil, then germination may take place.

Pink lady's slipper.

JUNE 3

Canadian Tiger Swallowtails vs. Eastern Tiger Swallowtails

Swallowtails are North America's largest butterflies, and their tropical relatives are the largest butterflies in the world. At this time of year, tiger swallowtails emerge from their chrysalises and seek nectar wherever they can find it, often in gardens. The two common species in the Northeast are the eastern tiger swallowtail and the Canadian tiger swallowtail. Those of us living in northern New England are most apt to see the Canadian tiger swallowtail, which replaces the eastern tiger swallowtail this far north, although both species can be found.

Canadian tiger swallowtail.

Eastern tiger swallowtail.

White-Tailed Deer Using Sense of Smell

White-tailed deer, being popular prey animals, have evolved extremely good senses of smell, sight, and hearing. Their elongated noses are filled with an intricate system of passages that contain millions of olfactory receptors—up to 297 million. By contrast, humans have just 5 million, and even those fabled smellers, dogs, have "just" 220 million. As the tongue in this photograph illustrates, a deer licks its nose to keep it moist. This helps odor particles stick to it and improves the deer's sense of smell. Not only do deer use their sense of smell to avoid predators, but they also use it, via seven scent glands on their head, legs, and hooves, to communicate with each other.

There are ways to tell these two swallowtails apart, although it can sometimes be difficult where their ranges meet. The Canadian tiger swallowtail is smaller than the eastern tiger swallowtail, but unless you have them side by side, this isn't a very useful field mark. The easiest way to tell the two species apart is to look on the underside of the butterfly's forewing and see if the yellow band along the margin is solid, indicating a Canadian tiger swallowtail, or if it is broken up into spots, indicating an eastern tiger swallowtail.

Bunchberry Flowering

Bunchberry.

The smallest member of the dogwood family, bunchberry, carpets the floor of coniferous woods right now, along with pink lady's slippers, Canada mayflowers, and clintonia. The small white flowers of bunchberry are as striking as the red fruits that replace them later in the summer.

White-tailed deer licking nose.

JUNE 4

Adult barred owl with eastern chipmunk.

Adult barred owl with red-backed vole.

Barred owl delivering red-backed vole to nestling.

Barred Owl Parents Feeding Nestlings

Young barred owls are fed by their parents from the day they hatch until late summer/early fall. During their first two weeks, the adult male delivers food to the adult female in a bill-to-bill exchange. The female tears the prey into swallowable bits and feeds them to her offspring. During this time the female does little hunting, but after about two weeks of brooding the young, she also begins to capture prey. At about this time, the young begin consuming whole prey on their own. Female prey deliveries are greatest immediately following sunset and immediately before sunrise, while male prey deliveries remain fairly constant throughout the night.

Lady Beetle Eggs Hatching

Most people know these insects as ladybugs, but since they aren't true bugs, entomologists prefer the names ladybird beetles or lady beetles. By whatever name you call them, these insects, like about 88 percent of all insects, pass through four separate stages of metamorphosis during their lives: egg, larva, pupa, and adult.

The first three stages of a lady beetle's life each last anywhere from seven to twenty-one days, depending on weather and food supply. An adult lady beetle lives for three to nine months. There are about 450 species of these beloved insects in the Northeast. The larvae of all lady beetle species look about the same and are predators of many garden pests.

Introduced multicolored Asian lady beetle larva.

JUNE 5

Common Loons on Eggs

Common loons usually return to northern New England from their coastal wintering waters sometime in April or May. Males and females pair up after they arrive at their ponds, and several weeks later they breed and build a new nest or renovate an old one, with the male choosing the actual nest site. Successful nests sites are often reused from year to year, especially if the male returns.

Common loon on nest.

Common loon nest with egg.

Loon on nest obtaining nesting material.

Common loon adding vegetation to nest.

Protection from wind, waves, and predators is paramount. Because their legs are positioned so far back on the body, loons are awkward walkers, at best. Thus, they usually build nests adjacent to water so they can easily slip on and off of them.

The nest is constructed during the day by both adults and is made of vegetation that the loons collect close to the nest. A loon often sits on the nest while collecting material, stretching its head down into the water to retrieve vegetation for the nest.

Two eggs are laid, usually between mid-May and early June. After being incubated by both parents, the eggs hatch in roughly twenty-eight days. Material continues to be added to the nest throughout incubation.

JUNE 6

Red Squirrel Gardens in the Woods

Red and gray squirrels remain active year-round, and thus need to have access to food throughout the year. For this reason, they must store seeds and nuts in the warmer months for consumption during winter and early spring, when food is much harder to find. While gray squirrels tend to bury nuts and seeds individually for this purpose, red squirrels often cache many seeds, mostly conifers and maples, in each spot, dispersing

Sugar maple seedlings.

Ground-Nesting Birds

Bird nests come in all shapes, sizes, materials, and locations. There are cavity nests, platform nests, burrow nests, scrape nests, and cup nests. Birds that nest on the ground typically build one of two types of nests: scrape nests, which are simple depressions in the ground with perhaps some stones or leaves added to provide camouflage and insulation, and cup nests. Due to their location, ground nests are the most accessible type of nest for predators. As a result, both the eggs and the incubating adults tend to be well camouflaged. Frequently the adult birds engage in some form of display to distract approaching predators, and the young of most ground-nesting birds are precocial—capable of locomotion and feeding themselves almost immediately after birth.

- Common loon
- Ring-necked duck
- Northern harrier
- Ruffed grouse
- Wild turkey
- Killdeer
- Spotted sandpiper
- Wilson's snipe
- American woodcock
- Herring gull
- Whip-poor-will
- Eastern towhee
- Song sparrow
- Dark-eyed junco
- Bobolink
- Eastern meadowlark

Common loon on nest.

Killdeer on nest.

Ruffed grouse nest.

Dark-eyed junco nest.

American bittern.

these caches throughout the woods. During the winter, red squirrels use their memory, and sometimes their sense of smell, to locate these buried treasures. Inevitably some are overlooked, and in many of these cases, the seeds germinate. Finding little patches of multiple seedlings, such as this miniature stand of sugar maples, is a good indication that at least one red squirrel overwintered in the vicinity.

Young Eagles Preparing to Fledge

For several weeks prior to their first flight from the nest, bald eagle nestlings practice flapping their wings to the point of lifting themselves several inches up into the air. This develops their wing muscles, flight coordination, and landing ability.

Juvenile bald eagle.

Witch Hazel Cone Gall Aphids Reproducing

The witch hazel cone gall aphid is responsible for the cone-shaped structures visible on some witch hazel leaves at this time of year. The life cycle of this aphid is intense—several generations are produced in one summer. As witch hazel leaves unfurl and start to grow in the spring, the aphid

Witch hazel cone galls.

Open witch hazel cone gall.

injects a leaf with a chemical that causes the plant to form a cone-shaped gall around the aphid. She proceeds to reproduce asexually and fills the gall with fifty to seventy female offspring. The walls of the gall provide them all with food and shelter. The second generation develops wings and disperses to repeat the process. The third generation includes both males and females. Toward the end of summer they reproduce sexually, and the females lay eggs on the branches of witch hazel, where they overwinter. The following spring the eggs hatch and the cycle begins again, allowing the aphid population to increase dramatically in a relatively short period of time. At lower altitudes these aphids have a secondary host (river birch), but at higher ones they have fewer generations and only one host, witch hazel. It has not been determined whether the aphids are two separate species.

JUNE 7

Indian Cucumber Root Flowering

Indian cucumber root, a member of the lily family, is in flower. It grows 1 to 2 feet tall and has one or more tiers of leaves that emerge from the same point on the stem. Plants that are going to flower usually put out two tiers of leaves, with

Indian cucumber root.

their distinctive yellow flowers arising from the second tier. The flowers nod below the leaves, while the dark purple fruit that forms later in the summer rises above them. As its name implies, the small tuber of this wildflower is edible and resembles a cucumber in texture and taste; it should be harvested very sparingly, if at all.

Rose Chafers Eating and Being Eaten

Seemingly overnight, the flowers of roses and peonies, as well as the foliage of many trees, shrubs, and other plants, are besieged by tan beetles called rose chafers. The reason for their sudden appearance has to do with their life cycle.

Adult rose chafers emerge from the ground in late May and early June. Adult beetles feed on plants for three or four weeks, generally until late June, when they mate, lay eggs in the soil, and then die. Two to three weeks later, the eggs hatch into small, white, grub-like larvae that feed on the roots of grasses and weeds. The larvae spend the winter in the soil below the frost line before pupating and emerging as adults in the spring.

Rose chafers contain a toxin that can be deadly to birds, but apparently not to crab spiders. As testimony to their drive to reproduce, a rose chafer, minutes after this picture was taken, mounted and attempted to mate with the rose chafer that was being consumed by the crab spider. Sparing spiders could save your roses.

Butterflies Obtain Nutrients from Scat

Nectar from flowers, sugar from running sap at yellow-bellied sapsucker holes and broken branches, and overripe fruit provide most, but not all, of the nutrition that butterflies need. The males of some species, such as the pictured white admiral, also "puddle" for mineral salts on damp earth, at muddy puddles, and on scat or animal carcasses to get amino acids and other vital nutrients. They need this nutritional boost to generate spermatophores, the packets of sperm and nutrients that are transferred to the female during mating.

White admiral on raccoon scat.

Rose chafer being eaten by crab spider.

JUNE 8

Snapping Turtles Laying Eggs

Every June, female snapping turtles leave their ponds to bury their eggs in sandy soil, where the eggs will develop for the next three months without any parental care or supervision. As is the case with many other reptile eggs, the

Snapping turtle laying eggs.

Spotted sandpiper.

temperature of an individual snapping turtle egg during the middle one-third of embryonic development determines whether the developing turtle will be a male or female. Males are generally produced at lower temperatures than females, between 72 and 80 degrees. At a warmer temperature, around 86 degrees, female turtles develop.

Spotted Sandpipers Nesting

Spotted sandpipers are a relatively easy shorebird to identify, with their spotted breasts, their constant body-bobbing, and the stiff beat of their wings in flight. Although they are shorebirds, they can be found near freshwater ponds and streams throughout North America.

Spotted sandpipers differ from most birds in that the male and female roles are completely reversed when it comes to breeding, in everything from courtship to parental care. The females establish and defend a territory, often arriving on nesting grounds before the males. Females court the males, performing display flights as well as strutting displays on the ground. Males, usually

less aggressive and smaller in size, do the lion's share of incubating the eggs and brooding the young chicks.

Ragged Robin Flowering

Ragged robin is native to Europe and has become so abundant in the northern United States that it borders on being considered an invasive plant. Usually found in wet areas like marshes, fens, and wet meadows, this perennial can cover an area as large as an acre. When flowering, ragged robin is very noticeable—not only to humans, but also to the

Ragged robin.

many insects that pollinate it. Bees and butterflies, especially, flock to stands of this plant in order to obtain its nectar and white pollen. If you suck the base of the flower, you will taste the sweetness that attracts pollinators.

JUNE 9

Crab Spiders Guarding Egg Sacs

Spiders protect their eggs by wrapping them up in a sac they make out of very tough silk. Some species, such as garden, or black and yellow argiope, spiders, then die, leaving their egg sacs to withstand the elements, as well as potential parasites and predators, on their own. The female spiders of other species survive long enough to guard their eggs until they hatch, or even until the young spiderlings disperse, and these sacs are usually far less tough. Among species in which the female protects her eggs, some females, such as wolf spiders and nursery web spiders, carry their egg sacs with them at all times, while others, like jumping spiders and crab spiders, simply remain with the sac.

Crab spider with egg sac.

Sedges Flowering

Sedges are perennial, grasslike plants in the family Cyperaceae. Sedges, which are often found growing in thick clusters or tussocks in wetlands, have triangular stems and spirally arranged leaves. Many species of sedges are members of one huge genus, *Carex*, the species of which can be distinguished from other sedges in two ways. Sedges that are not in the genus *Carex* have "perfect" flowers: each flower has both male and female parts. *Carex* sedges, however, have unisex flowers: their male and female reproductive parts are in separate flowers. In addition, *Carex* sedges possess a highly modified bract called the perigynium that forms a bag-like sac enclosing each one-seeded fruit. The fruits of *Carex* form a spikelet that persists well into the winter months. One non-*Carex* sedge frequently seen in bogs is common cottongrass, which is named for its tufted seedhead.

Common cottongrass.

Black Bears Marking Territory and Mating

Black bear breeding season begins in May and lasts until early July, with mating occurring mainly during June. The female traverses her territory at three times her normal rate during this time, laying down a scent trail that the male follows. Both male and female periodically deposit their scent by intentionally straddling vegetation, breaking off small limbs, and biting, scratching, and rubbing on trees (and telephone poles, if available). Tree species often used for marking include white birch, balsam fir, striped maple, and red pine. When contact between the bears is eventually

Black bear claw scratches.   Black bear bite marks on
                              telephone pole.

made, they nuzzle and chew on each other's head
and neck and may even wrestle a little. During
mating, which occurs repeatedly for several days,
the male and female remain together.

JUNE 10

Eastern Bluebirds Having Multiple Broods

Eastern bluebirds can have up to three broods in
a given season, depending on weather conditions,
parasites, and predators. Thus, it's possible for
nest boxes to be
occupied by the
same female's
offspring for long
periods of time.
When eastern
bluebird eggs

Eastern bluebird nestlings.

Female eastern bluebird
with larva.

hatch, the nestlings are fed small, soft foods,
such as caterpillars or spiders. As they grow
larger, they are fed bigger insects, such as grasshoppers and beetles. After sixteen to twenty-one
days, the nestlings fledge, but the parents continue to feed their young for up to three weeks
after they have left the nest.

Ram's-Head Lady's Slippers Flowering

Because of the small size of its flower, the brevity
of its flowering period, and its rarity (it is critically
imperiled or imperiled throughout its range in the
Northeast), ram's-head lady's slipper is notori-
ously hard to find. Its preferred habitat is moist,
mossy bogs, but it can
also be found in mixed
woods and uplands.

The flowers, which
appear only if the plant is
at least four inches high,
mature in mid-May to
early June, often developing rapidly and typically
lasting only a week or so.
The sepals, lateral petals,
and particularly the lower
lip (a pouch made of
fused petals), produce
a sweet odor to attract
potential pollinators, such
as small bees. Once the
flower is fertilized, the
upper sepal lowers over
the opening of the pouch,
excluding additional visitors.

Ram's-head lady's slipper.

Red-Winged Blackbird Eggs Hatching

Unlike most birds' eggs, those of the red-winged
blackbird hatch asynchronously, spread over several days. During seasons when food is in short
supply, the young chicks which hatch last often
starve, as the earlier-hatched young, being larger
and stronger, are the first to be fed, and thus

Red-winged blackbird eggs and chick.

deprive their siblings of food. Having eggs hatch in succession is thought to be an adaptation that allows the size of the surviving brood and the amount of available food to balance.

JUNE 11

Blackburnian Warblers Singing

Male blackburnian warblers are relatively easy to identify by sight. Their intense orange breeding plumage is unmistakable, and they are the only

North American warbler with an orange throat. However, because they often forage for spiders and insects high in the canopy where they are hidden from sight, it is often easier to locate a blackburnian by ear. The singing of their thin, high-pitched song peaks soon after the males arrive on their breeding grounds.

Blackburnian warbler.

Pitcher Plants Flowering

The flowers of pitcher plants are just as unusual and fascinating as their insect-luring leaves. These plants blossom during a two-to three-week period in the spring, from late May through June. The drooping maroon petals typically prevent you from seeing the inner structure of the flower, which more

Pitcher plant flower.

or less resembles an upside-down umbrella. This "umbrella" forms a bowl that has receptive stigmas at each of its upraised tips. Within one to two days of the flower's opening, its stigmas become receptive, and the anthers shed their pollen, some of which falls into the umbrella. To get into the flower, an insect has to crawl over one of the stigmas, where pollen collected from a previous visit to another flower is deposited. Inside the flower, the insect may contact the anthers directly, or it may become coated with the pollen that has fallen into the umbrella. The only pathway out of the flower keeps the insect away from the stigmas, so self-pollination does not occur. Ants are almost invariably present in the flowers, attracted by the abundant nectar, but they are probably of little importance as pollinators. Queen bumble bees and flies appear to be the primary pollinators of pitcher plants.

Rosy Maple Moths Emerging

Many moths in the silk moth family, Saturniidae, emerge in June, including the giant silk moths such as luna moths and cecropia moths. A smaller member of this family, the rosy maple moth, also appears at this time of year. While its 1- to 2-inch wingspan doesn't compare to many

Rosy maple moth.

of the giant silk moths' 5- to 6-inch spread, its pink and white or yellow coloring is stunning.

Adults emerge from the soil in mid-May through mid-July in the late afternoon and mate in the late evening. Females begin laying eggs at dusk the next day in groups of ten to thirty on leaves of host plants, which include box elders, red, sugar, and silver maples, as well as some oaks. The eggs hatch in about two weeks. The larvae, referred to as green-striped mapleworms, occasionally do considerable damage to host trees when their population soars. In the Northeast there is only one brood per summer. The larvae pupate and overwinter underground.

JUNE 12

One-Flowered Wintergreen Flowering

A walk in cool, moist woodlands at this time of year may reward you with the sight and smell of one-flowered wintergreen in bloom. The 3- to 6-inch-tall nodding flower has five waxy petals with rounded tips and wavy edges. Its true beauty can only be appreciated if you get down on your hands and knees and look under the petals. At this angle and close range, you can not only see the ten stamens and five-lobed stigma, but you can breathe in the flower's delightful fragrance, which is very similar to that of lily-of-the-valley.

One-flowered wintergreen's blossom remains viable, without withering, for up to six weeks. After the flower is pollinated, the developing capsule becomes erect. Wintergreen seeds, along with orchid seeds, are the smallest in the plant kingdom—a single seed weighs around two-millionths of a gram. One-flowered wintergreen is in the Heath family, which also includes rhododendrons, mountain laurel, azaleas, blueberries, and cranberries.

One-flowered wintergreen.

American Woodcock Eggs Hatching

The aerial displays of courting male American woodcocks earlier in the spring resulted in many successful matings. Woodcocks, or timberdoodles, are members of the shorebird family Scolopacidae, many of which are ground nesters and have precocial young who are able to fend for themselves almost immediately after hatching. After being incubated for three weeks, the eggs

American woodcock hatched eggs in nest.

of woodcocks are hatching now. Young wood-cocks leave the nest a few hours after their down dries, but unlike many other precocial chicks, they depend on their mother for food for the first week. Three or four days after hatching, a chick starts to probe in the dirt for worms and other invertebrates with its long, flexible-tipped bill.

Red-Tailed Hawks Adding Greenery to Nests

Although red-tailed hawk eggs hatched last month, the adults continue to spruce up their nest periodically with fresh, green-leaved branches throughout the nesting period. This red-tail is flying home with a recently plucked sugar maple branch.

Red-tailed hawk.

Staghorn Sumac Flowering

The tiny, greenish-yellow staghorn sumac flowers that bloom at this time of year are a very import-ant source of nectar for several butterfly species, including banded and striped hairstreaks. This sumac is also a host plant for spring azure butterfly larvae. Stag-horn sumac flowers are recognized by pollination ecologists for attracting large numbers of native bees, which visit for its pollen and nectar. This flowering shrub also acts as a biological control, as it attracts predatory or parasitoid insects that prey upon pest insects.

Staghorn sumac flowers.

Ruby-Throated Hummingbirds Drinking Nectar

For years scientists assumed that hummingbirds passively extracted nectar from flowers with their tongue by capillary action, but it turns out that this is not the case. A hummingbird's forked tongue, which is twice as long as its beak, is lined with hairlike extensions or fringes called lamellae. When the tongue is inserted into a flower and immersed in fluid, it separates into two parts and the lamellae extend outward so that the open grooves between the lamellae lie flat. As the hummingbird pulls its tongue into its mouth, the forked tips come together and the lamellae roll inward, trapping the nectar within the tongue until it is swallowed. No output of energy is

Ruby-throated hummingbird with tongue out.

necessary on the part of the bird—this process is automatic, takes all of one twentieth of a second, and occurs thousands of times a day.

Giant Water Bugs Laying Eggs

Giant water bugs, also known as "toe-biters," have the largest eggs of any aquatic insect. The eggs pictured belong to a species in the genus *Lethocerus* and are usually attached to vegetation above the water line. The eggs of some of the other species of giant water bugs are carried on the backs of the males. These aquatic predators lie on the bottoms of ponds and streams, where they

Giant water bug eggs.

stalk and capture crustaceans, fish, amphibians, and even young turtles. They then inject their prey with powerful digestive saliva and drink the liquefied remains.

JUNE 14

Plantain Flowering

Many people consider plantains to be weeds. While their flowers are fairly inconspicuous and don't have the colorful petals or fragrance of many other flowers, their success at propagating is indisputable, given their abundance in fields and lawns far and wide.

Although not particularly eye-catching, the flowers of plantain species develop in an interesting way, as illustrated by the English plantain in the photo. Its flowers are packed tightly into a spike whose most obvious oddity is the ring of anthers on the mature flowers in the middle of the spike. Each flower has four pollen-bearing anthers and one stigma. Slender filaments allow the anthers to dance in the breeze as their pollen is dispersed by the wind. Below this ring of open flowers are old, dried up, dead flowers, and above it are the green sepal-covered buds of flowers yet to mature. Plantain's spike of flowers matures from the bottom up, so that the ring of stamens appears to move up the spike from the bottom to the top.

English plantain.

Alder Flea Weevils

Weevils are beetles in the family Curculionidae. There are more species in this family than in any other beetle group—over one thousand species in North America alone. Most weevils are small,

Alder flea weevil.

310 mm in length, and dark-colored. A weevil's most distinctive feature is the shape of its head, which is elongated to form a snout; its mouth is at the end of the snout.

Both larval and adult weevils are herbivorous and are frequently associated with crop destruction, because they often feed on stored grains and seeds. The cotton boll weevil is a famous example. The larva and adult of the local weevil pictured, the alder flea weevil, both feed on speckled alder leaves.

Brown-Headed Cowbirds Fledging

Brown-headed cowbird on eastern bluebird nest box.

Brown-headed cowbirds expend much less energy on producing the next generation than many species of birds, for this member of the blackbird family neither builds a nest nor raises its young. The female cowbird does lay eggs—sometimes more than three dozen in one breeding season—but she lays them in the nests of other birds. Over 220 species are parasitized by brown-headed cowbirds. Most host birds do not recognize the cowbird egg in their nest as different from

their own and proceed to incubate the egg and raise the young cowbird. This often occurs at the expense of the host bird's own chicks, for brown-headed cowbird eggs hatch earlier than the eggs of many other species, which gives the young cowbird a jump start on its fellow nestlings. The cowbird fledgling pictured here was raised by an eastern bluebird.

JUNE 15

One-Flowered Cancer Root Flowering

One-flowered cancer root, also known as one-flowered broomrape, produces up to five colorless flowering stalks, each of which bears a single, fragrant, white or lavender flower. Glandular hairs cover the petals, and two bright yellow ridges inside the flower may act as nectar guides for pollinating insects, although it is also self-pollinating. One-flowered cancer root has no chlorophyll in its sparse, scalelike leaves, so it cannot make its own food. This parasitic plant is classified as a holoparasite—it is entirely dependent upon other plants to supply its nutritional needs. These host plants often include sedums, as well as plants in the saxifrage and aster families.

The tiny one-flowered cancer root seedlings, with their limited food supply, must find a suitable host plant within a few days of germinating, or die. Chemicals released by the growing roots of the host guide the seedling's search. Once a host plant is located, cancer root's root hairs exude an adhesive substance that attaches its roots to those of the host plant. Enzymes break down

One-flowered cancer root.

the cell walls of the host, and a tuber-like connection, an haustorium, forms between the vascular tissue of the two plants, allowing the movement of water, minerals, and carbohydrates to flow in just one direction, from host to parasite.

Hooded Merganser Ducklings on the Water

In response to the calls of their mother, who waits below, hooded merganser ducklings typically leap from their cavity nests in trees within twenty-four hours of hatching. Long claws on their feet help them climb up to the opening of the cavity. The ducklings feed themselves on aquatic insects and invertebrates from day one and are capable of shallow dives as soon as they leave their nest. The mother, who has been their sole caretaker since she started incubating the eggs, often moves her brood downstream from smaller streams and ponds near the nest site to larger lakes, rivers, and bays. A month or two after they hatch, she leaves her young, often before they can fly.

Female hooded merganser and ducklings.

Pearl Crescents Mating

These mating pearl crescent butterflies may have used size, color, shape, vein structure, and/or pheromones to recognize each other. When

Mating pearl crescents.

mating, most male butterflies provide the female with a package of sperm and nutrients called a spermatophore, which she needs in order to produce and lay eggs. The female stores spermatophores from multiple matings in a sac called a bursa until she is ready to lay eggs. She fertilizes her eggs as she lays them, using the most recently received sperm first. For this reason, males of some species leave a substance that dries into a film on the female's abdomen after mating in an effort to keep her from mating with other males.

JUNE 16

Liverworts Reproducing

Liverworts, along with mosses and hornworts, are classified as bryophytes—non-flowering plants that lack vascular (conductive) tissue. It is possible, even likely, that liverworts were among the first plants to make the transition to life on land. You've seen them, even if you think you haven't. There are two forms: the greatest number of species are leafy liverworts; fewer, but better-known species are thalloid, or ribbonlike. Leafy liverworts cover fallen logs, tree trunks, rocks, and soil in large swaths, while one of the most

Liverwort.

Archegonia.

Moose Infested with Flies

At this time of year, moose have to tolerate a multitude of flies on and around their hindquarters. These "moose flies" can be seen throughout the spring and summer in dense swarms over and on the rumps of moose—five hundred or more may accompany a single moose. Unlike most other biting insects, both male and female moose flies feed on their host's blood. Although not considered a serious pest—moose tend to pay little attention to them—moose flies may be responsible for sores often found on the hind legs of moose. It is thought that female moose flies may be stimulated by gases released by the moose when it is defecating, after which the female flies descend and deposit eggs into crevices in the moose's scat.

common thalloid liverworts, *Marchantia polymorpha*, may even be a pest in your garden.

Like all land plants, liverworts have a two-stage life cycle in which they alternate between a generation that produces sperm and eggs and one that reproduces by spores. Plants of the sexually reproducing generation, called gametophytes, are photosynthetic and free-living. The spore-producing generation does not photosynthesize, but develops and lives on the gametophyte. The stalked, palm tree–like structures on *Marchantia* bear egg-producing, flask-shaped archegonia on the underside of their fronds, and the stalked disks hold sperm-producing antheridia. Both are less than an inch tall and are produced on separate plants, unlike 80 percent of liverwort species, which produce their sex organs on the same plant. Liverwort sperm must swim into an archegonium in order to fertilize the single egg inside, which requires the presence of a film of rainwater or dew. The second generation, the sporophyte, develops inside the archegonium from the fertilized egg. As its name implies, this plant produces spores, which will grow into gametophytes, thus continuing the cycle, which is called the alternation of generations.

Moose being bothered by moose flies near its hind quarters.

JUNE 17

Mallard Eggs Hatching

When mallard ducklings hatch they are fully covered with down that dries in about twelve hours. At this point, they begin moving around in the nest and may even wander a few feet away, but for the most part their mother broods them until the family leaves the nest for the water. This

Wasps

The term "wasp" is a general name that applies to a large group of insects in the order Hymenoptera, many of which do not have "wasp" in their common name, leading to some confusion. Wasps can be broken down into two groups: those that lead communal lives and those that live solitary lives. The majority of wasp species are solitary wasps.

The most highly organized social wasps have a communal nest site, cooperative brood care, overlapping generations within a colony of adults, and division of labor into reproductive and non-reproductive groups. They rely on their venom for defense. Paper wasps, hornets, and yellow jackets are all social wasps.

Paper wasp nest.

Solitary wasps do not share any of these characteristics. They live alone, all adults are fertile, and they build cells of mud above ground or burrows underground in which their larvae develop by themselves. They rely on their venom to hunt prey. Mason wasps and pollen wasps are solitary wasps.

Great golden digger wasp at nest hole.

Hen mallard and ducklings.

departure usually takes place on the morning after they hatch. The mother leads them to water as she vocalizes up to two hundred times a minute.

Adult Stoneflies Emerging

Stoneflies spend their larval stage on the bottom of streams, in among the stones for which they're named. Larval stoneflies of some species feed on decomposing organic matter, while others are predators. The adults have such short life spans that very few species feed at all. Those that do, feed on algae, lichens, nectar, or pollen.

After shedding its skin ten to twenty-two times, depending on the species, the larva crawls out of the water, splits its skin one final time, and emerges as a winged adult. Most species emerge in the spring or early summer, though some mature in the fall or winter. Most larvae spend ten to eleven months under water and live on land for only one to four weeks as adults. The adults spend their days hiding on the branches or leaves of streamside vegetation and crawl around at night.

Adult stonefly.

Big brown bat.

Big Brown Bats Giving Birth

Female big brown bats form maternity colonies, where the mothers cluster with their young. The pups are born naked and blind and weigh just three grams. They are nursed during the day and left at the roost during the night, when their mothers leave to feed. In about three to five weeks, the pups begin to fly and explore on their own. Maternity colonies disperse in late July and August.

JUNE 18

Twinflower Blooming

Twinflower.

Carl Linnaeus, known as the father of modern taxonomy, came up in the mid-1700s with the two-part binomial naming system of genus and species that is universally recognized as the system now used to assign scientific names to all living things. During his lifetime he named close to eight thousand plants and many animals, including *Homo sapiens*. Linnaeus used the names of many of his supporters and detractors as inspiration for naming plants. The most beautiful of plants were often named in honor of his supporters, and he named common weeds or unattractive plants after his detractors. Twinflower, reported to be Linnaeus's favorite plant, was named *Linnaea borealis* in his honor by his close friend and teacher, Jan Frederik Gronovius.

Red-Shouldered Hawk Parents Caring for Nestlings

Red-shouldered hawks typically have two to five chicks, often in early June. They are born covered with thick, buff-colored down and soon grow a second set of white down that is even thicker. The female red-shouldered hawk does nearly all of the feeding of the young, just as she does all of the brooding.

Adult red-shouldered hawk with two chicks.

Growth and development is rapid; by the time they are five days old, the nestlings can shoot their feces over the edge of the nest. At about two weeks of age, the chicks are frequently standing up, lying down, and flapping their wings. Whitewash on bushes below the nest is a sign that it is active.

By the time they are three weeks old, the nestlings begin to eat delivered prey on their own, but the parents continue to offer food to them long after the young have fledged at the age of six weeks. While small mammals such as chipmunks, mice, and voles are the predominant prey brought to nestlings and fledglings, insects, snakes, frogs, and toads also make up part of their diet.

Group of showy lady's slippers.

JUNE 19

Showy Lady's Slippers Flowering

Just fifty years ago, showy lady's slippers could be found over most of the Northeast. Habitat loss and an exploding deer population are considered major factors in their decline, making them endangered or on the verge of extinction in many areas. Although rare, showy lady's slippers are still locally abundant, particularly in fens, peat wetlands that get their water from groundwater or surface water.

As with pink and yellow lady's slippers, one of showy lady's slipper's three petals is greatly modified into a large inflated pouch called the labellum. The pouch's hot pink color can vary widely from year to year, depending on the ambient temperature. Cooler conditions appear to produce more intense color.

The petals on either side of the pouch attract pollinators with an alluring odor, but the insects that enter the pouch are in for a disappointment, as lady's slippers produce little or no nectar. Once inside, visiting insects are guided toward the flower's pistil and stamens by very

fine, slanting hairs on the inner surface of the pouch. After an insect has entered the constricted passageway that leads to the reproductive parts, it cannot turn around and must pass first by the pistil and then by the stamens. Although lady's slippers produce seedpods with tens of thousands of seeds, their seed germination rate is low, and it takes about eight years from seed to flower, so it is fortunate that these plants reproduce well by growth of their underground rhizomes.

Showy lady's slipper.

Burying Beetles Providing Larvae with Food

Burying beetles are the undertakers of the animal world. They belong to a group of large, often black and orange, beetles that bury dead and decaying animals such as mice and small birds in order to provide their larvae with food. Burying beetle antennae are equipped with receptors that are able to detect a mouse, within an hour of its death, from up to 2 miles away. Males and females pair up at the carcass and will fight off rivals to take possession of and bury it. They are capable of moving a mouse-size carcass several feet until they find soil soft enough for burial. The female lays her eggs on or beside the buried body.

Burying beetle.

Burying beetles are unusual in the beetle world in that both males and females continue to care for the larvae after they hatch, feeding them from the corpse. Elsewhere in the insect world, such behavior is typically exhibited only by social insects like bees, ants, wasps, and termites.

JUNE 20

Chimney Swifts Roosting

Chimney swifts, or "flying cigars," a name derived from their silhouette, are among the most aerial of all land birds. Not only do they feed on the wing, but they also drink by skimming water with their beaks, bathe by slapping their breasts against surface water, and collect nesting material by breaking off dry twigs with their feet, all without ever touching ground. Except for when roosting or nesting, chimney swifts are airborne.

Mated pairs seek out a chimney, building, or hollow tree in which to nest. They cannot stand or perch like most other birds, but their toes are equipped with long, sharp claws for gripping vertical surfaces. Communal roosting typically takes place during migration, but some non-breeding individuals remain in communal roosts throughout the summer, sometimes

Chimney swifts.

sharing a chimney with a nesting pair.

Chimney swifts are diurnal and spend the day flying at a mean speed of 30 miles per hour as they hawk insects in the air while issuing their high-pitched chip notes. One swift can eat over one thousand insects per day. As darkness approaches, the non-breeding swifts head for nearby chimneys and hollow trees. Once inside, they grasp the vertical walls and remain there for the rest of the night. It is not unheard of for a chimney to serve as a roosting site for several hundred chimney swifts through the summer, and during fall migration the number of birds can climb to several thousand.

Wolf Spider Eggs Hatching

Female wolf spiders provide both their eggs and young with a considerable amount of maternal care. They actually carry their egg sac around with them, attached to the spinnerets at the end of their abdomen, as they hunt for food and go about the rest of their lives. The mother is careful to keep her egg sac from touching the ground and to make sure that it receives a sufficient amount of sunlight each day, presumably to enhance incubation. She also mends any tears that appear in the sac. The eggs hatch in one to two weeks, and four to twenty-two days later, the mother perforates the egg sac, either part way or all the way around the seam, by rotating the sac

Wolf spider with young.

about anywhere at this time of year, including inside the nostrils of humans, some of whom are allergic to them.

All pines have separate male and female cones on the same tree. Male pine cones, which produce pollen, are much smaller and more papery, occur in clusters, and remain on the tree for a much shorter period of time than most female pine cones. By July they will litter the ground beneath pines before they quickly disintegrate. Although it may mean that those allergic to the pollen have to endure a brief period of sneezing, this "golden smoke" makes it possible for pine trees to produce the next generation of seeds.

with her legs as she makes tiny holes in it with her mouthparts. Within three hours, spiderlings crawl out of the sac through the holes made by the mother, climb onto her abdomen, and remain there for days or weeks, depending on the species.

Pine Pollen Dispersing

If you've recently noticed yellow clouds near pine trees or a layer of yellow dust on your car or pond, you are witnessing the annual dispersal of pollen by male pine cones. Light and fluffy so as to be easily carried by the wind, these minute pollen grains can be found just

JUNE 21

Green Frogs Calling

Male green frogs are calling to attract mates. Scientists have actually differentiated six different green frog calls, but the one most familiar sounds much like a loose banjo string being plucked.

Green frogs, like most frogs, have a single vocal sac that acts as a resonating chamber. Wood frogs, northern leopard frogs, and pickerel frogs have paired vocal sacs. While spring peepers, bullfrogs, and gray tree frogs have single sacs that bubble out beneath their chins when they call, the inflated sac of the green frog is subtler.

Pine pollen.   Male red pine cones.

Male green frog.

Green frog eggs.

There is only a slight swelling of the throat and sides of its body when it is calling.

With their calls, male green frogs not only attract females, but also stake out territories that are 3 to 20 feet in diameter. The female green frog chooses her mate and then lays three thousand to five thousand eggs that the chosen male fertilizes externally.

Calopogon Deceiving Bumble Bees

A visit to a bog or marshy area at this time of year may well reward you with the sight of a striking orchid known as calopogon, or grass-pink. You'll immediately notice fine white hairs on the upper lip of the flower, which act as a

Calopogon.

"pseudopollen" lure for naïve, recently emerged bumble bees. This upper lip, or labellum, is hinged at its base, so that when a bee lands on the fake pollen, its weight swings the lip down. This delivers the bee smack on its back onto a structure below called the column. The column is a structure peculiar to orchids that combines pollen-producing male parts with a receptive female stigma. In the case of calopogon, if the bee has just visited another flower of the same species, it carries two saddlebags of pollen on the first segment of its abdomen. When the bee lands upside down on the column, the pollen packets land precisely on the stigma to bring about pollination. As the bee pushes backward to escape the flower, it picks up another load of pollen.

Veery Eggs About to Hatch

Female veeries build a nest on or near the ground, occasionally under a small overhang, where it is usually well concealed. Twigs, weeds, and grapevines are placed on top of a pile of dead leaves. The female repeatedly presses her body into this pile as she shifts her position to create a cup-shaped nest. She then lines the nest with soft bark strips, rootlets, and grasses. The pale blue eggs of a veery resemble those of other thrushes, particularly those of hermit and wood thrushes.

Veery nest.

JUNE 22

Trailing Arbutus Setting Fruit

The fruit of trailing arbutus, also known as mayflower, is maturing. While this plant's flower is familiar, its fruit may not be. Although it develops from the flower, and therefore is in the same location—under trailing arbutus's leathery leaves, next to the ground—it is not as showy or as noticeable. In addition, each of the aromatic pink and white flowers that blossomed in early spring

A drone honey bee that lost its life after successfully mating with a queen.

Trailing arbutus fruit.

only bore two fleshy white fruits. Like many spring wild-flowers, the seeds of trailing arbutus have elaiosomes, fleshy attachments that attract the ants that are the seeds' main dispersal agents.

Trailing arbutus flowers.

European Honey Bees Swarming and Drones Mating with New Queen

A honey bee colony has one fertile, egg-laying queen, several hundred male drones, and thousands of sterile female worker bees. The drone's only function is to mate with and fertilize a queen.

Honey bee hives can get overcrowded at this time of year, and when they do, the old queen leaves with roughly 60 percent of the workers and forms a cluster, or swarm, of bees nearby. Once scout bees have found a tree cavity in which to establish a new hive, they relocate.

A young virgin queen in the old hive then takes several mating, or nuptial, flights.

Every year the nuptial flights take place in the same location, which is somehow located by drones and by the virgin queens who were not

alive the year before. On these flights, she mates in midair, 200 to 300 feet above the ground, with from one to more than forty drones. The drones are usually not from the queen's hive and may be from several other hives. On average, the queen mates with twelve drones. Although brief, honey bee mating is dramatic. The drone inserts his endophallus, or internal penis, into the queen's sting chamber, and with great force injects his sperm into her. The force with which this is done is so powerful that it ruptures the endophallus, thus separating the drone from the queen. The drone dies shortly thereafter.

The queen stores up to six million live sperm from her mating flights and retains them for the remainder of her life, which is two to three years for a long-lived queen. The more times a queen has mated, the more attractive she is to her worker bees because of pheromone alterations, and the longer she is allowed to live before being replaced by the workers. Unlike the drones she mates with, the queen may live several more years.

JUNE 23

Ruffed Grouse Eggs Hatching

If you stumble upon a female ruffed grouse whose eggs have recently hatched, be prepared for her fury! A mother defending her chicks will charge at a predator with her crest raised, tail spread, and ruffs (black neck feathers) erect.

Ruffed grouse nest just after eggs hatched.

Fiercely protective, female grouse with young are known for their aggressive behavior. A large grouse weighing 2 pounds will tackle a perceived predator, like a human, that weighs more than fifty times as much as itself.

Ants Dispersing Seeds

Bloodroot seeds, as well as the seeds of as many as 5 percent of flowering plants, have a fatty appendage called an elaiosome attached to them that is very attractive to ants. The ants collect the seeds and take them down into their tunnels, where they feed the elaiosomes to their larvae. The actual seeds are discarded underground, often in the ants' compost, where the seeds' chances of germinating are enhanced. The dispersal of seeds by ants is referred to as myrmecochory.

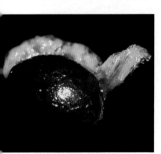

Bloodroot seeds.

Virginia Opossums Giving Birth and Weaning Young

Virginia opossums have a long breeding season in the Northeast—from January through July. After a brief twelve- to thirteen-day gestation period, one to twenty-one embryonic-looking, honey bee-size baby Virginia opossums are born. Most female opossums have thirteen teats, and the first thirteen babies that attach themselves to these teats are those that have a chance of surviving. When giving birth, the female opossum sits on her rump, with her tail in front of her. This places the newly born opossums 1½ to 2 inches from their mother's pouch, which is as close as possible. With relatively well-developed front legs, the baby climbs into its mother's pouch. Once a young opossum attaches itself to a teat and begins sucking, the teat swells in its mouth and secures the baby to its mother. In about two months, the babies detach themselves, but they remain in the pouch and nurse periodically for about another month, until they are fully weaned and beginning to eat solid food.

JUNE

Virginia opossum.

195

JUNE 24

Iridescent Dogbane Beetles Emerging

Dogbane beetles appear suddenly, usually in early summer, when dogbane is flowering. Look on the leaves and blossoms of the host plant, also called Indian hemp, for this blue-green beetle with a metallic copper and crimson shine to it.

The leaves of dogbane, which the beetles consume, contain latex that makes their mouthparts very sticky. To avoid this, beetles eat the outermost parts of the leaves, which contain less latex. The plant tissue also contains cardenolides, chemicals that are bitter and toxic to most insects. However, some of the insects that eat dogbane, including dogbane beetles, have adapted to consume and store these chemicals in their bodies. They use them as a defense from predators by releasing them when they are disturbed.

Dogbane beetles mate about once a day, usually early in the day. After choosing a female and mating, the male beetle rides on the back of the female to keep her from mating with other males. The female lays her eggs in large groups of protective capsules on the leaves and stems of dogbane. The larvae, after hatching, make their way into the soil, where they feed on the roots of dogbane, and overwinter there.

Dogbane beetle on dogbane flowers.

Male dogbane beetle riding on female.

Cattails Flowering

Cattails reproduce vegetatively, forming clones by sending up shoots from their creeping horizontal stems, or rhizomes, but they also reproduce sexually, by seed. Separate male and female cattail flowers form in cylindrical spikes at the tip of a stalk, with the female flowers located directly below the male.

The female cattail flowers mature before the male flowers above them, thus minimizing self-pollination. Soon after producing clouds of pollen, the male flower spike dies, leaving the seed-laden,

Male and female cattail flowers.

sausage-shaped female spike below. One spike produces roughly 220,000 seeds. Each seed has tiny hairlike appendages that aid in its dispersal. These hairs form on the outside of the spike, giving it a surface similar to felt.

Red Fox Kits Enjoying Carefree Summer

The first summer of a red fox's life is by far the most carefree period it will ever experience. Days are spent playing tag, king of the mountain, and

Red fox kits.

Red fox kits at play, learning to pounce.

Red fox kit investigating a leaf.

Male Yellow-Bellied Sapsuckers Helping Females Raise Young

Often when the male and female of a species' plumage is similar, as in woodpeckers, they share rearing responsibilities. Without fail, the male yellow-bellied sapsucker parent keeps up with his mate in numbers of visits to their nesting hole, the amount of food he collects and brings to the nest, and keeping the nest clean.

Male yellow-bellied sapsucker at nest hole.

hide-and-seek. Just like human babies, the kits put everything from sticks to bones and feathers in their mouths in an effort to discover as much as they can about the world around them. Mock fights, pouncing on each other, and tumbling in the dirt are daily activities from which they learn important skills. Food is delivered to them by their parents, coats are groomed by their parents, and life is good.

Forest Tent Caterpillars Molting

The larval, or caterpillar, stage of a moth or butterfly is the only stage that has chewing mouthparts, and a larva spends most of its waking hours eating. This consumption of food results in massive growth, making its skin, or exoskeleton, very tight. When this happens, a hormone called ecdysone is produced and prompts the caterpillar to molt. During the molt, the caterpillar shrugs off its old exoskeleton, under which is a new and larger exoskeleton. An old exoskeleton is visible to the left of the caterpillar

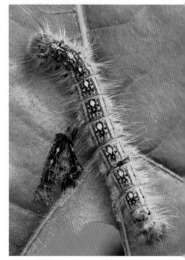
Forest tent caterpillar and molted skin.

Red fox kits at play.

in the photo. After the molt, while the new exo-skeleton is still soft, the caterpillar swallows a lot of air, which expands its body. After the exoskel-eton hardens, the caterpillar lets the air out, thus leaving room for growth. Caterpillars molt four or five times as they grow.

JUNE 26

Canada Goose Goslings: Contour Feathers Replacing Down

Within twenty-four hours of hatching, downy Canada goose goslings leave their nest and are capable of walking, swimming, diving, and feed-ing. Like many species of waterfowl, their growth is rapid. Contour feathers on the wings and tail begin to emerge in about three weeks (note the wing feathers of the gosling in the photo). Feath-ers on a gosling's head, neck, and back are the last to appear. Just before a gosling develops the ability to fly, the last fluff of down, which is on top of its head, disappears.

Canada goose gosling.

Gray Fox Kits Exploring

In the past century, gray foxes have become nearly as common as red foxes in the North-east, but due to their more secretive nature,

Gray fox kits.

we do not see them as often. Because of their mixed coloration of gray and red, gray foxes are often mistaken for red foxes, but there are two easy ways to distinguish them. The red fox has a white-tipped tail, whereas the tip of the gray fox's tail is black. The gray fox is the only mem-ber of the dog family capable of climbing trees; its semi-retractable claws enable it to pursue tree-dwelling animals such as squirrels. Gray fox kits can be seen near their den as they investigate and play with nearby objects, such as feathers left over from previous meals.

Viper's Bugloss Flowering

Even if it weren't such a beautiful and vibrantly colored flower, viper's bugloss would be notable just for its name. "Bugloss" is of Greek origin,

Viper's bugloss.

Common bladderwort.

from a word signifying an ox's tongue, and alludes to the roughness and shape of the plant's leaves. Some say the dead flower head resembles a snake, and in the 1600s this plant provided a popular cure for snake bites.

Viper's bugloss is particularly popular with bees. It is long flowering, and it produces nectar throughout the day, unlike most other plants, whose nectar run lasts only a short period of time. With an unlimited supply of viper's bugloss, honey bees can collect between 12 and 20 pounds of nectar a day—an acre of viper's bugloss provides enough nectar to produce anywhere from 300 to 1,000 pounds of honey.

JUNE 27

Common Bladderwort Flowering

Common bladderwort is a free-floating, carnivorous flowering plant. On its finely divided, submerged leaves are tiny sacs which, though once thought to be flotation devices, are actually highly specialized traps that capture, hold, and digest food for the plant. These sacs have a double-sealed, airtight door on one end. When this door is closed, the sac, or bladder, expels water through its wall, creating a partial vacuum inside. Trigger hairs surround the door, and the instant an organism bumps against a hair, it twists and breaks the seal of the door. Water rushes into the vacuum, pulling the victim along with it. As the bladder fills with water, the pressure inside and out equalizes, and the door automatically closes, caging the plant's prey. This entire process takes two-thousandths of a second. As enzymes digest the prey, special cells in the bladder's wall pump out the water and reestablish the vacuum, preparing the trap to spring again.

American Toadlets Emerging from Ponds

The American toad tadpoles that hatch in May and June begin to transform into terrestrial toadlets after about three weeks. Metamorphosis is a complex series of external and internal changes. The digestive system, which was

American toad tadpole with two legs and a tail.

American toadlet on a penny.

adapted to an herbivorous diet, changes to accommodate a carnivorous one, lungs are formed, gills are absorbed, legs appear, and the tail is absorbed. When these changes have taken place, the young toads leave the water but tend to linger near the pond for days or weeks before dispersing.

Water Scorpions

Although called water scorpions, these water bugs aren't even closely related to scorpions, which are arachnids. The name comes from the superficial resemblance of their body shapes. Both have grasping front legs, but the water bug's "tail" is really a breathing tube that acts like a snorkel. Water scorpions are insects and possess three pairs of legs, three body parts, and two pairs of wings. Despite their almost exclusively aquatic lifestyle, water scorpions can and do fly.

Bog Plants Flowering in June

- Leatherleaf, *Chamaedaphne calyculata*
- Bog rosemary, *Andromeda polifolia*
- Labrador tea, *Rhododendron groenlandicum*
- Bog laurel, *Kalmia polifolia*
- Common cottongrass, *Eriophorum angustifolium*
- Pitcher plant, *Sarracenia purpurea*
- Rose pogonia, *Pogonia ophioglossoides*
- Calopogon, *Calopogon tuberosus*
- Large cranberry, *Vaccinium macrocarpon*
- Small cranberry, *Vaccinium oxycoccos*
- Wild blueberry, *Vaccinium sp.*
- Rhodora, *Rhododendron canadense*
- Sheep laurel, *Kalmia angustifolia*

Labrador tea.

Pitcher plant.

Leatherleaf.

Cottongrass.

Cranberry.

Bog rosemary.

Calopogon.

Sheep laurel.

Wild blueberry.

Rhodora.

Water scorpion.

The long-bodied water scorpions in the genus *Renatra*, also called water stick insects or needle bugs, can reach up to 5 inches in length. Water scorpions are predators that mostly eat other invertebrates, but they have been known to take tadpoles and minnows as well.

The male water scorpion produces chirping noises, much like those of a cricket, to attract females. After mating, the female lays several eggs attached to aquatic vegetation.

JUNE 28

Red-Tailed Hawk Nestlings Growing

Gone are the white down feathers of newly hatched red-tailed hawks. They have been replaced by a juvenile plumage that closely resembles the adult's, but with two major differences. The primaries, the outermost flight feathers, of juveniles are pale compared to the adult's dark-colored primaries, and they lack the red tail for which this bird is named.

Juvenile red-tailed hawk.

Moose Antlers Growing

Antlers grow faster than any other mammal bone—a big bull moose can grow an 80-pound rack in a summer, adding a pound of bone a day. While genetics has an influence on antler growth and size, nutrition is by far the most important factor, and males in high quality habitats grow much larger antlers.

In the early stage of growth, antlers are covered with a fuzzy skin called velvet, which contains a tremendous concentration of nerves as well as a supply of blood. The velvet nourishes the growing antlers for about five months, during which time the antlers are extremely sensitive to touch, and if injured, may be permanently misshapen. Eventually, when the bone stops growing, the velvet is shed. Bull moose then use their antlers to attract and fight for mates, as well as to root plants from the pond floor. A month or two after they have served their purpose of securing a mate, antlers are shed.

Bull moose in velvet.

In moose, antlers may act as large hearing aids. Moose with antlers have far more sensitive hearing than moose without, and a study of antlers using an artificial ear confirmed that the antler behaves like a parabolic reflector.

American bullfrog.

American Bullfrogs Calling

American bullfrogs are the largest frogs in North America, weighing up to a pound and measuring up to 18 inches in length. Male bullfrogs are very aggressive and will defend their territories against other male bullfrogs, both physically and with a special call.

The bullfrog's advertising call is used to attract a mate and begins to be heard in late spring or early summer. Described as a rumbling *jug-o-rum* reminiscent of lowing cattle, this call has a low frequency and can be heard over half a mile away.

JUNE 29

Northern Flying Squirrels Giving Birth

Northern flying squirrels are considered crucial to the health of their environment because of their

feeding activities, which disperse tree seeds and the spores of symbiotic fungi throughout the forest. These gliding rodents typically breed once a year, sometime between mid-March and early June. Five to seven weeks later, two to four young are born. At birth, their ears and eyes are closed and their toes are fused. Within a month or so, they are covered with hair, they can hear and

Northern flying squirrel.

see, and their teeth are erupting. Before they are two months old, they venture out of the nest and are eating solid food. They are most active a few hours after sunset and a few hours before sunrise.

Fishflies Emerging

Adult stoneflies, fishflies, and dobsonflies all have aquatic larval stages, and the long-winged adults resemble each other quite closely. Mouthparts and antennae are helpful in distinguishing the three. Fishflies have small mandibles and feathery antennae, whereas dobsonflies and stoneflies have threadlike antennae and larger mandibles—especially noticeable on dobsonflies, whose pincers are huge. Fishflies and

Fishfly.

dobsonflies are in the same family, Corydalidae. Fishflies spend several years in the water as larvae before emerging as adults. These terrestrial adults live for up to a week.

Ring-Necked Snakes Laying Eggs

Adult ring-necked snakes measure 1 to 2 feet from the tip of the nose to the tip of the tail. The ring-neck is named for the yellow/orange ring

Ring-necked snake.

around its neck, but it also has brilliant orange scales on its belly. This snake is fairly common throughout the Northeast but is not often seen due to its nocturnal habits and secretive nature. The three or four eggs that female ring-necked snakes lay in late June and July are deposited in or under rotting logs and stones. Several females have been known to use the same nest. The eggs hatch in late August or September, and the young snakes feed on the same prey as adults—small toads, frogs, salamanders, earthworms, smaller snakes, insects, and grubs.

JUNE 30

Wild Turkeys Nesting

Wild turkey nest.

Female wild turkeys have a very primitive nest, consisting of a shallow depression scratched in the ground. The nest site varies—it can be in dead leaves in the woods at the base of tree, under a brush pile, or in an open hay field. During incubation the hen may add dead leaves and other nearby vegetation to the nest. The number of eggs ranges from four to seventeen, but turkeys engage in dumping—laying eggs in other turkeys' nests—so it is possible to find up to twenty-six eggs in a nest where this has occurred. Like those of all ground-nesting birds, turkey eggs are subject to heavy predation.

Jumping Spiders Preying on Insects

Jumping spiders are aptly named, as they can spring more than fifty times their own body length to land on unsuspecting prey. They hunt actively rather than by catching prey in a web, and they have excellent vision, with four big eyes in front of and four smaller eyes on the top of the head.

Jumping spider with prey.

Jumping spiders have three-dimensional vision, which allows them to estimate the range, direction, and nature of potential prey—essential skills for a predator that catches prey by pouncing on it.

European Skippers Flying in Fields

Roughly one-third of all butterfly species in North America belong to the skipper family. Most species possess stout bodies, wide heads, and relatively small wings. An early morning walk from mid-May to mid-July through almost any field, especially one with lots of timothy grass, which the larvae eat, will result in a flurry of tiny orange-brown wings rising into the air. It is likely that the butterflies stirred up are European skippers that have been roosting at night on grass stalks. During the day they feed on the nectar of a variety of low-growing field flowers, including orange hawkweed, thistles, ox-eye daisy, fleabane, white clover, red clover, selfheal, Deptford pink, common milkweed, swamp milkweed, dogbane, and vetches. These abundant butterflies were accidentally introduced into Ontario, Canada, in 1910, and their range has been expanding ever since.

European skipper on red clover.

Female common green darner.

JULY

Biosurveillance and Solitary Wasps

The wasps we are most familiar with—paper wasps, yellow jackets, hornets—are all social wasps. They live in a colony with one queen, a few male drones, and hundreds or thousands of female workers, depending on the species. They work as a unit for the benefit of all. Ninety percent of wasp species, however, live solitary lives, with every female not only laying eggs, but also constructing the cells in which they are laid and provisioning them with food.

The cells of one species of solitary wasp, *Cerceris fumipennis*, are built, like those of many other solitary wasps, in hard-packed sandy soil, such as you find on baseball diamonds and unpaved parking lots. Their nests consist of a central tunnel, with five to twenty-four cells excavated off of it. The entrance to the nest has a mound of sand, similar to an ant mound, but the hole is larger, roughly the diameter of a pencil. You rarely see just one nest. Although they live independently, these solitary wasps nest close to one another to take advantage of the special features of the habitat. Where you find one, you usually find several or even hundreds.

C. fumipennis, like many solitary wasps, doesn't actively care for its young. Rather, the female stashes a supply of food in each underground cell and then lays an egg in it and, when the egg hatches, the larva has plenty to eat until it pupates and emerges as an adult. It is the nature of the food this wasp collects for its offspring that has inadvertently made it an efficient agent of biosurveillance, the use of another species to survey for a pest species. *C. fumipennis* generally preys only on members of the Buprestid beetle family to feed her larvae, and the emerald ash borer (EAB) beetle is a member of this family. A clever biologist recognized the potential of this wasp to help detect the presence of the emerald ash borer in any area where *C. fumipennis* lives. Biologists and citizen scientist volunteers now track the prey that *C. fumipennis* collects and brings back to its nest, keeping an eye out for metallic green beetles. There are several emerald ash borer look-alikes, so some green specimens are sent to a specialist for identification.

The effects of the emerald ash borer, a native of Asia, were first observed in North America in 2002. The beetle has since been found in much of

C. fumipennis rarely, if ever, stings a handler.

C. fumipennis has three creamy yellow patches between her eyes and a single yellow band around her abdomen.

Quite often *C. fumipennis* drops its prey just as it approaches its nest. Scientists have not determined why they do this.

When it has located prey, *C. fumipennis* alights on it, climbs over it, inserts her stinger into the base of the beetle's leg and injects a paralytic venom. She then carries the paralyzed beetle back to her nest, positioned beneath her body. Keeping it alive delays decomposition and provides larvae with relatively fresh food.

the eastern half of the United States. It was found in Massachusetts in 2012 and in Connecticut, through biosurveillance, and New Hampshire in 2013. Although the adult emerald ash borer does some damage to ash foliage, it is the larvae feeding on the inner bark of all species of ash that do the most damage, as they destroy the trees' ability to transport water and nutrients. Tens of millions of ash trees have been killed, with much

more devastation predicted. One-third to one-half of an infested tree's branches may die in one year, and most of the canopy will be dead within two years of when the first symptoms appear.

Once the presence of the emerald ash borer has been determined, quarantines are put into place to prevent the transportation of trees, logs, and firewood outside of the quarantine areas. Thus, the early detection of this beetle in any given area is key to stopping its spread. *C. fumipennis* has proven to be more efficient at finding emerald ash borers than any man-made device.

North American River Otters

North American river otters, the most aquatic members of the weasel family other than sea otters, are found across America wherever there is enough water to support them. Although they are active year-round and during both day and night, it is much more common to come across signs of a river otter than to see one.

During the winter, the river otter's overland journeys are well documented by their tracks and the belly grooves left when they slide in the snow. In summer, signs of an otter's presence are more subtle and often are related to its scent marking. Each hind foot has scent glands, which are constantly leaving information for other animals. Like the rest of the members of the weasel family, the otter has highly developed anal glands and is an active and frequent scent marker. It is these markings that one looks for at this time of year.

When river otters are on the move, they often travel along well-worn paths or along streams, typically covering about 2 to 3 miles of shoreline a day. They tend to mark their route frequently, often on elevated surfaces or where they enter and exit the water. The most common and obvious markings are latrines and scrapes and rolls.

River otters defecate on land and their spraint, or scat, can assume many forms, from tubular to patty-shaped. Regardless of its initial shape, it disintegrates rapidly into a pile of fish

The amount of the lighter colored spraint (otter scat) on the darkened ground in this latrine indicate that several otters frequent this spot.

North American river otters can swim up to 7½ miles per hour, dive to 65 feet, and spend up to four minutes underwater on a single breath.

All four feet of an otter are webbed, greatly enhancing their swimming ability.

Otters roll on the ground frequently, distributing oil from their glands throughout their coat in order to keep it water repellent. This action also helps dry their fur, fluffing it up and renewing its ability to insulate the otter.

scales, bones, and perhaps some broken bits of crayfish shells. Several otters may use the same spot on land over and over, creating a "latrine." Otter latrines are often found on a narrow strip of land between two bodies of water. Another frequently-used site is a narrow peninsula that juts out into a river, lake, or pond. Latrines may also be near holes in a bank where otters come out of the water.

Otter latrines are also referred to as "brown outs," as acid tends to build up and kill the vegetation. Various other otter signs may be present at these spots, including circular scent mounds of earth and vegetation that the otters make and then mark with their gland secretions and/or spraint or urine. Otters also tend to roll in these areas (which are also called "rolls," "haulouts," "landings," and "scrapes"), spreading oil throughout their coat in order to make it waterproof while simultaneously scent marking.

Like beavers, otters are well equipped for an aquatic existence. They are excellent swimmers and they can dive to a depth of 60 feet, thanks to their webbed feet, streamlined body, and powerful tail. Valves in their ears and nose automatically close when they go under water, and sensitive whiskers compensate for their compromised vision, hearing, and ability to smell when submerged. Their thick, water-repellent fur equips them for the coldest water.

North American river otter.

Orb-Weaving Spiders

Roughly half of all spiders ambush or use snares and traps to capture prey. The other 50 percent spin webs to catch their meals. There are many different types of webs, among them sheet, funnel, cob, and mesh, and several families of spiders create flat webs with sticky spirals that are called orb webs.

One of the most common of these families, and the most diverse, is the Aranaidae. While not every spider in this family spins an orb web, the vast majority do. You are probably familiar with at least one or two species in this family—E. B. White's Charlotte is a member of this family, as is the black and yellow argiope, or garden spider, that is quite common. While they come in all sizes, colors, and shapes, members of this family all have eight eyes in two rows, eight legs, and three-clawed feet. Identification to species often requires microscopic inspection of genitalia; you are doing well if you can determine the genus of an orb-weaving spider.

When starting a web, the spider releases a sticky thread that is blown away with the wind. If the breeze carries the silken line to a spot where it sticks, the first bridge is formed. The spider tightens it and then cautiously crosses along the thin line with its serrated claws, a smooth hook

Otter scat, or spraint, usually consists of fish scales and bones and crayfish parts.

Look for river otters in saltwater marshes, open beaches, and tidal pools, as well as in streams, lakes, and ponds. A very adaptable animal, the otter is at home in both lowlands and mountains and is found in both warm and cold climates. Its adaptability does not, however, extend to tolerating polluted water. It is generally true that if you find otters, you've also found relatively clean water.

Otters are usually on the move, traveling a circuit through their home range, visiting ponds and streams along the way. They are rarely in one place for an extended time—just long enough to leave sign and perhaps catch one or two, usually non-game, fish.

and a series of barbed hairs on the end of each leg, reinforcing the single strand with one or more lines of silk. It then walks across this thread and releases another, looser, thread below it, which it attaches at both ends. The spider climbs

Black and yellow argiope.

Black and yellow argiope wrapping prey.

Orb-weaving spider wrapping prey.

Orb web.

to the middle of the loose thread and lowers itself down on a vertical strand of silk to form a Y shape. This is the basis of the frame. After adding more frame lines, the spider spins radius threads from the center of the web out to the frame. The spider then lays down more non-stick silk to form a spiral, which extends from the center of the web to the outer edge. Next the spider spirals inward, this time laying out sticky thread, as it retraces and eats the non-sticky spiral. The end result is a web with non-sticky radius threads on which the spider can walk, and a sticky spiral for catching insects.

One feature of the webs of some orb-weavers is a thick, white band of silk through the center of the web, called a stabilimentum. The web of the black and yellow argiope usually includes such a band. There are many theories as to its function, including a lure for prey, a marker to warn birds away from the web, and camouflage for the spider when it sits in the center of the web. Recent research suggests that the stabilimentum decreases the visibility of the silk to insects, resulting in more food for the spider.

Most orb-weaver webs are vertical, and the spider usually hangs toward the center of the web with its head down, monitoring the radius threads for vibrations. Occasionally spiders are hidden off to the side of the web, but with at least one foot in contact with it. Orb-weaving spiders typically have poor eyesight, as they do not depend upon their eyes for spotting prey. Their feet, not their eyes, receive information through web vibrations, which tell them whether a leaf, a dangerous insect such as a wasp, or an edible insect has been caught. If it is suitable for eating, the spider rushes out and paralyzes the prey by biting it and then rapidly wraps it in silk. Sometimes the prey is eaten (actually drunk, after enzymes have liquefied the innards) then and there, but often the spider will return to feed at a later time.

Most orb-weavers are nocturnal, but some are active during the day. Many build a new web every twenty-four hours. Generally, in the evening the spider consumes its old web, rests for an hour or so, and then spins a new web in the same general location. For this reason, unlike the webs of other spiders, early in the morning orb webs are pristine, without holes or the dried-up exoskeletons of insects that have been caught and devoured by the web spinner.

Orb-weaving barn spider repairing web.

JULY 1

Red-Shouldered Hawk Nestlings Soon Fledging

After spending six or seven weeks in the nest, young red-shouldered hawks are ready to fledge. They are not completely independent, however, as their parents will continue to feed them for the next several weeks, and the fledglings will roost at or near their nest at night.

Red-shouldered hawk nestling.

Common Milkweed Flowering

The pollen of common milkweed flowers is contained in two sacs resembling saddlebags, with a black appendage joining them. The two halves snap onto an insect's leg when it lands on the flower. The pollen

Common milkweed flower.

sacs (pollinia) hang inside a slit between each of the five cups, or hoods, that contain nectar. An insect lands on the slippery flower, attracted by the scent, and one or more of its six legs may slip down between the hoods into a slit, where the pollinia automatically attach to the leg. The insect withdraws the leg upon leaving, and the attached pollinia may fall off onto the next milkweed flower, pollinating it.

In about 5 percent of milkweed flowers, insects become trapped because they cannot extract their legs from the slit. It is sad but not uncommon to see a helpless insect dangling from a common milkweed flower.

Honey bee with pollinia.

Fly caught in stigmatic slit.

Beavers Grooming

Beavers are constantly grooming and oiling their fur to keep it clean and waterproof. A grooming beaver usually sits upright with its tail between its back legs and protruding in front of it, exposing the cloaca—the single opening for all the functions of the scent, reproductive, and excretory organs. The beaver gets oil from

Beaver grooming.

Two beavers engaged in mutual grooming.

Ovenbird nest.

Ovenbird.

its oil glands with its front feet, and then rubs it all over its body, using all four feet. The second toe of each hind foot

Split nail on beaver's hind foot.

has a split nail which the beaver uses to distribute the waterproofing oil and to comb debris out of its fur. Without a coating of oil, a beaver's fur would soon become saturated, and the animal would not be able to tolerate cold water. Occasionally, beavers groom each other with their teeth, a practice referred to as mutual grooming.

JULY 2

Ovenbirds Nesting

Ovenbirds, the warblers responsible for the *teacher-teacher-teacher-TEACHER* song that reverberates throughout deciduous woods at this time of year, are known not only for their song, but also for their unique ground nests. It is the resemblance of their nest to an old-fashioned domed oven that is the source of the ovenbird's common name.

The materials the female uses to build the nest—leaves, bits of plant stems, bark, pine needles, rootlets, moss, and a lining of deer and/or horse hair—and its roofed structure make it all but invisible to most passersby. More often than not, the female ovenbird chooses a site with an especially thick leaf layer on which to build her 6½-inch-diameter nest. She enters and exits through a side entrance that is roughly 2 inches wide and just over 1½ inches high. The female incubates and broods the young, and both parents feed them, approaching and leaving the nest on foot along several partially concealed routes. As the nestlings grow, the top of the nest is frequently pushed back, exposing the nest cup. No attempt is made by either parent to reconstruct the roof before the young fledge in a week to ten days.

Robber Flies Hunting

Robber flies often perch on the leaves or stems of low plants, waiting until suitable prey flies by and then attacking it in the air. They have long, strong, spiny legs for grabbing prey and piercing-sucking mouthparts for consuming it. Robber flies mostly seek out bees, beetles,

Robber fly.

Energy-Saving Tactics of Avian Nest Builders

Birds locate, collect, and recycle bark, twigs, leaves, lichens, hair, rootlets, snake skins, and countless other natural materials when constructing a nest, all of which takes a considerable amount of time and energy. If an ample supply of material is located in one spot, both time and energy spent by a nest-building bird are greatly reduced. Nests that have served their purpose and then have been abandoned, as most songbird nests are, are a goldmine for a bird that nests later in the season.

Pictured is a cedar waxwing which has discovered an empty Baltimore oriole nest. The oriole nestlings have fledged, never to return, and it is highly unlikely that the parents will ever use the nest again. Waxwings, which are relatively late nesters, take advantage of the female oriole's labor-intensive material collecting. Fiber by fiber the waxwings pull this nest apart, recycling the material they remove by constructing their nest with it. The need for hours of searching for suitable nesting material is eliminated. There is no such thing as waste in the natural world.

Robber fly with prey.

bugs, dragonflies, grasshoppers, flies, leafhoppers, and wasps. Once they capture an insect, they pierce it with their short, strong proboscis, or mouthpart, and inject their saliva into it. The saliva of robber flies contains enzymes that paralyze the insect and digest its insides, which the robber fly then drinks.

American Toads Breathing with Skin and Lungs

Like all amphibians, American toads breathe through their skin as well as with their lungs. Unlike mammals, amphibians do not make regular and rhythmic breathing movements but bring air into their lungs sporadically as the need arises. When a toad is inactive, the skin usually absorbs enough oxygen to meet its needs. During and after activity, a toad often supplements its supply of oxygen by actively breathing air into its lungs.

Cedar waxing recycling Baltimore oriole nest material.

American toad.

Air enters the toad's mouth through its nostrils, and by raising the floor of its mouth, the toad forces air into its lungs.

JULY 3

Sac Spider Shelter Serves as Nursery and Coffin

It is not unusual to come across a rolled-up leaf, for the larvae of many moths create shelters in this fashion, using silk as their thread. Less common, and more intricate, are the leaf "tents" of sac spiders. With great attention paid to the most minute details, a female sac spider bends a leaf (often a monocot, with parallel veins, as in photo) in two places and seals the perfectly aligned edges with silk. She then spins a lining for this tent and lays her eggs inside. There she spends the rest of her life, guarding the eggs. She will die before the eggs hatch and her body will provide her offspring with their first meal.

Folded leaf containing sac spider and egg sac.

Dark-Eyed Juncos Incubating Second Brood Eggs

In the Northeast, dark-eyed juncos typically have two broods in a summer. Four or five eggs are usually laid, one per day. The eggs lie on a soft lining made from the hair of a white-tailed deer.

Dark-eyed junco nest.

Unlike most songbirds, dark-eyed juncos build their nests in a wide variety of sites, from on the ground to 8 feet high in trees. Often they are well hidden by surrounding grass in a small cavity on a sloping bank, under a protruding rock, or among tree roots. They have been found under fallen tree trunks, on supports underneath houses on stilts, in barns or lofts between hay bales, in vines on the sides of buildings, on window ledges and light fixtures, and in hanging flower pots.

Spongillaflies Pupating

In its larval stage, a spongillafly is under water, where it feeds exclusively on fresh water sponges that live in the still waters of large rivers, lakes, and wetlands. The beautiful silken net, as well as the small cocoon inside the net, are spun by a spongillafly larva after it crawls out of the water and chooses a spot on land on which to pupate. This entire structure is less than ¼ inch in diameter.

Spongillafly cocoon.

213

JULY 4

Barred Owls Fledging

The fledging of flightless barred owl chicks takes place four or five weeks after they hatch. Typically, they perch on the rim of the nest cavity before climbing to a nearby branch. If there are no branches close by, the chicks will drop to the ground and climb a nearby tree, where they perch and are fed by their parents. Juvenile barred owls

Barred owl about to fledge.

Barred owl beating wings from nest hole.

Barred owl fledgling.

begin short flights at approximately ten weeks of age, attaining longer flights by twelve weeks. They are now learning to hunt but continue to be fed by their parents until late summer or early fall.

JULY 5

Common Loon Eggs Hatching

Peeps can be heard from inside a common loon egg before the chick starts to crack it open with its temporary "egg tooth." The chicks are covered with sooty black down, which is often dry within an hour of hatching. Both chicks and parents are usually in the water and off the nest for good within twenty-four hours of when the eggs hatch.

Adult common loon on nest with two recently hatched chicks.

Shinleaf Flowering

Shinleaf, also known as pyrola, is an evergreen perennial that is most noticeable at this time of year, when it is flowering. The common name, shinleaf, refers to its medicinal properties. It contains a drug closely related to aspirin. The leaves reportedly have analgesic properties and were used as a poultice on bruised shins and other sores and wounds.

Shinleaf.

Shinleaf's fragrant blossom is distinctive in that the style of the female pistil is proportionally far longer than in most flowers and extends beyond the waxy, white petals. There are several species of pyrola in the Northeast, varying in leaf shape and flower color and arrangement. All of them belong to the family Ericaceae, which includes blueberries and cranberries. Look for this 4- to 12-inch plant in shady, damp woods, and when you find one, peer under the petals to see the orange-tipped stamens.

Damselflies Laying Eggs

These two damselflies have mated, and the female is laying eggs. The male is still clasping the back of her head to prevent another male from removing his sperm from the female and replacing them with his own. Damselflies lay their eggs both in the water and on plants. The pictured female (bottom damselfly) is in the act of using her ovipositor, the thin black structure at the tip of the abdomen, to puncture a cattail leaf and insert her tiny egg into the plant tissue. The holes in the leaf blade above

Male (top) and egg-laying female (bottom) damselflies.

the hole she's currently making are the sites of previously laid eggs. Thousands of these holes may be drilled during her brief life.

JULY 6

Life and Death in a Milkweed Patch

Like all insect-pollinated flowers, common milkweed must attract insects in order to get its pollen dispersed. Some flowers have bright flashy petals that serve this purpose, while others,

Checkered beetle.

Mating small milkweed bugs.

Virginia ctenucha moth

Jumping spider and fly.

White admiral butterfly.

Grasshopper.

like milkweed, have a sweet fragrance and even sweeter nectar. Not only is the nectar very rich in sugar, being up to 3 percent sucrose, but the supply is renewed over the life of an individual flower. Honey bees, bumble bees, wasps, beetles, flies, moths, and a variety of butterflies move from flower to flower, drinking nectar from the blossoms and inadvertently pollinating them. These insects, as well as monarchs, are greatly affected by the current precarious health of the common milkweed population.

Monarchs are closely associated with milkweed because the larvae only eat plants in the milkweed family, but many other insects inhabit a milkweed patch.

JULY 7

Paper Wasps Exchanging Food

Like all adult wasps, bees, and ants, paper wasps are limited to liquid diets: the passageway between their head and abdomen, where food is digested, is so narrow that pieces of food will not fit through it. Wasp larvae (the white, grub-like organisms in the upper third of the pictured wasp nest cells) are able to eat a wider range of food, due to mouthparts and their body structure. Adult paper wasps capture caterpillars and other insects and feed them to their larvae. The larvae then digest their food and produce saliva rich in nutrients. The adult wasps proceed to scrape their abdomens across the nest, producing a vibration that signals to the larvae to release some of their carbohydrate-rich saliva, which the adults then drink. Cells covered with white paper nest material contain wasp pupae.

Watershield Flowering

Watershield is a perennial aquatic plant whose bright green, shield-shaped leaves float on the surface of shallow water in lakes and ponds. Its small purple flowers bloom from June through September, but each individual flower lasts only two days. On the first day, the female flower parts, the stigma, style, and ovary, are mature. After receding into the water overnight, the flower reemerges with mature male flower parts, the stamens, filaments, and anthers. The anthers burst open, releasing pollen to the wind, and the flower is then withdrawn below the water, where the fruit develops.

The horizontal rhizomes, or stems, of watershield, as well as the undersides of the leaves and developing buds, are covered with a thick, jellylike slime. Botanists theorize that it may deter snails from grazing on these plants. Watershield secretes a number of chemicals that kill or inhibit growth of a wide range of bacteria, algae, and other plants.

Paper wasps and nest.

Watershield.

Common Wood Nymphs Mating

Every step taken in a shrubby meadow this time of year is likely to flush a common wood nymph, which, after some erratic flying, settles back down beneath the grasses, hidden from view. These butterflies are in a group called "satyrs" which consists of mainly medium-sized, brown butterflies. They belong to the Nymphalidae family, also known as brush-footed butterflies, or four-footed butterflies. The reason for these common family names is clear if you examine a common wood nymph or other butterflies in this family, including monarchs, painted ladies, fritillaries, or checkerspots. They look as though they only have four legs. Being insects, however, they have six. The front two legs are folded up in front of the head and are extremely small and bristly. These

Common wood nymphs mating.

reduced legs are present in all brush-footed butterflies and are not used for walking or clinging. Rather, the bristles on these legs are sensory organs, used for smelling and tasting. The butterfly's proboscis is coiled up between this front pair of legs.

JULY 8

Black-Throated Blue Warblers Are Incubating a Second Brood

Male and female black-throated blue warblers differ strikingly in appearance, so much so that the two sexes were considered separate species by

Female black-throated blue warbler on nest.

early naturalists, including John J. Audubon. The male is a brilliant blue, but the female is dull gray and is practically invisible when she is on a nest.

Black-throated blue warblers have from one to three broods in a summer, the first usually in June; a second, if there is one, in July; and, rarely, a third in late July or early August. The nest is usually within 3 feet of the ground and is built of thin strips of birch bark and bits of rotten wood bound together by cobwebs and saliva. Fibers, rootlets, needles, and mammalian hair line the nest. Female black-throated blue warblers are known for sitting tightly on their nests until a potential threat is very close, at which point they drop to the ground and, similar to killdeer, engage in a distraction display, feigning injury to a wing.

Helleborine Flowering

Helleborine is a common woodland plant which is easily overlooked due to its inconspicuous, small, greenish purple flowers. However, this modest member of the orchid family brings pollination to a new level. Apparently, its structure is not

Helleborine.

217

attractive to insects, so helleborine has evolved a different strategy to get its flowers pollinated. It produces nectar that contains a number of compounds with narcotic properties, including a minute amount of oxycodone, a drug which has an effect similar to morphine on organisms that ingest it. Botanists suggest that when insects drink the oxycodone-laced nectar, they become sluggish, which prolongs the amount of time they spend at the flower and increases the chances that the flower will be pollinated.

JULY 9

Avian Air Sacs

Birds have an efficient breathing system which makes use of their lungs but also uses seven to twelve air sacs within the bird's body. Common loons use their air sacs for more than respiration, however. By changing the amount of air in the sacs, loons can vary the depth at which they float. When a deep breath fills the sacs with air, the loon is more buoyant. During dives, loons compress their feathers, which forces air out from between them, and decrease the amount of air in their sacs by exhaling. The ability to deflate their air sacs also allows loons to quietly sink to the water's surface so that it's easier for the chicks to climb aboard.

Common loon and chicks.

Twisted stalk fruit.

Twisted stalk flowers.

Twisted Stalk Fruiting

Twisted stalk's common name is apt, for not only are the stems bent slightly where the leaves clasp them, but there is a 90-degree bend in the flower stalk after it emerges from the base of the leaves, causing the flowers to hang down from the stem. Earlier in the summer, delicate, greenish white, bell-like flowers hung on their twisted stalks. Those that were fertilized are currently developing into bright yellow to red fruit which make the plant obvious even in the moist, shady woods where it grows. Although considered edible by some, the berries of twisted stalk—also called watermelon berry—can be mistaken for poisonous ones, so eating the fruits is not recommended.

Clymene Moths Active

The clymene moth is notable for the striking upside-down cross pattern on its forewings. Because of this design, some people refer to it as the crusader moth. A member of the tiger moth family (as is the woolly bear/ Isabella tiger moth), the clymene moth can be seen flying day or night. Typically,

Clymene moth.

they inhabit deciduous forests and fields adjacent to them, where the black, bristly larvae feed on a wide variety of plants, including willows, oaks, and members of the aster family. In contrast to its white forewings, the clymene moth's hind wings are bright yellow. Its long proboscis allows it to reach deep inside the nectar-bearing hoods of common milkweed.

JULY 10

Bobolinks Fledging and Preparing to Migrate

Between their "backward tuxedo" appearance and their long, bubbly song, male bobolinks are hard to miss. The female's plumage is more subtle,

Male bobolink.

Female bobolink.

with lots of browns, so that she blends in well when on her ground nest in hayfields, meadows, or pastures. The most notable accomplishment of this member of the blackbird family is its annual migration between breeding grounds in the northern U.S. and southern Canada and its wintering grounds in northern Argentina, Paraguay, Brazil, and Bolivia: a round-trip of approximately 12,500 miles, the longest of any North American songbird.

Grassland birds such as bobolinks, eastern meadowlarks, upland sandpipers, and a number of sparrows have been in decline for decades. Many of

these birds build their nests on the ground, raise young, and forage for insects and grains in summer months. If you own or manage a hayfield that hosts bobolinks or any other grassland species, consider delaying mowing until after mid-July so that these birds have time to fledge their young and get them ready for their strenuous migratory flights.

Beaked Hazelnut Fruit Developing

Beaked hazelnut is named for its fruit: a nut with a tubular husk that resembles a beak. The surface of the husk is covered with fine filaments that can irritate the skin. Rich in protein and fat, the hard-shelled nuts are a preferred food of ruffed grouse, hairy woodpeckers, blue jays, white-tailed deer, and squirrels. Beaked hazelnut, a shrub in the birch family, is quite versatile. Native Americans ate the nuts roasted and raw, pounded them for use in cakes, and used their oil as a cure for coughs and colds, as well as an astringent. The wood of beaked hazelnut was carved into arrows, hooks, and spoons, and the long, flexible shoots were twisted into rope. A European species of hazelnut is used for commercial production of hazelnuts (also called filberts) in the United States.

Exterior and interior of beaked hazelnut fruit.

219

Bald-faced hornet.

Hoverfly Mimics Bald-Faced Hornet

Adult hoverflies are in the Syrphidae family and are often referred to as syrphid or flower flies. They feed on pollen and nectar and are often seen hovering at or crawling on flowers. Some species of hoverflies have black and yellow bands on their abdomens and mimic stinging wasps, including yellow jackets and bald-faced hornets. Predators such as birds, ambush bugs, and spiders might hesitate before eating an insect that can sting, and hoverflies take advantage of this. This is an excellent example of Batesian mimicry—when a harmless species evolves to imitate a harmful species that has the some of the same predators.

Hoverfly.

JULY 11

Common Loon Chicks Hitching a Ride

The first few days in the lives of common loon chicks can be quite precarious. As soon as their down dries, the chicks are quick to leave their nest and enter the water, where they are not as vulnerable to land predators. However, there are dangers everywhere. Parents keep a close eye on their buoyant young to protect them from predators both above and below the water, such as bald eagles and largemouth bass. For the first two weeks or so, parents protect their young by ferrying them around on their backs much of the time.

Adult loon and chicks.

Dog Vomit Slime Mold

Slime molds are organisms that reproduce using spores. Technically, they are not plants, animals, bacteria, or fungi. One look at dog vomit slime mold and you know how it got its common name. The pictured stage in dog vomit slime mold's life cycle is called a plasmodium, which is essentially one giant cell with thousands of nuclei. The plasmodium moves by slowly flowing over the ground, gradually engulfing and consuming fungi and bacteria that are present on decaying plant matter. This particular slime mold can often be found on mulch that is regularly watered. Dog vomit slime mold is harmless to

Dog vomit slime mold plasmodium.

people, pets, and plants. In fact, it is edible. In some parts of Mexico people scramble it like eggs and call it *caca de luna*.

Spittlebug Nymphs Feeding

A spittlebug is the nymphal stage of an adult froghopper. During its immature stage, it is referred to as a spittlebug, because while feeding on the sap of a plant, it pumps excess water out of its abdomen which, combined with body secretions, turns into sticky bubbles which fall down over the upside-down-feeding nymph. The spittle provides thermal protection and prevents the nymph from drying out while it feeds in the sun. While seemingly drawing attention to the nymph's presence, the spittle has a very bitter taste that would-be predators find unappealing. As an adult, the froghopper earns its name from its ability to jump one hundred times its length.

Spittlebug nymph.

Indian Pipe Flowering

The very first Indian pipes are starting to poke up through the forest floor. Lacking chlorophyll, this parasitic plant cannot make its own food; instead it gets energy from underground fungi that, in turn, derive their energy from the trees they are connected to. You can tell whether or not an Indian pipe flower has been pollinated by its position. Prior to being pollinated, the flower head bends toward the ground; after pollination and fertilization, its stem straightens, and the flower faces skyward.

Unfertilized Indian pipe.

Abbott's Sphinx Moth Larvae Feeding

Abbott's sphinx moth larvae feed on grape and Virginia creeper leaves during the night. During the day they tend to rest on the woody vines of the plants they are eating, and because they are well camouflaged, they remain hidden from most humans' eyes.

Fertilized Indian pipe.

Older larvae have two color forms, one resembling unripe green grapes; the other is brown and looks much like a branch. In their last stage, or instar, both forms have a rear eyespot which looks like a human eye, right down to the white reflection spot, which scares off potential predators. If the caterpillar is pinched or prodded, it squeaks and tries to bite the attacker.

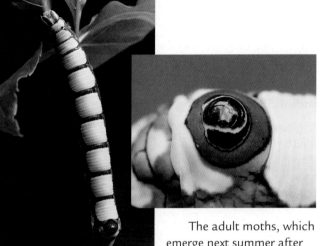

Green form of Abbott's sphinx moth larva.

The adult moths, which emerge next summer after pupating all winter, also defend themselves with both color and behavior. They are brown with yellow bands on their underwings, which makes them look something like a bumble bee, and when they fly, they create a buzzing noise.

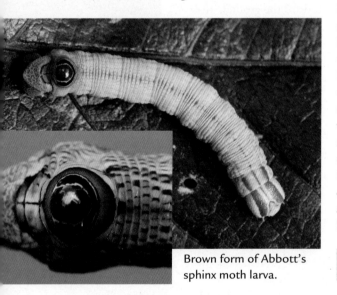

Brown form of Abbott's sphinx moth larva.

Young Striped Skunks Defending Themselves

There is a reason why coyotes, foxes, and most other predators (one exception is the great horned owl) keep their distance from striped skunks. Whether newborn or several years old,

skunks are capable of using their musk-filled anal glands to send an accurately aimed spray toward anything that threatens them. They are reluctant to spray, however, as they only have a few teaspoons—about half an ounce—of musk in their glands, enough for five or six sprays, and once that's gone, they are defenseless for about ten days, while it builds up again. Hence, plenty of warning is given in the form of stomping front feet, erect hair, raised tail, and chattering before a skunk contracts the muscles surrounding its anal glands and shoots a pungent, yellowish spray as far as 10 feet away.

The organic compounds that make the smell of skunk spray so offensive are called thiols, or mercaptans. Thiols are also found in garlic and onions and form parts of the keratin in hair. If you or your dog happen to be at the wrong end of a skunk's partially everted anus, the best way to neutralize the smell is to use a mix of one quart of 3 percent hydrogen peroxide, ¼ cup of baking soda, and one teaspoon of liquid dish soap.

Young striped skunk.

JULY 13

Juvenile Bald Eagles Fledging

For several weeks before leaving their nest, young bald eagles flap their wings, occasionally lifting themselves off the nest several inches in the air. Eventually they succeed in making short flights to nearby branches and then back to their nest. The young eagles are strengthening their wing

Juvenile bald eagle.

Juvenile bald eagle.

Organ Pipe Mud Dauber Wasps Making Cells and Laying Eggs

There are two groups of wasps: social wasps, such as hornets, yellow jackets, and paper wasps; and solitary wasps, species that live solitary lives and typically hunt prey for their larvae, while the adults consume nectar.

Female organ pipe mud dauber wasp applying ball of mud.

Female organ pipe mud dauber wasp at nest with spider.

Spiders and organ pipe mud dauber wasp egg inside mud cell.

Organ pipe mud dauber wasp larva and spiders inside mud cell.

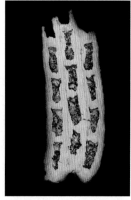
Back side of organ pipe mud dauber wasp nest.

muscles, practicing landing, and beginning to master flight.

When they are between eight and fourteen weeks old, bald eagles leave the nest. Many fledge successfully, but up to half of the nest departures are unsuccessful, with the young ending up on the ground, where they may stay for weeks before flight is mastered. During this time, the parents usually continue to feed their young, but the juvenile eagles are far more vulnerable to predators. If the flightless, grounded juveniles are approached or threatened, or if they simply want to move from one spot to another, they walk or run. As they gain flight and foraging skills, fledglings may continue to use their nest as a feeding platform for several weeks after leaving it.

JULY

223

Mud daubers are solitary wasps. The female organ pipe mud dauber builds cells out of mud in which she puts prey, usually spiders, that she has stung and paralyzed, but not killed. She then lays an egg on top of the comatose spiders and seals the cell. After the egg hatches, the larval wasp consumes the still-fresh spiders, pupates, emerges as an adult wasp, and chews its way out of the cell.

JULY 14

Milkweed Longhorn Beetles Mating

In this pictured pair of mating milkweed longhorn beetles, the female milkweed longhorn beetle feasts on a milkweed flower bud while the male milkweed longhorn beetle satisfies his appetite as well.

Born last summer from eggs laid on the stem of a milkweed plant, longhorn milkweed beetle larvae feed on the plant's stems and roots. When fall approaches, they burrow into the ground for the winter and, after pupating in the spring, they emerge as adult beetles. Look for holes in the tips of milkweed leaves, left when these herbivorous insects feed. When they are disturbed, milkweed longhorn beetles are capable of making a squeaking noise by rubbing rough spots on their thorax, or middle section, together.

Mating milkweed longhorn beetles.

Scarab Beetle Antennae

Beetles in the family Scarabaeidae share several characteristics, including specialized antennae. The last three to seven segments of each antenna form flat plates, or lamellae, that can be expanded like a fan (Japanese beetle) or folded together into a club (June beetle). When these plates are separated, they are being used as sensory devices to detect odors. When folded together, the antennae are used as clubs by some species of fighting male scarabs.

Japanese beetle.

June beetle.

Great blue heron nestlings.

Great Blue Heron Nestlings Growing

It won't be long before great blue heron chicks are spreading their wings!

Green Frog Tadpoles Changing Inside and Out

It's hard to believe, when you think about the structure and form of a tadpole—a plant-eating creature designed for aquatic locomotion—and that of a meat-eating terrestrial frog which is adapted for jumping on land, that they are one and the same organism. The visible changes in this transformation are dramatic enough—legs emerging, head shape changing, tail being absorbed—but the internal changes a tadpole undergoes are just as impressive. Everything from a tadpole's respiratory, urogenital, and sensory systems to its digestive system (the intestines become much shorter due to the change in diet) is undergoing significant changes.

JULY 15

Loon Parents Feeding Chicks

Both loon parents provide their very young chicks with small fish, crayfish, and the like several times an hour, especially early and late in the day. This continues, in a more limited way, long after the young loons can provide for themselves, right up until the parents migrate in the fall, prior to their young migrating. The chicks' initial buoyancy and their lack of experience prevent them from procuring their own food for the first month or so, although they soon learn how to chase fish. Often food delivery takes place when the chick is in the water, but occasionally it occurs while the chick is on the parent's back during its first week or two of life.

Green frog tadpole metamorphosing into adult.

Meal delivery.

Red fox kits.

Eastern kingbird with blueberry.

JULY 16

Red Fox Kits Growing Up

Just two months ago, red fox kits were fuzzy balls of sand-colored fur. They have grown in their third coat since birth, and finally they really are "red" foxes. Their noses have lengthened, and they are almost as big as their parents. Even though they look like grown-ups, the kits' continued playfulness gives away their age.

JULY 17

Eastern Kingbirds Feeding Nestlings

Eastern kingbirds are busy raising their nestlings this time of year. Kingbirds are members of the tyrant flycatcher (Tyrannidae) family, and, as this name suggests, they feed primarily on insects.

During cold and wet or hot and dry weather, especially as the summer progresses, an eastern kingbird's diet is supplemented with fruit, including cherries, serviceberries, blackberries, elderberries, nightshade, and blueberries. During fall migration, eastern kingbirds eat even more fruit, and it makes up most of their diet on their South American wintering grounds. Nestlings are fed both insects, such as the female widow skimmer dragonfly in the photographs, and fruit.

Eastern kingbird feeding dragonfly to nestling.

Ants Considered Milkweed Nectar Thieves

Ants are some of the most common insects to visit milkweed, and they forage day and night. However, they are considered "nectar robbers" because they rarely pollinate the milkweed

Ant drinking from one of common milkweed's five hoods that contain nectar.

flowers they drink from. In addition, because ants are constantly draining milkweed's supply of nectar, the flowers they visit are less likely to attract good pollinators, such as moths and butterflies.

JULY 18

Harvestmen Harvesting

Harvestmen—also known as daddy longlegs—and spiders are closely related and share many characteristics, but they also have significant differences. One is that harvestmen do not possess venom glands, or the digestive enzymes capable of breaking down the insides of prey into a liquid.

Some species of harvestmen are omnivores, eating both plant and animal matter, and others are scavengers. Unlike fellow arachnids (spiders, ticks, scorpions, and mites) that drink their food, harvestmen ingest small particles, breaking them down with their chelicerae, or mouthparts, which resemble miniature, toothed lobster claws. In this photograph, the harvestman is holding a deer fly with its pedipalps, appendages used to grasp food. Its chelicerae are too small to discern, but they efficiently reduced the deer fly into bits that were swallowed within ten minutes.

Least Sandpipers Migrating

Least sandpipers are the smallest shorebirds in the world, weighing only an ounce and measuring 5 to 6 inches long. Their fall migration has begun, with individuals leaving their breeding grounds in the subarctic tundra and far northern boreal forest to winter in Central and South America. Banded birds have revealed that the eastern population of least sandpipers undertakes nonstop transoceanic migrations of about 1,800 to 2,500 miles, from the Gulf of St. Lawrence and the Northeast to northeastern South America. Not much bigger than a sparrow, this common but declining shorebird can be seen refueling on mud flats throughout the Northeast during its fall migration.

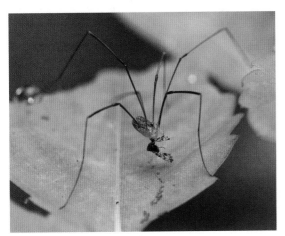

Harvestman and deer fly.

Least sandpiper.

Canada Lilies Being Pollinated

Flower shapes, colors, odors, nectar, and flowering time all serve to attract certain pollinators, be they mammals, birds, or insects. Flowers attractive to hummingbirds tend to be large, tubular-shaped, and red, orange, or sometimes yellow. These flowers usually have a large supply of dilute nectar, which they secrete during the day. Since birds do not have a strong response to scent, the flowers they visit tend to be odorless.

Canada lilies, found throughout eastern North America, have a distinct tubular shape. A ruby-throated hummingbird's long, thin beak allows it to reach nectar that is inaccessible to many other creatures. In order to do this, the hummingbird must go deep into the flower—so far that its neck and chest press up against the orange pollen-laden anthers of the Canada lily flower. When the hummingbird moves on to the next Canada lily, some of this pollen is likely to end up on the flower's stigma, and pollination will be accomplished. Note that the stigma, in the center of the lily, is longer than the anthers, thereby discouraging self-pollination.

Canada lily and ruby-throated hummingbird.

JULY 19

Great Golden Digger Wasps Digging Nests for Eggs and Provisioning Them with Food

The great golden digger wasp is a solitary, predatory wasp whose hunting and nesting techniques are programmed and rarely vary. Having overwintered underground in a nest dug by its mother, the adult female wasp emerges, often in late July or August, and begins preparations for the next generation. She digs several nests in packed, sandy soil, using her mandibles to cut the earth. Emerging backward to the surface of the ground with a lump of soil between her forelegs and head, she flips the soil with her forelegs beneath her body and scatters it to the sides with her hind legs. In this manner she excavates several cells off a central 4- to 6-inch-deep tunnel.

The wasp seeks out prey—usually a grasshopper, cicada, or cricket—and then stings and paralyzes it. If the prey is small, she flies it directly to the nest. If prey is too large, the wasp will walk it across the ground, dragging it by its antennae. She then drops the prey several inches from the nest hole. After crawling down into the nest for a brief inspection, she pulls the prey down into one of the cells while walking backward. After an insect has been placed in a cell, the wasp lays an

Great golden digger wasp—note mandibles.

Great golden digger wasp dragging grasshopper prey by antennae.

egg on the insect. The egg hatches within two or three days, and the wasp larva begins eating the insect. Because the prey is not dead, the larva's food is relatively fresh. The developing wasp overwinters in the nest and emerges the following summer to begin the process all over again.

Turkey Vultures Staying Cool

Turkey vultures have an ingenious way of staying cool on hot summer days. They defecate on their legs, and evaporation cools the birds while strong acids kill bacteria.

Caddisfly Larvae Building Shelters, Pupating, Emerging, and Mating

Caddisfly larvae are aquatic, and you find them crawling along the bottoms of ponds and streams. They are closely related to butterflies and moths, and one of the features they have in common is that the larvae have silk glands in the lower lip. They use this silk to build portable cases or attached retreats out of natural materials. Some species build elongate tubes out of pieces of plants, sand, sticks, or pebbles and live in them while they drag them along with them wherever they go. Other species attach their cases with silk to crevices or at the bottoms of stones in streams. Each species of

Turkey vulture.

caddisfly constructs an identifiable kind of case, and you can often tell the genus or even species of a caddisfly by the appearance of its case.

The larval stage of a caddisfly can last two to three months or up to two years, depending on the species. Most species spend the winter as active larvae. When it is ready to pupate, the larva attaches its case with silk to something immoveable, such as a large rock. Inside its case, the larva spins a cocoon and pupates inside. In two to three weeks, the sharp-jawed pupa cuts its way out of the cocoon and floats to the surface of the water, where it emerges as a winged adult, often using its pupal skin as a raft for support during this process. Adult caddisflies live for about thirty

Caddisfly larva in case.

days, during which time the males form mating swarms to attract females. After mating takes place, the egg laying begins.

JULY 20

White-Tailed Deer Fawns' Summer Coats

White-tailed deer fawns are close to two months old now and will retain their spots until their gray winter coat grows in this fall. The dappling of the spots enhances a fawn's ability to remain camouflaged until it is large enough and strong enough to outrun most predators. However, it doesn't hide them from biting insects. During the summer months,

White-tailed deer fawn.

229

when white-tailed deer, including fawns, have a relatively thin, cool coat of hair, they are vulnerable to biting insects such as female horse flies and deer flies. These flies make tiny slices with their bladelike mouthparts in their host's skin in order to have access to their blood.

Monarch Eggs Hatching

If you look under the tender, young leaves at the top of milkweed plants at this time of year, you may be lucky enough to find a monarch egg. They are very small—the size of a grain of rice—pale yellow, and pointed at one end. Usually only one egg is laid on any given milkweed plant.

Leaf pieces cut by leafcutter bee for cell construction.

Monarch larva emerging from and eating its egg.

After about four days, the egg hatches and a monarch larva's first meal consists of its own egg shell. It then moves on to nearby milkweed leaf hairs, and then the leaf itself. Often the first holes it chews are U-shaped, a shape thought to prevent sticky sap from flowing into the section of leaf being eaten and clogging the larva's mandibles.

Leafcutter Bees Creating Cells and Laying Eggs

Leafcutter bees are solitary and are about the size of a honey bee, but they are much darker, almost black. They construct cigar-shaped nests, often in soil, in holes in wood made by other insects, or in plant stems that contain several cells. Leafcutter bees make the cells by cutting and folding leaves of almost any deciduous tree. After gathering and storing a ball, or loaf, of pollen inside the

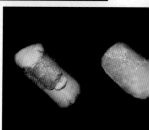

Open leafcutter bee cell showing bee egg and pollen supply for larva.

cell, the bee lays an egg and seals the cell shut. When the egg hatches, the larval bee feeds on the pollen and then spins a cocoon and pupates. The adult bee emerges from the cocoon and usually overwinters inside the cell. In the spring, the bee chews its way out of the cell. Leafcutter bees pollinate wildflowers, fruits, and vegetables and are also used as pollinators by commercial growers of blueberries, onions, carrots, and alfalfa.

JULY 21

Ichneumon Wasps Laying Eggs with Ovipositors

Ovipositors and stingers are similar in structure and position, but not necessarily in function. Female ichneumon wasps have lengthy ovipositors; some species have ovipositors that are

Ichneumon wasp on Queen Anne's lace.

Ichneumon wasp laying egg inside caterpillar.

Common loon chick gets a fishing lesson.

longer than their bodies. These wasps use their ovipositors to lay their eggs, and the larger species may use it as a stinger to defend themselves. The females of many other types of wasps have a defensive stinger that is not involved with egg laying. Males do not have ovipositors or stingers.

Some ichneumon wasps lay their eggs in the ground, but most are parasitoids. They inject their eggs into the larva, or sometimes the pupa, of another insect, usually targeting beetles, butterflies, moths, ants, bees, wasps, flies, and spiders. The larva of each species of ichneumon wasp has a taste for a particular host. The egg hatches, and the wasp larva feeds on the insides of the insect or spider until it is ready to pupate, by which time the host is usually dead. Adult ichneumon wasps drink nectar, if they feed at all.

Common Loon Chicks Learning How to Catch Prey

During the first two or three weeks, the parent loon, having caught a crayfish, small fish, or other prey, swims right up to its young and offers the chick its next meal. The chick grasps the food while it is still in its parent's beak. The parent lets go, and the chick attempts to swallow the crayfish. In the beginning, the chick often drops its meal. The parent then dives down to retrieve it and once again offers the same crayfish to the chick. This sequence of events can happen over and over until the chick finally manages to hold onto and shift the crayfish into a head-first position in order to swallow it.

By the third week or so, this beak-to-beak service begins to be replaced by a practice designed to teach the chick how to capture its own meals. The parents drop the food they've caught for their chick into the water in front of the chick, forcing the chick to dive and develop the skills necessary for survival.

Tree Swallow Nestlings Well Fed and About to Fledge

Tree swallow parents begin feeding their four to seven nestlings as soon as they hatch, and they continue doing so until their young leave the nest, and sometimes for several days afterward. The adult carries food in its bill and places it directly into the open mouth of a begging nestling. The small insects gathered by the parent may be formed into a rounded ball, or bolus, which they hold in their mouth or throat. Both parents feed the nestlings, together averaging about ten to twenty deliveries per hour. During periods of peak nestling demand, the two parents may feed as many as seven thousand insects in a single day to their chicks.

Tree swallow nestling with full beak.

Adult tree swallow feeding nestling at nest box.

Tortoise Beetle Larvae Making Fecal Shields

Instead of discarding feces, or frass, some insects use their waste matter for defensive purposes such as "fecal shields." These are coverings over the back of the larval insect that are made largely of feces and provide either physical or chemical barriers to predators. Adult tortoise beetles have a type of shield, but it is formed from expanded, hardened forewings and is not a fecal shield. The larvae of these beetles, however, do have fecal shields which serve as chemical deterrents,

Tortoise beetle larva with fecal shield.

preventing most predators from even touching them. The deterrent in the feces comes from the beetles' food source, plants in the order Solanales. Tortoise beetle larvae have what is known as a fecal fork on their last abdominal segment, which they hold over their body. The larva maneuvers its muscular, telescopic anus, or anal turret, in such a manner as to excrete feces and bits of shed exoskeleton onto the fecal fork, forming a fecal shield "umbrella."

Round-Leaved Sundew Flowering

Sundews are familiar to most people because of their carnivorous lifestyle. They trap and dissolve insects with the glandular hairs that cover their leaves. At this time of year, round-leaved sundew unfurls a single curled-up stalk with flower buds running up one side of it. The buds open in succession, one at a time, when they reach the apex of the bending flower stalk, revealing tiny white or pink flowers.

Round-leaved sundew flower.

Elfin saddle fungi.

Red grasshopper mites.

JULY 23

Elfin Saddle Fungi Fruiting

A group of fungi called ascomycetes, or sac fungi, all produce their spores in saclike structures. This group includes, among others, morels, false morels, cup fungi, and saddle fungi. Sac fungi in the genus *Helvella* are known as elfin saddles, and the caps of their fruiting bodies come in a variety of shapes, including ears and cups as well as saddles. Most are not brightly colored, but rather white, cream, buff, brown, gray, or black. *Helvella* species grow on the ground or, in a few cases, on rotting wood. Species are defined by the shape of their caps and the texture of their outer surface and stem.

Red Grasshopper Mites

If you examine a grasshopper this time of year, chances are great that you will find tiny, red mites. These red grasshopper mites, close relatives of ticks, go through four stages: egg, larva, nymph, and adult. The six-legged larvae attach to the base of a grasshopper's wings, as well as to its feet, antennae, or other parts, and proceed to suck the grasshopper's blood. Eventually, the larvae molt and become eight-legged nymphs. The nymphs, as well as the adults, are free living and feed on grasshopper eggs. Each red grasshopper mite nymph requires more than two grasshopper eggs to become an adult. An adult male red grasshopper mite requires three grasshopper eggs for reproducing, and each female needs seven to eight eggs. After breeding, a female mite deposits up to four thousand eggs. Entomologists believe that mites reduce grasshopper survival and reproduction dramatically.

Young Wood Frogs Emerging from Ponds

Wood frog tadpoles are in a race against time. They must develop into frogs before the temporary pond, or vernal pool, where they live dries up. After roughly two months, this begins to happen. Tiny juvenile wood frogs can be found in adjacent woods, where they will remain until next March or April, when they will awake from hibernation in the forest floor and head back to their natal pools to breed.

Juvenile wood frog.

JULY 24

Muskrats Busy Feeding

Muskrat feeding on aquatic vegetation.

For the most part, muskrats are herbivores. They consume with relish the leaves, stems, and rhizomes of emergent aquatic plants such as cattails, bulrushes, sedges, horsetails, water lilies, and arrowheads. To a lesser extent, they also eat fish, frogs, and invertebrates, including crayfish and clams. Muskrats are voracious eaters—captive muskrats eat 25–30 percent of their weight daily. When their numbers are very high, muskrats can cause what is referred to as an "eat-out," where they mow down everything in sight. Like beavers, muskrats can close their upper lips behind their incisors in order to cut plants underwater without taking in water and choking.

Muskrat that has been digging cattail rhizomes.

Wool Carder Bees Collecting "Wool"

Female wool carder bee.

This female wool carder bee is in the act of "carding wool." A male wool carder bee sets up his territory and protects the nectar and pollen of the flowers in it from other insects in the hopes of attracting a female bee. If he succeeds, mating takes place, after which the female scrapes hairs off plant stems and leaves within the male's territory. She often chooses hairs from woolly lamb's ears or other fuzzy plants. As she collects the hairs, she forms them into a ball and flies with this to a cavity that she lines with the hairs. The cavity consists of several cells, in each of which she deposits an egg, along with pollen collected from her mate's territory. She then seals the cell. When the egg hatches, the larval bee has a soft bed and a meal awaiting it. Look for the ball of hairs between the legs of the bee in the photograph.

Stinky Squid Fungus Fruiting

Stinky squid fungus.

The fruiting body of a stinky squid fungus, a member of the stinkhorn family, is very distinctive. Its shape is markedly different from that of most fungi, as it has three or four separate orange arms that are fused at the top. If your eyes don't detect this fungus, your nose most certainly will. The fungus emits a strong, putrid odor from the dark green, spore-bearing slimy material, the gleba, found on the inner surfaces of the arms. This smell attracts insects, primarily flies, which inadvertently disperse spores when they get them stuck on their feet. Look for round, egglike, whitish structures at the base of stinky squid fungi—these are young fruiting bodies that have yet to develop arms.

JULY 25

Male Ruby-Throated Hummingbirds Leading Life of Leisure

Equality of the sexes has yet to reach some avian species. Among them is the ruby-throated hummingbird, the only species of hummingbird that breeds in the Northeast. After courtship and mating takes place, the male has next to no contact with his mate(s). He might visit them during nest construction, but he does not lift a feather to assist in raising their offspring.

By herself, the female selects a nest site, builds a nest in six to ten days, lays two eggs, incubates the eggs for twelve to fourteen days, broods the chicks for nine days, and removes their waste for the first two days. She feeds them in the nest for twenty-two to twenty-five days and for four to seven days after they fledge. Males spend the summer feeding, preening, bathing, stretching their wings, fanning their tails, sleeping, roosting, sunbathing, and chasing all other hummingbirds away from feeders. Not a bad life for him, but an exhausting one for her.

Male ruby-throated hummingbirds.

Female Black and Yellow Mud Daubers Collecting Mud and Making Cells

There are many species of mud daubers, those wasps that build mud cells in which they lay eggs and in which their larvae develop. The female black and yellow mud dauber gathers mud at the edge of a pond or puddle, rolls it into a ball, grasps it in her mandibles, and flies with it back to her nest site, which is in a spot protected from rain, often on a man-made building. Here she constructs several cylindrical mud cells in which she places spiders that she has stung and paralyzed. After laying an egg and sealing the cell, she repeats the process several times and then covers the small group of cells with mud. The mud dauber larvae feed on the fresh spiders, pupate in the fall, overwinter inside the cells, and chew their way out to emerge as adult wasps the following spring.

Black and yellow mud dauber grasping ball of mud in mandibles.

JULY 26

Moose Submerge to Reach Aquatic Plants

Moose are herbivores that have a preference for aquatic vegetation in the summer. In addition to walking along the shore of a pond or lake to feed, they will swim out in the water for a meal. A moose will sink, much like a submarine, until

Moose eating aquatic vegetation.

only the top of its back is visible, and then it, too, completely disappears. Seconds later, the moose's head reappears, with its mouth full of green plants. After consuming these plants, the moose often submerges again and again, pulling up mouthfuls of vegetation each time it goes underwater. When moose are feeding on submerged vegetation, they are capable of reaching plants in water that is over 18 feet deep, and they can remain under water for up to fifty seconds or longer before resurfacing. It is thought that they remain submerged by paddling and perhaps by releasing air from their lungs.

Elm Coxcomb Aphids Soon to Leave Galls

An elm coxcomb gall is about 1 inch long and about ¼ inch high. It derives its common name from the similarity of its irregular edge and reddish-brown color at maturity to a rooster's comb. The galls dry, harden, and turn brown as they age. They are caused by aphids, which may be seen through a slit opening in the underside of the gall. This insect has a

Elm coxcomb aphid larva.

complex life cycle: it forms galls on elm leaves in early summer and feeds on grass roots later in the summer. It eventually returns to the elm tree and lays eggs between the scales of leaf buds, where the eggs overwinter.

Indigo Buntings Nesting

Indigo buntings have an extended period of nesting that runs from May into September, and they may have up to three broods. The female chooses the nest site and builds the nest. A nest built early in the breeding season may be constructed in eight to ten days, whereas nests built later in the summer only take about two days to construct. The female lays three or four eggs, incubates them, broods and feeds the nestlings, and disposes of the nestlings' fecal sacs. Indigo bunting nests are often parasitized by brown-headed cowbirds.

Indigo bunting nest with eggs.

Indigo bunting nestlings.

JULY 27

Juvenile Green Herons Becoming Independent

Green herons are typically solitary and secretive birds, but if you find one, you often have an extended period of time to observe it, as these herons often slowly stalk their prey or pose, still as a statue, sometimes for minutes at a time,

Juvenile green heron.

while waiting to strike at a fish, frog, or invertebrate. Three characteristics tell you if a heron is a juvenile bird: tufts of down on its head, a streaked neck instead of the adult's solid rufous neck, and yellow legs rather than the adult's orange legs. Green herons are one of very few bird species that are known to occasionally use tools such as insects, earthworms, twigs, or feathers to catch their food. They simply drop the lure in the water and wait for small fish to appear.

Cicadas Shedding Skins and Calling

As the hot, humid days of summer arrive, a high-pitched insect song issues from the tree tops. These hot-weather bugs are male cicadas—bug-eyed, 1-to 2-inch-long insects that create their courtship song not by rubbing wings or legs together, as crickets and grasshoppers do, but by contracting their abdominal muscles over and

Annual cicada.

over to create clicks that coalesce into the song we hear. We don't often see an adult cicada, for this insect lives way up in the canopy. We also don't see a cicada in its youth, for a cicada nymph spends the better part of two to seventeen years underground (depending on the species), feeding on root juices and shedding its skin periodically as it grows.

The emergence of cicadas is triggered by the temperature of the soil they are in: once the soil 8 inches below

Shed cicada skin.

the surface rises to 64 degrees, annual cicadas are on the move. They crawl up through the soil, climb up a tree or shrub, clasp the bark, and proceed to split and shed their nymphal skin for the final time. It is these skins that we occasionally find on vegetation. The winged adults mate, and the female deposits her eggs in a slit she cuts in the bark of a tree. When the eggs hatch, the larvae simply drop to the ground and begin burrowing.

JULY 28

Chicory Flowering

Chicory is in the composite family (Asteraceae), along with sunflowers, asters, and many others. The flowers, each of which lasts only a day, are clustered, so that what appears to be one flower is actually many, each of which has petals and reproductive parts. This compact grouping of flowers makes pollination very efficient for its

Bee.

Fly.

Bumble bee.

Sweat bee.

Hoverfly.

goldfinches, wild turkeys, and other seed-eating birds, as well as small mammals, will be feeding on chicory seeds come winter.

Dragonflies Mating

Dragonflies and damselflies form what is called a "mating wheel" when they mate. It is a complicated dance: first, the male curls his body around to transfer sperm from his testes, which are at the tip of his abdomen, to a receptacle just behind his legs. He then grasps the female at the back of her head with clasping appendages at the tip of his abdomen. The female then curls her abdomen forward so that its tip reaches into the male's receptacle, where she is inseminated. A male can remove a previous

visitors. Chicory is easy for bees to spot, and in a short time a bee can visit many flowers.

The structure of the flower allows chicory to self-pollinate if cross-pollination fails. For cross-pollination, chicory relies on visiting insects, which it attracts with nectar as well as pollen. It is pollinated mainly by honey bees, leafcutter bees, and ground-nesting bees, but many other insects, including flies and beetles, visit this flower. As insects gather nectar and pollen, their bodies become dusted with white pollen grains. Thanks to these diligent pollen collectors and transporters, American

Mating male (top) and female (bottom) dragonflies. (Small red spherical objects on female's abdomen are mites.)

male's sperm from a female, so after mating a male may continue to grasp the female and accompany her while she lays her eggs in order to prevent his sperm from being removed.

JULY 29

Cecropia Moth Caterpillars Molting

The caterpillar, or larval, stage of a butterfly or moth is the only stage in which the insect has chewing mouthparts. Thus, it is the stage during which a great deal of eating takes place. As the caterpillar eats, it grows larger and periodically molts its skin, or exoskeleton, revealing a new, larger skin underneath the old one.

Most moth and butterfly caterpillars molt their skin four or five times. The stage in between each molt is referred to as an instar. The caterpillar that hatches from the egg is the first instar; the second instar appears after the first molt, and so on. Cecropia caterpillars molt four times and thus have five instars, each a little larger than the last. After the fourth molt, the fifth instar spins a cocoon.

The caterpillar in this photograph has just molted its skin and partially eaten it. The remaining skin is attached to the plant just above the caterpillar's head and bears colored tubercles.

Wild Turkey Nests Raided

The eggs and young of ground-nesting birds are extremely vulnerable, and wild turkeys are no exception. Eggs survive long enough to hatch in only about half of all wild turkey nests. Predators, including raccoons, opossums, skunks, crows, and ravens, are typically opportunistic feeders and look for the easiest and most accessible meals available. Because of this, ground-nesting birds like wild turkeys often have larger clutches of eggs than tree-nesting birds.

Cecropia caterpillar and molted skin.

Raided wild turkey nest.

JULY

239

Caterpillars

Some insects, including butterflies and moths, go through four life stages of development. This process is referred to as holometabolism, or complete metamorphosis. An egg is laid, the egg hatches into a caterpillar (larva), which then forms a pupa, which transforms into an adult butterfly or moth. Every stage is vital to the development of the insect, but the larval, or caterpillar, stage has some unique features.

First Meal

As soon as most caterpillars hatch, they begin to eat the shell of their egg. The outer layer, or chorion, is rich in protein and provides the new caterpillar with a nutritious start.

Eating Mouthparts

The larval stage is the only stage in which a moth or butterfly has eating mouthparts and can chew. It does little else but eat, in order to have the energy to complete its metamorphosis, and, if it is a female, to develop eggs. Some caterpillars consume twenty-seven thousand times their body weight: a tobacco hornworm can increase its weight ten thousand-fold in less than twenty days.

Molting

Caterpillars can increase their body mass by as much as one thousand times or more. As a caterpillar eats, it grows, and because its outer skin, or exoskeleton, is not very flexible, the caterpillar must molt several times to accommodate its larger size. It sheds the old skin and replaces it with a new, larger skin beneath the old skin. After the molt, while the new skin is still soft, the caterpillar swallows a lot of air, which expands its body. Then, when the cuticle hardens, it lets the air out and has room for growth. The stage between molts is called an instar, and most caterpillars have five or six instars before they pupate. The number of instars a caterpillar goes through is dependent upon the species and environmental conditions.

Muscles

Some caterpillars have as many as 4,000 muscles in their body. By comparison, humans have about 640 muscles. A caterpillar's head capsule alone consists of 248 individual muscles.

Eyes

Caterpillars have six pairs of simple eyes, or ocelli. Ocelli, also called stemmata, are small, simple eyes that can detect changes in light intensity, but cannot form an image. Ocelli are composed of pigments and light-sensitive cells called photoreceptors. They are usually located in two clusters of six eyes on the sides of a caterpillar's head.

Legs

Caterpillars have six true legs, just as adult butterflies and moths do. Most caterpillars have eight pairs of legs—three pairs of so-called true legs in the front and five pairs of prolegs behind them. Prolegs help the caterpillar hold onto plant surfaces and allow it to climb. The three pairs of legs on a caterpillar's thorax are true legs, which remain through adulthood. The prolegs are left behind with the caterpillar's skin in the final molt.

Silk Production

Using modified salivary glands along the sides of their mouth, caterpillars can produce silk. Some caterpillars, like gypsy moths, disperse by "ballooning" from the treetops on a silken thread. Others, such as eastern tent caterpillars or fall webworms, construct silk tents in which they live communally. Bagworms use silk to join leaves together into a shelter. Caterpillars also use silk when they pupate, either to suspend a chrysalis or to construct a cocoon.

American lady caterpillars.

Defenses

Caterpillars are prey for all kinds of predators, and they have evolved some very effective defenses using their appearance as well as their behavior and biochemistry. Some caterpillars, such as the early instars of black swallowtails, look like bird droppings. Certain inchworms in the family Geometridae mimic twigs and bear markings that resemble leaf scars or bark. Other caterpillars, like monarchs, use the opposite strategy, making themselves visible with bright colors to advertise their toxicity. A few caterpillars, such as Abbot's sphinx moth and tiger swallowtail, display large eyespots to deter birds from eating them. The hairiness of some caterpillars discourages many predators. Behavioral adaptations, such as playing dead (thanatosis), are also employed by caterpillars, which which drop to the ground if approached, as are chemicals, such as the swallowtail butterfly's smelly gland (osmeterium) that projects from its head if it is threatened, and the saddleback moth caterpillar's poisonous spines.

Life Span

Most caterpillars live from about two weeks to a month. For many moths and butterflies, this is the longest part of their life cycle.

Hog sphinx moth caterpillar.

Pale tiger moth caterpillar.

Eight-spotted forester caterpillar.

Splendid dagger moth caterpillar.

241

Haircap Moss Spores Maturing

The green spores of haircap mosses are maturing now and can be seen by removing the "hairy cap" and prying off the lid of the spore capsule, as in the sporophyte seen below.

Capsule cover (seta).

Capsule and lid (calyptra).

Spores.

Juvenile spring peeper next to Japanese beetle and on finger for scale.

Spring Peepers Metamorphosing

Roughly two months ago, spring peepers could be heard calling from temporary as well as permanent ponds, as males sang to attract mates. After mating took place, the females each laid hundreds of eggs, attaching them singly or in packages of two or three to vegetation. After they hatch, it takes roughly two to three months for peepers to metamorphose into tiny, four-legged, land-dwelling adult frogs.

They are now finding their way to shrubby growth and woodlands near ponds, where they are fairly well hidden in the leaf litter or on the lower leaves of shrubs. Here in the shade, they feed on small insects and spiders. Roughly ¼-inch long at this stage, these small tree frogs will only reach 1 or 1½ inches in length when fully grown.

Hummingbird Clearwing Moth

The hummingbird clearwing moth is a species of sphinx moth that is named for its habit of hovering at flowers (as hummingbirds do) while it gathers nectar with a long proboscis. In fact, these moths are often mistaken for hummingbirds or bumble bees. Transparent wings, a light brown thorax, and a dark chestnut

Hummingbird clearwing moth.

abdomen are field marks to look for. The hummingbird clearwing is a diurnal moth and is often seen visiting pink or purple flowers.

Goldenrod Spindle Gall Moth Larvae Growing

There are three galls commonly found on goldenrod: the goldenrod ball gall, a round swelling in the stem caused by a gall fly; the goldenrod bunch gall, with leaves at the top of the plant bunched into a mass and caused by a gall midge; and the goldenrod spindle gall, whose elliptical stem swelling is caused by a moth. Not only do these galls provide shelter for the insects living within them, but they are nutritious and serve

Goldenrod spindle gall.

as the insect's food supply.

The spindle galls are home to the larval stage of the goldenrod gall moth. In the late fall, the adult female moth lays an egg on a low goldenrod leaf, where it overwinters. The larva, or caterpillar, hatches out the following spring and makes its way from the now-dead leaf to a newly sprouted goldenrod, where it eats its way through a bud and into the stem. The goldenrod plant reacts to this invasion by forming an elliptical swelling around the area where the larva took up residence. The larva feeds and develops all summer. Prior to pupating, it chews a tunnel all the way through the gall and spins a silk cover over the exit hole. The larva then returns to the cavity in the middle of the gall and pupates. In the fall, the adult moth crawls down the tunnel, bursts through the thin layer of silk, mates, and lays eggs.

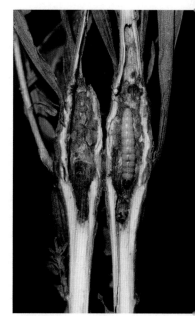

Goldenrod gall moth larva inside spindle gall.

Goldenrod spindle gall exit hole.

AUGUST

Praying Mantis

Mantises have been a source of intrigue to humans for centuries. The Greeks considered them prophets, the French believed mantises could lead lost children home, and the Chinese used them to treat a number of illnesses. These imposing predators were introduced into North America in 1869 to control insect pests. In the Northeast, there are three species of mantises, the most common of which is the European mantis, commonly known as the praying mantis. (The largest family in the order Mantodea is Mantidae—mantids. *Mantis* is a genus in this family. Thus, all mantises are mantids, but not all mantids are mantises.)

One look at the physical attributes of a praying mantis tells you why it is such a formidable predator: angled and enlarged front legs equipped with spikes for snaring and pinning prey, a short but very flexible neck that enables it to be the only insect that can look over its shoulder, five eyes that allow it to detect prey 50 feet away, and green or brown cryptic coloration.

Exactly how does a praying mantis utilize these adaptations to procure its prey? Usually it waits motionless and well camouflaged until a meal comes within striking range, but occasionally it slowly pursues prey until it gets within reach. The actual strike is phenomenally fast—thirty- to fifty-thousandths of a second. As for the prey it secures, they are tremendously varied in types and sizes, including insects, turtles, mice, frogs, birds, and salamanders.

Mantises are known for their unusual form of copulation, referred to as "sexual cannibalism," where the female mantid consumes the male.

While it is true that in several species of mantids, the male is sometimes eaten by the female prior to, during, or after copulation, this does not occur all of the time. The notion that cannibalism is an integral part of all mantid copulation is misguided. When it occurs, this behavior may be due to the physical condition of the female (fecundity, hunger, etc.), the fact that many of the reported observations took place in a laboratory setting, or a number of other factors.

Once copulation has taken place, the female lays between fifty and three hundred eggs. They are laid in the middle of a foamy mass called an ootheca that she whips up and then shapes with

Praying mantis.

American bittern.

appendages on her abdomen. This walnut-sized mass is usually attached to a twig, often in an overgrown field. It is soft and sticky at first, but soon becomes hard and water-repellent. The eggs overwinter and hatch in the spring. Tiny praying mantises emerge from the mass through a special section of pliable overlapping scales. They look much like the adults, but lack wings. The new-born's first meal is often its own sibling.

Spectacular Stinkhorns

While the vast majority of any given fungus is under the ground and not visible, its fruiting body appears above ground. "Mushroom" is the name we commonly give to the fruiting body of many fungi. The fungus kingdom has some unusual fruiting bodies, but perhaps none are as unforgettable as those in the family Phallaceae, the stinkhorns. Although these fungi are more prevalent in the tropics, several species can be found in the Northeast and their fruiting bodies typically mature in July, August, and September. Closely related to earthstars and coral fungi, stinkhorns are saprophytes, feeding off decaying organic matter, especially wood chip mulch. Like most fungi, they do not cause disease in plants or animals, but contribute to the breakdown and recycling of dead plant and animal remains

All stinkhorns in the genus *Dictyophora*, including netted stinkhorn, possess a veiled skirt that hangs down from the top of the fungus. Flies are attracted to netted stinkhorn due to the smell of the brown spore mass, or gleba, at the top of the fungus.

Ravenel's stinkhorn is named after Henry Ravenel, a mycologist and botanist from South Carolina. This 4- to 6-inch fungus bursts out of its egg and grows to its full length within hours. The immature form, or egg, is considered a delicacy in some parts of the world. Clusters of Ravenel's stinkhorn are commonly found in late summer and early fall.

Also known as the devil's dipstick and dog stinkhorn, the elegant stinkhorn lacks a cap and has the typical phallic shape of many stinkhorns. Smelling like rotting meat, elegant stinkhorn attracts a variety of insects, predominantly flies, which come to eat the smelly slime, or gleba, and in so doing accumulate spores on their legs, ready to be redistributed to whatever decomposing matter the fly next visits. Elegant stinkhorn is considered an aphrodisiac in China.

into humus, minerals, and nutrients that can be utilized by plants.

The fruiting bodies of the different species of stinkhorns exhibit a tremendous variety of shapes and colors. Many are single stalks, some are spherical, and others latticed. Some resemble a part of the male anatomy, some have tentacles, and others look like Chinese lanterns or crab claws.

As different looking as the stinkhorn species are, they all share two traits. Stinkhorns all arise from egg-like structures located in damp, decomposing material. Some mycologists refer to them as "witch's eggs." They are attached to the ground with threadlike mycelia—the true body of the fungus. The outer layer of the egg (peridium) is white or reddish, with two or three layers. The outermost layer is extremely thin and flexible, while the innermost layer is thicker and gelatinous. You can occasionally see remnants of the peridium on the top of the stinkhorn as well as at its base, where it is referred to as a volva. When the fungus is mature, the peridium opens up and the stinkhorn grows rapidly. Within hours, some stinkhorns grow several inches, due to the uptake of water. The cells of many of these fungi are extra-large and divide rapidly, but the fruiting body can be short-lived, wilting and collapsing within twenty-four hours of appearing.

A second trait that all stinkhorns share is implied by their name—they all smell quite putrid and can be detected even by humans from quite a distance away. The reason stinkhorns produce this rotting meat–like odor has to do with reproduction. The smell comes from the slimy, sticky spore mass, or gleba, that the fungus produces, often at the tip of a stalk or other structure. It attracts flies and other insects, which, after stepping in and consuming some of the mass, become very effective spore dispersal agents. This reproductive strategy for getting spores dispersed is very similar to some of the pollination tactics flowering plants came up with millions of years later.

Stinkhorns have attracted attention for several centuries and will probably continue to do so for many more. Pliny the Elder wrote about them in *Natural History* in the first century A.D. The first booklet ever written about a specific mushroom was about stinkhorns; it was written in Holland in 1564. The stinkhorns have been connected to witchcraft, disease, and the devil—but if you can overlook their smell, a more interesting family of fungi would be hard to find.

Antlions

Antlion—the very name conjures up visions of an improbable combination of two distinctly different creatures. In fact, the name is derived from the ferocious, leonine nature of the predaceous larva that consumes ants. A member of the insect family Myrmeleontidae, the antlion matures into an adult winged insect that closely resembles dragonflies and damselflies but has longer clubbed antennae and a different pattern of veins on its wings. Only the larval stage is referred to as an antlion; its mission is to consume enough food to metamorphose into an adult. While the adult may eat small flies, pollen, and nectar, its month-long life is consumed more by reproduction than feeding.

Antlions are known for the manner in which they capture their prey. They look for a sandy spot, meandering here and there, creating trails and designs in the sand, for which they are nicknamed "doodlebugs." Once soft sand is located, the larva excavates a pit about 2 inches deep and 3 inches wide at the edges. It goes about this by first making a circular groove in the sand. The antlion larva then starts to crawl backward, using its abdomen as a plow to shovel up the soil. With one of its front legs, it places a pile of loosened particles on its flat head, and then with a jerk of its head, it throws the pile up and outside of the circle it made. This head-jerking reflex occurs over and over as the larva gradually shovels its way toward the center and deepest part of the pit.

After the last headful of sand has been flicked out of the pit, the remaining sand then settles at the critical angle of repose—the steepest angle the sand can maintain without collapsing in on itself. At this point, the slightest disturbance will cause the sand to collapse.

It takes an antlion about fifteen minutes to excavate a pit, after which it hides at the bottom, with only its pincerlike mandibles exposed, ready to grab unsuspecting prey. When an ant or other small insect or spider accidentally falls into the pit, its weight causes the sand to collapse below it, drawing the victim toward the center, where the antlion is lying in wait under a thin layer of loose sand. Climbing back up to the top of the pit is practically impossible, but if the ant attempts to do so, the antlion, with quick jerking movements of its head, showers it with sand. The sand either hits the ant, which then falls down into the pit, or causes the loose, sandy slopes of the pit to collapse, carrying the ant down with them.

Once the ant is in the grip of the antlion's mandibles, the antlion quickly injects venom and digestive fluids into it, through a groove that runs the length of each mandible. The gastric juices digest the soft parts of the ant inside its exoskeleton within a few hours. The dissolved nutrients are sucked up through the same mandibular grooves, after which the antlion hurls the indigestible ant carcass out of the pit. After a few more head tosses of the loose sand that has accumulated at the bottom of the pit, the antlion resumes his careful watch at the center of the pit.

From its manner of catching prey to its anatomy and its copulation process, there is nothing ordinary about antlions. The antlion's digestive system is unusual, to say the least. For one thing, it has no mouth opening. Secondly, while antlions excrete some fluids, their digestive tract lacks an external opening for solid waste. Feces accumulate within the antlion's body during the entire larval stage, which can be as much as three years. Some of the waste is processed into silk for making a pupal case, and the remainder is voided by the adult when it emerges from the case. Because digestion occurs outside of the larva's body, there is a minimal amount of solid waste, which, given the antlion's anatomy, is a decidedly good thing.

After about three weeks of pupating inside a hollow, ¼-inch-diameter ball of sand and silk that the larva makes, the adult emerges, usually at night, and climbs up a nearby plant or tree, where it waits for about twenty minutes while its wings expand and harden so it can fly. For the next month or so, its goal is to mate and, if it is a female, lay eggs.

Mating adults are said to be quite acrobatic, with the male attaching his abdomen to a perched female's abdomen and then hanging below her, suspended only by his genital apparatus, while copulation ensues for the next two hours.

Antlions are easier to find in their larval stage than when they're adults, as adults are nocturnal. Look for antlion sand pits—there are often several clustered together—in soft

Antlion.

Pincers exposed while antlion lies buried at bottom of pit.

Antlion pupa case with exit hole.

Antlion pits in sand.

sand beneath trees or under overhanging rocks; the larvae prefer dry places that are protected from the rain. Their hunting antics are entertaining to watch.

American toad.

AUGUST 1

Banded Longhorn Beetles Mating

Banded longhorn beetles spend their larval life boring into decaying as well as live trees, depending on the species. As adults, they leave their wooden tunnels to find food—nectar and pollen—and new trees to tunnel in and to mate. Male banded longhorn beetles have a transparent hose-like appendage called an aedeagus, which extends from the tip of their abdomen. They insert it into the female and sperm capsules pass through it from the male to the female as they breed. After breeding, the males retract their aedeagi, so they are not visible. Other insects possess aedeagi in different shapes and sizes, but those of longhorn beetles are considered to be among the most impressive.

Mating banded longhorn beetles. Note male's aedeagus.

American Toad Skin Secretions Both Lethal and Beneficial

The skin of toads contains two kinds of glands. Mucous glands secrete a transparent mucus that acts as a lubricant in water and also helps keep a toad's skin stay moist on land. Granular glands are filled with toxins that protect toads from predators, such as mammals, birds, and snakes. The two large parotid glands behind the head of an American toad exude a milky, poisonous secretion that can cause serious inflammation of the eyes or digestive tract, vomiting, and even death. A little known fact is that the potency of a toad's toxic secretions is so profound that hedgehogs use it for enhancing their own protection by taking these secretions into their mouths and then licking it on their quills. Its presence on the quills is thought to increase pain or the potential for infection in the hedgehog's predators.

Toad toxins also can be beneficial. They protect toads' skin from microorganisms and help repair wounds. Toads, especially those belonging to genus *Bufo*, such as the American toad, are considered to be an outstanding source of useful granular gland secretions. Compounds derived from toad skin secretions have been used as painkillers and to treat cardiac problems, multi-drug–resistant bacteria, HIV infection, and cancer. They do not cause warts.

Creeping Snowberry Fruiting

Creeping snowberry, a well-named perennial plant, can be found growing in acidic soil, creeping along the forest floor, sometimes forming an expansive carpet of greenery. Tucked among its tiny leaves at this time of year are snow-white berries, which developed from the plant's greenish-white flowers. Both the leaves and the

Creeping snowberry fruit.

berries smell mildly like wintergreen. Creeping snowberry belongs in the heath family, along with blueberries, huckleberries, and cranberries. Other than the bristles on the underside, the leaves of creeping snowberry could easily be mistaken for those of small cranberry. The fruit is actually edible (it also tastes a bit like winterberry), but you will have to compete with deer, hares, grouse, robins, and bears for it.

AUGUST 2

Small Purple Fringed Orchid Flowering

Small purple fringed orchid.

Small purple fringed orchid flowers from late July until late August, and occasionally into September. Its labellum, or modified petal that forms a lip, is deeply fringed and three lobed. Three small petal-like sepals form a hood over the two pollen sacs, and two small lateral petals spread out at the sides. At the back of the flower is a long, slender, curving, purplish spur. Because of its resemblance to a butterfly, it is also referred to as the butterfly orchid.

Small purple fringed orchid is primarily a wetland species found in wet meadows, fens, bogs, swamps, and the edges of streams. A very similar species, the large purple fringed orchid, has flowers about 1 inch wide, as opposed to the ½-inch-wide petals of small purple fringed orchid. Often occurring in large colonies, the flowers of small purple fringed orchid vary in color from white to deep purple. The range of this orchid is moving northward and to higher elevations due to the effect of global warming.

Snails Feeding

Most terrestrial snails are herbivorous, feeding on a wide range of vegetation. A snail's mouth is on the bottom of its head near the shorter pair of tentacles, or eyes. Snails (and all mollusks) consume their food not with mouthparts, like insects, or teeth, like mammals, but with a rasping tongue, or radula. Snails don't bite their food, but rather, rasp or scrape it. The radula is covered with rows of tiny "toothlets" that rasp particles away from vegetation and move them back toward the snail's gullet. Different species of snails have differently shaped toothlets. The radula is used by the snail not only to process food, but to clean bits of dried mucus from its shell. If you listen hard, you are supposed to be able to hear a rasping sound when the latter is occurring. If you look closely, you can just barely see the orange radula of the land snail in the photograph.

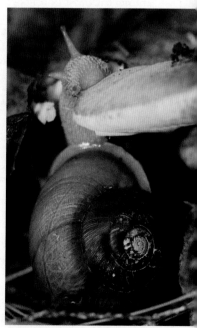
Snail with radula exposed.

Hog moth larva.

Checkered rattlesnake plantain and its flowers.

Hog Moth Larvae Feeding

The horn on this caterpillar immediately tells you that it is a species of sphinx, or hawk, moth in the family Sphingidae. It is specifically known as the Virginia creeper sphinx or hog sphinx. The latter name is due to the jowls formed when the caterpillar's head retracts. Hog sphinx larvae feed on grape, Virginia creeper, and porcelain berry (ampelopsis).There are roughly twelve species of eastern sphinx moths that feed on grape, with hog sphinx being one of the most common.

AUGUST 3

Checkered Rattlesnake Plantain Flowering

Checkered rattlesnake plantain is an evergreen plant (each leaf lives for about four years) belonging to the orchid family. It has broad, rounded leaves, like plantain, that bear a design somewhat reminiscent of snakeskin. For the latter reason, it was used by Native Americans to treat snakebites. Botanists think it must have been used on bites from non-venomous snakes, for medicinally it does not cure a venomous snakebite.

This species is quite similar to downy rattlesnake plantain, the most common species of rattlesnake plantain in the Northeast, but its leaves lack the broad central stripe down their middle, and its flowers are not as tightly clustered. At this time of year, checkered rattlesnake plantain's tall flower stalk is bedecked with tiny, delicate, white orchids, each the size of a baby fingernail, which are well worth examining through a hand lens.

Hermit Thrushes Still Singing

The woods have become relatively quiet in the last few weeks. A majority of songbirds have mated and nested, so there is no need to reinforce pair bonding with song. However, some late nesters, including the hermit thrush, are still on eggs and the males are still singing.

The hermit thrush makes up for its rather drab appearance with its melodious, haunting,

Hermit thrush.

Bumble Bees vs. European Honey Bees

Bumble Bees

- Thick and fuzzy body with yellow, orange, and/or black coloring
- Live in poorly drained soils
- Colonies of five to fifty bees
- Only female workers can sting, and they can do so multiple times.
- Drones leave colony and never return.
- Queen lives one year.
- Do not produce a honey surplus; all but queens die in fall and queens hibernate, so no need.
- Queens are the only bee to overwinter; they hibernate at the nesting site.
- Feed on nectar
- Native to U.S.

Bumble bee.

European Honey Bees

- Small, fuzzy, tan body with sleek abdomen
- Live in hollow trees and man-made hive bodies
- Colonies of thirty thousand to sixty thousand bees
- Only female workers can sting. They can only sting once, and then they die.
- Few drones leave nest to mate with queen, rest don't leave hive until end of the summer.
- Queen lives four to five years.
- Produce honey surplus; bees overwinter and need food.
- Large portion of the colony remains active and overwinters with the queen.
- Feed on nectar
- Introduced by Europeans

European honey bee.

flutelike song. It is similar to that of its close relative, the wood thrush, but it starts with a single, clear note, which the wood thrush's song lacks. The hermit thrush doesn't sing during migration or on its wintering grounds, so we are now privileged to hear its last lyrical songs of the year.

Robber Fly Mimics Bumble Bee

Some species of robber flies enhance their chances of securing prey—and of not being preyed upon—by mimicking other, more threatening insects, such as bumble bees. The short, straight antennae and the presence of only two wings, instead of four, tell you the pictured insect is in the order Diptera, or true flies. The pointed, stout proboscis, bearded face, fleshy feet, and long, tapering abdomen narrow it down to a species of robber fly. Robber flies in the genus *Laphria* resemble bumble bees—they are typically quite hairy, with black bodies and yellow stripes on their abdomens. Like other species of robber flies, they hunt by perching and snagging prey, such as other robber flies, bees, wasps, or beetles, in the air. They often return to their perch, inject the prey with enzymes that dissolve its innards, and then have a long drink.

Robber fly with Japanese beetle prey.

AUGUST 4

White-Tailed Deer Fawns Still Nursing

A doe giving birth for the first time usually has one fawn. The following year, and until she is quite old, twins are the norm. Triplets are fairly common, quadruplets are known, and there are at least two records of quintuplets. Fawns nurse for eight to ten weeks before being weaned and it's apparent from this doe's udder that her young are still nursing.

White-tailed deer doe.

Milk Snake Eggs Hatching

Most snakes—about 70 percent—lay eggs, while others give birth to live young. Milk snakes belong to the former group. Sometime between April and late June, female milk snakes lay three to twenty eggs in rotting logs or moist, warm, leaf litter—locations that offer protection from predators and cold weather. Eggs laid in June are now hatching, and 7- to 10-inch milk snakes are each using their egg tooth to slice through their egg and enter the world. Newly hatched milk snakes

Newly hatched milk snake.

have especially vibrant colors, including oranges, reds, purples, and yellows, which become duller as they age. Milk snakes are most active during the day but are rarely seen due to their secretive nature.

Net-Winged Beetles

The colorful net-winged beetle is common in fields and roadsides where wildflowers grow, as it feeds on nectar. Like other beetles, it has two pairs of wings, with the outer pair (elytra) protecting the inner, more delicate pair that are used for flight. Net-winged beetles fly with their elytra spread and slowly flutter, mothlike, through the air.

Unlike most other beetles, net-winged beetles' elytra are not hard, but soft and leathery. A close look reveals ridges running down the length of them. These ridges rupture easily and contain noxious fluids. When the beetles are

Net-winged beetle with elytra spread.

attacked, the ridges burst and fluids are released. Because of this effective defense, net-winged beetles have many mimics, including other beetles and moths.

AUGUST 5

Pinesap Flowering

Pinesap, like its close relative, Indian pipe, is a flowering plant that lacks chlorophyll and, therefore, cannot make its own food. Often found under pine trees, pinesap ranges in color from yellow to pink, red, orange, brown, or some combination of these. Often, pinesap that flowers in the summer is yellowish, while pink is more dominant in the fall. Pinesap gets its nutrients from other plants' roots, but not directly. Mycorrhizal fungi are the middlemen, connecting the roots of pinesap with those of the fungi's host plant, allowing nutrients to be passed along from the host plant to the pinesap. Being the beneficiary of a fungi-dependent relationship makes pinesap a mycoheterotroph.

Pink pinesap.

White pinesap.

White-Marked Tussock Moth Caterpillars Feeding

The tussock moths (subfamily Arctiinae) get their name from the tufts of hairs, or setae, that are present on the larva's upper side. The larvae of most species, including the white-marked tussock moth, have yellow, orange, or red defensive glands on their abdomen. They are boldly marked, warning predators of their chemical

White-marked tussock moth caterpillar.

protection. Their host plants are varied and numerous—the white-marked tussock moth caterpillar feeds on more than 140 different plants. The larvae of gypsy moths, also in this family, have more than 500 host plants. As you might guess, the woolly bear, or Isabella, tiger moth is also in this family. The setae of some species of tussock moths are urticating—they can cause irritation when they break off and lodge in skin. In some species, these structures are hollow, and toxic fluid is injected through them. Most adult moths are brown or gray, do not eat, and live only long enough to mate.

Goldenrod Crucial to Honey Bee Survival

Because goldenrod is a prolific producer of nectar and pollen late in the year, it is one of the most important flowering plants for honey bees.

Viceroy vs. Monarch Butterfly in the Northeast

Viceroy and monarch butterflies are very similar looking. By observing their markings, size, and flight pattern, it is possible to distinguish the two species.

Viceroy	Monarch
Black line across the hind-wing near the outer edge	No black line
Smaller than monarch	Larger than viceroy
Flight is fast and erratic	Floating flight, with "flap, flap, glide" pattern
Overwinters as larva	Migrates to Mexico in fall
Emerges by late May	Arrives mid- to late June

Viceroy.

Monarch.

Blooming in the late summer and fall, this bright yellow–flowered composite provides nectar for the bees to build up stores of its strong- tasting, dark-amber honey for winter. Goldenrod also provides pollen to help stimulate the colony to produce brood late into the fall. The pollen adds considerable amounts of protein, fats, and minerals to the diet of the late-season bees.

Honey bee collectin goldenrod pollen.

Great Blue Herons Cooling Off

Birds have a number of ways of keeping cool. They do not sweat, nor do they technically pant, but birds do have several behavioral adaptations that can reduce their temperature. Often, while exposed to the relentless heat of the sun, great blue heron nestlings resort to what is called gular fluttering. They open their mouths and flutter their neck muscles, promoting heat loss—an avian version of panting. An easier behavior to observe is the position adult great blue herons will often assume on a hot day. They droop their wings while standing, which allows air to circulate across their body and sweep away the excess heat.

Great blue heron nestlings cooling off.

Adult great blue heron cooling off.

American Caesar's Mushrooms Fruiting

American Caesar's mushroom is a member of the *Amanita* genus, although it differs from most *Amanita* species in at least two ways. It is one of the few edible *Amanitas*—most species are

255

American Caesar's mushroom rupturing through its protective white membrane, or universal veil, as it matures.

American Caesar's mushroom maturing.

Mature American Caesar's mushroom.

Young Isabella tiger moth larva.

poisonous, so consumption is discouraged unless an expert identifies the fungus. Secondly, unlike some *Amanita* species, American Caesar's mushroom does not usually have any warts or patches on its cap.

The common name of this mushroom traces back to the fact that its close relative, Caesar's mushroom, which grows in Italy, was a favorite of the emperors of the Roman Empire, the Caesars. Both of these species of *Amanita* are mycorrhizal, forming a symbiotic beneficial relationship with the roots of certain trees. Look for American Caesar's mushrooms fruiting under pine and oak.

Second Brood of Isabella Tiger Moth Eggs Hatching

Typically, we start seeing woolly bear caterpillars in October, when they are searching for sheltered spots in which to spend the winter as larvae. However, there are woolly bears right under our noses throughout the summer. In the Northeast there are two broods of Isabella tiger moths, whose larval stage is the woolly bear. The caterpillars that hibernated last winter emerged from hibernation this past spring, pupated, transformed into adult Isabella tiger moths, and proceeded to mate and lay eggs. Those eggs hatched, the larvae grew, pupated, emerged as moths, and mated. The eggs of this second

brood have recently hatched. These woolly bear caterpillars, which are currently no bigger than the length of your baby fingernail, will be eating dandelions, grasses, nettle, and meadowsweet nonstop for the next two months in order to survive the coming winter.

AUGUST 7

Broad-Necked Root Borers Laying Eggs

This egg-laden, 2-inch-long female broad-necked root borer is searching for just the right spot to lay her eggs. She repeatedly extends and retracts her ovipositor, the pointed, egg-laying structure at tip of her abdomen, in an attempt to find soil soft enough

Female broad-necked root borer.

for her to insert a clump of eggs into the ground. When the eggs hatch, the larvae tunnel downward to feed on the roots of a variety of shrubs and trees. They overwinter as larvae, and in the spring they pupate and the adults emerge above ground. This life cycle is thought to take three years.

Turtlehead Flowering

Turtlehead, a member of the plantain family, can be found growing along stream banks and wetlands throughout eastern North America. Its long, arching upper lip, or hood, overlaps the lower lip like a turtle's beak, giving turtlehead its common name. The male parts of the flower mature before the female parts, and when pollen is being produced, the lips are very hard to pry open. Pollinators are primarily bumble bees, which are one of the few insects that have the strength to open the flower. When the female pistil matures, the lips relax a bit, so entry is easier, but access to the nectar at the base of the flower is restricted by a sterile stamen to long-tongued

insects. Thus, it is specifically long-tongued bumble bees that are able to both enter the flower and reach the nectar. If you look on the sides of the flowers, occasionally you will find where impatient bumble bees have chewed through to the nectar, avoiding the struggles involved in entering the flower in the traditional manner.

Wild Turkeys Flying

Wild turkeys spend most of their time on the ground, and often it is assumed they cannot fly. While the wild turkey has the second heaviest maximum weight of any North American bird, second only to the trumpeter swan, it is able to lift itself off the ground and take flight. In fact, a wild turkey is very well adapted for explosive, short-distance flight, perfect for escaping predators.

When startled or threatened, the bird squats slightly just before taking off and then explodes upward with help from its powerful legs. Turkey wings are highly cupped, which enables quick takeoff, and the breast muscles that power a turkey's wings are built for rapid but brief exertions. Wild turkeys can fly up to 55 miles per hour for short distances; a wild turkey rarely flies more

Turtlehead being pollinated by bumble bee.

Wild turkey taking off.

than about 100 yards, which is usually enough to bring it to safety. What is even more surprising is that, under duress, wild turkeys can swim. They tuck their wings in close, spread their tails, and kick.

AUGUST 8

Spiders Using Spinnerets

Most spiders have six spinnerets—organs located on their abdomens from which silk is extruded. The individual spinnerets move independently yet in a highly coordinated manner. Each spinneret is dotted with many tiny spigots, through which various types and thicknesses of silk are extruded. The strong muscles that move the spinnerets also force liquid silk through the narrow spigots. This pressure, as well as external pulling by the spider, rearranges the liquid silk molecules into a solid but flexible thread. Although spider web silk is only about one-millionth of an inch thick, weight for weight, it is stronger than steel (but not as strong as Kevlar).

Orb spider using spinnerets to spin silk web.

Tricolored Bumble Bees Foraging

At this time of year, tricolored bumble bees, also called orange-belted bumble bees, can often be found foraging on the flowers of goldenrod. These colorful bees collect both protein-rich pollen and nectar. Pollen collection requires more finesse, as the pollen must be scraped off the bee's hairs and packed into pollen baskets, a special section of the outer surface of each hind leg that is flattened and surrounded by spikey hairs. As a result, it is usually older bees that forage for pollen. The bees collecting nectar, which is swallowed and transported in an internal crop, do not fill their crop to capacity, because if they did, the added weight would cause them to expend more energy flying than the amount of energy the nectar would provide for the colony. The foraging range of a bumble bee is anywhere from 3½ to 12 miles.

Tricolored bumble bee.

AUGUST 9

Hemlock Varnish Shelf Fungi Fruiting

As its name implies, hemlock varnish shelf has a shiny, varnished appearance and is usually found growing on hemlock, spruce, and pine. This shelf fungus belongs to a group of fungi called polypores. Unlike many fungi that produce their spores on gills, polypores produce spores inside hundreds of tubes found on the underside of its fruiting body. Each tube ends with a pore, or opening, through which its brown spores are released.

Hemlock varnish shelf.

Baltimore checkerspot butterfly.

A similar species of mushroom that grows on hardwood trees has been used extensively in China and Japan for general good health, as well as for a variety of ailments, including insomnia, arthritis, hepatitis, and cancer. Hemlock varnish shelf is believed to have medicinal properties as well.

Baltimore Checkerspot Eggs Hatching

At this time of year, just as turtlehead is flowering, a butterfly known as the Baltimore checkerspot is mating and laying bright red eggs, often on the underside of turtlehead's leaves. English plantain, false foxglove, and hairy beardtongue are also host plants for Baltimore checkerspots. When the eggs hatch, the tiny larvae proceed to spin a web that envelopes them and the leaves of the plant that they are eating. They eat profusely, enlarging the web as they expand the area to include uneaten leaves. Eventually, as fall approaches, they will spin a pre-hibernation web, where they remain until late fall, when they migrate down into the leaf litter. While most butterflies and moths overwinter as eggs or pupae, the Baltimore checkerspot remains in its larval stage until spring, when it forms a chrysalis, pupates, and emerges as an adult butterfly.

Juvenile Eastern Newts Emerging from Ponds and Transforming into Red Efts

Eastern newts, 4-inch-long, red-spotted, olive-green salamanders that inhabit most ponds, breed throughout the summer and well into the fall. Their eggs hatch in three to five weeks, and the aquatic larvae are equipped with gills with which they breathe for the next three months or so. By late summer and early autumn, the 1½-inch-long larvae start to reabsorb their gills and develop lungs and a rough-textured skin. These tiny, young salamanders begin to emerge from ponds and

Baltimore checkerspot larvae on turtlehead.

A juvenile eastern newt that just emerged from a pond and has yet to attain the red color of a red eft, shown on a finger for scale. The darker patch on its neck just before its foreleg is where gills were once located.

Red eft coming out of water.

Ambush bugs are usually brightly colored yellow, red, or orange and have thickened front legs that are used to capture prey up to ten times their own size. They live up to their name, patiently lying in wait, motionless, often in goldenrod flowers where they are very well camouflaged, for unsuspecting prey. The ambush bug, upon sighting prey, suddenly seizes the prey in its powerful forelegs and quickly dispatches it with a stab from its sharp beak. It then injects digestive enzymes into its prey, after which it drinks the liquid innards.

This time of year you often see the smaller males riding around on the backs of the larger females while the females continue to feed. This behavior is part of the courtship ritual—males actively guard their mate prior to and following copulation. Mating takes place side by side, after

live on land, gradually turning reddish orange. We refer to the juvenile eastern newt salamander during its terrestrial stage as a red eft. After spending two to five years on land, red efts return to the water, regain their green coloration, and live the rest of their life as aquatic eastern newts.

Adult eastern newt.

Ambush bugs courting.

AUGUST 10

Ambush Bugs Courting

Ambush bugs are true bugs, in the order Hemiptera. Although insects are often referred to as "bugs," technically, only insects in this order are considered and referred to as bugs by entomologists. All true bugs have piercing and sucking mouthparts and wings that are membranous and clear at the tips, but hardened at the base.

which the female deposits her eggs among the leaves or on the stems of flowering plants. Look for ambush bugs in yellow and white flowers, especially goldenrod.

Sundews Capturing Food

Sundews are carnivorous plants often found in acidic bogs, fens, and cedar swamps. They have numerous small leaves arranged in a circular, or rosette, pattern that are covered with reddish,

Round-leaved sundew with damselfly.

Grass of Parnassus.

glandular hairs, or tentacles, that exude a sticky secretion at their tips. Insects, attracted to the glistening sticky droplets that resemble dew, land on a leaf and become stuck. The movement of the struggling insect triggers cell growth in the glandular hairs, and they begin folding over the insect within sixty seconds. An anesthetic is released by the plant's hairs, causing the insect to become motionless. Digestive enzymes are then secreted that liquefy the insect's internal organs so that they can be absorbed by the plant's hairs. Although insect prey is not vital to sundews, the nitrogen the plants receive from the insects enables them to thrive in environments where nitrogen is in short supply. The pictured damselfly has been captured by a round-leaved sundew's glandular hairs, which have rendered it motionless and have started to grow and fold over the tip of the damselfly's abdomen and its wings.

AUGUST 11

Grass of Parnassus Flowering

Grass of Parnassus, also known as bog-star, was named for Mount Parnassus in central Greece. It is not a type of grass; rather, it belongs to the family Celastraceae and can be found growing in fens, bogs, and swamps. The striking green lines on its petals guide flies, bees, and other pollinating insects to the flower's supply of nectar.

The structure of grass of Parnassus's flower is far from typical. In between its five functioning stamens and five petals there is a whorl of five sterile stamens, each of which is three pronged. The spherical tip of each prong mimics a glistening droplet of nectar. These stamens do not actually produce any nectar—they are there purely to attract pollinators. The actual nectar is located near the base of these false, or sterile, stamens.

Only one of the five true stamens in the flower is active at any one time, and it produces pollen on average once every twenty-four hours. In order to promote cross-pollination, the stigma opens up to receive pollen only when all the stamens are empty.

Young Beavers Out and About

Most beavers are born between May and early July, weighing 1 pound and measuring a foot long. They are fully furred and their eyes and ears are open. Kits can swim within hours after birth but are too buoyant to submerge themselves until they are several days old. They first leave the lodge at about two weeks of age, but rarely are seen until they are about one month old, at which point they weigh about 7 or 8 pounds.

Adult beaver with this year's young.

Tachinid fly.

Lobster mushroom.

Initially their fur isn't water-repellent. By three to four weeks of age, the young beavers' anal glands, used in greasing their fur, are functional, and they can waterproof their fur.

Tachinid Flies Seeking Hosts

There is a family of flies, Tachinidae, in which every one of the ten thousand species is a parasitoid, a type of parasite that kills its host. A majority of tachinid flies develop inside another insect. Usually the host insect is a caterpillar, sawfly larva, beetle, or true bug. Because tachinid flies are parasitoids of plant-eating insects, they are considered beneficial in controlling insect pests of plants. A typical tachinid fly is similar to a housefly in size and shape, and, like the pictured species, *Hystricia abrupta*, has an abdomen studded with long, stout bristles.

AUGUST 12

Lobster Mushrooms Fruiting

Lobster mushrooms are so named because they look a bit like lobsters—reddish orange "shells" on the outside with white inside. A lobster mushroom is actually two fungi in one: the parasitic fungus, *Hypomyces lactifluorum* (the red-orange outer crust), and the mushroom being parasitized (the white inner flesh, usually a *Russula* or *Lactarius* mushroom). *Hypomyces lactifluorum* has only been known to parasitize non-poisonous mushrooms, and it has been eaten for hundreds of years without any known problems. Still, it is possible that it could parasitize a poisonous mushroom, rendering it harmful to the forager.

Darners Laying Eggs

Females of different species of dragonfly have different techniques for laying their eggs. Most skimmers, cruisers, and clubtails dip the tip of their abdomen to the surface of the water while hovering or flying and release their eggs. Most darners, such as the black-tipped darner pictured, have a sharp-edged ovipositor with

Cattail leaf with egg slits.

Black-tipped darner.

which they slit a stem or leaf of a plant on or near the water. They then push their egg into the plant tissue exposed by the slit. Because they are stationary during this process, female darners are vulnerable to predation by fish and frogs at this time. A close look at the bottom third of cattail leaves this time of year will tell you whether or not darners are in the vicinity, because the slits they make are very apparent.

Cedar Waxwings Nesting

While the nestlings of most species of birds have fledged, some cedar waxwings are still incubating eggs. Known for being one of the last species to nest, a waxwing on a nest in mid-August is probably on its second brood. Both the male and female collect nesting material, but it is the female who does most of the nest construction and all of the incubation of the eggs. The cup nest is constructed with a wide variety of material, including twigs, grasses, cattail down, moss, string, horsehair, dead leaves, cloth, shredded bark, roots, leaves, ferns, stalks of herbs, and flower blossoms. Occasionally, the exterior of the nest is decorated with ornate plant material, such as the lichen *Usnea*, or old man's beard, in the photograph.

Cedar waxwing eggs.

Cedar waxwing on nest.

AUGUST 13

Slime Mold on the Move

Coral slime mold.

Slime molds look like a fungus and reproduce with spores like fungi do, but are no longer classified as fungi. Slime molds are made up of individual organisms that form a mass called plasmodium. They can be bright orange, red, yellow, brown, black, blue, or white. These large masses act like giant amoebas, creeping slowly along and engulfing food particles—decaying vegetation, bacteria, fungi, and even other slime molds—along the way. If a slime mold is cut up into pieces, the pieces will pull themselves back together.

The most common species are in a group called plasmodial slime molds. They share one big cell wall that surrounds thousands of nuclei. Proteins called microfilaments act like tiny muscles that enable the mass to crawl at rates of about $\frac{1}{25}$ of an inch per hour. A slime mold mass can actually navigate and avoid obstacles. If a food source is placed nearby, it seems to sense it and head unerringly for it.

As long as conditions are good, that is, enough food and moisture and favorable pH, the mass thrives. But when food and water are scarce, the mass transforms itself into spore-bearing fruiting structures. These typically form stalks topped by spherical fruiting bodies called sporangia. The sporangia contain spores that are carried by the rain or wind to new locations. After they have been dispersed, each of these spores will germinate and release a tiny amoeba-like organism, which, if it successfully finds and fuses with another similar organism, can then begin to feed and develop into a new plasmodium.

The pictured slime mold, coral slime, is one of the more common slime molds. It is unusual in that it produces its spores externally on small stalks, not in sporangia, which gives it a fuzzy appearance when it is mature.

Larvae of Twelve-Spotted Tiger Beetle Hunting Prey

The larvae of the twelve-spotted tiger beetle live in tunnels that they dig in the sand and that can be up to a foot deep. The larvae have hooks located on the back of their abdomens to anchor them to the side of the burrow. Tiger beetle larvae are predators, like the adults, and after digging a tunnel, the larva crawls up it until just the top of its head is visible. From this position the larva watches for prey wandering by. When it sees a potential meal, such as the pictured chalk-fronted corporal dragonfly, it flips backward incredibly fast and grabs its prey, pulling it down as far as it can into its tunnel, where the larva safely feasts on its catch. In this case, the portion of the chalk-fronted corporal's abdomen that was inside the tiger beetle tunnel was completely consumed except for the outer skeleton.

Woodchucks Fattening Up

Woodchucks are eating fast and furiously as the days get shorter, in an effort to put on a layer of fat that will sustain them through hibernation. They typically spend the middle of the day sunning themselves, but early mornings and evenings will find these herbivorous rodents eating and putting on a layer of fat equaling about a third of their weight. They lose anywhere from 20 to 37 percent of their body weight during hibernation. If they don't gain enough weight now, they won't survive until green grass and other plants are available again in the spring.

Chalk-fronted corporal.

Twelve-spotted tiger beetle larva.

Woodchuck.

AUGUST 14

Ruffed Grouse Taking Dust Baths

During the summer and fall, some species of birds bathe in substances other than water. Often dust or sandy soil is the material of choice, but rotten wood and weed particles are also used. It is believed that this behavior is a means of ridding the bird of parasites like lice and mites.

After sitting down on the ground and scraping the sand all around it into a pile, the bird kicks its feet and beats its wings in the pile, getting the sand in among all of its feathers and next to its skin before standing up and shaking it all out. Usually, some feathers come out as well, and if you are familiar with different birds' feathers, it is often possible to determine what species of bird has taken a bath. The pictured dust bath is sprinkled with ruffed grouse feathers and is located in the midst of many anthills, which is typical of this species. Another favorite location where ruffed grouse often choose to bathe is the entrance of an old mammal burrow.

Eastern chipmunk grooming.

Ruffed grouse dust bath site.

Eastern Chipmunks Grooming

Chipmunks are known for their personal hygiene. Much of their grooming takes place after eating, when they've been holding a seed or nut in their front paws while eating it. They often sit up on their haunches and proceed to lick the insides of both front paws, after which they typically rub their faces, presumably to clean whiskers and facial hairs that might have gotten a bit of food on them. Chipmunks, like some birds, also take dust baths, during which they saturate their fur with sand and then shake it out, in an attempt to rid themselves of the mites and fleas that are known to plague them.

Ants Tending Spiny Witch Hazel Gall Aphids

Aphids are responsible for the formation of two different galls on witch hazel, one of which grows on branches and is covered with spiny points. It is called the spiny witch hazel gall, and it provides aphids with both food and shelter while they are developing inside the gall. Their two-year life cycle involves birches as their next host.

The pictured spiny witch hazel gall has split open enough to allow ants to discover and have

AUGUST

265

Spiny witch hazel gall.

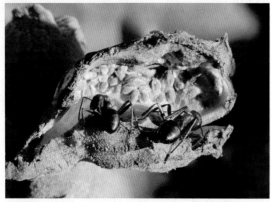

Aphids and ants inside spiny witch hazel gall.

access to the aphids. Once the ants enter the gall, they stroke the resident aphids with their antennae, stimulating the aphids into producing droplets of tasty "honeydew" from the tips of their abdomens, which the ants find irresistible. In return, the ants protect the aphids from predators.

AUGUST 15

Katydids Cleaning Antennae

Grasshoppers, crickets, katydids, and a few other close relatives belong to the order Orthoptera. Although many katydids look like grasshoppers, they are more closely related to crickets. One group of katydids is referred to as coneheads, because their heads develop into a pointed or rounded cone. The only conehead katydid commonly found in the Northeast is the sword-bearing conehead.

Katydid antennae, like those of crickets, are at least as long as their body and usually

considerably longer. Insect antennae are among the most sensitive and selective chemical-sensing organs in the animal kingdom. They detect information crucial to an insect's survival, including odors, sounds, humidity, and air speed. Antennae are capable of these feats because they are covered with sensory receptors that bind to free-floating molecules.

Experiments with cockroaches, ants, and flies confirm that insects engage in antennal grooming—removing foreign materials from the surface of their antennae with their mandibles—primarily to maintain acute olfactory reception. Pheromones, chemical signals that are vital to insect communication, are used to convey alarm, attract a mate, mark territory, and lay out trails, among other things, and clean antennae enhance these messages.

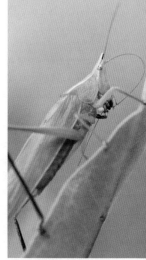

Sword-bearer conehead katydid.

Wild Cucumber Flowering

Wild cucumber, a member of the gourd/melon/cucumber family, Cucurbitaceae, is native to North America but spreads much like an invasive plant. The white to pale green flowers on this vine flower in late summer and are very fragrant. The flowers are unisexual, or monoecious, with separate male and female flowers on the same plant. The male flowers mature weeks

Wild cucumber flowers.

before the female flowers, thus discouraging self-pollination. The delicate flowers bear no resemblance to their prickly fruit, seen in four to six weeks.

Great Horned Owl Fledglings Still Being Fed by Parents

Great horned owls are one of the earliest nesting birds—you can find them on nests in January, February, and March, even in northern New England. Eggs are incubated for about a month, typically in March or April, with young usually hatching in May or June. The nestlings remain in the nest for six or seven weeks before fledging, and it is four or five more weeks before they can fly. The fledglings follow their parents around and continue to be fed and cared for by them until fall. At this time of year, when they are begging their parents for food, you can hear their distinctive calls.

Great horned owl fledglings.

AUGUST 16

Cauliflower Coral Fruiting

Ramaria botrytis could easily be mistaken for a head of cauliflower—right down to the thick branches and large, fleshy base—growing on the

Cauliflower coral.

forest floor under both conifers and hardwoods. It is also known as clustered coral, and its spores are produced on the outer surface of its branches. Cauliflower coral is considered edible, although it can affect some digestive systems negatively.

Waterfowl Molting

All North American birds replace their old, worn plumage with new feathers at least once a year, a process known as molting. Most birds have what is called a sequential molt, in which their flight feathers are lost one at a time simultaneously from each wing. This allows many birds to continue flying while molting. However, during their annual molt, waterfowl undergo a simultaneous wing molt, losing all of their primary wing feathers at once, preventing them from being able to fly for a month or more while their new

Canada goose feathers.

primaries are growing in. During this period, they are extremely vulnerable, as attested to by this photograph. If you look closely at the remains of the Canada goose's wing on the right in the photograph (dark feathers), you'll see that the new primaries have almost, but not quite, grown out of their sheaths, making them not quite functional. It is apparent that this bird was unable to take flight during its molt in order to escape its predator.

Summer Moose Scat in Clumps

The form of moose scat, as well as that of most members of the deer family, is highly dependent upon the type of food that they eat and the amount of moisture and fiber in it. In the summer, when the moose diet includes succulent green leaves and semi-aquatic and aquatic vegetation, as well as twigs and bark of deciduous

trees, moose scat ranges from pellets clumped together to plops or patties. In the winter, when their diet is mostly fibrous conifer twigs and bark, they produce individual pellets.

AUGUST 17

American Goldfinches Fledging and Flocking

American goldfinches are late nesters—it is not uncommon for them to be raising young in August, and occasionally even into September. Their nesting is timed to coincide with the ripening seeds of milkweed and thistle in order to take advantage of the seeds as a source of food for themselves and their nestlings, as well as the dispersal down attached to the seeds that is used as nesting material. Many songbirds feed their nestlings protein-rich insects, but American goldfinches are an exception.

The fledglings remain dependent on their parents for about three weeks after they leave the nest. Once the young birds can fly and feed themselves, they tend to collect into flocks, which often include adult birds. These flocks gradually increase in size, and by late September to early October they may number in the hundreds. Many young remain in the northern parts of their range during the winter.

Summer moose scat.

Winter moose scat.

American goldfinch nestling.

268

Buttonbush Producing Seeds

Buttonbush fruit.

During the summer, buttonbush's ½-inch-diameter white flower balls can be spotted along shorelines and in wetlands. The fragrance of this shrub's flowers attracts many pollinators, especially bumble bees and butterflies, whose tongues are long enough to reach the deep nectaries. After pollination, the two hundred or more flowers on each head produce small nutlets that are dispersed by water and consumed by waterfowl, particularly surface-feeding dabbling ducks, American bitterns, rails, and northern bobwhites.

Dragonflies and Damselflies Spearing Prey with Lower Lip

Dragonflies and damselflies are unique among aquatic insect larvae in that they have a greatly enlarged hinged lower lip, or labium, which they can rapidly extend outward to capture prey.

Cast skin of dragonfly larva from which adult dragonfly emerged.

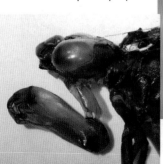

Dragonfly labium.

When retracted, the prehensile labium fits like a mask over the face or is folded flat beneath the insect's head. There are no muscles at the hinge joint, leading entomologists to believe that the labium is extended by increased blood pressure caused by abdominal muscle contraction. The lip unfolds at a right angle and extends extremely rapidly, faster than most prey can react.

AUGUST 18

Comb Tooth Fungi Fruiting

Tooth fungi produce their spores on spinelike teeth that hang down toward the ground, instead of on gills or in tubes. There are four species of tooth fungi in North America, all of which are edible. Combtooth fungus's delicate branches are covered with rows of fleshy spines, most of which are under half an inch in length and look like

Comb tooth fungus.

tiny white icicles. Look for this fungus on fallen branches, logs, and stumps of hardwoods, particularly maple, beech, oak, and hickory.

Juvenile Gray Tree Frogs Well Camouflaged

A gray tree frog starts life as a ¼-inch, yellow tadpole. Eventually it may reach 2½ inches in length, its body turns olive green, and it has a red tail. Upon metamorphosing into a frog, the gray tree frog turns a bright emerald green and gradually develops into a mottled gray-green adult. The

Juvenile gray tree frog.

Adult gray tree frog.

two color phases of the juvenile and adult frog are so different it is hard to believe that they are the same species.

Eyed Click Beetles

Although the eyed click beetle looks ferocious with its large, black eyespots—its actual eyes are below its antennae—it is harmless to humans. Like all members of the click beetle family, it gets its name from the sound it makes when it flips itself upright. Click beetles possess a spinelike structure as well as a

Eyed click beetle.

notch under their thorax. When they release the spine from the notch, it snaps and they are propelled into the air. Click beetles use this mechanism to right themselves if they are on their backs. Entomologists believe predators are deterred not only by the false eyes, but also by the beetle's catapulting action. Eyed click beetle larvae, called wireworms, spend most of their two- to five-year life in the soil feeding on decaying plants and other insects before emerging as adults.

AUGUST 19

Birds Transporting Ticks

Several recent studies demonstrate that wild birds transport ticks and their associated diseases during migration. In addition, a number of bird species are able to contract *Borrelia burgdorferi*, the bacterium causing Lyme disease, and transmit it to uninfected ticks that parasitize the birds for a blood meal. Since ground-feeding species like northern cardinals, gray catbirds, song sparrows, and American robins spend a significant amount of time foraging for food at the optimal height for ticks, they are excellent hosts and have all demonstrated the ability to infect ticks with *Borrelia burgdorferi* during their first blood meal. Look carefully at the pictured song sparrow's neck and you will find a tick.

Song sparrow with embedded tick.

AUGUST

ddisfly egg mass. Recently hatched caddisly larvae.

Adult caddisfly.

Velvety fairy fan.

Caddisflies Laying Eggs

The 1- to 2-inch-long jelly masses with tan dots, often located about two-thirds up cattail and other emergent aquatic vegetation leaves at this time of year, are egg masses laid by a caddisfly. The location of these eggs makes sense, as caddisflies spend their larval stage at the bottom of ponds and streams, where they build themselves camouflage cases of pebbles, leaves, or sticks, depending on the species, which they drag along with them. After pupating and emerging as adults, caddisflies mate and lay eggs on submerged vegetation or where the newborn larvae can easily drop into the water.

Velvety Fairy Fan Fruiting

Velvety fairy fan lives up to its name. Its brown stalk is fuzzy, and it is tiny and fan-shaped. It is also called spatula mushroom, for equally obvious reasons. This fungus belongs to order Helotiales, which also includes earth tongues, jelly drops, and other small fungi that grow on plant stems, wood, and wet leaves. Because of its diminutive size—⅜ inch high—it is often overlooked. The fruiting bodies are often found in clusters that appear in August and September.

AUGUST 20

American Lady Larvae Building Nests

The American lady (formerly known as the American painted lady) larva is very distinctive, with its branched spines and white bands across

American lady larval nest in pussytoes.

American lady larva and shed skin.

American lady.

its abdomen. One of its favorite foods is pussytoes, a member of the aster family. Larvae make nests at the tops of host plants by binding leaves, chaff, and bits of the flowers with silk. The larvae hide inside these nests during the daytime and come out at night and on overcast days to feed. Occasionally, you can find a shed skin inside the nest. Soon after the larva forms a chrysalis and pupates, a butterfly emerges and starts its migration south, where it spends the winter.

Jack-in-the-Pulpit Corms Growing Larger

Jack-in-the-pulpits have underground, vertical swollen stems referred to as corms, which store nutrients that allow them to withstand extremes in temperature, as well as droughts. They also provide the plant with the energy it needs to produce leaves and flowers. A large corm is likely to produce a female plant, which needs more energy to produce seeds, a smaller corm a male. If the plant lacks enough nutrients to produce a flower, its corm will be very small.

Jack-in-the-pulpit corm.

Jack-in-the-pulpit.

All parts of jack-in-the-pulpit, including the corm, contain a high concentration of calcium oxalate crystals, which are known to cause a burning sensation if eaten. However, Native Americans roasted or dried them before grinding them into flour for bread (they called them Indian turnip or Iroquois breadroot), or using them to treat colds or as a contraceptive.

Double-Crested Cormorants Begin Flights South

Double-crested cormorants, whose double crest is visible on adults only during the breeding season, begin migrating this month, with peak numbers reached in late September and early October. The migration route of Northeast cormorants is primarily along the coast and river valleys, with stops at fall staging areas to refuel. These fish-eating birds winter primarily in the Florida wetlands and along the coast as far north as the Carolinas.

Double-crested cormorant.

AUGUST 21

White Goldenrod Flowering

White goldenrod, also called silverrod, is the only member of the genus *Solidago* in the East that doesn't have bright yellow flowers. This native

White goldenrod.

species of goldenrod is found growing in sandy soil, often along roadsides. It flowers July to October, and, unlike the familiar Canada goldenrod, which has its flowers at the tip of the plant, white goldenrod has its flowers clustered in the axils of the leaves. The flowers can appear to be pale yellow due to the yellow color of its stamens and pollen. White goldenrod, like all goldenrods, produces a large number of seeds in the fall that are consumed by a variety of birds.

Moth Eyes and Biomimicry

Because moths need to use every bit of light available in order to see in the dark, their eyes are highly non-reflective. This trait is also helpful in decreasing the chances of predators spotting them. Scientists, through biomimicry, have come up with a number of technological advances thanks to studying the structure of moth eyes, including the development of a film that can be applied to solar cells that helps keep

Plant Succession

Succession is the natural change in the types of plant species that occupy a given area over time: the orderly procedure of one plant community gradually replacing another. This process includes the colonization, establishment, and extinction of plant species. Each community of plants that moves into an area changes the environment, specifically affecting the amount of sunlight, temperature, and humidity, which in turn eliminates certain species and allows others to move in. Temporary plant communities are replaced by more stable communities until equilibrium is reached between the plants and the environment.

One example of the progression of plants in a disturbed area:

Colonization by *early successional*/pioneer plants:
- Grasses
- Meadowsweet
- Goldenrods
- Steeplebush

Transitional woody plants that move in:
- White pine
- Trembling aspen
- Grey birch
- Black cherry

Late successional:
- Sugar maple
- American beech
- Yellow birch
- Eastern hemlock

Steeplebush.

White pines.

Sugar maples.

Luna moth.

sunlight from being reflected off them before the light can be utilized. Man-made materials based on the structure of moth eyes could someday reduce the radiation dosages received by patients getting X-rays while improving the resolution of the resulting images. Research on recreating the pattern found on moths' eyes onto plastic could lead to reflection- and glare-free display screens for televisions, cell phones, computer monitors, eyeglasses, speedometers, and more.

Porcupines' Feet Adapted to Arboreal Life

Due to their woody diet, porcupines spend a lot of their life climbing on and clinging to trees. In addition to strong, curved nails that fit into bark crevices, the soles of their feet have a pebbly surface with very little fur. The bumpy texture increases the surface area and the friction when a porcupine's feet are in contact with a branch,

Porcupine footpad.

helping the porcupine hold onto the tree trunk and branches. Even so, examination of porcupine skeletons confirms that many have fractures that have healed, indicating that, although porcupines' bodies are adapted for tree climbing, a significant number of porcupines still experience falls.

AUGUST 22

Ants Using Mandibles

Ants go through complete metamorphosis, passing through four stages: egg, larva, pupa, and adult. Like honey bees, ants have queens, female workers, and male drones in their colony. The female worker ants have a series of jobs that they perform in a certain order. A young worker spends the first few days of its life caring for the queen and young. After that, she maintains the nest, and eventually she forages for food. Like most insects, ants lack grasping forelegs and compensate for this by using their mandibles as hands. When the nest is disturbed, work-

Ants carrying larvae.

ers rush to rescue the eggs, larvae, and pupae by clasping them in their mandibles and transporting them to safety. They also use their mandibles to carry food, to construct nests, and for defense.

Virgin's Bower Flowers Developing Fruit

Virgin's bower, also known as old man's beard, devil's darning needles, and clematis, is often noticed later in the fall, when its female flowers have produced fruits with long, silky tails—remnants of the female flowers' pistils. However,

Virgin's bower—flowers.

Virgin's bower—mature fruit.

Virgin's bower—young fruit.

Spiders Molting Exoskeletons

Like other arthropods, spiders have a protective hard exoskeleton that is flexible enough for movement but can't expand like human skin. Thus, they have to shed, or molt, this exoskeleton periodically throughout their lives as they grow and replace it with a new, larger exoskeleton. Molting occurs frequently when a spider is young, and some spiders may continue to molt throughout their life.

At the appropriate time, hormones tell the spider's body to absorb some of the lower cuticle layer in the exoskeleton and begin secreting cuticle material to form the new exoskeleton. During the pre-molt period, a new, slightly larger, inner exoskeleton develops and is folded up under the existing exoskeleton. This new, soft exoskeleton is separated from the existing one by a thin layer called the endocuticle. Before molting, the spider secretes fluid that contains digestive enzymes between the new inner and old outer exoskeletons. This fluid digests the endocuticle between the two exoskeletons, making it easier for them to separate.

Once the endocuticle is completely digested, the spider is ready to complete the molt. At this point, a spider pumps hemolymph (spider blood) from its abdomen into its cephalothorax in order to split its carapace, or headpiece, open. The spider then slowly pulls itself out of the old exoskeleton through this opening.

Typically, the spider does most of its growing

Shed spider exoskeleton.

this vigorous native vine produces cascades of fragrant white blossoms at this time of year. Male and female flowers are borne on separate plants and are pollinated primarily by bees, wasps, and flies. The toxic leaves are avoided by herbivorous mammals, but the larvae of many moths and midges consume them, and they provide cover and nesting habitat for many songbirds. Virgin's bower is often mistaken for the invasive sweet autumn clematis. The two species can easily be distinguished by their foliage—the leaf margins of virgin's bower are toothed, while those of sweet autumn clematis are smooth.

immediately after losing the old exoskeleton, while the new exoskeleton is highly flexible. The new exoskeleton is very soft, and until it hardens, the spider is particularly vulnerable to attack.

AUGUST 23

Common Aspen Leaf Miners Mining

A leaf miner is the larval stage of an insect (primarily moths, sawflies, and flies) that feeds on plant leaf tissue. Most of these insects feed for their entire larval period within the leaf, creating tunnels between the upper and lower leaf surfaces. Some will pupate within the leaf mine, while others cut their way out when they are full-grown and pupate in the soil.

Leaf miner trail in poplar leaf.

The pattern of feeding tunnels, as well as the pattern of droppings, or frass, within them (darker sections of tunnels), combined with the species of plant on which they occur, can sometimes identify the species of insect that created the mines. A moth larva, the common aspen leaf miner, leaves delicate, serpentine mines that are diagnostic of this species.

Damselflies Capturing Prey

Damselflies, nature's more delicate version of a dragonfly, spend most of their life under water, first as an egg and then as a nymph. Eventually, after a year or so, they crawl out of the water onto nearby vegetation, shed their nymphal skin for the final time, and emerge as winged adults. A damselfly's beauty belies its behavior—most damselflies are voracious predators, both as aquatic nymphs as well as adults. In flight, they hold their bristly hind legs in a basket shape to

Damselfly with prey.

scoop up their prey. The prey is then transferred to their front legs, which hold it while the damselfly devours it.

AUGUST 24

Green Frog Listening Device

A frog's tympanic membrane, or tympanum, is the circular patch of skin directly behind its eye that we commonly call its eardrum. It functions much like our eardrum does—it transmits sound waves to the middle and inner ear, allowing a frog to hear both in the air and below water. In addition, the membrane serves to keep water and debris from entering a frog's ears. In some

Male green frog.

Female green frog.

species of frogs, such as the green frog, American bullfrog, and mink frog, their gender can be determined by the size of their tympanum relative to their eye: the male's tympanum is larger than its eye, while the female's is equal in size or smaller than its eye.

Goldenrod Bunch Gall

Goldenrods are host to about fifty species of gall-making insects, two-thirds of which are midges, or tiny flies. Goldenrod bunch galls, also called rosette galls, are the result of an egg being laid in the topmost leaf bud of Canada goldenrod by a midge. The stem of the goldenrod stops growing, but the leaves don't. The resulting rosette of leaves provides shelter and food for the midge larva, as

Goldenrod bunch gall.

well as a host of other insects, including other midges. Adult goldenrod bunch gall midges emerge from the galls in the fall, and females lay eggs in the soil. The larvae hatch within one to two weeks and spend the winter underground, emerging as adults in the spring to start the cycle all over again. The goldenrod bunch gall midge lays either all male or all female eggs.

Young Cooper's Hawks Fledging

After a month of living in a nest that measures roughly 7½ inches across and 3 inches deep, Cooper's hawk nestlings are more than ready to stretch their wings. Although they've been dismembering prey—mostly birds and a few small mammals brought to them by their parents—since they were three weeks old, catching prey is a skill they have yet to acquire. For roughly ten days after they leave their nest, the young hawks return to it for continued prey deliveries by their parents and for roosting. During this time, the fledglings learn to catch their own prey and they become independent, but they continue to stay together near their nest for the next month or so.

Juvenile Cooper's hawks.

Queen Ants Mating and Removing Wings

Ants are social and live in colonies consisting of one or more queens, female workers, and males. In most species, the non-sexually mature female ants are wingless; only the males and the queen(s) have wings. Periodically, usually three to five days after a heavy rain, the winged ants emerge from the colony in large swarms in order to mate and create more colonies. Swarming behavior is usually synchronized with other nearby colonies, so large numbers (hundreds or thousands) of winged ants suddenly appear. After mating, the males die, and the queens shed their wings and use the remaining wing muscles as a source of nutrients during the early stages of colony development. The shedding of wings is not a passive activity. The pictured ant, in the process of removing her fourth and final wing, makes use of her legs to accomplish this task.

Queen ant removing her wings.

Two-month-old juvenile common loons.

Aging Juvenile Loons by Plumage

This year's common loon chicks are now roughly two months old. Even without knowing when it hatched, you can estimate the age of a chick by looking at its feathers. Their color and type, either down or contour, can give you a good idea of how many weeks old it is. Common loon chicks are born covered with sooty black down. By the time they are three weeks old, they have replaced this natal down with a second, gray-brown down. Juvenile feathers start appearing soon thereafter, replacing the down; the age of a chick can be estimated by the amount of down that remains. By eight weeks of age, the chicks have just small tufts of brown down remaining on their head and neck. By nine weeks of age, their entire body, including the head and neck, are covered with smooth, gray contour feathers and there is no sign of down.

Nodding Ladies' Tresses Flowering

The downward "nodding" curve of its tubular flowers gives nodding ladies' tresses part of its common name. The two to four spiraling rows of

Nodding ladies' tresses.

bright white flowers form a spike that resembles a woman's braid to some. This relatively common member of the orchid family stands out in moist meadows of green grasses in August. A perennial, nodding ladies' tresses grows between 4 and 12 inches tall and is pollinated by both long- and short-tongued nectar-seeking bees. It is one of the few orchids that have a fragrance.

AUGUST 26

Sulphurs Flying

Sulphurs are a group of butterflies that are usually some shade of yellow, orange, or white and have a wingspan between 1½ and 2½ inches. The three species likely to be seen in the Northeast are the clouded sulphur, the orange sulphur, and the pink-edged sulphur. Distinguishing one species of sulphur from another can be quite challenging. Sulphurs perch with their wings closed and are commonly seen drinking nectar from flowers, as well as puddling in muddy areas, where they obtain salts and other minerals.

Joe-Pye Weed Flowering

Joe-Pye weed is in the composite family and is named for a Native American herbalist and healer, Joe Pye, who used it for treating typhus.

You will often find Joe-Pye weed and boneset, a close relative, growing together in wetlands. Butterflies, especially tiger swallowtails and fritillaries, bees, and flies visit this plant's flowers looking for the fragrant nectar deep within them. While the flowers are popular with insects, the seeds are not a major source

Sulphur butterfly.

Joe-Pye weed.

of food for wildlife. Among the few birds that eat Joe-Pye weed seeds are mallards, ruffed grouse, wild turkeys, and swamp sparrows. Look for the pinkish purple flowering heads of Joe-Pye weed in the transition zone between cattail wetlands and fields of goldenrod.

AUGUST 27

Spiders Spinning Sacs and Laying Eggs

Female spiders that have mated have many strategies for where to lay their eggs and whether or not to remain with them once they are laid.

Some species of ground spiders attach their egg case to the surface of a rock, plant, or building and remain nearby.

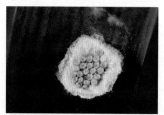

Spider egg sacs.

Some spiders, such as those in the genus *Argiope*, attach their egg sac to vegetation and then die. Some spiders, including wolf spiders, attach the egg sac to their spinnerets and carry it around with them. Nursery web spiders carry their egg sacs in their chelicerae, or mouthparts.

Many species of spiders build egg cases that are thick, have a heavy weave, and can be spiny, spiky, and presumably quite unpleasant for any potential egg sac predators, while others are suspended from leaves or twigs, making it difficult for predators to reach them.

Twelve-Spotted Skimmers Flying

Twelve-spotted skimmers are classified as king skimmers due to their large size and conspicuous coloration and wing patterns. Male twelve-spotted skimmers have a grayish bloom on their

Male twelve-spotted skimmer.

Female twelve-spotted skimmer.

abdomens, and each wing has three dark spots with white spots in between them. Females have brown abdomens and no white spots on their wings. All summer you can see males flying back and forth short distances along the shores of ponds and over water, hovering as well as perching. They are very territorial and patrol over water, loop-the-looping with competing males. A small number of twelve-spotted skimmers occasionally take part in Atlantic Coast migrations.

Skunk Cabbage Fruit Maturing

After the flowers of skunk cabbage, located on the knob (spadix) sitting inside a modified leaf (spathe), have been pollinated and fertilized in early spring, the fruits begin to mature. The spathe withers and dies, and the stalk that carries the fruit head elongates, growing along the surface of the ground. Initially, the fruit head is green and dark purple, measures 2 to 3 inches in diameter, and has a convoluted exterior

resembling that of a brain. Inside this compound fruit, a circle of ten to fourteen seeds lines the periphery. By August, the fruit heads will have fallen apart, and the seeds will lie on the ground, where they will likely germinate or be eaten by squirrels, ruffed grouse, or wood ducks.

AUGUST 28

Insects Mating

In some insect species, there are no signs of rituals preceding mating. Most insects, however, engage in routines that are uniquely characteristic of the species. Females are often stroked by the males with their legs or antennae. Dance patterns may be performed, wings may be fluttered or moved in circles, or short flights may occur. "Songs" are produced in a variety of ways, by rubbing wings or wings and legs, or with abdominal plates.

In some species, the rituals take place and lead to mating in the late summer or fall, and

Skunk cabbage fruit.

Ladybug beetles.

Black blister beetles.

Craneflies.

Hover flies.

Locust borers.

Skippers.

Damselflies.

AUGUST 29

Black Bears Seeking Protein

Although insects and animal matter make up less than 10 percent of the annual black bear diet, they are a crucial part of it. Black bears get most of their animal protein from ant brood, hornet larvae, tent caterpillars, march fly larvae, grubs (especially June beetle grubs), and snow fleas. Among the preferred sources are bee and hornet larvae. Berries and other fruit do not have a great amount of protein, but they do have some. Blackberries, for example, have two grams of protein per cup. If the summer berry crops fail, insect brood is especially important.

When tearing apart a bee hive, yellow jacket nest, or bald-faced hornet nest, bears do get stung, particularly on their ears and faces, as their fur is fairly impenetrable. Appar-

Bald-faced hornet nest torn apart by a bear.

ently the reward is worth the aggravation. After filling themselves with brood, and in some cases, honey, black bears shake vigorously in order to rid themselves of any insects that are caught in their fur.

Juvenile Spotted Salamanders Emerging from Vernal Pools

In April, spotted salamanders breed and lay eggs in their ancestral vernal pools. Four to seven weeks later, their eggs hatch and half-inch, gilled larvae emerge. It takes the aquatic larvae roughly two to four months to transform into juvenile spotted salamanders. At this point, they

many of the eggs laid go into diapause, a type of hibernation, until spring, when they will hatch. Some fall-mating insects include ladybug beetles, walkingsticks, paper wasps, bald-faced hornets, yellow jackets, crickets, katydids, grasshoppers, and praying mantises.

Juvenile spotted salamander.

are 1 or 2 inches long, depending on the temperature, shade, and other conditions of their natal pool. The spotted salamander larvae lose their gills, develop lungs, and begin life on land. In two or three years, they will return to the same pond, but only to breed. The rest of the year they lead a subterranean life, often in small mammal burrows.

Bumble Bees Raising Queens and Males

Unlike honey bees, whose queen and workers overwinter, only new queen bumble bees survive the winter. The entire colony, minus the

Bumble bees emerging from pupal cases.

queen, dies once cold weather arrives. Queen bumble bees mate in the fall and overwinter underground, often in an abandoned chipmunk or mouse burrow or in soft soil or compost, where they can survive temperatures down to five degrees below zero due to a kind of antifreeze they produce. In the spring, the queens emerge and start new colonies.

This late in the summer, colonies begin producing new queens as well as males in order to allow the colony to reproduce. The male bees leave the nest and do not normally return. They spend their time feeding on nectar and trying to mate with the new queens that have left their nest in order to mate before hibernating.

AUGUST 30

Northern Walkingsticks Mating

In an effort to look even more like a stick, the wingless northern walkingstick can stretch its front pair of legs out straight in front of it, to either side of its two long antennae. In addition to being very well camouflaged, some species of walkingsticks will rock their bodies side to side, resembling a twig swaying in the breeze. Worldwide, walkingsticks range in length from an inch to over a foot, and they are often green or brown. Those in the Northeast are usually about 3 inches in length.

Mating and egg laying begins in late August, peaks during mid-September, and dwindles in late

Northern walkingsticks mating.

October until most of the green foliage is no longer present. Egg laying often takes place in the canopy of trees, with each female dropping one egg at a time. If there are enough walkingsticks, it can sound like it is raining. The eggs overwinter on the ground in the leaf litter until spring, when the nymphs hatch. Hatching tends to occur when the humidity is 80 percent or higher because the moisture in the air serves as a lubricant, allowing the nymphs to get out of their eggs easily.

Ruby-Throated Hummingbirds Migrating

Finally, female and juvenile ruby-throated hummingbirds can come to hummingbird feeders without fear of being driven off by male hummingbirds, since the males have, for the most part, headed for warmer climes. All summer, the males do their very best to have sole occupancy of feeders. When the time for hummingbirds to migrate south arrives in the Northeast, males leave first, then females, and last, juveniles. The fall migration of hummingbirds occurs around the time of peak jewelweed flowering, suggesting that this flower is an important nectar source during this time and may influence the timing of migration.

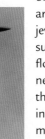

Male (top) and female (bottom) ruby-throated hummingbirds.

Spotted jewelweed.

Red Trillium Seeds Being Dispersed by Ants

The flower of red trillium, also known as stinking Benjamin and wake robin, is familiar to many, as it is one of our more common spring ephemerals. The three reddish-maroon petals (some populations have white, yellow-green, or paler red petals) are the same color as, and smell faintly like, rotten meat. Lacking nectar, these flowers rely on deception to bring in pollinators, primarily flies and beetles, that are attracted to dead animals.

Once a red trillium flower is pollinated, the chocolate kiss–shaped red fruit begins to develop. The seeds of red trillium (as well as 5 percent of all flowering plants) have oily appendages, called elaiosomes, that attract a number of insects, particularly ants. The elaiosomes, also called "ant snacks," contain lipids and protein highly sought after by ants. The ants carry the seeds down into their underground tunnels, where they feed the elaiosomes to their larvae and dispose of the seed in their compost pile, where they put their droppings, or frass, as well as dead ants. Conditions for germination are ideal here; understandably, there is a greater germination rate for seeds with elaiosomes than those without them.

Red trillium.

Red trillium fruit and seeds bearing elaiosomes.

284

AUGUST 31

Parasitoids and Parasites

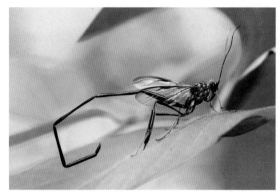

Pelecinid wasp with mites.

Black swallowtail larva.

Black swallowtail chrysalis.

By definition, a parasitoid is an organism that lives on, or in, a host organism and ultimately kills the host. The pictured pelecinid wasp is a parasitoid. Its host is the grub, or larval stage, of the June bug beetle. The female pelecinid wasp uses its long abdomen to probe into the soil until it locates a June bug grub, and then it lays an egg on the grub. When the egg hatches, the wasp larva burrows into and feeds on the grub, eventually causing its death.

A parasite is much like a parasitoid, deriving nutrients from a host, but, unlike a parasitoid, a parasite does not usually kill its host. Parasites are often much smaller than their host, and frequently live in or on their host for an extended period of time. In this photograph, a parasitoid, the pelecinid wasp, is host to reddish parasitic mites located on its thorax.

Black Swallowtail Larvae Soon to Form Chrysalises

In its younger days, the black swallowtail larva resembles a bird dropping, but in successive molts a green or white, yellow, and black pattern develops. Often discovered in vegetable gardens on carrot, parsley, and dill plants, it also feeds on wild members of the celery/carrot/parsley family (Apiaceae), including its favorite, Queen Anne's lace. Seeds as well as leaves are rapidly consumed as the chrysalis forms inside the caterpillar's skin, which it will soon shed for the last time. After overwintering as a pupa inside the chrysalis, the adult black swallowtail will emerge the following spring.

Meadowsweet and Steeplebush Flowering

Meadowsweet and steeplebush can easily be confused. Not only are their flowers similar—both plants are in the rose family—but steeplebush is also known as meadowsweet and hardhack. However, there are differences. Steeplebush gets its name from its steeplelike clusters of rose pink flowers. Meadowsweet's creamy white to pink fragrant flowers do not usually form a spike. Steeplebush's species name, *tomentosa*, means deeply woolly, which the underside of its leaves and twigs are. Meadowsweet's twigs and leaves lack hairs.

Steeplebush and meadowsweet.

SEPTEMBER

Dragonfly Migration

Bird migration is well documented and is a familiar concept to most individuals, but birds are not the only animals that depart from cool climates in search of warmer ones in the fall. Monarch butterflies are also long-distance migrants, and so are many other insects, including other species of butterflies, moths, locusts, and dragonflies.

Migration by dragonflies has been recorded sporadically for several centuries. European records of the phenomenon date back to 1494. Today, dragonfly migration takes place on every continent but Antarctica. Recently there has been renewed interest in this topic, and in 1998 an extensive review of observations and literature about massive swarm migrations of dragonflies in eastern North America concluded the following: Most swarms are sighted between late July and mid-October, with a peak in September. The majority of large flights occur along topographic features, such as lakeshores and coastlines, and massive swarm migrations are correlated with northerly winds following the passage of cold fronts. As is the case with monarchs, it is most likely that the offspring of the fall migrating adults are the dragonflies that return in the spring. The common green darner is the predominant species involved in the majority of these flights.

Migrant Species

There are approximately 326 species of dragonflies in North America. Of these, only about sixteen to eighteen are regular migrants, with some making annual seasonal flights, while others are more sporadic. It is not always easy to differentiate migrant dragonflies from those that aren't migrating, but dragonflies flying together in large swarms that move in a common direction for sustained periods are considered migrants. Well-documented, annual, long-distance migratory species of dragonflies in North America include the common green darner, the wandering glider (which migrates twice the distance the monarch does), spot-winged glider, black saddlebags, and variegated meadowhawk. The first four of these species are found regularly in the Northeast.

Radio Telemetry Revelations

A new collaborative, the Migratory Dragonfly Partnership, has greatly increased what is known about dragonfly migration by attaching miniature radio transmitters to the thoraxes of migrating common green darners and following them for up to twelve days. Information has also been gleaned from the study of isotopes. Radio telemetry reveals that the common green darner, weighing about 1 gram, flies over 400 miles during a two-month migration. There are interesting similarities between bird and dragonfly migration behavior. Like migrating birds, dragonflies stop over at feeding spots to refuel along the way. During migration, common green darners often spend as much or more time feeding in areas as they do making long flights. On average, they migrate southward every three days, covering roughly 30 to 40 miles in five to seven days. Common green darners migrate exclusively during the day, regardless of wind direction, but only after two nights of successively lower temperatures. Like many migrating songbirds and hawks,

Monarch chrysalis.

dragonflies appear to avoid flights over extensive open water, even if it means going miles out of their way. Dragonflies begin their adult life in the fall with very little fat, undeveloped ovaries, and functional but incompletely developed flight muscles. They quickly increase muscle mass and fat stores—more so than local breeding dragonflies that don't migrate—and some species periodically lay eggs in ponds along their migratory route during their southward flight. The extent of the southward migratory flight of dragonflies has not been determined, but it is known that they reach Florida and even Mexico in substantial numbers.

Spring Dragonfly Migration

Large swarms of dragonflies are a more common sight in the fall than in the spring. Various indicators lead entomologists to believe that there is a spring migration, though it may be more protracted than the fall migration. Adult dragonflies in various locations in the Northeast have a history of appearing several weeks before the first sign that resident adults are emerging, indicating that the early arrivals are migrants. Mature dragonflies have also been observed mating and laying eggs in northern areas in early spring in locations where they could not have already emerged. Substantial numbers of common green

Female common green darner.

darners have appeared with warm air masses in early spring in the Northeast, remaining at a given site for only a few days, indicating migratory behavior. Unlike birds, common green darners observed migrating northward in the spring do not have much wing wear, which strongly suggests that they are not the same individuals involved in the autumn migration.

Moose Courtship: The Rutting Season

Autumn is not commonly associated with the breeding season, yet many animals, including cottontail rabbits, red squirrels, muskrats, martens, white-tailed deer, and moose, are in the throes of courtship at this time of year. From mid-September through October, the males, or bulls, of North America's largest member of the deer family (excluding caribou), the moose, are going through the annual ritual of establishing hierarchy within their ranks, luring potential mates, and mating with them. These behaviors are collectively referred to as rut.

Although capable of breeding as yearlings, bull moose rarely have the opportunity to do so at such a young age, due to the small size of their body as well as their antlers. But as they mature in subsequent years, they actively engage in courtship. Long before copulation occurs, a series of actions take place that determine not only which bulls mate, but which cows they mate with. To begin with, the normally solitary bull moose form small groups in the fall and then establish a hierarchy within their group. This is accomplished primarily through mock fighting, also called sparring. It is not a particularly aggressive behavior; in fact, sparring is quite low-key. Usually two bulls, frequently of different sizes, carefully position their antlers together. Gentle pushing ensues for up to an hour, demonstrating one bull's strength over the other. If the less dominant bull feels that the larger male is becoming too aggressive, he may give a submissive whine, which serves to slow down the action, or even to end it altogether. At

Young bull moose with shredded velvet hanging from antler.

Cow moose urinating (scent marking).

the end of the sparring match, it is obvious to all concerned who ranks higher than whom. Another behavior, called antler thrashing, also takes place at this time of year. Two competing bulls approach each other in a swaying gait, rocking their antlers from side to side as they get closer and closer to each other. If one opponent doesn't retreat, a serious fight can follow.

In addition to dealing with competition, bull moose are also busy advertising their availability to potential mates. They do so by scent marking, through both glandular secretions and urine. There are two main avenues for this advertisement: wallows and tree scent posts. During the mating season, the bull moose's urine is particularly pungent and can be smelled at quite a distance, even by humans. The bull paws the ground repeatedly, creating a shallow depression called a wallow, and then squats and urinates into this pit. He then proceeds to lie down in his own urine, occasionally rocking from side to side, thoroughly soaking his sides and underbelly. Just to make sure he is well anointed, he then stomps in the urine, splashing a mixture of mud and urine onto the underside of his face, neck, and antlers. This behavior is usually quickly rewarded with the appearance of a female, or cow moose, who urgently seeks to enter the

wallow, sometimes even driving the male out of it in order to do so. The cow occasionally will even drink the bull's urine. It is obvious that the bull's urine contains pheromones that cows find highly attractive; they may even stimulate the cow to come into estrus. Cows also participate in scent marking, including urinating on or near shorelines.

A second means by which bull moose announce their availability to cows is to scent mark small trees and shrubs by stripping away the bark with their lower incisors or antlers and rubbing their forehead against the tree's inner wood. This way, pheromones, which are thought to convey the bull moose's status, health, sexual availability, and perhaps even more information to cow moose, are deposited on the tree for all passersby to smell. Bulls also thrash their antlers back and forth against shrubbery and saplings while leaving their scent. The sound of their antlers beating against vegetation is thought to signal the bull's dominance to other males, as well as serving to attract females.

Although normally silent (except for cows with calves), both male and female moose call during rut. Bull moose utter a low, *moo*-like plea, broken off short with an upward inflection at the end, or a throaty gulp. The call of the cow

SEPT

Balsam fir thrashed by bull moose antlers.

Moose wallow.

moose is longer and more like a domestic cow's, but not nearly as loud. At this time of year, bull moose have one thing on their mind, and they are diligently rushing through the forest, listening for grunting cows and challenging rival bulls with their bellows.

Serious fighting, as opposed to sparring, commonly occurs at the peak of rut, between two large males of nearly equal dominance. When true confrontation finally arrives, and more than one moose finds a receptive cow, there is no mistaking the bulls' behavior. The hair along the middle of their backs becomes erect, heads are held below the level of their shoulder blades, and ears are held downward. They may initially engage in jousting, where they place their antlers together and then attempt to position themselves advantageously. Aggressive fighting often follows, in which the two bulls attempt to gore each other in the side—or the rump, if one decides to retreat. Repeated slamming of antlers, charges, and attempted gorings may take place. If the opponents are evenly matched, these fights can last for hours, with bouts of jousting intermixed with vigorous pushing and attempts to wound each other. Usually, one male ends up retreating, but occasionally one bull is killed or dies later

from wounds sustained during combat. Although moose have died with their antlers locked, it is a rare occurrence.

Mating usually occurs within a day or two of a serious fight between bull moose, after which the male remains with the female for seven to twelve days. He then leaves to take another mate, and another and another until the end of the rutting season. Cow moose, on the other hand, usually mate only once.

Feet Made for Climbing

Fall finds a lot of animals climbing for a lot of different reasons. Some species of spiders crawl up vegetation, where they leave overwintering egg sacs. Many insects and spiders climb behind loose bark, where they will hibernate through the winter. Tree-climbing birds seeking these invertebrates as well as nuts and fruits are increasingly busy climbing up trunks as the temperature drops. Squirrels are climbing up and down trees to collect and then cache nuts for the coming winter. The feet of these climbers and many others have adapted in a variety of ways that facilitate their ascents and descents.

Insects have a foot-like appendage, the tarsus, which usually bears either small claws, bristles, or both. Their claws are composed of chitin, the same material contained in their exoskeleton. On the undersurface of many insect feet, often

Cecropia caterpillar true legs (3 front pairs) and prolegs (5 hind pairs).

Orb-weaving spider.

between the claws, there are adhesive pads, called pulvilli, that are covered with tiny hairs, or setae. These pulvilli grip or adhere like suction cups when the insect walks upside down on the undersurface of plants, in part due to an adhesive fluid that is secreted. Most caterpillars, the larvae of moths and butterflies, have eight pairs of legs—three pairs of true legs in the front of the caterpillar, and five pairs of false legs, or prolegs, behind the true legs. The tips of a caterpillar's six true legs are armed with a single small claw, while the tips of its prolegs are surrounded by numerous little hooks, called crochets, that help them grip surfaces. The six true legs in the front of the caterpillar develop into the legs of the moth or butterfly that the caterpillar will metamorphose into, and each of the adult's legs bears two small, grasping claws at its tip. The caterpillar's prolegs are shed with the last larval skin.

Comblike claws, surrounded by bristles, enable most spiders to secure a footing on a single thread of silk. Some spiders have only two claws and some have none. Clawless feet are thickly covered with bristles. These adaptations enable spiders not only to walk on silk, but also to climb vegetation in order to hunt insects and to attach their egg sacs in the fall. Jumping spiders, which catch their prey not in a web but by moving swiftly and pouncing, have feet that are

Wood frog.

even more modified, with about 624,000 fine, feathery hairs called setules and claws made of flexible chitin.

Certain frogs, especially those dwelling in wooded habitats, such as tree frogs, have large, round, adhesive discs, or toe pads, at the tips of their toes. The skin on these pads consists of hexagonal cells separated by deep channels into which mucous glands open. The combination of the structure of the bottom of the discs, the angle they hold their toes, and the mucus that moistens them enables gray tree frogs and spring peepers, to climb the smoothest bark in the woods.

Birds have many different sizes and shapes of feet, depending on the habitat in which they live and how they use their feet. Nuthatches and brown creepers, both of which spend a great deal of time climbing up and down tree trunks looking for invertebrates, have sharp claws and strong toes for gripping the bark. Most birds have four toes, but some have three, and, rarely, two. Many of those with four toes have three pointing forward and one backward. Woodpeckers, cuckoos, owls, and ospreys have what is referred

Female downy woodpecker.

to as zygodactyl feet—the first and fourth toes are directed backward and the second and third toes forward. While owls and ospreys use this toe arrangement to grasp prey, woodpeckers use it to reach places where their prey resides. Woodpeckers spend a lot of time clinging to tree trunks while they drill holes in search of insects, and because of the position of their toes, they are able to have a secure grasp of the tree. Cuckoos are arboreal birds for the most part and benefit from increased grasping prowess.

Mammals' feet have an endless variety of modifications that enable them to climb all manner of structures. Squirrels have four long, slender toes on their front feet, each with needle-sharp claws, and five toes and claws on each back foot. The palms and toes are covered with numerous knobs, or pads, which may be used for gripping smooth surfaces. In addition, the hind feet of red and gray squirrels are reversible, which is advantageous when they are climbing down vertical surfaces headfirst or hanging from a branch while reaching for nuts with their front

Red squirrel.

feet. Raccoons can also reverse the direction of their hind feet when descending trees headfirst. Porcupines are well equipped for climbing, with their long, curving claws and pebbled soles. They, like black bears, climb down a tree backward, in part because they cannot reverse the direction of their hind feet. Most primates, along with and opossums, have opposable thumbs, which enables them to do any number of tasks, including climbing almost any place they wish to go.

From the tiny feet of bats, whose sharp claws enable them to climb and hang upside down, to the common fly, whose suction-cupped feet enable it to climb over, under, and across just about any surface, the range of foot structures is enormous. Human feet seem relatively unimpressive in comparison.

292

SEPTEMBER 1

Nursery Web Spiders Guarding Young

Some species of nursery web spiders mate and lay eggs in the early fall. The female nursery web spider lashes leaves together with silk to form a protective shelter, or "nursery web," for her egg sac and hatching offspring. The mother stands guard over her spiderlings, aggressively defending her young until they have had their first molt, after which both the spiderlings and the adult female disperse.

Nursery web spider and young.

Brachonid Wasps Pupating and Emerging

Tobacco hornworms, which are often found feeding on tomato plants and are mistaken for tomato hornworms, are often the host of a species of a brachonid wasp (a type of ichneumon wasp) that parasitizes beetle, moth, fly, and sawfly larvae. The adult wasp lays her eggs inside the hornworm with her long ovipositor. The eggs hatch, and the wasp larvae feed on the caterpillar. Eventually, the wasp larvae emerge and spin silk pupa cases, or cocoons, on the skin of the dying hornworm larva. Inside the cocoon they transform into winged adults within four to

Brachonid wasp larva spinning cocoon.

Brachonid wasp cocoon.

Tobacco hornworm larva with brachonid wasp cocoons.

Adult brachonid wasp.

eight days. Because they parasitize hornworm, cabbage worm, aphid, and gypsy moth larvae, brachonid wasps are considered important biological control agents. If you want to discourage tobacco hornworms in your tomato patch, allow the wasps to complete their metamorphosis. This accomplishes both the demise of the hornworm and an increased population of brachonid wasps.

293

SEPTEMBER 2

Yellow Jacket Nests

Yellow jackets commonly build nests in rodent burrows, making opportunities to examine a yellow jacket nest few and far between. A black bear dug down into the pictured yellow jacket nest to feed on the nutritious larvae, leaving the remains of the nest visible after it departed.

The paper nest is made from fibers scraped from wood and mixed with saliva. There are multiple tiers of vertical cells, similar to nests of paper wasps, but enclosed by a paper envelope around the outside that usually contains a single entrance hole, much like a bald-faced hornet nest. If the rodent hole isn't spacious enough, yellow jackets will increase the size of the underground cavity by moistening the soil and digging.

Yellow jacket colonies, which are begun each spring by a single reproductive queen, can reach populations of between fifteen hundred and fifteen thousand individuals, depending on the species. Except for the queens, all of these yellow jackets live only one season. From spring to mid-summer, nests are in the growth phase, and larvae require large amounts of protein. Thus, workers forage mainly for other insects at this time. By late summer and early fall, however, the colonies grow more slowly or cease growing altogether and require large amounts of sugar to maintain the queen and workers. Foraging yellow jackets are particularly interested in sweet things at this time of year.

Workers in the pictured colony will only live a few more weeks, yet they immediately set about rebuilding their damaged hive.

Snakeroot Flowering

Large patches of snakeroot can be found flowering in Northeast woods at this time of year. Snakeroot is a benign-looking perennial with clusters of tiny flower heads at the tip of its stem, each containing multiple white flowers. Its name comes from its roots being used to make a poultice to treat snakebites.

Snakeroot contains a toxin called tremetol. An animal may die from eating either a large amount of snakeroot at one time or small amounts over a long period. When the plant is consumed by cattle, the meat and milk become contaminated with the toxin. If this contaminated meat or milk is consumed, the poison is passed on, and if enough is ingested, it can cause "milk sickness" in humans, a potentially lethal illness. Thousands of Midwest settlers in the early 1800s died from this disease— possibly including Abraham Lincoln's mother—because they were unfamiliar with the plant and its effect on their cattle. Snakeroot is also poisonous to horses, goats, and sheep. Today, small amounts are used by herbalists to treat a variety of ailments, from high blood pressure to insomnia.

Yellow jacket hive dug up by black bear.

Snakeroot.

SEPTEMBER 3

Small Milkweed Bugs Feeding

At this time of year you can often find orange and black bugs on milkweed leaves. If they are black with an orange X on their forewings, they are small milkweed bugs. The red and orange combination of colors, which many insects that feed on milkweed possess, warns predators that, because of the milkweed toxins they ingest, these insects may be bad for their health. Adult small milkweed bugs feed mainly on milkweed seeds, but they also consume the nectar of a variety of flowers and occasionally an insect.

Small milkweed bug drinking insides of ant.

Juvenile Broad-Winged Hawks Fending for Themselves

Broad-winged hawk chicks spend their first five or six weeks in the nest being fed small mammals, toads, nestling birds, and a variety of invertebrates by their mother. They then fledge, but for the next two weeks the young birds continue to use the nest as a feeding and roosting site, and food is still being provided for them. At about seven weeks of age, they begin capturing their own prey, but they will remain on their parents' territory for the next month or two.

Juvenile broad-winged hawk.

Earwigs Mating

Earwigs are elusive insects, primarily because they are nocturnal, and during the day they tend to hide in crevices where we seldom look. When we do see them, the first thing often noticed is their cerci, the pair of pincers, like tiny forceps, at the tip of their abdomen. These pincers are used primarily to capture prey (earwigs are scavengers for the most part, but some are omnivorous) and for copulation. Male earwigs have curved pincers, while females have straight ones.

After mating in the fall, the male and female earwig spend much of the winter together, tucked away in a crevice. By the time spring arrives, the male has left and the female has laid her eggs, which hatch in about a week's time. In many species of earwigs, the mother remains with the nymphs, as earwigs are one of the few insects that provide maternal care for their eggs and offspring.

Male earwig.

295

Fungal Spore Production

A fungus is neither a plant nor an animal, but is classified as a separate kingdom. The body of a fungus consists of many branching, threadlike filaments called hyphae, which are collectively called mycelium. Because mycelium grows underground or under loose bark or rotting logs, its fine, often white, hyphae are usually not visible. However, the fruiting bodies produced by the mycelium—mushrooms, shelf fungus, puffballs, and the like—are very evident. These are the structures which produce reproductive bodies called spores.

Spores are formed either in saclike structures called asci or on the surface of club-shaped structures called basidia. Fungi with asci are called ascocarps and include morels, false morels, and cup fungi. The form they take varies tremendously, from the concave surface of cup fungi to the pockets of morels. Asci often release spores by bursting at their tips.

Basidiocarps include mushrooms, puffballs, coral fungi, jelly fungi, stinkhorns, and bird's nest fungi. The tissue that creates spores, called hymenium, is found on several different types of structures, including gills, pores, jell, and teeth. Mushroom *gills* are thin, papery structures that hang vertically under the cap of a mushroom. Gills are classified according to their attachment to the stem of the mushroom. *Pores* appear as small holes on the underside of the cap. These holes are the ends of a series of tubes within the mushroom cap. Spores are produced on the sides of these tubes, and eventually they are released and fall down the tube, out the pore, and into the air. The long, thin, spiny *teeth* of tooth fungi hang downward and produce spores. The teeth are always oriented so that they will be exactly perpendicular to the earth. The teeth are also tapered, allowing the spores that are produced on their surface to fall straight down without disturbing the lower parts of the teeth.

Ascocarps:

Morel—pockets.

Cup fungi—surface of cup.

Basidiocarps:

Oyster mushroom—gills.

Elegant stinkhorn—jell.

Bear's head tooth—teeth.

Bolete—pores.

Shelf fungus—pores.

Giant Swallowtail Larvae Feeding

The giant swallowtail, the largest butterfly in North America, with a 4- to 6-inch wingspread, is extending its range northward. Because of the larva's preference for plants in the citrus family, this butterfly has historically been considered a more southern species. However, warming temperatures and the presence of the common prickly ash tree, a member of the citrus family, has allowed it to extend its range into the Northeast.

The larval stage, or caterpillar, is equally as impressive as the adult butterfly. Its defense mechanisms include looking very much like a bird dropping—even appearing shiny and wet—making it seem unpalatable to most insect eaters. In addition, if it is threatened, a bright red, forked structure called an osmeterium emerges from its forehead and a very distinctive odor that repels insect eaters is emitted.

Giant swallowtail larva with osmeterium extended.

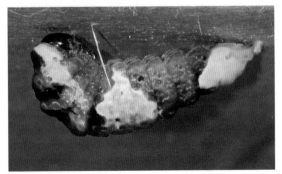

Giant swallowtail chrysalis.

Turkey tail fungus.

Turkey Tail Fungi Fruiting

One of the most common woodland fungi is a shelf fungus known as turkey tail fungus. Its common name was derived from the banding pattern on its fruiting body that resembles the tail of a displaying turkey. The color of the bands can be quite variable. Turkey tail fungi are polypores—they produce spores inside pores located on the underside of the fungus. Turkey tail fungus is found growing on wood, which it decomposes, recycling the nutrients and minerals in the wood and releasing them over a long period of time for use by other forest organisms.

SEPTEMBER 5

Bottle Gentian Flowering

Even if it were not one of the last plants to flower in the fall, bottle gentian would stand out because of its brilliant bluish purple, bottle-neck-shaped blossoms. Getting inside the flowers is a monumental task for pollinating insects, so much so that only fairly large species of bumble bees attempt—much less manage—to do so. It takes several seconds of pushing and shoving for a bumble bee to get its head through the

Bumble bee inside flower.

Bumble bee's tongue.

Cross-section of the bottle gentian flower, showing the central pistil surrounded by withered stamens.

minuscule opening at the top of the gentian blossom. Eventually the bumble bee's body follows, sliding down into the flower. While the whole bee sometimes disappears, usually its hind legs poke out of the flower while its long tongue reaches the copious amount of nectar that awaits inside the flower.

Like many other flowering plants, bottle gentian times the maturation of its reproductive parts to discourage self-pollination. Male pollen-bearing stamens mature first, and by the time the female pistil is mature, the stamens have gone by, so the flower's pistil can't receive its own pollen and thus self-pollinate.

Spiders Spinning Egg Sacs and Laying Eggs

Over their long evolution, spiders have developed different silks, produced by seven different glands, for various functions: ballooning, webs, wrapping prey, dragline, egg sacs, and so forth. The tubuliform gland is responsible for the large-diameter silk fibers used in the construction of egg cases. Unlike other silk glands, which synthesize protein throughout a spider's lifetime, the tubuliform gland synthesizes silk for only a short time in a spider's life, just before eggs are laid.

Spider eggs inside silk sac.

This silk is synthesized only by female spiders and is the stiffest type of silk, making it a very protective covering for eggs.

Spider egg sac.

Shorebird Migration

Of the more than 650 species of North American breeding birds, more than half are migratory. As a group, shorebirds undertake some of the most spectacular long-distance migrations of any North American birds. Nearly two-thirds of the shorebird species that breed in North America journey from their Arctic nesting grounds to winter in Central and South America and then return

Spotted sandpiper in winter plumage.

298

to the Arctic the following spring. Many species traverse more than 15,000 miles in this annual circuit. Some fly at altitudes exceeding 10,000 feet and achieve cruising speeds approaching 50 miles per hour. From sightings of marked individuals, we know that at least some birds engage in nonstop flights that cover nearly 2,000 miles in less than two days.

SEPTEMBER 6

Monarch Butterflies Migrating

Peak monarch migration occurs during the first two weeks of September. Monarchs typically cycle through four generations during the breeding season and the final generation migrates to Mexico. Monarchs emerging in late summer live much longer than monarchs emerging in June and July: the late-summer butterflies have a six- to nine-month lifespan versus six to eight weeks for the mid-summer ones. This allows monarchs east of the Rocky Mountains the time needed to migrate up to 3,000 miles to central Mexico—a trip that takes roughly two months—to live through the winter, and to begin a return trip, although the overwintering individuals make it only about halfway back. Mating and laying eggs as they go, the returnees and succeeding

Monarch.

generations of monarchs continue the trip back to the Northeast. With luck, the great—or great, great—grandchildren of the butterflies that are migrating to Mexico now will grace our milkweed patches next summer.

Painted Turtle Eggs Hatching

Young painted turtles.

Painted turtle eggs hatch in late summer, usually in late August or the first half of September. The young turtles remain inside the nest cavity for varying amounts of time. Here in the Northeast, in the northern part of their range, they often overwinter in their nest and emerge the following spring. Further south, the hatchlings emerge and make their way to nearby ponds in the fall.

SEPTEMBER 7

Pandorus Sphinx Larvae Soon to Pupate

The family Sphingidae consists of sphinx (also called hawk) moths. In their larval stage, these moths are often referred to as hornworms, because of the horn, eyespot, or hardened button they all possess at the far end of their bodies.

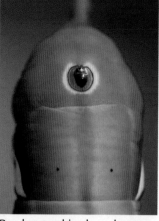

Pandorus sphinx larva . Pandorus sphinx larva button.

Wood thrush.

Pandorus sphinx pupa and cast larval skin.

Many gardeners are familiar with the tobacco hornworm—Carolina sphinx moth—a voracious consumer of tomato plants.

Before overwintering as pupae, hornworm larvae feed continuously. The pictured Pandorus sphinx feeds on both grape and Virginia creeper foliage. This species of hornworm comes in four colors—green, orange, pink, or cinnamon—and can grow to a length of 3½ inches before pupating. Each of the white spots surrounds a spiracle, a tiny hole through which air enters the hornworm's body. The horn is present up until the last instar, or stage, of the larva's life, at which point it is replaced by a button. Soon the larva will burrow into the soil, spend the winter as a pupa, and emerge as an adult moth in the spring.

Wood Thrush's Rictal Bristles

A close look at the head of a wood thrush reveals specialized feathers, or rictal bristles, projecting from its beak. These stiff, sturdy, specialized feathers are found in a wide variety of bird families, and are especially visible in owls, hawks, eagles, woodpeckers, flycatchers, night-jars, thrushes, and thrashers. There are several theories about their function. They may provide protection for the bird's eyes as it consumes struggling prey, and they may also provide tactile feedback, similar to whiskers on a cat or dog.

SEPTEMBER 8

Milkweed Tussock Moth Caterpillars Feeding

Female milkweed tussock moths lay their eggs in masses on the underside of milkweed and dog-bane leaves, which the hatching caterpillars eat. The caterpillars are gray and hairy, but quickly they develop the tufts of hairs that give them their name and make them resemble little mops. When still fairly young, the caterpillars stay together, skeletonizing the leaves they consume, leaving only the strongest veins that contain sticky latex. As they mature, the caterpillars tend to wander, and it is unusual to find large groups of them on a single leaf. At this point, they often cut through

Cluster of young milkweed tussock moth larvae.

bottom, typically resulting in all females from the top eggs and all males from the bottom eggs. In some locations, the hatchlings emerge from the nest in hours or days, and in others, primarily in locations warmer than the Northeast, they remain in the nest through the winter. When they emerge above ground, the hatchlings, without any adult guidance, make their way to the nearest body of water, which can be up to a quarter of a mile away, and once there, they seek shallow water.

SEPTEMBER 9

Calico Paint Moth Larvae Feeding

a vein in order to prevent the latex from reaching the area of the leaf where they are feeding, a tactic also used by older monarch caterpillars. Like monarchs, milkweed tussock moths are toxic to predators, because as larvae they have consumed the cardiac glycosides contained in milkweed and dogbane leaves.

Snapping Turtle Eggs Hatching

Every fall, roughly three months after they're laid, snapping turtle eggs hatch underground. The hatchlings' gender is determined by the temperature of the soil in which they were incubated during the summer. Eggs at the top of the nest are often significantly warmer than those at the

In the Northeast, calico paint moths, also called brown-hooded owlets, produce two generations a summer. The larvae of the first generation mature in July; the second generation matures from late August into October. Calico paint larvae are often found on aster and goldenrod plants, resting on stems in plain sight during the day. First-generation larvae feed on leaves, and the second generation consumes the flowers of the plants. The comparatively drab, brown adult moths they turn into can often be found on wild bergamot and common milkweed flowers in the early evening.

Calico paint moth larva.

Recently hatched snapping turtle emerging from nest.

Red-Osier and Silky Dogwood

Some of the most prolific flowering shrubs in the Northeast are dogwoods. In the spring, their flowers attract attention, and at this time of year, their colorful fruit stands out. There are many

Silky dogwood.

Red-osier dogwood.

species of dogwood, two of which are red-osier dogwood and silky dogwood. These shrubs can be hard to tell apart, as they both have white flowers, red stems, and similar foliage. In the fall, however, the color of their fruit differs. The mature berries of red-osier dogwood are dull white, and those of silky dogwood are blue with white blotches. The color of their pith, or central stem tissue, also differs. The pith of red-osier dogwood is white, whereas the pith of silky dogwood is salmon colored.

The fruit of dogwoods is an extremely important source of food for many migrating songbirds, as well as resident birds. Wood ducks, northern cardinals, eastern bluebirds, gray catbirds, purple finches, evening grosbeaks, American robins, yellow-bellied sapsuckers, wood and hermit thrushes, red-eyed and warbling vireos, cedar waxwings, and downy woodpeckers all consume dogwood berries.

Dung Beetles Feeding on Bear Scat

Wherever there is scat, or dung, there are dung beetles. This is a photograph of a dung beetle residing inside a black bear's large, apple-filled scat, which will provide it with food for a long time. Some species of dung beetles, called rollers, shape pieces of dung into balls, roll them away, and bury them to eat later or lay their eggs on. Some species, called tunnelers, bury dung by tunneling underneath the pile of scat. And a third group, dwellers, actually live inside dung piles.

Most dung beetles prefer the scat of herbivores. There are always bits of food that do not get digested, and these bits are what a dung beetle feeds on. Dung beetle larvae eat the solids, while adult beetles drink the liquids contained in the scat. A given species of dung beetle typically prefers the dung of a certain species or group of animals and does not touch the dung of any other species.

Dung beetles have a brain that is the size of a grain of rice, yet they are very sophisticated insects. They are capable of using celestial clues, such as the Milky Way, in order to roll balls of

Bear scat and burrowing dung beetle.

Dung beetle.

dung in a straight line. They are known for "dancing," which helps them orient themselves after their path has been disrupted. Dung beetles use their dung balls to regulate their temperature and cool off. In warm climates, around noon, when the sun is at its peak, dung beetles will routinely climb atop their dung balls to give their feet a break from the hot ground. Thermal imaging has shown that dung balls are measurably cooler than the surrounding environment, probably because of their moisture content. And dung beetles keep track of the number of steps they take and the direction from which they came, instead of landmarks, in order to return to their nest with a ball of dung.

Even though they are remarkably clever, dung beetles can be duped! A flowering plant native to South Africa, *Ceratocaryum argenteum*, produces large, round nuts that are strikingly similar in appearance, smell, and chemical composition to antelope droppings, which the dung beetles roll away and bury, effectively sowing a new generation of *C. argenteum*.

SEPTEMBER 10

Eastern chipmunk.

Eastern Chipmunks Clucking

Especially in the fall, and sometimes in the spring, the woods are full of eastern chipmunks clucking. It is unusual to hear this call during the summer, but once leaves have started to fall off the trees, giving chipmunks a clearer view of the sky, the chorus begins. One chipmunk starts calling, and the message is passed on to other relatives, who join in. These vocal little rodents are

thought to be warning each other of the presence of an aerial predator, perhaps a hawk or day-hunting owl.

Bald Eagles Migrating

Bald eagles are present throughout the Northeast year-round, but some individuals migrate southward along the Atlantic Coast or inland along the Appalachian Mountains. Most bald eagle migration occurs from late August through early December, with peak adult migration occurring the first two weeks of September. Typically, bald eagles migrate alone and during the middle of the day, when they take advantage of thermals, riding them up and then gliding southward until they reach another thermal.

Bald eagle.

Ants "Milking" Treehoppers

Certain species of treehoppers release a sugary liquid called honeydew, made mostly from excess plant sap that they consume. Ants farm these treehoppers, much as they farm aphids, for their honeydew. An ant strokes a treehopper with its antennae, causing a droplet of honeydew to appear at the tip of the treehopper's abdomen, which the ant then consumes. Both insects benefit from this mutualistic arrangement. The ants get

Larva and adult treehopper

Eastern gray squirrel with acorns.

honeydew, and in return, provide protection for the treehoppers from predators. The plant indirectly benefits from the ants, as well, for if the ants were not there, the treehoppers' honeydew would fall onto the plant, causing mold growth on fruits and leaves.

Ants tending treehoppers.

SEPTEMBER 11

Eastern Gray Squirrels Collecting and Caching Nuts

Many species of squirrel, including the red squirrel, are "larder hoarders"—each squirrel stores its food in one central area that it defends aggressively against invaders. Gray squirrels, however, are "scatter hoarders," collecting and burying one nut at a time throughout home ranges up to seven acres in size. It has been estimated that up to 25 percent of the nuts that gray squirrels cache are stolen by other gray squirrels. Gray squirrels are clever enough to deceive potential thieves; they engage in deceptive caching. Carrying a nut, a squirrel will repeatedly dig a hole and then fill it in, without depositing the nut. They also will cover a spot with leaves, even though they have not buried anything in this location. Where gray squirrel densities are high,

the squirrels often keep a cache in its original location for only about three days before moving it to a new location.

Virginia Ctenucha Moths Mating

The Virginia ctenucha moth is a day-flying moth. It is notable for the iridescent blue on its thorax and abdomen, its orange head, and its yellow feet, or tarsi. Like the Isabella tiger moth, which come from woolly bears, Virginia ctenucha moths are in the tiger moth family, Arctiidae, and like all members of this family, they have an organ on their thorax that has membranes that produce ultrasonic vibrations. These sounds are used for mating and defense purposes. Virginia ctenucha moths overwinter as caterpillars and pupate in the spring in cocoons that the larvae construct using their own hairs.

Virginia ctenucha moths mating.

SEPTEMBER 12

Indian Cucumber Root Fruiting

Indian cucumber root is a member of the lily family that grows to be 1 to 2 feet tall and has one or more whorls of leaves (a whorl is several leaves coming off the stem at the same point). Indian cucumber root plants that are going to flower usually put out two tiers of leaves, with their distinctive flowers arising from the second tier. The flowers nod down below the leaves, while the dark purple fruit that forms and ripens at this time of year rises above them.

Female horntail (note slender ovipositor).

Male horntail on bark.

Male horntail.

Indian cucumber root.

Pigeon Tremex Horntails Laying Eggs

Horntails, also known as wood wasps, are non-stinging, wood-eating insects that lay their eggs deep within trees. Both male and female horntails have a pointed spine at the tip of their abdomen; females also have a long, slender ovipositor. Horntails get their name not from their spine or ovipositor, but from a knob at the tip of their abdomen.

Pigeon tremex horntails are active in late summer and early fall. A mated female inserts her ovipositor several inches into a dead or dying tree and lays an egg, where it is safe from most, but not all, predators. Along with the egg, the adult horntail deposits some white rot fungus, which she stores in special abdominal glands. The fungus breaks down and softens the wood for the horntail larva to eat and is required for the successful development of the horntail. Infection of trees with white rot fungus accelerates decay and further weakens the structure of affected trees. The larva typically begins consuming the soft, fungus-ridden wood around it, and then chews its way to the inner bark so as to provide a means of exiting the tree when it becomes an adult. The larva then returns to feed on inner wood. It completes its metamorphosis and emerges from the tree within a year as a winged adult horntail.

The horntail larva is not safe in the tree, though: a parasitic insect, the giant ichneumon wasp, has a 3-inch ovipositor capable of drilling into trees. There are several theories about how the female wasp detects the presence of horntail

305

larvae deep within the tree. One theory is that she may lay her antennae on the outside of a tree and pick up the vibrations of horntail larvae gnawing away in their wood chambers. Another theory proposes that the female wasp uses her antennae to smell the frass, or droppings, of the horntail as well as the wood-softening fungus. Once she locates a horntail larva, the ichneumon wasp paralyzes it and then lays an egg on it. The ichneumon wasp larva feeds on the paralyzed horntail larva, consuming it completely within two weeks. The larva then pupates and remains dormant under the bark until the following summer, when the adult emerges.

Grasshoppers mating.

SEPTEMBER 13

Grasshoppers Mating

Grasshoppers are courting, mating, and laying eggs that will overwinter and hatch next spring. In addition to adopting different poses and flashing brightly colored wings, male grasshoppers attract females by producing calling songs. Some females also produce sounds, but they are usually infrequent and very soft. The males rub their hind femur against a forewing, or rub a forewing against a hindwing in order to make their calls, a process called stridulation. Tympana, or structures on their abdomens that are similar to eardrums, allow both male and female grasshoppers to hear. Because the songs are species specific, females can readily identify males of the same species.

When two grasshoppers pair up, the smaller male grasshopper usually mounts the female and the female curls her abdomen up to reach the aedeagus, the male's reproductive organ, from which she receives a package of sperm called a spermatophore. The mating process can take from forty-five minutes to more than a day, depending on the species. When her eggs are fully formed, the female pushes the ovipositor at the end of her abdomen ½ inch to 2 inches into

the ground and produces a glue-like secretion that cements the soil around the egg mass she deposits, forming a protective pod. Each pod may contain twenty-five to three hundred eggs, depending on the species of grasshopper.

Beechdrops Flowering

Beechdrops are parasitic plants that obtain nutrients from the American beech tree. They insert a rootlike structure called a haustorium into a beech root and absorb enough nutrition to sustain themselves and produce flowers between August and October. Beechdrops belong to a family of plants, broomrape, whose members live as root parasites. Being annuals, beechdrops don't live long enough to damage their host trees. Because they lack

Beechdrops.

Grasshopper, Katydid, and Cricket Sound Production

Grasshoppers, katydids, and crickets all belong to the order Orthoptera. Most have specialized structures for producing sounds that they use to communicate with other members of their own species. Although some females make muted sounds, it is the males that produce calling songs that communicate their species, location, and readiness to a potential mate.

Even though it is mainly the males calling, both sexes have organs that allow them to hear. Grasshoppers have these organs located on their first abdominal segment. The hearing organs of katydids and crickets are located at the base of their tibia.

The way in which most Orthopterans produce sound is through a method called stridulation—rubbing parts of their bodies together that are modified to enhance the sound. The ways in which grasshoppers, katydids, and crickets stridulate differ. Grasshoppers use a variety of parts, but most commonly rub their hind femur against their forewing and rub their forewing against their hind wing. Often visual signals or movement accompanies the song. Katydids and crickets rub their forewings together. At the base of one of the two forewings there is a specialized vein with ridges called the stridulatory file. The opposite forewing has a hard, sharp, upward-projecting structure, the scraper. When the wings are opened and closed during stridulation, the scraper rubs the file, producing sound.

Katydid.

Cricket.

Grasshopper.

chlorophyll and obvious leaves—their leaves are scalelike and are pressed flat against their stem—beechdrops are easily overlooked. Keep an eye on the forest floor near American beech trees for these 5- to 18-inch plants, which are flowering this month.

Gold and Brown Rove Beetles Active

Rove beetles are the largest family of beetles, with approximately sixty thousand species, a majority of which are nocturnal. Most rove beetles have short wing covers, or elytra, which leaves much of their abdomen exposed. This allows you to see the gold and brown rove beetle's last three abdominal segments, which are a striking golden color. Intricately folded underneath the short elytra are fully functional wings.

Gold and brown rove beetle on scat.

Adult female gold and brown rove beetles deposit their eggs on scat, carrion, or fungi, which their larvae feed on. As an adult, the gold and brown rove beetle uses its large mandibles to consume maggots, mites, and other small arthropods.

SEPTEMBER 14

Destroying Angel Fruiting Bodies Appearing

Several species of poisonous mushrooms in the genus *Amanita* in the Northeast are referred to as "destroying angels," but the most widely

307

Destroying angel.

distributed and commonly encountered is *Amanita bisporigera*. It has a smooth white cap, gills, a skirt-like ring underneath the cap and surrounding the stem (annulus), and a swollen stem base enclosed in a cuplike structure (volva). As it ages, this mushroom often acquires an odor reminiscent of rotting meat. Destroying angels are mycorrhizal with oaks—the underground portion of the fungus surrounds a tree's rootlets with a sheath and helps the tree absorb water and nutrients, while the tree provides sugars and amino acids to the fungus. Caution: Destroying angels are among the most toxic mushrooms known, and they closely resemble other white mushrooms that are edible.

Orange-Humped Mapleworm Larvae Feeding

Between July and September, orange-humped mapleworms can be found feeding on the leaves of maples, especially sugar maple. These caterpillars will eventually develop into tan moths known as prominents. As a defense mechanism while feeding, the larva sometimes elevates its rump,

Orange-humped mapleworm larva.

which resembles a second head, bearing "antennae," which are actually prolegs. Orange-humped mapleworms will soon be spinning cocoons in leaf litter, where they will overwinter as pupae.

Broad-Winged Hawks Migrating

Mid-September is the peak of broad-winged hawk migration in the East. This small, stocky bird of prey tends to migrate in flocks, called kettles, that can consist of thousands of birds circling higher and higher as they rise on thermals and then peel off at the apex, soaring southward to the next thermal. Satellite transmitters reveal that in the fall, broad-winged hawks migrate an average of 4,350 miles to northern South America, traveling roughly 69 miles each day.

Broad-winged hawk.

SEPTEMBER 15

American Ginseng Fruiting

American ginseng is a perennial plant in the ivy family that is commonly used in Chinese and herbal medicine. It is found in hardwood forests in the Northeast, but due to overharvesting, it has become quite rare. (Daniel Boone and Davy Crockett are said to have made large sums of money in ginseng trafficking.) Ginseng has a light tan, gnarled root that often looks like a human body, with stringy shoots for arms and legs. It used to be assumed that, if a plant looked like a part of the human body, it could be used to cure that body part. Because ginseng's root resembles the entire human body, it was used to treat just about any ailment. American ginseng was used

Fruit of American ginseng.

by Native Americans as a stimulant and to treat headaches, fever, indigestion, and infertility. Today, it is associated with alternative medicine as a treatment for diabetes, cancer, colds and flu, ADHD, immune system deficiency, and sexual impotency.

Black Bears Gorging

Black bears are omnivores as well as opportunists. They will eat almost anything that they can find, but the majority of their diet consists of grasses, roots, berries, nuts, and insects. In the fall, prior to going into hibernation, black bears enter a stage called hyperphagia, which literally means excessive eating. They forage practically nonstop—up to twenty hours a day—building up fat reserves for hibernation and increasing their body weight up to 100 percent in some cases. Their daily food intake goes from 8,000 to 15,000 to 20,000 calories.

Corn regurgitated by a black bear.

Signs of their foraging for grubs and beetles can be found with relative ease at this time of year if you live where there are black bears. A less-common sight is an indication that a bear's eyes were bigger than its stomach, such as the regurgitated corn in this photograph.

If you do share territory with black bears, be forewarned that they have excellent memories, especially for food sources. Be sure not to leave food scraps or pet food outside, and don't start feeding the birds until late December, when most black bears have entered hibernation.

Green Lacewing Larvae Using Corpses as Camouflage

Green lacewings are aptly named for the prominent venation of the adults' wings. Some species in this insect family even have "ears" in the larger veins that allow them to detect the ultrasonic sounds made by hunting bats.

Lacewing larvae and adults are both predators of soft-bodied insects like aphids. Lacewing larvae have long, hollow mandibles with which they puncture prey and suck out the liquefied contents, leaving the woolly husks. Some species of lacewing larvae have hairy backs, and they camouflage themselves when dining on woolly aphids by sticking aphid husks on these hairs.

Green lacewing larva covered with aphid husks.

Adult lacewing.

These "trash packets" camouflage the lacewing larvae from predators, including ants that would otherwise attack the larvae if they recognized that they were lacewings and not woolly aphids.

Beechnuts Ripening

Birds and mammals that rely on beechnuts as a staple of their diet include black bears, white-tailed deer, fishers, porcupines, wild turkeys,

Yellow-shouldered slug.

ruffed grouse, wood ducks, tufted titmice, and numerous small rodents, among others. There is a good reason for beechnuts to be in demand—they have roughly the same protein content as corn, but five times the fat content. Beechnuts also have nearly twice as much crude protein and twice the fat of white oak acorns and about the same fat content as red oak acorns. In the Northeast, there is often an alternate-year pattern of American beechnut production,

American beechnut.

with one year good and the next poor. Research has shown that high beechnut production in the fall is correlated with a high percentage of reproducing female black bears in the coming winter.

Yellow-Shouldered Slugs Feeding

This bright yellow green, ½-inch-long, oval creature is the larval stage of an ochre-winged hag moth. Possessing suction-cup prolegs, the yellow-shouldered slug glides, rather than crawls, over the leaf it is consuming. Perhaps this is why these caterpillars show a preference for smooth-leaved trees and shrubs, such as basswood, beech, cherry, maple, and oak. The yellow-shouldered slug pupates inside a cocoon all winter, and in the spring a small, brown moth with a ½-inch wingspread emerges.

Grape Phylloxera Bugs Migrating

At this time of year, many wild grape leaves are covered with spiny little galls containing grape phylloxera—a family of true bugs that are closely related to aphids. These bugs are one of the most destructive grape pests worldwide, affecting both roots and foliage. In the late nineteenth century, the phylloxera epidemic destroyed almost all European grapes.

The life cycle of grape phylloxera is complex, due to the fact that generations with different life cycles may develop at the same time. In the spring, a female hatches from a fertilized egg that had been laid on the wood of a grape vine. She migrates to a leaf, where she produces a gall and grows to maturity in about fifteen days. She fills the gall with eggs and dies soon afterward. Nymphs that hatch from the eggs escape from the gall and wander to new leaves, where they in turn produce galls and eggs. There maybe six or seven generations of this form during the summer.

Grape phylloxera galls.

In the fall, nymphs migrate to the roots, where they hibernate through the winter. The following spring they become active again and produce root galls. The root-inhabiting wingless females may cycle indefinitely on the roots year after year. In late summer and fall, some of the root-inhabiting phylloxera lay eggs that develop into winged females. These females migrate from the roots to the stems, where they lay eggs of two sizes; the smaller ones develop into males and the larger ones into females. Mating occurs, and the female then lays a single fertilized egg that overwinters on the grape stem. It is this egg that gives rise to leaf-inhabiting generations.

SEPTEMBER 17

Jack-in-the-Pulpit Fruits Maturing

After the spathe, or hood, dies back, the fruit of jack-in-the-pulpit is more obvious, especially as the green berries turn brilliant red at this time of year. Eventually, the stem withers and the seedhead falls to the ground. The tissues of jack-in-the-pulpit, particularly the roots, contain high, toxic levels of oxalic acid. The berries, if eaten, cause a burning sensation in the mouth and throat due to physical cuts caused by the crystals of calcium oxalate. Although cattle, goats, pigs, and sheep are susceptible to the toxin, white-tailed deer, wild turkeys, and wood thrushes appear to consume Jack-in-the-pulpit without distress.

Jack-in-the-pulpit.

Juvenile Great Egrets Dispersing

Although great egrets do breed sporadically in the Northeast, they are not overly common. The likelihood of a sighting increases as summer progresses, due in large part to the phenomenon of post-breeding dispersal. After young great egrets have fledged, individuals wander well outside their typical breeding range, as far north as southern Canada. This northward dispersal of juvenile birds peaks in August and September.

Great egret.

Hickory Tussock Moth Caterpillars Molting

Most tussock moth larvae, such as this hickory tussock moth caterpillar, are densely covered with hairlike structures called setae that bear microscopic barbs. Many people are sensitive to these setae and get an itchy rash if they handle a tussock moth caterpillar. Even touching the cocoon of a tussock moth can cause irritation, as the setae are woven into it. Many tussock moths display warning coloration, such as their black, white, red, orange, or yellow setae.

What looks like two hickory tussock moth larvae in the photograph is actually one adult

Hickory tussock moth caterpillar and shed skin.

caterpillar (left) and the skin it outgrew and shed (right). Many caterpillars shed or molt their skin several times before pupating. You can find hickory tussock moth caterpillars feeding on hickory, walnut, ash, oak, and many other trees. After spending the winter in the leaf litter as a pupa inside a cocoon, a small, spotted, tan moth emerges in the spring.

SEPTEMBER 18

Juvenile Pickerel Frogs Active before Hibernation

If you remember visiting a pond last April or May and hearing a low, snoring sound—the mating call of the male pickerel frog—you might see the

Juvenile pickerel frog.

results of those snores if you revisit the pond now. Young pickerel frogs the size of quarters are currently abundant on the banks of the ponds in which they spent the summer as tadpoles, as well as in nearby vegetation. After emerging from the water sometime between July and September, many of these first-year frogs move into nearby fields, meadows, and damp woods. They are only a few weeks away from burying themselves in mud at the bottom of a pond, where they will hibernate all winter.

Blackberry Seed Gall

Blackberry is host to numerous gall-making insects, including mites, midges, and gall wasps, and their temporary homes, the galls, are more obvious now that blackberry bushes have lost their leaves. Some galls house one inhabitant; others, including the blackberry seed gall caused by a tiny cynipid wasp, have multiple residents. A cluster of small, globular, seedlike galls within which the gall wasp larvae live are pressed together in a lump sur-

Blackberry seed gall.

rounding the cane. Each of these $\frac{1}{10}$-inch-diameter chambers bears a spine, and together they create a reddish brown, hairy mass.

Eastern Cottontail Replacing New England Cottontail

There are two species of cottontails in the Northeast—the New England cottontail and the eastern cottontail. Although they are two separate species, these two rabbits look very similar—the eastern cottontail is slightly larger, has longer ears, and its eyes are half again as large as the New England cottontail's.

Eastern cottontail.

The New England cottontail was the only rabbit east of the Hudson River until the eastern cottontail was introduced in the late 1800s. Today the New England cottontail is restricted to less than a fifth of its range in the early 1900s; the eastern cottontail can be found throughout the Northeast. A combination of dwindling habitat due and inferior eyesight has led to this decline; the eastern cottontail has adapted to changing habitat.

SEPTEMBER 19

Rose Hips Ripening

Rose hips, the fruits of roses, are packed with nutrients and fatty acids and are therefore attractive to a variety of wildlife, including bears, beavers, rabbits, skunks, squirrels, mice, deer,

Rose hip.

thrushes, and ruffed grouse. Humans cannot eat the hairy seeds of rosehips because they irritate our intestines, but teas and jellies made from rosehips are rich in vitamin C. Rose hip seeds have been shown to germinate better after they've passed through an animal's digestive system.

Slugs Mating

Slugs are hermaphroditic, possessing both male and female organs; however, most species mate, with one slug pursuing the slimy trail of another. If a slug is in mating mode, there is a chemical present in its slime that conveys this information to other slugs. When two receptive slugs first encounter each other, there can be extensive interaction prior to mating. The pursuer often mouths the tip of the tail of the slug it's pursuing to confirm that it's receptive. The pursued slug may shake its tail vigorously to signal that it's not interested, in which case they go their separate ways. If the leading slug is receptive, mating eventually takes place, with sperm being transferred from each slug to the other through penises that extend half the length of their bodies. During this process, the sexual organs are entwined; occasionally, in some species, the organs get stuck. If this happens, one slug gnaws off the other's penis in a process called apophallation. The penis is not replaced, and the slug lives the rest of its life as a female. The opening you see on the side of the slug is its respiratory opening, or pneumostome.

Courting slugs.

Spring peeper.

Fruit of black walnut.

Spring Peepers Calling

The *peep*s of male spring peepers can be heard fairly consistently this time of year. Unlike in the spring, these calls are coming not from bodies of water, but from the woods nearby. And they are single *peep*s from individual peepers, not the chorus of "sleigh bells" one hears in the spring. This phenomenon occurs so regularly in the fall that herpetologists have given it a name—fall echo. Scientists speculate that the calling of peepers is triggered by light and temperature conditions, when fall climate conditions are similar to those of spring.

SEPTEMBER 20

Black Walnuts Ripening

The fatty meat of black walnuts is highly prized by both humans and other animals. Before the nut itself can be consumed, one has to crack the outside shell of the nut, which is no mean feat. (Because of its hardness, the shell has a number of commercial uses, including metal cleaning and polishing, oil well drilling, paints, explosives, and cosmetic cleaners.) While humans struggle with this task, rodents, particularly red squirrels,

seem to manage it with ease, thanks to their incisors. If you look closely at the edges of the chewed hole as well as the inner surface of the shell, you will see the tiny incisor marks of a red squirrel. They typically chew a hole on both sides of the nut so that they can gain access to both halves of the meat.

Blue-Headed Vireos Reaching Peak of Migration

Blue-headed vireos, formerly called solitary vireos, are fairly distinctive birds, though perhaps not aptly named. While their white "spectacles," or eye rings, are readily apparent, their blue heads are somewhat subtle. Blue-headed vireos are the last species of vireo to migrate, beginning in August and peaking at the end of September or beginning of October. After spending the winter in the southern United States or Central America, they head north, one to two weeks earlier than any other species of vireo.

Blue-headed vireo.

Juvenile common garter snake eating worm.

Young Common Garter Snakes Feeding

Common garter snakes mate soon after emerging from hibernation in April or May, and four months later the females give birth to live young. The newborn snakes are 5 to 9 inches long at birth and from day one have to fend for themselves. Their diet at this early stage consists of earthworms, insects, slugs, tadpoles, small frogs, and fish. Earthworms are their preferred diet, and garter snakes are known for their ability to find them, even underground. Earthworms produce a chemical substance in their skin that is attractive to, and easily detected by, common garter snakes. If there is an abundant supply of food, the young snakes can grow as much as 1½ inches a month during their first year.

Juvenile common garter snake.

Pokeweed Fruiting

All parts of common pokeweed are somewhat toxic to humans, pets, and livestock. Roots are the most poisonous, leaves and stems are intermediate in toxicity (toxicity increases with maturity), and berries are the least toxic. Even so, the fruit of pokeweed has been widely used by people over the years. Native Americans used it to treat cancer, rheumatism, itching, and syphilis. They also ate young pokeweed shoots, first boiling them several times.

Pokeweed.

Juice from the berries was once used to make ink and dye. Even today, pokeweed is still used—by the food industry to make red food coloring and by farmers to reduce the swelling of cows' udders. Research has shown that pokeweed contains a compound that appears to enhance the immune system, and it has had some anticancer and antivirus effects in animals.

Black and Yellow Argiope Spider Eggs Hatching

Black and yellow argiopes, often referred to as garden spiders, are one of the most conspicuous orb web-spinning spiders—their webs are often 2 feet in diameter. Female black and yellow argiope spiders measure 1½ inches, males about ¾ of an inch. At this time of year, they and many other spiders are busy mating and laying eggs, which the females wrap in a multilayered sac of tan silk

SEPT

315

Black and yellow argiope.

that resembles a large marble in size and shape. Inside a black and yellow argiope's egg sac are between three hundred and fourteen hundred eggs, enveloped in hundreds of very fine, insulating strands of silk. In northern New England, the eggs hatch in the fall and the spiderlings overwinter inside the sac, where they remain dormant unless the weather warms appreciably, in which case they become active and resort to cannibalism, there being no insects in the sac.

Black and yellow argiope egg sac.

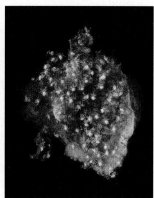

Newly hatched spiderlings inside egg sac.

White-Tailed Bucks Rubbing

Rising levels of testosterone circulating in a male (buck) white-tailed deer's blood toward the end of summer result in the maturation of antlers and the drying up of the velvet that was providing nutrients to them. It used to be thought that bucks engaged in rubbing their antlers against saplings at this time of year in order to remove the velvet, but research has shown there is much more behind this behavior. Rubs are visual and olfactory sign posts that transmit important information to other bucks and does in the area, including individual buck identification, breeding readiness, age, and hierarchy. The positioning of the antlers against a tree is not random—a buck generally rubs the base of his antlers and his forehead skin against the tree. The skin between antlers contains a multitude of scent-producing skin glands called apocrine glands, the same glands used during emotional sweating in humans. These glands typically are inactive during the summer months, but in response to rising testosterone levels they become increasingly active in the fall. Mature, dominant bucks have the most active glands.

Buck rubs have been the subject of much research. More rubs are made in years of good acorn production than in poor ones. Young bucks appear to make fewer rubs than older bucks, and they tend to start rubbing much later in the fall, so rubs you find now were most likely made by mature bucks. Older bucks may make more than twelve hundred rubs during the roughly ninety-day rubbing period, which equals about fifteen rubs per day.

White-tailed deer antler rub.

SEPTEMBER 22

Tree Buds Have Formed

Because tree buds tend to swell and increase greatly in size in the spring, this is often the season when we first notice them, and it is natural to assume that this is the time of year when trees produce buds. In fact, trees produce their buds in

American beech bud.

the summer. If you look in the axils of leaves on any tree right now, you will see full-size buds. These little packages of miniature leaves, branches, and flowers will remain on trees all winter, tightly closed and, in most species, protected from the elements by modified leaves called bud scales. Come spring, when trees are once again taking up quantities of water, their buds will swell, scales will fall off, leaving scars, and tiny, pristine leaves will appear.

Box Elder Bugs Congregating

The base of box elder trees is the gathering site for hundreds of box elder bugs, which are congregating prior to hibernating. While these insects feed on a variety of plants, box elder seeds are their food of choice, so very little damage is done to the trees. Various developmental stages of box elder bugs can be found at these hibernation sites, including the immature red nymphs as well as the black adults. In addition to gathering at the base of box elders, these bugs also seek shelter inside cracks and crevices of exterior house walls. If these cracks allow access to the inside

Box elder bugs.

of a house, the bugs will enter. Even though they are harmless, box elder bugs are considered a household pest by those whose homes are invaded. Be forewarned that they will stain red and produce a foul odor if squashed.

Wood Turtles Heading to Streams for Winter Hibernation

The wood turtle's common name comes from the resemblance of each segment of its top shell, or carapace, to the cross-section of a tree, complete with radiating growth rings. Unlike other turtles,

Wood turtle.

Wood turtle in stream.

American toad.

which favor either land or water, wood turtles reside in both aquatic and terrestrial habitats. They require streams and rivers for spring mating, feeding, and winter hibernation, but they also require terrestrial habitats for summer egg laying and foraging.

In slow-moving streams and rivers, they feed on fish and insects. On land, usually within 300 yards of a stream, they forage for snails, slugs, berries, and mushrooms. Wood turtles are known for stomping their feet on the ground, presumably mimicking the vibrations of rain. Earthworms then come to the surface, and the turtle snaps them up.

SEPTEMBER 23

American Toads Burrowing

Come September, American toad sightings in the Northeast are few and far between. In response to the dropping temperatures and dwindling daylight, these amphibians seek sheltered spots where they will hibernate for the next few months. They either dig burrows in the ground or use existing mammal tunnels or crevices for their hibernacula. To avoid freezing temperatures,

toads will go as much as a foot underground, where they will remain until the ground temperature is well above freezing in the spring.

Juvenile Cedar Waxwings Feeding

Possibly because of the importance of summer fruits in their diet, cedar waxwings are late nesters, but by late August adults have begun their migration to the southern states and Central America. This year's young are beginning this roughly 900-mile flight now, a month after their parents have left. You can often find waxwings feeding in crabapple and other fruit trees, where they stop over to refuel during their flight. Juvenile birds lack the sleek look of adults—the red

Juvenile cedar waxwing.

waxlike feather tips for which this bird is named have not developed, and their plumage is a much duller color than that of the adults.

SEPTEMBER 24

Cut-Leaved Grape Ferns Releasing Spores

Botrychium is a genus of plants referred to as grape ferns. Several species of grape ferns occur in the Northeast, all of which are true ferns, but they are not closely related to the plants we generally think of as ferns. They do share some characteristics with them, however. Like other ferns, grape ferns do not have flowers; they reproduce with spores, not seeds. Typically, a single shoot divides into two blades—one of which is sterile and does the photosynthesizing, and one of which is fertile and bears spores. The resemblance of the plant's clusters of spore cases to miniature clusters of grapes gives this group of ferns its name. Cut-leaved grape fern is one of the most common species of grape ferns in the Northeast. It is roughly 6 to 8 inches tall, and its yellow spores mature at this time of year.

Cut-leaved grape fern.

Ruffed Grouse Well Camouflaged

Cryptic coloration is exemplified in the plumage of ruffed grouse. Their mottled gray, brown, buff, and black feathers make them almost invisible once leaves have started to fall, especially when they remain motionless, as they often do in the presence of danger. Ruffed grouse plumage

Ruffed grouse.

occurs in two color morphs, gray and red/brown; the gray phase predominates in northern parts of its range, the red phase in the south.

Milk Snakes Basking

This is the time of year when snakes take advantage of sunny, mild days by basking in the sun and warming their bodies. It is possible to come across basking milk snakes as late as November, because they are fairly cold and heat tolerant. Soon, however, they will be retreating into their hibernacula, where they are protected from severe cold; being ectothermic, snakes cannot control their body temperature. Rock crevices, abandoned woodchuck burrows, rotting tree stumps, and old foundations are favorite overwintering sites for milk snakes. Here, they gather in groups and go into brumation, a less active state, waking in the spring to mate before emerging.

Milk snake.

SEPTEMBER 25

Chicken of the Woods Fruiting

A bright orange and yellow shelf fungus on a living or dead tree this time of year is likely to be chicken of the woods. The fruiting bodies of this fungus can grow in fairly impressive clumps of up to 100 pounds. They don't appear until well after the fungus has attacked the tree, and because this fungus causes heart rot, the center of the living tree on which it grows is often hollow. Young chicken of the woods, particularly the growing edge of the fruiting body, is sought after by fungi

Camel cricket.

camel crickets are attracted to damp cellars and crawl spaces, giving us an opportunity to admire their impressive legs. Often mistaken for spiders, camel crickets have long legs, but only six, not eight, of them. Their two hind legs are obviously longer and stronger than the other four, and enable this cricket to jump 3 feet high, a skill they use for defense against predators. Invasive species of camel crickets from Asia, including the greenhouse camel cricket, may currently outnumber native species.

Chicken of the woods.

foragers because its taste resembles chicken—hence, its common name. Although it has been considered one of the "foolproof" fungi that can be eaten, similar species have been found that are not edible, so forage with caution.

Camel Crickets Entering Houses

Camel crickets are named for their camel-like humpback appearance. We don't often see these wingless insects—they prefer dark, damp environments, such as under stones and logs, where they can find fungi to eat. However, in extreme weather conditions, such as excessive rainfall or extended periods of hot, dry weather,

Thistle Seeds Dispersing

Many members of the composite family, including thistles and dandelions, have sepals that have been modified and reduced to special feathery bristles known collectively as

American goldfinch.   Thistle seeds and flower.

SEPT

the pappus. In thistles, the bristles are united into a ring around each seed. This ring of bristles, or pappus, serves as a parachute, enabling the wind to disperse a thistle seed up to a mile or more away—if American goldfinches don't eat it first.

SEPTEMBER 26

Blinded Sphinx Moth Larvae Burrowing

Sphinx moths, also known as hawk moths, are a group of long-tongued moths that possess the most acute color vision of any animal. The larva has a "horn" (eyespot or hard button) on its abdomen and is known as a hornworm. Both

Rock polypody.   Rock polypody sori.

Blinded sphinx moth larva.

the tobacco hornworm and tomato hornworm are sphinx moth larvae. The larva of the blinded sphinx moth is the most common sphinx moth larva in many of the Northeast's woods. Its bright green color and granulated skin camouflage it well among the leaves of the oak, hophornbeam, cherry, and poplar trees that it eats. The larva burrows into the soil in the fall and pupates through the winter. An adult moth emerges the following summer and mates, but does not feed.

Rock Polypody Releasing Spores

Rock polypody, also called rock cap fern, is a perennial plant most often found growing on rock surfaces, usually in moist, shady woods. Being a fern, rock polypody reproduces by spores. Sporangia, structures that produce and contain spores, are found on the undersides of the fertile frond leaflets. The sporangia form round clusters called sori. The sori of common polypody are orange brown when mature and lack the protective covering, the indusium, that some other fern species have. At this time of year, the mature spores are being dispersed by the wind.

The ability of common polypody to tolerate extreme desiccation—the leaves roll up when moisture isn't available and resume their normal state when moist conditions return—means it is well adapted to the extreme moisture fluctuations of rock surfaces. Its evergreen fronds are consumed in the winter by ruffed grouse, wild turkey, and white-tailed deer.

SEPTEMBER 27

Sensitive Ferns Killed by Frost

Sensitive fern is aptly named—it is extremely sensitive to frost. When temperatures dip down to 32 degrees or below at this time of

Sensitive fern.

year, it is common to see susceptible parts of sensitive ferns blackened from the frost.

Coral Fungi Fruiting

The branching fruiting bodies of coral fungi, also known as clavarioid fungi, bear a striking resemblance to aquatic coral. These fungi come in a rainbow of colors—white, yellow, orange, red, purple, and tan, depending on the species. Typically found growing on the forest floor or on rotting wood, coral fungi bear their spores on the sides of their branches, not on, or in, gills or pores, like many fungi. All fungi that look like coral were originally lumped into one group, but DNA analysis has determined that, while these fungi may look alike, they are very different and taxonomically they belong to many different families. While many species are edible, some species are poisonous, and distinguishing between the two can be extremely challenging.

Fisher Scent Marking

Many mammals have scent glands that they use to mark territory and to advertise their presence to other members of their own species. The glands are often located around the mouth, eyes, paws, and genital area. While deer have interdigital glands located between their toes, members of both the cat and dog families have scent glands located on the pads of their feet. When these animals walk, they leave a scent trail on the ground, dispersing pheromones that convey critical information to members of their own species, such as their sex, age, reproductive status, and health.

Scent glands (dark spots) on metacarpal pad of fisher foot.

While it is common knowledge that members of the weasel family, including weasels, mink, otters, martens, and fishers, have anal scent glands, the fisher and marten also have scent glands on the large metacarpal pads found behind toe pads of their hind feet.

Coral fungi in a variety of colors.

SEPTEMBER 28

Striped Skunks Digging for Insect Larvae

Lawn divots.

During the summer, invertebrates make up roughly half of a striped skunk's diet. One of their preferred foods is beetle larvae (grubs), particularly immature June bug larvae, which reside an inch or so beneath the surface of the soil. Swirls, or divots, are created when a skunk is actively looking for food and probes the ground with its nose. If and when a skunk smells a protein-rich

Striped skunk.

earthworm or grub in the ground, it digs a hole in order to retrieve it. These cone-shaped holes are dug at night, when skunks are active, and often appear after a heavy rain, when grubs move closer to the surface of the wet ground, making it possible for a skunk to smell them. When the soil dries, the grubs move back down into deeper soil, and skunks will no longer be able to smell them—thus, no more holes will be dug. Because skunks are eating voraciously in order to put on fat for the winter, signs of digging activity are frequently seen in the fall.

Pine needle divots.

Common Loons Molting

Adult loons begin a full body molt (minus their wing feathers) in the late summer and early fall, prior to migration. The black and white breeding plumage of adult loons in summer is replaced by the gray-brown plumage of winter. This process typically begins at the base of the bill and spreads

323

Common loon beginning fall molt.

across the head and over the upper back. The process of molting can extend through migration on into December.

SEPTEMBER 29

Northern Tooth Fungus Fruiting Bodies Appearing

Northern tooth fungus is an unusual combination of both a shelf (bracket) fungus and a toothed fungus. Typically, a shelf fungus produces spores inside pores located on its underside. Northern tooth fungus, however, produces spores on pendant, spine- or toothlike projections on its underside. This fungus usually has several tiers of shelves that grow in tight, thick layers and change from white to light tan as they age.

Northern tooth fungus.

Northern tooth fungus is a parasite of living trees, especially sugar maples, causing the central heartwood of the living tree to rot. The only sign that a maple has this fungal parasite is the appearance of these shelflike fruiting bodies in late summer or fall. Often, trees with this fungus become weak and are blown over by the wind. Like most shelf fungi, northern tooth fungus is considered to be inedible.

Spiderlings Hatching and Dispersing

Many spider eggs hatch in the spring, but some species of spiders produce eggs that hatch in fall. Most spiderlings stay within the egg sac until they undergo their first molt—their small cast skins can be seen inside the old egg sac. After molting, they emerge and cluster together, still living largely upon the remnants of yolk sac in their abdomens. In several days, the spiderlings are ready to disperse. This is necessary to avoid competition for food and to prevent cannibalism among hungry siblings.

Some species, especially ground dwellers, disperse by walking, often over relatively short distances. Others, particularly foliage dwellers and many web builders, mainly disperse by ballooning. To balloon, spiderlings crawl to the top of a blade of grass, a twig, or a branch; point their abdomens up in the air; and release a strand of silk. Air currents catch the silk, often called gossamer, and lift the spider up and carry it off. Aerial dispersal may take a spiderling just a few feet away or much, much farther—spiderlings have been found as far as 990 miles from land. Charles Darwin noted spiderlings landing on the rigging of the *Beagle*, 62 miles out to sea.

Spiderlings dispersing.

SEPT

Common milkweed pod and seeds.

Beaver lodge.

Beaver dam.

Seeds Dispersing

Did you know that only 2 percent of common milkweed flowers develop into pods, and all the seeds in a pod come from one flower?

SEPTEMBER 30

Beavers Refurbishing Lodge and Dam

At this time of year, the industriousness of beavers determines whether they survive the winter. A beaver colony has three major tasks to tend to in the fall: refurbishing their lodge, strengthening and repairing their dam, and cutting and storing their winter food supply. They tend to perform these tasks in this sequence, tackling the lodge first. If the water level is high, the beavers will raise the floor of the lodge and the roof of the sleeping chamber. They also add new material, both mud and sticks, to the exterior of the lodge to strengthen the entire structure. Mud, sticks, and vegetation are also added to the dam to reinforce it.

Beaver transporting branch.

Beaver.

OCTOBER

Poison Ivy

The only characteristic that holds true for any poison ivy plant is that its leaves are divided into three leaflets. Other than this, poison ivy is a master of disguise. Botanically speaking, it is a deciduous woody vine, but it can also take the form of a shrub or thick ground cover. The vine itself can be thin and sprawling, or ropelike and up to 4 inches thick. While the compound leaves always have three leaflets, they can be rounded or pointed, shiny or dull, and their margins toothed or smooth. It is understandable why this plant is frequently not recognized.

North American poison ivy was described in 1612 by Captain John Smith in Jamestown, Virginia, as resembling English ivy, but "causeth redness, itchynge, and finally blysters." While poison ivy was relatively common in southern United States at this time, it has only become well established in the Northeast during the past one hundred years or so. Much of the Northeast was cleared in the 1800s, and poison ivy quickly moved into the open, sunny pastures, where it thrived. However, grazing held it in check. As farming declined in the twentieth century, there was no holding back the natural spread of this member of the cashew/sumac family, and poison ivy spread rampantly through both fields and woodlands.

At this time of year, poison ivy is at its most beautiful, for its green leaves turn a brilliant red in the fall. The 3-inch clusters of flowers that were produced in the spring have developed into white berries that persist well into winter. Botanists feel that the color change of poison ivy leaves at the very time that its fruit is ripening is no coincidence. In fact, this process has been given a name—foliar fruit flagging. The red color of the leaves is thought to attract birds, including many fall migrants, which eat the fruits and disperse the seeds in their droppings, often many miles from the original vine. Whether or not the red color of its leaves serves as an avian lure, poison ivy does provide food for over sixty species of birds. Those for whom poison ivy berries are a preferred food include northern mockingbirds, black-capped chickadees, ruffed grouse, hermit thrushes, ruby-crowned kinglets, starlings, yellow-rumped warblers, white-throated sparrows, wild turkeys, northern flickers, and both hairy and downy woodpeckers.

While poison ivy provides much needed sustenance for birds, especially during the most trying season of the year, its negative effect on approximately 40 to 50 percent of the humans that come in contact with it can't be ignored. All parts of the plant except the pollen contain resinous compounds called urushiols that cause inflammation of the skin, blistering, and itching. The compounds can be transferred to people by direct contact with the plant or with objects or animals that have been exposed to the plant, including tools, pets, and clothing. The smoke produced when burning poison ivy also contains droplets of these compounds, which are easily breathed in and carried to the lungs. You can be affected year-round by this plant, and the compounds remain active on objects and in dead plants for years—century-old herbarium specimens of poison ivy have produced rashes on botanists.

Should you not be part of the population that is immune to these compounds, wash your skin in soap and cool water as soon as possible

Common loon in fall.

Poison ivy leaves: "Leaves of three, let it be; berries white, take flight."

Although toxic to humans, poison ivy berries provide much needed sustenance for birds in the winter.

if you come in contact with a poisonous plant. It only takes ten minutes for the compounds to be absorbed by the skin, so time is of the essence. The sap of crushed jewelweed or touch-me-not is a remedy that some swear by, as are plantain and sweetfern sap. No one can be complacent, however, as immunity can be ephemeral; present one year and gone the next.

Poison ivy is very sensitive to carbon dioxide, and even slightly elevated levels of CO_2 have proven to increase its growth. In the past fifty or sixty years, during which time the amount of carbon dioxide in the atmosphere has increased by roughly 22 percent, poison ivy's growth rate has doubled. The amount of urushiol has not only increased, but it is also more potent.

Porcupine Courtship

Porcupines are one of the few mammals that breed in the fall. At the onset of the breeding season, male porcupines travel farther afield, expanding their range in hopes of finding a female. When a male encounters a receptive female, a form of behavior referred to as a

The male porcupine's courtship of a mate is very elaborate, but it is worth the energy expended, as 90 percent of female porcupines are impregnated each year.

guarding episode begins. Typically, the female sits on a branch of a tree, and the male sits on a lower branch of the same tree, guarding his potential mate from the advances of other male porcupines. If another suitor ambles along and becomes interested in the female, he may challenge the resident male, and a vicious battle can ensue wherein the porcupines use every weapon available to them, including teeth, claws, and quills. The guarding episode can last several days.

Once mutual interest has been established between two porcupines, a very peculiar ritual usually takes place. The excited male does a three-legged walk usually with the left forepaw holding onto his genitals. An alternative behavior that has been observed involves the male holding a long stick in his forepaws and straddling and riding it, while the female does the same. Yet a third scenario has the male rubbing his genitals on objects while producing a low whining sound. One would assume that any one of these behaviors would not only get the attention of the female, but convince her of her suitor's ardor.

OCT

Males can become quite aggressive with other males when it comes to staking a claim on a female porcupine, to the point of using their quills on each other.

However, there is more to come. At some point during this demonstrative declaration, the male squirts high-velocity jets of urine directly at the female, thoroughly wetting her. If she's not ready to mate, she walks away; if she is ready, she presses her quills against her body, raises her hind quarters, and arches her tail over her back, so that the male has a safe surface for his chest and forepaws when he mounts her. Apparently, with mice, male urine accelerates estrus in the female, and this could be the case with their rodent relative, the porcupine, as well.

The male's timing has to be just right for his objective to be met. This is even more difficult than it sounds, as there are a mere eight to ten hours during which the female is physically receptive. Perhaps this is why there is nothing ambiguous about the signals that the male porcupine gives the female.

This extensive effort of courtship and mating is not without its reward. After a seven-month gestation, the female porcupine gives birth to one young porcupette that weighs approximately 1 pound, is fully furred, has its eyes open, and has 1-inch-long soft quills, which harden within an hour. In eighteen short months, it will be sexually mature.

Cocoons

It has been estimated that 45 to 60 percent of all animal species on the planet are insects that undergo complete metamorphosis. These insects hatch from eggs as wormlike larvae that eventually enter a pupal stage before emerging as adults. Some of these insects have silk glands and spin silken cases, or cocoons, around themselves just before transforming into pupae.

Cocoons are as varied as the larvae that spin them; they differ in size, durability, structure, material, shape, and color as well as how they are attached to a substrate. Although cocoons are most often associated with moths, other insects, including beetles, fleas, winged members of the order Neuroptera, and caddisflies, also create them. Some of these cocoons are quite intricate, many incorporate material from the surroundings, and all are well designed to protect the pupae within.

The aquatic spongillafly larva emerges from water and spins a tiny, densely woven inner cocoon surrounded by a lacy net.

Black flies spin pouch-like underwater cocoons.

The larvae of more than ten species of sawfly feed on pine needles. Needles as well as bark are eaten by the larvae before they spin cocoons in July and pupate. The cocoon is cylindrical and is finely textured, somewhat glossy, and brown. It measures roughly ⅓ inch long by ⅛ inch wide. Cocoons are most frequently spun on the host among the needles, at the bases of the small branches, or on the trunk in bark crevices. They are usually attached lengthwise to branches. Occasionally, they are found on non-host trees, shrubs, or grasses. When ready to emerge, the sawfly cuts the circular end of the cocoon to create an opening.

Ichneumon wasp larvae spin cocoons similar to sawflies, but they are marked with blotches of white or gold.

Flea cocoons are found in cracks and crevices on the ground or among debris. The adults

OCT

The aquatic *Climacia sp.* spongilla-fly larva emerges from the water and spins a tiny cocoon (3–7 mm). It then covers it with a silken net made up of little hexagons.

Adult sawflies emerge from their cocoon through a neatly cut hole at one end.

lie motionless, sometimes for months, inside the cocoons until stimulated by the vibrations of a potential host, at which time they spring into action.

By far the largest cocoons found in the Northeast are those of giant silk moths, ranging from 1½ inches to 4 inches in length. Even at this size, these cocoons can be very difficult to find, as they are so well camouflaged. The larvae spin their tough, papery silk cocoons with a spinneret located near their mouths.

The promethea moth larva spins a 2-inch-long cocoon that it wraps in a single leaf and then spins silk around the stem of the leaf so that it remains attached to the twig through the winter. In the spring, the adult moth emerges through a valvelike structure at the upper end of the cocoon.

Luna moth cocoons are much more flimsy than other silk moth cocoons, with very thin walls, making emergence relatively easy for the adult moth. These cocoons are usually enclosed in a leaf and are found on the ground.

Polyphemus moth cocoons are usually enclosed in one or several leaves and typically fall to the ground in the fall. Both ends are closed until the spring, when the pupa secretes a fluid that dissolves the gummy substance that binds the silken cocoon together.

The purpose of cocoons is to protect the pupae they contain. While some dark-colored cocoons do absorb heat, most provide little direct insulation. They may, however, reduce the rate at which the temperature of the pupa within them changes.

Polyphemus moth cocoon.

Protection from elements other than the cold is provided in a number of ways. Cocoons are certainly helpful in physically protecting many pupae overwintering inside cocoons that are on the ground, covered by soil and/or snow. They provide a barrier between the pupa and ice crystals that may form on the surface of the cocoon. The silk of some cocoons is so tough that it discourages predators. Other cocoons are more or less waterproof. Last but not least, the silk of many cocoons has antibacterial and antifungal properties.

OCTOBER 1

Saddleback Caterpillars Preparing to Pupate

There is a group of moths (family Limacodidae) which are known as slug caterpillar moths due to the manner in which they travel during their larval stage, secreting a semifluid silk from their ventral pores as they move. The caterpillars come in all sizes and shapes. Among them is the saddleback caterpillar, which is much more colorful than the brown adult moth it eventually turns into. Saddleback caterpillars are best known for their stinging (urticating) spines. Reputedly far worse than that of a bee, the sting of the saddleback caterpillar may be the most potent of any North American caterpillar. The larva's bright colors serve to warn predators of its toxicity. Soon these

OCT

Saddleback caterpillar.

caterpillars will be spinning cocoons, which can contain spines as well, in which they will pupate until emerging as moths next spring.

Common Loons Migrating

Most of the eastern U.S. and Canada common loon population shifts from freshwater inland breeding locations to coastal marine wintering areas, although some remain at inland freshwater sites throughout winter. Research shows that the very large loons in Maine, New Brunswick, and eastern New Hampshire do not migrate far and primarily overwinter in the Gulf of Maine, while smaller loons from other New England and New York breeding populations migrate to Long Island Sound south to New Jersey.

Some common loons begin their diurnal migration to their wintering territory in late summer, but most loons leave their breeding territory in September in higher latitudes and October in lower latitudes, and arrive at their destination by the end of November. Breeding pairs and their offspring do not migrate together. Parents generally migrate first, usually separately; the young remain on their lakes after adults have departed, until near freeze-up, and often migrate in groups. Although they often migrate singly, common loons do form groups—in some places, hundreds or thousands of birds—on large bodies of water before and during migration. These are referred to as staging areas. When migrating over land, loons can reach an altitude of 1½ miles; over water they usually fly within 300 feet of the surface.

Common Garter Snakes Basking

Snakes take advantage of sunny, mild autumn days by basking in the sun to warm their bodies. It is possible to come across basking common garter snakes as late as November, as they are more cold tolerant than many species of snakes. Most, however, will soon be retreating into their hibernating sites, or hibernacula, where they are protected from severe cold. To further protect them, a high level of glucose acts as antifreeze in snakes.

The ideal hibernaculum not only serves as a temperature buffer, but also conceals its occupant from potential predators, permits gas exchange, and prevents excessive desiccation. Rock crevices, abandoned woodchuck burrows, rotting tree stumps, and old foundations are favorite hibernacula for snakes and other hibernating animals. Common garter snakes typically

Common loon.

Common garter snake.

overwinter in groups, and some even share their hibernacula with other species of snakes, including smooth green snakes, ring-necked snakes, and red-bellied snakes.

OCTOBER 2

Deciduous Leaves Turning Color

The reds and purples of fall foliage come from a group of pigments called anthocyanins. Unlike carotenoids (orange pigments), xanthophylls (yellow pigments), and tannins (brown pigments), which are present in leaves throughout the growing season, anthocyanins are produced toward the end of summer. The green pigment chlorophyll begins to break down in the fall and isn't replaced, allowing other pigments to be visible. At this time, phosphate, which has been helping break down the sugar that the plant has made during the warmer months, begins to decrease in the leaf, and this triggers the production of anthocyanin pigments. The amount of anthocyanin produced is, in part, determined by the weather—the brighter the sun, the more anthocyanin is produced, and cold, but not freezing, nights all but guarantee brilliant foliage. The production of this pigment is not for show only. Anthocyanin protects a leaf from fall sunlight damage, therefore allowing it to continue to produce nutrients for the tree until it falls off.

Hobblebush.

False Solomon's Seal Fruiting

False Solomon's seal's leaves are starting to lose their chlorophyll, bringing attention to their bright red fruit. This member of the lily family's flower arrangement differs from true Solomon's seal's whose flowers dangle down below the leaves singly or in pairs. There are several theories as to the derivation of false Solomon's seal's name, ranging from the appearance of its leaf scars (King Solomon was said to be responsible for their markings, which resemble a signet ring with Hebrew letters) to its six-pointed flowers that resemble the Star of David, which was commonly called Solomon's Seal.

False Solomon's seal often appears in clusters, as the stems are the annual growths off of a perennial rhizome, the subterranean stem of a plant. In the spring, each stem develops a terminal cluster of small, white, star-shaped flowers. Bees and beetles are the chief pollinators that enable the plant to produce green berries that turn red in the late summer and fall (soil pH affects the final coloration of the fruit formed). The roots of false Solomon's seal have been used medicinally in a number of ways, but one of the more unusual ways of utilizing this

False Solomon's seal.

plant was that of a Native American tribe in California that used an effusion of crushed false Solomon's seal roots to stun fish and facilitate their harvest from streams.

OCTOBER 3

Woolly Bears on the Move

Woolly bear caterpillar.

Legend has it that the more black at either end of a woolly bear caterpillar (the larval stage of the Isabella tiger moth), the harder the winter that lies ahead, and the more brown, the milder the winter. However, the coloration of a woolly bear has more to do with its diet and age than the coming winter's weather. Woolly bears molt their exoskeleton (skin) up to six times. The more they eat, the more frequently they molt, and each time they molt, a brown section is added. The longer the summer—and thus time for woolly bears to eat—the greater the ratio of brown to black on a woolly bear. A mostly brown woolly bear is more an indication of an early spring or late fall than it is a forecast of the coming winter's severity.

Moose Advertising

As part of the rut, or breeding season, that they are in the middle of, bull moose seek to advertise their wares as far and as wide as possible.

Information regarding the moose's dominance is conveyed visually to cow moose, as well as other bull moose, by the size of a bull moose's antlers. Additional information is conveyed olfactorily through the transfer of urinary pheromones via the bull moose's bell, or dewlap, the structure located under the chin of both bull and cow moose.

A moose's bell increases in size with age; the pictured moose is just a yearling. While there are many theories as to the function of the bell—thermoregulation during the heat of summer, extra insulation for a moose's chin when bedding down in snow, and a secondary indicator of sex and age—it has been confirmed that the bell is an olfactory device that plays a role in communication.

During rut a bull often digs a depression, or wallow, in the ground in which he urinates. He then proceeds to stamp and wallow in this depression, thoroughly soaking his antlers, belly, and bell with his pheromone-laden urine. Cows are attracted to this pungent scent. Suspended from the bull's body, the bell is an excellent way of dissipating these pheromones into the air—an innovative means of sexual advertising.

Bull moose.

OCTOBER 4

Red-Winged Blackbird Diet Changing from Insects to Seeds

During the breeding season, insects make up the bulk of the red-winged blackbird's diet, but during the rest of the year, plant seeds are preferred. While the seeds of ragweed, corn, oats, and smartweed are more staple food sources, cattail seeds are not overlooked. At maturity, and under dry conditions, the cattail spike bursts, releasing the seeds—some estimates are as high as 228,000 seeds per spike. When this happens, blackbirds take advantage of the easily accessible source of food, but the minute size of each seed, just .0079 inch long, means a great deal of work per meal.

Male red-winged blackbird.

Northern Two-Lined Salamanders Seeking Hibernacula

Northern two-lined salamanders are usually found near open water, along stream beds, or in swamps and other wetlands. Named for the two black stripes running down its back, this amphibian typically ventures out in search of invertebrate prey shortly after dark. Adults can detach their tails to escape capture. The tail continues to move as the salamander escapes from a snake or other predators, including various mammals, birds, and larger salamanders.

In winter months, adults may remain active in springs, streams, or water-laden soil if the temperature in these places remains above freezing.

Northern two-lined salamander.

In northern New England, adults usually overwinter up to 31 inches below the surface in the soil of a stream bank.

OCTOBER 5

Dark-Eyed Juncos Protected by Countershading

Countershading is a common color pattern in animals in which the upper side of the animal is darker than the lower side. This color pattern provides camouflage for the animal when viewed from the side, above, or below by balancing the sunlight on the animal's back and the shadow beneath the animal so as to blend the animal's

Dark-eyed junco.

side profile with its surroundings. In addition, when viewed from below, a counter-shaded animal with a light belly blends into the light coming from the sky above. When viewed from above, the darker back of a countershaded animal blends into the darker ground colors below. Because birds spend a considerable amount of time in the air, this defensive coloration is very beneficial.

Blister Beetles Defending Themselves

Blister beetles are aptly named, for when they are disturbed they emit a yellow, oily, defensive secretion called cantharidin from their joints, which causes blisters when it comes in contact with skin. This toxin deters many potential predators and is especially effective against ants. As little as 100 milligrams is reported to be fatal to humans if ingested, and this amount can be extracted from just a few beetles. Humans used to crush and dry blister beetles and use the resulting concoction for gout and arthritis. It was also used as a popular aphrodisiac known as Spanish fly. Because of its toxicity, it is no longer widely used in medicine.

Cantharidin is, however, indirectly used by tree-nesting nuthatches. With a limited number of tree cavities, there is competition among animals using them to raise their young, especially between squirrels and nuthatches. Nuthatches have been seen with short-winged blister beetles in their beaks, sweeping them on the bark around tree cavity entrances. The nuthatches don't eat the beetles; they use them strictly as tools. It is assumed that the birds do this so as to repel squirrels with the cantharidin that is smeared on the tree.

Bear's Head Tooth Fungi Fruiting

Bear's head tooth fungus, also known as lion's mane, monkey head, and icicle mushroom, is fruiting now. This delicious, fleshy fungus, with a taste somewhat reminiscent of lobster, is among the safest, most unmistakable of all of North America's species of edible wild mushrooms; it looks like a cluster of white fungal icicles hanging off a decaying log, stump, or dead tree trunk. Bear's head tooth fungus fruits on a number of different deciduous trees, particularly beech, maple, birch, oak, walnut, and sycamore. Distinguishing among the species of *Hericium* can be tricky, but all species are edible and tasty. Even so, it is wise to have someone very familiar with edible fungi confirm identification of any fungus that may be consumed.

Bear's head tooth fungus.

Short-winged blister beetle.

OCTOBER 6

Paper Wasps Still Flying

Worker paper wasps collect nectar from late-blooming flowers such as mustard and goldenrod right up until the first hard frost, after which both they and their queen die. Mated female offspring of the queen are the only survivors in the colony, and they seek overwintering sites such as rotting logs. In these protected spots they tuck their wings and antennae under their bodies, and hunker down for the winter. If predators such as spiders don't kill these new queens, and if they don't emerge early due to a warm winter or starve due to lack of food, the young queens begin building nests and laying eggs in the spring. After establishing colonies and producing queen offspring, their year-long life ends in the fall.

Hermit thrush.

Paper wasp.

Hermit Thrushes Migrating

The hermit thrush is often one of the last thrushes to leave its breeding grounds in the fall—peak migration is between the end of September and the middle of October. High pressure, clear skies, and wind from the north usually produce many sightings of this bird at this time of year. Unlike many other species of thrushes that winter in Central or South America, the hermit thrush is not a long distance migrant and does not cross the Gulf of Mexico. Typically, it makes several two- to six-day stopovers to refuel before reaching its wintering grounds in southern U.S. and Mexico.

Porcupines Foraging

There are a few weeks in September and October when acorns and beechnuts are mature enough to eat but haven't yet fallen to the ground. Porcupines take advantage of this nutritious supply of food that is not yet accessible to small rodents, deer, and turkeys, and they climb oak trees to

Oak nip twigs discarded by porcupine.

Acorn caps remain on nip twigs.

Incisor marks on nip twig.

consume acorns. Because an average porcupine weighs between 12 and 35 pounds, it is unable to climb to the end of a branch, where acorns are located, so it nips off the tips of fruit-bearing branches and then eats the acorns, leaving the caps still attached to the branch. When all the acorns on a branch have been eaten, the branch is discarded. You can often find these branch tips, or nip twigs, on the ground beneath large oaks on a good mast year and, inevitably, some fall to the ground. The end of the twig is usually cut at a 45-degree angle, and often you can see the lines made by the porcupine's incisors.

Porcupine.

Raccoons Fattening Up

In the Northeast, raccoons spend the fall fattening up, for little, if any, food is consumed during the winter. Acorns, hickory nuts, beechnuts, and hazelnuts are favorite sources of fat. When insects are available, they form a large part of a raccoon's diet—delicacies include larvae of dug-up yellow jacket and bumble bee nests, honey bees, and the honey the bees have stored for the winter. Injured birds and rabbits, mice, bats, wild grapes, and an occasional crayfish provide raccoons with enough sustenance so that fat makes up almost 50 percent of their body weight as they head into winter.

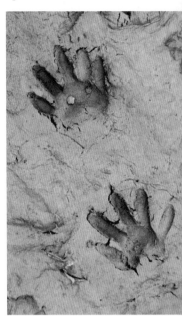

Raccoon tracks.

On the coldest winter days, raccoons will seek shelter in hollow trees, sometimes holing up for as long as a month at a time. Communal denning sometimes occurs, with up to twenty-three raccoons occupying the same den. Considered deep sleepers, raccoons do not lower their metabolism significantly, and therefore are not classified as true hibernators.

Eastern Chipmunks Storing Food

By the end of this month or the beginning of November, most eastern chipmunks will have gathered and stored their winter food supply underground in a special chamber which they will visit every two or three weeks throughout the winter to feed. Up to half a bushel of nuts and seeds

OCT

337

Eastern chipmunk.

Yellow-fuzz slime mold.

can be stored here, which means many trips from the food source to the larder. In order to minimize the number of trips, chipmunks manage to cram their cheek pouches as full as possible. The contents found in one chipmunk's two pouches include the following: thirty-one kernels of corn, thirteen prune pits, seventy sunflower seeds, thirty-two beechnuts, six acorns.

Yellow-Fuzz Cone Slime Forming Fruiting Bodies

Yellow-fuzz cone slime is a slime mold that is found in clusters on rotting wood. Neither a plant nor an animal, slime molds are known for the dramatic transformations they go through from the time they first appear to their disintegration. Slime molds are slimy and mold-like when they first emerge, but they soon change color, shape, and texture as they develop. Yellow-fuzz cone slime was named for its reproductive stage—when its gelatinous plasmodium starts fruiting. It forms tiny, round, shiny, spore-bearing sporangia that can be orange to yellow in color. When the spores are mature, the tops of these sporangia open up, creating goblet-shaped cups filled with yellowish, fuzzy threads interspersed with pale yellow spores. These threads are thought to be involved in the dispersal of the spores. The stages of yellow-fuzz cone slime are so different that you might well not recognize that they are the same species.

OCTOBER 8

Dead Man's Fingers

When it first appears above ground in the spring, the club- or finger-shaped fruit of dead man's fingers appears powdery white from the asexual spores that cover its surface. As it matures, it acquires a crusty, black surface. This is the sexual stage. The interior of the fruiting body of this fungus is white; just inside the outer surface is a blackened, dotted layer containing structures called perithecia which hold sacs of sexual spores. Dead man's fingers, unlike most fungi, which release their spores in a few hours or days, releases its spores over months, or even years. It can have many separate fingers, and sometimes

Dead man's fingers.

OCT

the fingers are fused, causing it to look somewhat like a hand. Look for this fungus growing on hardwood stumps and logs, particularly American beech and maples.

Red Squirrels Caching Winter Food Supply

Many animals cache food for later consumption—bobcats, fishers, chipmunks, beavers, and squirrels, to name just a few. If you find a mushroom hanging in an unlikely spot, such as from a tree branch or tucked into the bark of a tree where it didn't grow, it's likely that you have happened upon the work of a red squirrel. Red squirrels are known for their habit of snipping mushrooms and hanging them from branches and rough bark in order to dry them before collecting them and caching them for dining on later in the winter.

Mushroom cached by red squirrel.

Northern Cardinal Diet Reflected in Plumage

The diet of a northern cardinal consists mainly of seeds, fruits, and insects; the average annual consumption is 29 percent animal and 71 percent vegetable matter. As fall progresses, the proportion of vegetable matter in its diet increases until it reaches a high of 88 percent during winter. Cardinals' red plumage results from the ingestion of carotenoid pigments obtained from their diet during the fall molt in

Northern cardinal.

September and October. Fruits and insects are high in carotenoids, while most seeds are poor sources.

OCTOBER 9

Canada Geese Migrating

This is the time of year when the honking of migrating Canada geese can be heard as the familiar V-shaped formation passes overhead. Many of these birds have a long, arduous migration, and they need to conserve as much energy as possible. The V formation greatly boosts their efficiency and range. Geese flying in a V formation have slower heart beats than geese flying solo, and they can achieve a distance 71 percent

Migrating Canada geese in V formation.

greater than single birds. The birds in front make this possible by enduring the most air resistance and, at the same time, improving the aerodynamics of the birds behind them by reducing the drag by up to 65 percent. Canada geese constantly rotate positions in order to share flight fatigue.

Slugs Laying Eggs

Slug and eggs.

If you spend enough time looking under rotting logs at this time of year, you are bound to come across clusters of thirty or so tiny, pearly white eggs. With the right climate conditions, slugs will

mate and lay eggs twice a year—once early in the spring and once in late summer. Thirty to forty days after mating, the female slug lays her eggs under leaves and mulch, in or under a rotting log or in some other cool and moist location. The eggs hatch in ten to one hundred days, depending upon the temperature—the warmer it is, the faster they hatch.

Slug eggs.

New England Asters Providing Bees with Late Season Nectar

At a time of year when nectar and pollen sources are few and far between, New England aster provides many species of bees with food. This composite seems designed specifically for easy pollination. Its wide open flower shape provides a flat surface for insects to land on, and because the nectar and pollen are not hidden deep inside the flowers, both long- and short-tongue bee species can easily access them. Unlike honey bees, bumble bees do not have a large store of honey in their nests, so they need pollen and nectar throughout the season. The few flowers such as New England aster that blossom as late as October are visited frequently and in large numbers. Only the queen bumble bee overwinters, but the workers continue collecting nectar and pollen until they die in late fall.

New England aster flowers close at night, when fewer pollinating insects are flying. If an unusually cool period arrives during the time when New England aster is blooming, the blossoms close. Although it may seem that the aster is losing pollination opportunities during a cold day, bees are not very active in cool weather.

Bumble bees on New England aster.

OCTOBER 10

Yellow-Orange Fly Agaric Fruiting

The yellow-orange fly agaric is common in the Northeast, especially where conifers grow. In the West, this mushroom is often a bright red color, but in the East it's typically orange or yellow. When certain gilled mushrooms, including many *Amanita* species such as yellow-orange fly agaric, first form, they are encased in a membrane called a universal veil. As the mushroom enlarges and matures, the veil ruptures, with remnants of it remaining on the mushroom's cap.

Fly agaric fungi got their name from the custom of placing little pieces of the mushroom in milk to attract flies. The flies became inebriated, crashed into walls, and died. This mushroom is poisonous, as are many *Amanita* species, and hallucinogenic when consumed by humans. The toxins affect the part of the brain that is responsible for fear, turning off the fear emotion. Vikings, who had a reputation for fierceness, are said to have ingested this mushroom prior to invading a village.

Woolly Aphids

Woolly aphids are just that—aphids that have special glands that produce waxlike filaments which resemble white wool. When the "wool" is brushed aside, the dark aphid bodies below are visible. Colonies of woolly aphids often congregate in cottony masses while sucking the sap of a host plant or tree; in such a mass they are somewhat camouflaged in that they can easily be mistaken for mold or a fungus. When woolly aphids take flight, the wax strands catch the wind and allow them to drift, making them look more like seeds than edible prey.

Yellow-orange fly agaric.

Woolly aphids.

Seed Dispersal by Wind

Flowering plants have evolved many ways of getting their seeds dispersed to a location where there is less competition for sunlight and moisture than directly under the parent plant. Because plants have limited mobility, they use a number of different agents to accomplish this, including wildlife, water, force (expulsion), and wind.

Wind is the most primitive form of seed dispersal. Most plants whose seeds are dispersed by wind have several characteristics in common. Their seeds are usually relatively small and quite light. Most produce a very large number of seeds in order to increase the chances of some of them landing in a spot conducive to germination.

The two primary adaptive structures that wind-dispersed seeds utilize are a feathery pappus (modified sepals) attached to the seed which acts as a parachute in plants such as dandelions, goatsbeard, asters, coltsfoot, milkweed, and thistle; and wings. The spinning that the wings promote slows the seed's fall so that the wind might carry it some distance away from the parent plant. Maples, ashes, American basswood, and hophornbeam, among others, have winged seeds.

Clematis.

Dandelion.

Thistle.

Goatsbeard.

Box elder

White ash.

American basswood.

OCTOBER 11

Witch Hazel Flowering and Dispersing Seeds

Witch hazel is the only shrub in the woods of North America that has ripe fruit, flowers, and the following year's leaf buds on its branches at the same time. As colorful fall foliage disappears, the yellow, strap-like petals of witch hazel's fragrant flowers brighten denuded woods—one of nature's final fanfares of the fall. The flowers, which are pollinated by moths that are still active this late in the season, develop into small, hard capsules that remain dormant throughout the winter. These capsules mature throughout the following summer and in the fall expel two shiny black seeds 10 to 20 feet away from the tree. The

Witch hazel flower, fruit, and leaf bud.

seeds take another year to germinate, making the length of time from flowering to germination approximately two years. In the photo, the yellowish tan capsules were formed this summer, and the one brown, year-old capsule (furthest to right) has opened and dispersed its seeds.

Millipedes Migrating

We don't often see millipedes because of their preference for secluded, moist sites where they feed on decaying vegetation and other organic matter. Compost piles, heavily mulched shrub

Millipede.

or flower beds, rotting logs, or the soil under logs and stones are likely spots to find these arthropods. Millipedes overwinter as adults and are often seen migrating in the fall, presumably in search of overwintering sites that will provide added protection.

Woodchucks Heading to Winter Burrows

Woodchucks are one of the few species of mammals that enter into true hibernation. When the temperatures dip into the forties, usually in

Woodchuck.

October in the Northeast, most woodchucks leave their summer burrows and head for the woods, where they dig a tunnel that ends in a chamber that is well below the frost line. Here they curl up in a ball and live off of the additional 30 percent of body weight they put on in the fall. In order to survive until March or April, a woodchuck's metabolism slows way down. Its heartbeat goes from one hundred beats a minute to five, and its body temperature goes from 96 degrees down to 47 degrees.

OCTOBER 12

Deciduous Leaves Falling

The falling of a leaf is the final step in an ordered series of events referred to as senescence. This process allows trees to conserve resources, prepare for a dormant period, and shed inefficient tissues. When leaves become unable to produce food due to a lack of chlorophyll, a process of shutting down and sealing off begins. Leaves are shed through a number of biological actions that take place at the base of the leaf's stem, or petiole. The walls of some cells weaken, while those of adjacent cells expand. The expansion of the latter causes pressure against the weaker-walled cells, resulting in these two groups of cells tearing away from each other, causing the leaf to fall. The tree forms a protective barrier, the leaf scar, on the wound where the leaf had been attached to the branch, sealing it off from pests and the environment.

Beaver Lodges Vary in Design

Beavers are hard at work refurbishing their mud and stick lodges in preparation for winter, when their movements will be restricted and they will spend both day and night inside their lodge. When we think of a beaver lodge, we picture a mound of sticks and mud in the middle of a beaver pond. This was not always the case, however, and still isn't today. The earliest and most primitive beaver lodges consisted of a burrow in the side of a high bank with the entrance under water. The next advance was the addition of sticks and mud piled over the top of the bank as added protection

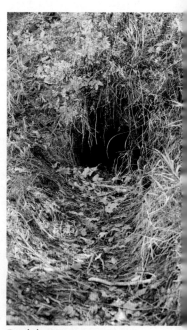

Bank burrow.

Falling sugar maple leaf.

Bank lodge.

Middle-of-pond lodge.

Brown snowberry clearwing larva.

from predators. Eventually, beavers started building a complete lodge on top of the bank which had an underwater entrance. The most advanced design is the lodge we most commonly associate with beavers—one that is built from the bottom of the pond and is completely surrounded by water. It requires the greatest amount of work but offers the greatest amount of protection to the beaver.

Snowberry Clearwing Larvae Soon to Pupate

The snowberry clearwing, a type of sphinx moth, is one of several daytime-flying "hummingbird moths," so called because of their ability to hover while drinking nectar from a flower and because of the humming sound they make, much like a hummingbird. The yellow and black bands of the snowberry clearwing's abdomen also cause it to be mistaken for a bumble bee. The most distinctive thing about this moth is that a large portion of its wings are transparent, due to scales falling off.

Snowberry clearwings are often seen around the time that bee balm is in bloom, in July and August. The females entice the males with a pheromone that they produce from glands at the tip of their abdomen. After mating, the females lay their tiny, round, green eggs on their larval food plants. Like many sphinx moths, the larvae have horns at the end of their bodies. Most snowberry clearwing larvae are green, but they can be brown, as well. Both colors enable them to be well camouflaged as they feed on the leaves of honeysuckle, viburnum, hawthorn, snowberry, cherry, mint, and plum. The caterpillars are active until late fall, when they drop to the ground, spin a loose cocoon, and pupate, partially protected by leaf litter. The pupa spends the winter hidden under the leaves, and the adult moth emerges the following spring.

Green snowberry clearwing larva.

Adult snowberry clearwing moth.

OCTOBER 13

White-Throated Sparrows Migrating

Although the breeding and winter ranges of white-throated sparrows overlap, most, if not all, populations are migratory. During their flight southward in the fall, white-throated sparrows stop during the day to refuel on seeds, fruits, and insects, if available. Females winter further south than males. Winged euonymus, or burning bush, is an invasive shrub that produces vast quantities of capsules, each containing up to four seeds. White-throated sparrows as well as many other species of birds find these bright red seeds attractive and inadvertently disperse them far and wide.

Note the long ovipositor at the tip of this female field cricket's abdomen between the two sensory organs, called cerci. Male crickets lack ovipositors.

White-throated sparrow.

Crickets Courting, Mating, and Laying Eggs

In late summer and autumn, crickets court by rubbing their forewings together, a practice referred to as stridulation. At the base of each forewing is a specialized vein with a series of hard teeth, or ridges—the stridulatory file. Only one file is fully functional, and in crickets it is usually the one on the left wing. On the inner, lower edge of the right forewing is the scraper, a sharp, hard projection that rubs against the file when the cricket opens and closes its wings during stridulation. In most species, it is the male crickets that sing, but both sexes have "ears," or tympana, on their front legs. After mating, the female cricket deposits her eggs in the soil or in plant tissue, depending on the species.

Cinnabar Polypore Fungus Fruiting

It is very hard to miss a fruiting cinnabar polypore fungus due to its electric red-orange coloration on both upper and lower surfaces. It is in a group of fungi known as polypores, which usually grow on dead trees, are shaped like shelves rather than umbrellas, and have many tiny holes, or pores, on the underside, where spores develop.

Cinnabar fungus.

Cinnabar polypore is called a white rot fungus, as it breaks down more cellulose and less lignin in dead trees, causing the rotted wood to feel moist, soft, spongy, or stringy and appear white or yellow. Look for it on dead cherry, birch, and beech trees.

OCTOBER 14

Oak Apple Galls

Galls are abnormal plant growths that are primarily caused by insects, but also by fungi, mites, nematodes, and bacteria. Each insect has a specific plant host, and each gall a distinctive shape. Of the two thousand gall-producing insects in the United States, fifteen hundred of them are wasps or gnats. Plants in the oak, daisy, rose, and willow families have the greatest number of galls, with oaks having over eight hundred different types. The insect typically lays an egg in a growing part of the plant—the twigs, leaves, or leaf bud. The larva hatches and the plant reacts to it by forming a growth around the larva. The pictured gall, an oak apple gall, is caused by a wasp, *Amphibolips confluenta*. These golf ball–sized galls were named for their resemblance to apples. One larval wasp lives in the center of each oak apple gall, where it feeds and eventually pupates and emerges as an adult wasp. The hole in the pictured gall was chewed by the exiting wasp.

Oak apple gall.

Northern Redbelly Snakes Heading for Hibernacula

Northern redbelly snake.

Northern redbelly snakes come in two colors— brown or gray—but both color morphs have red bellies. About a foot long, this secretive snake inhabits a variety of habitats and seeks shelter under logs, rocks, and other cover. Mating takes place primarily in the spring, after the snakes emerge from hibernation, and females give birth to one to twenty-one live young in the late summer or fall. Mass migrations of northern redbelly snakes take place in October and November, when these snakes travel to their hibernation sites, or hibernacula. Northern redbelly snakes often hibernate in groups of their own and other small snake species, taking refuge in anthills, abandoned animal burrows, and old building foundations.

White-Tailed Deer Transitioning to Winter Diet

A white-tailed deer's diet consists of a wide variety of herbaceous and woody plants, the ratio of one to the other being determined by the season. Fungi, fruits, and herbaceous plants form much of the summer diet. Once these disappear, dried

White-tailed deer.

leaves and grasses, acorns, beechnuts, and woody browse become important autumn and early winter food. After snowfall, the winter diet consists mostly of woody browse—twigs, leaves, shoots, and buds—from many different trees, maples, birches, and cedars among them. Come spring, deer seek out buds, twigs, and emerging leaves.

OCTOBER 15

Common Juniper Cones Mature

Common juniper is one of the few evergreen shrubs in the Northeast and has one of the largest ranges of any woody plant. You often

Fruit of common juniper.

find it in old pastures and meadows, where its sharp needles protect it from most herbivores. It is a member of the pine family, and even though its fruits look like berries, structurally they are cones with fleshy scales. Whereas most of the cone-bearing members of the pine family disperse their seeds in the wind, common juniper uses birds and mammals to distribute them. Cedar waxwings, evening grosbeaks, and purple finches consume many juniper berries, and many other songbirds are frequent visitors. White-footed mice and white-tailed deer occasionally eat the fruits as well. While not aiding the dispersal of seeds, humans do use the fruit to flavor gin.

Bumble Bees Basking

Bumble bees are some of the earliest bees to emerge in the spring and are often the last to be seen in the fall. They can regulate their body temperatures by shivering or basking in the sun. This enables bumble bees not only to stay active longer in the season, but also during wet or cooler weather. Look for them on sunny patches of ground at this time of year, soaking up the sun's heat, with antennae at half-mast.

Bumble bee basking.

North American River Otters Leaving Sign

In the winter, river otter slides are very noticeable, but if you know what to look for, you can find signs of this member of the weasel family year-round. Their scat is unlike most other animal scat in that it has little form and often disintegrates into a pile of fish scales. Sometimes river otters create what are called "rolls"—areas near water that they repeatedly visit to defecate, urinate,

OCT

Otter brown-out.

and roll around on the ground. If used frequently enough, rolls become so acidic that they turn black with dying vegetation. These areas are called "brown-outs." Like beavers, otters possess oil glands and waterproof their fur with oil. It is possible that in addition to marking territory at a roll, they are distributing this oil throughout their coat when they are rolling on the ground.

OCTOBER 16

Striped Skunks Raiding Eastern Yellow Jacket Nests

A common sign of striped skunk activity is excavated ground nests of yellow jackets. If they've met with success, skunks will often leave sections of empty paper cells scattered about the nest site. Apparently, even though yellow jackets can sting

Yellow jacket nest dug up by striped skunk.

multiple times, they are not very effective at discouraging foraging skunks. Should you be so inclined, a close examination of skunk scat this time of year will reveal the skins and seeds of fruit and bits of insect exoskeletons, as well as the bones and hair of small rodents.

Striped skunk.

Red Squirrel Middens

Red squirrels often have a chosen spot in which they remove the scales of the cones of conifers in order to reach the seeds inside. Consequently, large piles of cone scales, called middens, are

Midden of cone scales.

Red squirrel's cache of green spruce cones.

scattered throughout coniferous and mixed woods. At this time of year, green cones are collected and stored, both above- and underground. Note tunnel entrance at the base of the midden.

OCTOBER 17

Big Brown Bats Entering Hibernation

Big brown bats, one of the most widespread mammals of North America, are one of the last species of bat to be seen flying in the fall. A

relatively hardy species, the big brown bat can tolerate conditions that other bats can't. However, once cold weather arrives and the nighttime temperatures dip down into the thirties, they go into hibernation.

During October, November, and December, big brown bats seek out caves, buildings, and mines in which to hibernate. Some may migrate short distances to find an appropriate location for hibernating, but many find hibernacula close to their summer residence. Individuals often become active for brief periods during the winter months, sometimes even changing hibernation sites. Big brown bats can live as long as eighteen to twenty years in the wild, but, unfortunately, most big

Big brown bat.

brown bats die during their first winter because they do not store enough fat to survive their entire hibernation period.

Snow Geese Migrating

The snow goose is one of the most abundant species of waterfowl in the world. Their migration in the East peaks from mid- to late October, as they travel from their breeding grounds on the western shores of Greenland and most of the eastern Canadian Arctic down the St. Lawrence Seaway to their coastal wintering areas ranging from Massachusetts to North and South Carolina. Flocks of hundreds, even thousands, of birds stop to refuel in staging areas—agricultural grain fields along their route. If you happen to be near one of these staging areas, you may well hear snow geese before you see them—their honking resembles the distant sound of baying hounds. The naturalist J. B. Grinnell described the sight of their approaching tiny, white, moving shapes as resembling "snowflakes drifting lazily across the azure sky."

Snow geese.

Willow-Beaked Gall Midges Overwintering inside Galls

Willows are host to a great number of gall-making insects, including tiny flies called midges. The most common species of willow gall midge is the willow beaked-gall midge. In the spring, after

Insect Galls

Galls are abnormal plant growths that are caused primarily by insects, but also by fungi, mites, nematodes, and bacteria. Each gall-making insect has a specific plant host, and each gall a distinctive shape. Of the two thousand gall-producing insects in the United States, fifteen hundred of them are gall wasps or gall gnats. Plants in the oak, daisy, rose, and willow families have the greatest number of galls, with oaks having over eight hundred different types. An insect typically lays an egg in a growing part of the plant—twigs, leaves, or leaf buds—in the spring, and the plant reacts to a chemical secretion, the egg, or the burrowing larva by forming a growth around it. This growth, or gall, often provides shelter and food for the larva living within it. Many galls have one inhabitant, while others are colonial.

Goldenrod ballgall, made by the goldenrod gall fly *Eurosta solidaginis*.

Kernel flower gall (oak), made by the wasp *Callirhytis serricornis*.

Insect Galls

Poplar petiole gall, made by the moth *Ectoedemia populella*.

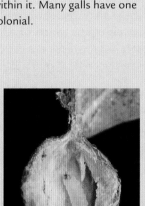

Poplar petiole gall moth larva.

Banded bullet gall (oak), made by the wasp *Dryocosmus imbricariae*.

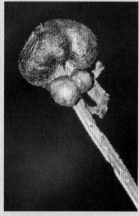

Blueberry stem gall, made by the wasp *Hemadas nubilipennis*.

Hackberry nipplegall, made by the jumping plant louse *Pachypsylla celtidismamma*.

Deciduous oak gall, made by the wasp *Dryocosmus deciduous*.

Willow beaked-gall, made by the midge *Rabdophaga rigidae*.

mating, the adult female midge lays an egg in a willow bud (often terminal) that is just starting to expand. The egg soon hatches, and the larva burrows deeper into the bud. The larva's feeding and the hormonelike chemicals in its saliva contribute to the conversion of a bud into gall tissue. The larva remains inside the gall through the winter, where it has a constant supply of food (the interior of the gall) and shelter. In the spring the larva pupates, an adult midge emerges and the cycle begins all over again. Some gall midges are crop pests, but willows are not significantly damaged by them.

OCTOBER 18

Mossy Rose Gall Wasp Larvae No Longer Feeding

In the spring, the 4 mm-long cynipid gall wasp lays up to sixty eggs (through parthenogenesis) inside a leaf bud of a rose bush. A week later,

the eggs hatch, and the larvae begin feeding on the leaf bud tissue. This stimulates the abnormal growth of plant tissue, and a mossy rose gall, covered with a dense mass of sticky, branched filaments, is formed. The gall provides the larvae with food and shelter through the summer. In late October, when the mossy rose gall is at its most colorful, the larvae stop eating and pass into the prepupal stage, in which they overwinter inside the gall. In February or March, the prepupae undergo a final molt and become pupae. If the pupae aren't extracted and eaten by a bird during the winter or parasitized by another insect, adult wasps exit the gall in the spring and begin the cycle all over again.

Spreadwing Damselflies Mating and Laying Eggs

Damselflies and dragonflies are still flying, mating, and laying eggs at this time of year in the Northeast. Certain damselflies, known as spreadwings, perch with their wings partially open, unlike most other damselflies. Another

Mossy rose gall.

Resting pair of spreadwing damselflies.

telltale spreadwing sign is that they often perch at roughly a 45-degree angle. Spreadwings are weak flyers that fly low and for short distances. When sexually mature, the males tend to spend their days perched on vegetation along a pond's shoreline. The females, like most dragonflies and damselflies, return to the water only when ready to breed. Spotted spreadwings are one of the latest species of damselflies active in the fall; the two in the photo were resting before resuming egg laying. The male (at top of photo) grasps the female's "neck" to prevent other males from replacing his sperm, while the female uses the sharp ovipositor at the end of her abdomen to slice into emergent vegetation and lay her eggs, which end up in the water when the plants die.

Large Milkweed Bugs Siphoning Seeds

Only 2 to 4 percent of common milkweed flowers eventually produce mature pods. Each pod contains an average of 226 seeds, all from one flower. Resembling overlapping fish scales, the seeds are arranged in a way that allows the wind

Cluster of large milkweed bugs on common milkweed.

to successively, from the top to the bottom of the pod, catch their silk parachutes and disperse them.

Just as milkweed pods are opening and seeds are maturing, large milkweed bugs, whose eggs are laid on the milkweed plant, congregate on the pods to feed on the seeds. Each of these bugs may be in any one of the five stages, or instars, of metamorphosis. Like all true bugs, their mouthparts, or rostrum, are not adapted for biting and chewing food, but

are designed for piercing and sucking. The rostrum consists of two side-by-side tubes. The milkweed bugs use one tube to pump digestive enzymes into the tough milkweed seeds and the other to siphon up the softened plant material. Like other milkweed feeders, milkweed bugs obtain poisonous compounds from the milkweed plant that are used for defense, and their orange and black coloration warns predators of their toxicity.

Large milkweed bug siphoning plant material.

OCTOBER 19

White-Tailed Deer Communicating with Pheromones

Animals communicate with their own species through strong smelling chemicals known as pheromones. Many mammals have glands that generate pheromones. The messages these smells convey vary according to the pheromone that is used— they can indicate alarm, territorial boundaries, the age of an animal and/or its sex, what place in the hierarchy an animal has, or the receptiveness of an animal during the breeding season, among other things. White-tailed deer have scent glands where you might not expect

White-tailed doe.

them—their heads, legs, and feet. Their primary glands and their functions are:

Forehead—Leaves scent on antler rubs and over-hanging branches

Preorbital, near the eye—Does use it to communicate with fawns

Interdigital, between the two toes of each hoof—Leave a foul-smelling yellow substance on the ground with every step a deer takes

Nasal, inside nose—May produce a scent, or may just lubricate the nose

Preputial, on inside of a buck's penile sheath—Function unknown

Tarsal, inside of hind legs near middle joint—Urinated on to spread scent; used intensely by bucks during rut

Metatarsal, outside of hind legs between ankle and hoof—Function unknown

Eastern Box Turtles Entering Hibernation

Box turtles, with their hinged bottom shells, or plastrons, can retract inside their shell and then close their top (carapace) and bottom shells together, leaving no flesh exposed. While this protects them during the warmer months, they must seek further protection from cold winter

Eastern box turtle.

Box turtle's hinged plastron.

weather when they hibernate. They are, like all reptiles, ectothermic, or cold-blooded, and are the same temperature as the air around them. When the temperature drops in October and November, box turtles stop eating, become lethargic, and attempt to burrow into loose soil, mud, or abandoned mammal burrows. As winter progresses and the soil temperatures drop, the turtles burrow deeper and deeper into their hibernacula.

Bird Nests Visible

When leaves start falling from deciduous trees, bird nests appear out of nowhere. Most song-birds abandon their nest after raising one brood, never to return to it. An empty nest sits where it was built until the elements break it down, another animal recycles the material from which it was made, or a mouse takes over winter occupancy. After the leaves fall, but before winter and other creatures deconstruct the nests, is the ideal time for discovering what species were nesting in your area this past summer.

Just as each species of bird has its own distinctive song, each species also builds a unique nest. It is often possible to determine what species built a nest without ever setting eyes on the bird. The size, shape, material used, and habitat in which a nest is built are remarkably similar for

The combination of this nest's size (3-inch outer diameter), location (3 feet off the ground), and material (yellow birch bark strips, grasses, cocoons, and black rootlet lining) pinpoint the builder as a black-throated blue warbler.

Common clubmoss spore-bearing strobili.

Common clubmoss.

all birds of a given species. Eastern phoebe nests mainly consist of mud covered with moss. Gray catbirds incorporate grape vines into their nests and line them with rootlets. Ovenbird nests are on the ground and roofed over like old-fashioned ovens. While federal permits are necessary to collect these nests, they can be admired and identified without a permit.

OCTOBER 20

Common Clubmoss Releasing Spores

Clubmosses are small, flowerless, evergreen, spore-producing plants. They form large colonies that creep along the forest floor, with some species resembling miniature conifers and others assuming a more horizontal form. Common clubmoss is known by several common names, among which are running clubmoss, staghorn clubmoss, wolf-paw clubmoss, foxtail clubmoss, running ground-pine, running pine, running moss, and princess pine. Because of this, its scientific name, *Lycopodium clavatum*, is often used.

This species bears dense leaves with long, whitish to colorless hairlike tips. This fern ally—related to but not a true fern—reproduces with spores, not seeds, which are found in cone-like structures called strobili located at the end of a stalk. At this time of year, if you tap one of the strobili, you may see a yellow cloud of spores released into the air. In the past, clubmoss spores were used as photographic flash powder because they explode when lit.

Belted Kingfisher Plumage

Some belted kingfishers remain in the Northeast through the winter if there is open water where they can catch fish. They are one of the few species of birds in which the female is more colorful than the male—the common pattern of sexual dimorphism is reversed. In polyandrous species, where the female mates with

Male belted kingfisher.

multiple males and the males provide most of the parental care, the male's plumage is often less colorful than the female's. Male belted kingfishers have only one "belt," or pectoral band, across their breast, which is primarily blue gray. Females possess this band, as well as rufous sides and a second, rufous, band across their lower breast. Juveniles have a partial second (rufous) belt.

Shaggy Mane Fruiting Bodies Liquifying

Shaggy mane is one of a group of mushrooms known as inky caps. Both of these common names reflect the appearance of the mushroom at different stages of its development—the cap has white, shaggy scales, and as the mushroom matures its gills liquefy into a black substance that was once used as ink. Most inky caps have gills that are very thin and very close to one another, which does not allow for easy release of the spores. In addition, the elongated shape of this mushroom does not allow for the spores to get caught in air currents as in most other mushrooms. The liquefaction/self-digestion process is actually a strategy to disperse spores more efficiently. The gills liquefy from the bottom up as the spores mature. Thus the cap peels up and away, and the maturing spores are always kept in the best position for catching wind currents. This continues until the entire fruiting body has turned into black ink.

Young and old shaggy mane.

OCTOBER 21

Muskrats Constructing Lodges

Muskrats, in addition to digging bank dens, also build lodges in which to live. Muskrat lodges resemble beaver lodges, but are usually much smaller, only up to 8 feet high, and 4 feet wide, and are made of vegetation, not sticks, like beaver lodges. Most lodge construction occurs in May and early June, and again in October. Typically they are built in no more than two feet

Muskrat lodge.

of water. A single dry chamber, with the entrance below and the chamber above the water line, houses a pair of muskrats, and often several litters of young; the mother adds a chamber for each litter. Even though the walls of a muskrat lodge are up to a foot thick, mink, foxes and coyotes often dig into them in the winter. Two or three smaller versions of a lodge, called pushups, serve as protected feeding platforms.

Eastern Towhees Migrating

In general, eastern towhees in the northern part of their range are short distance migrants, whereas populations south of Virginia tend to be year round residents. The last of northern New

Male eastern towhee.

Green stain fungus.

Wood stained with green stain fungus.

England's migrating eastern towhees are departing for southern climes now. A few individuals are permanent residents in the Northeast and are seen intermittently during the winter, especially during warmer winters. We don't observe eastern towhees migrating, as they do so during the night, but we do see them when they stop to refuel on fruits, seeds or insects during the day.

Green Stain Fungus Fruiting

Sac fungi, or ascomycetes, are a division of fungi, most of which possess sacs, or asci, in which spores are produced. The relatively common *Chlorociboria aeruginascens* and its close relative, *Chlorociboria aeruginosa*, are in this group and are referred to as green stain fungi. The two differ only microscopically, by the size of their spores. Most of the time you do not see the actual fruiting bodies of these fungi. More often you come across the brilliantly blue-green stained wood for which these fungi, which grow on the rotting logs or barkless wood of poplar, aspen, ash, and especially oak, are responsible. Woodworkers call this wood green rot or green stain. Fourteenth- and fifteenth-century Italian Renaissance woodworkers used *Chlorociboria*-infected wood to provide the green colors in their intricate wood inlays. The blue-green discoloration is caused by the production of the pigment xylindein, which can inhibit plant germination and has been tested as an algaecide. Xylindein may make wood less appealing to termites and has been studied for its cancer-fighting properties.

OCT

OCTOBER 22

Mice Storing Food for Winter

Northern cardinal nest serving as mouse larder.

Mouse.

Mammals that stay active in winter often cache food in the fall for later consumption, when food becomes harder to find. White-footed mice and deer mice create larders, often in abandoned bird nests. Once their young have fledged, most songbirds never reuse their nest. Mice find these empty cup-shaped containers perfect for storing seeds that they collect in the fall. The mouse that took over this northern cardinal nest located in a rose bush has filled it with a sizable number of rose hips.

Giant Puffball Fruiting Bodies Appearing

The fruiting bodies of giant puffballs are quite distinctive looking—they typically grow to the size of a soccer ball, but the record specimen measured 8 feet 8 inches in diameter and weighed 50 pounds. It been calculated that a single 10-inch giant puffball has as many as seven trillion spores. If each of those spores grew and yielded a 10-inch puffball, the combined puffball mass would be eight hundred times that of the earth.

Giant puffball.

Look for giant puffballs in the fall, growing on lawns, grassy meadows and open woods, sometimes in clusters, sometimes singly. While this fungus is edible when young, it does resemble other inedible fungi, thus confirmation by a mycologist is recommended.

OCTOBER 23

Some Golden-Crowned Kinglets Migrating and Some Staying Put

A large number of golden-crowned kinglets pass through the Northeast on their way from Canada to more southern wintering grounds at this time of year, but some hardy souls choose to remain here year-round. Barely bigger than a hummingbird, golden-crowned kinglets are the world's smallest perching birds, each weighing about 5 grams, the weight of two pennies. Remarkably,

Golden-crowned kinglet.

OCT

some manage to survive the northeastern winter, although research shows that 87 percent of the population perishes every year.

Winged Female Woolly Aphids Leaving Sumac Leaf Galls

The saclike galls found on staghorn and smooth sumac are anywhere from marble- to Ping Pong ball–size, and usually become obvious in late summer when they often acquire a rosy pink blush. Inside the thin walls of this gall is one big hollow cavity, teeming with tiny orange woolly aphids *(Melaphis rhois)*. In the spring, female aphids lay an egg on the underside of a sumac leaf, causing the plant to form an abnormal growth, or gall. A number of parthenogenic generations are produced inside the gall, and then in late summer or early fall, the winged females fly to patches of moss, where they establish asexually reproducing colonies. According to biologist D. N. Hebert, these colonies produce the males and sexual females responsible for recolonizing sumac each spring.

Sumac leaf galls.

Woolly aphids inhabiting sumac leaf gall.

Eastern Coyotes Howling

Eastern coyotes are heard with some regularity in the Northeast, especially in the fall. The typical family unit consists of two parents and their young that have yet to disperse, often females. Together these four or five coyotes serenade us with a very distinctive chorus, often several times a night. One wildlife biologist described this chorus as starting with a few falsetto yips, then blossoming into something resembling maniacal laughter, with the yips stringing together into chattering howls. Coyotes use their voices to communicate with members of their family, as well as with other coyotes. If the family members have been off hunting by themselves, the howling serves to call the family back together again. The familial chorus also serves as a warning to other coyotes not to trespass onto their territory.

Eastern coyote.

Peak Activity Time

Crepuscular (dawn and dusk), diurnal (day), and nocturnal (night) are terms used to describe when an animal is active. This is determined by many factors, including when prey is active and climatic conditions.*

Primarily Nocturnal

Many animals that are active at night have a specially developed sense of vision which helps them to see in the dark, and they often have excellent hearing as well. A number of animals that used to be diurnal, such as beavers, have become nocturnal as a means of avoiding predation. Most of the following animals are nocturnal most of the time.

Earthworm.

Eastern coyote.

Flying squirrel.

- Majority of owls
- Frogs and toads
- Salamanders
- Mice
- Raccoons
- Mink
- Bats
- Beavers
- Eastern coyotes
- Flying squirrels
- Porcupines
- Virginia opossums
- Majority of moths
- Crickets
- Earwigs
- Fireflies
- Mosquitoes
- Earthworms

* These lists are generalized, meaning there are exceptions.

Primarily Diurnal

Many domesticated animals, such as cats and dogs, which associate with humans, have been converted from a nocturnal to a diurnal activity pattern. Often the eyesight of diurnal animals is not as acute as that of nocturnal animals.

White admiral.

- Turtles
- Majority of snakes
- Majority of birds
- Gray squirrels
- Red squirrels
- Eastern chipmunks
- Humans
- Butterflies
- Grasshoppers

Wood turtle.

Crepuscular

Many animals take advantage of dawn or twilight to feed, find water, and engage in other behaviors because their visibility may be somewhat compromised, and because many predators are not as active at these times of the day. Most of these animals are crepuscular most of the time.

- White-tailed deer
- Rabbits
- Black bears
- Moose

White-tailed deer.

OCTOBER 25

Black Vine Weevil Larvae Crawling Deep Underground

Black vine weevil larvae overwinter in the soil. In the spring, the flightless adults emerge and feed at night on the outer edges of leaves, causing the leaves to have a notched margin. They lay as many as five hundred eggs in the soil near the base of host plants. The larvae hatch in a week or two and feed on plant roots until cold temperatures drive them farther underground. The larval stage is quite destructive, especially to landscape plants such as rhododendron and azalea. Female black vine weevils have the ability to produce female offspring from unfertilized eggs. Fertilization of eggs is required to produce males, but no males have been observed in North America.

Adult black vine weevil on Jack-in-the-pulpit fruit.

Funnel Weaving Spiders Spinning Last Webs of the Year

A number of unrelated spider families in North America spin webs with funnel-shaped retreats. These spiders are all referred to as funnel weavers. The spider lies in wait in the funnel, and when an insect flies into or lands on the web, the spider rushes out, checks to see if it is prey, and if it is, bites it. Its venom is fast acting, and as soon as the prey is largely immobile, the spider drags it back into its funnel to safely consume it out of sight. Many species' funnel webs are horizontal, and found in grass and bushes, but others are vertical. Like most spiders, funnel weavers are nocturnal. Many species die in the fall, but a few live a year or two. If you find an inhabited funnel web, it is likely to be a female. Males spend most of their lives wandering in search of a mate and after finding one and mating a few times, often die.

Funnel weaving spiders are docile and nonaggressive, and their bite is rarely as bad as a bee sting. Funnel weaving spiders are sometimes referred to as funnel web spiders. True funnel web spiders are not found in North America, but in Australia, where their bite is considered harmful.

Web of funnel weaving spider.

OCTOBER 26

Meadowhawks Mating and Laying Eggs

Meadowhawks mating.

There is a genus of dragon-flies, *Sympetrum*, referred to as meadowhawks, which emerge and fly in late summer and autumn, breeding in ponds and foraging over meadows. Mature males and some females of certain species of meadowhawks become bright red on part or all of their bodies. When breeding, the male grasps his mate behind her head with the appendages at the end of his abdomen and often does not release the female until after she has laid her eggs, which she typically does by dipping the tip of her abdomen in the water. The reason for this continued connection is that a male dragonfly may remove sperm present in the female from any previous mating and replace it with his own packet of sperm, or spermatophore. In order to prevent this from happening and assure his paternity, a male dragonfly sometimes flies close to his mate, guarding her while she lays her eggs, or, in the case of meadowhawks, may fly in tandem with the female throughout the egg-laying process.

Female meadowhawk (bottom) laying eggs while accompanied by male (top).

Yellow-Rumped Warblers Migrating

Yellow-rumped warblers overwinter as far north as Newfoundland and the New England coast, in open brushy habitats where they feed on the fruits of bayberry and juniper—they are the only warblers able to digest the waxes found in bayberries. People in most of the rest of the Northeast only see them during migration and the summer breeding months. Yellow-rumps, or butter butts, as birders may call them, are quite conspicuous when they migrate through, as they do so in large numbers. At this time of year, their plumage is quite subdued, but after their spring molt they are very colorful and it is easy to see how they got their name.

Yellow-rumped warbler in fall plumage.

OCTOBER 27

Predaceous Diving Beetles Remaining Active

While meadows and fields are experiencing a sharp decline in insect life at this time of year, one habitat where insects remain active in the fall and often through the winter is ponds. Among the year-round active pond invertebrates are predaceous diving beetles, which can be seen rowing through the water, intermittently surfacing to thrust their abdomen above the water line in order to procure a bubble of air from which they breathe. A close look at their middle and hind legs reveals that they are fringed with long hairs to aid them in navigating the water in search of prey or detritus.

OCT

Predaceous diving beetle.

Predaceous diving beetles lay their eggs on and in plants above the waterline in early spring. When the eggs hatch, the larvae drop into the water. Mature larvae crawl out of the water to pupate in damp chambers on the shoreline. They emerge as adults and reenter the water, where they remain active under the ice through the winter. Water scavenger beetles look a lot like predaceous diving beetles, but they stroke first with one leg, then another, not simultaneously like predaceous diving beetles, and they come to the surface of water head first to secure air.

Brightly Speckled European Starling Plumage

The European starling's summer, or breeding, plumage shows purple and greenish iridescence, especially on the head, back, and breast. Following the annual mid-summer/fall molt, most head and body feathers have whitish or buff terminal spots. Through the winter, most of these light spots gradually wear away to produce the glossy black appearance of spring.

Galium Sphinx Larvae Nearing Pupation

The galium sphinx moth is also known as the bedstraw hawk moth because it is commonly found in bedstraw, its preferred food. In its larval stage, this caterpillar has the distinctive horn at the end of its body that most sphinx moth caterpillars have, but it can have a variety of markings and colors. Adult galium sphinx moths fly from June to August, often hovering like hummingbirds as they drink nectar from flowers. The larvae are present from mid-August to October, when they pupate and overwinter in loose cocoons in shallow underground burrows.

Galium sphinx larva.

European starling.

Galium sphinx moth.

OCTOBER 28

Balsam Fir Seeds Dispersing

Regular seed production in balsam firs begins when the trees are twenty to thirty years old. The cones mature and ripen in late summer, with seed fall beginning late in August, peaking in September and October, and continuing into November or later. Unlike the cones of most conifers, the scales and shorter bracts drop away with the seeds, leaving the central axis standing alone. Some historians think these snow-covered spikes inspired the Germanic people to decorate trees with candles or lights. Most of the seeds are spread by wind—some to great distances over frozen snow—and some are spread by rodents. Good seed crops occur at intervals of two to four years.

Gray catbird.

Balsam fir cones.

Balsam fir cone after scales and bracts have fallen off.

Gray Catbird Stragglers Passing Through

Gray catbirds begin their nocturnal migration to wintering grounds in late August and early September. The last of the stragglers are now passing through northern New England. Catbirds winter from the southern New England coast south to Panama, with concentrations on the U.S. Gulf Coast and the Yucatan Peninsula. Those individuals that winter in the Yucatan Peninsula and Central America cross the Gulf of Mexico, and in order to do so they put on so much fat—during fall migration their mass may increase to 150 percent of lean body mass—that it approaches the upper limit of what flight allows.

Shrew Eyes

Shrews have a very high metabolism and spend most of the day and night hunting for food. Subterranean worms and insects are their main prey, which means that a lot of their time is spent in tunnels, where there is little, if any, light. Consequently, shrews have little need for large eyes or excellent vision, neither of which they have.

While the sight of most shrews is probably limited to the detection of light, some species

Short-tailed shrew.

compensate by using other senses, including hearing and touch, to direct them. The short-tailed shrew has a well-developed repertoire of squeaks and clicks, including ultrasonic sounds, for navigation and predation.

OCTOBER 29

Tamarack Leaves Turning Yellow

Eastern larch is also known as tamarack, the Algonquian name for the species, which means "wood used for snowshoes." This tree strongly prefers moist to wet sites in acidic soils and is common in northern New England bogs. Eastern larch is the only species of conifer in the Northeast that drops all of its needles every year. The needles are borne on short shoots in groups of ten to twenty, and prior to falling off, they turn a beautiful golden color.

Tamarack.

White-Crowned Sparrows Passing Through

Most eastern white-crowned sparrows neither breed nor overwinter in the Northeast, but they do pass through twice a year on their migration to and from their breeding grounds in the Canadian tundra and their wintering grounds in the southern U.S. At the end of summer, each pair of white-crowned sparrows breaks up and they winter separately, but when both members of a pair return the next summer, about two-thirds of the pairs re-form.

White-crowned sparrow.

Fisher Diet

Contrary to what their name implies, fishers seldom eat fish. While they prey on a wide range of animals and even plants, their preference is for small mammals, which make up 80 percent of their diet; snowshoe hares; and porcupines. Because fishers are well equipped to kill porcupines, and because there is little competition for them, porcupines are an important prey of fishers—up to 35 percent of fisher diet samples contain the remains of porcupines, including quills and footpads

Fisher scat containing porcupine footpads.

OCTOBER 30

Wood Frogs Preparing For Winter

Wood frog.

In late fall or winter, as temperatures drop, wood frogs flood their bodies with blood sugar that acts as antifreeze in their circulatory system. However, wood frogs, and other frogs such as spring peepers and gray tree frogs, still partially freeze. Activity in their brain stops, arteries and veins freeze, their heart stops, and 45–60 percent of their body may freeze. They can remain in this state for two to three months, with the temperature remaining between 21 and 30 degrees. Yet within hours of being exposed to the spring's warming temperatures, wood frogs thaw out and start moving toward a body of water to breed.

Virginia Creeper Fruits Ripening

As you might assume from its appearance, Virginia creeper is in the grape family. This climbing woody vine clings to the surfaces over which it climbs with adhesive disk-tipped tendrils, which are actually modified flower stalks. The disks form only after the tendril has made contact with a tree or other surface, at which point the disk secretes a cementlike substance, keeping the vine attached to the substrate long after it has died. Although it superficially resembles poison ivy, Virginia creeper has five leaflets as opposed to poison ivy's three, and poison ivy tendrils lack terminal disks. Virginia creeper's brilliant red fall foliage is thought to attract birds, which consume the blue-black berries and disperse the seeds.

Virginia creeper leaves and fruit.

Virginia creeper tendrils.

OCTOBER 31

Black Bears Making "Nests"

If you look up when you are in a beech-maple forest, you may occasionally notice a sizeable cluster of twigs and branches fairly high up in an American beech tree. This nest of twigs is usually bigger than a squirrel's nest and not cup-shaped like a hawk's or owl's nest. In fact, it isn't a nest at all—it is a sign that a black bear has been sitting, usually in the crotch of the tree,

Black bear "nest."

OCT

pulling, biting, and breaking off branches primarily in order to eat beech nuts, leaves, buds, and catkins. When the bear has finished eating, it discards the branch into a pile.

Antmimic Spiders Hatching

Antmimic egg sac.

The roundish, flat, papery, ¼-inch diameter, metallic-looking structures with tiny bumps in the center often seen adhering to the top of a rock are spider egg sacs, most likely those of an antmimic spider—spiders resembling ants that often prey on ants—specifically one in the genus *Castianeira*. One would assume that the contents of the sac that were causing the bumps were eggs that were going to overwinter and hatch once warm weather arrives. This is true for a majority of spider egg sacs, but some, such as those of antmimic spiders, hold spiderlings that have already hatched and will remain in the sac throughout the winter.

Antmimic egg sac and spiderlings.

Ruffed Grouse Preening

Birds have up to twenty-five thousand feathers, and most birds preen, or clean, waterproof, and align their feathers several times a day. Ruffed grouse, as well as most other birds, possess a uropygial gland, or preen gland, on their rumps. The preen gland produces a waxy substance that helps waterproof feathers and keeps them flexible. Some birds, including owls, pigeons, parrots, and hawks, lack a uropygial gland and instead have specialized feathers that disintegrate into powder down, which serves the same purpose as preen oil.

Ruffed grouse reach back and rub their beaks on this gland and then distribute the wax on their body and wing feathers by stroking them toward the tip. The grouse grasps a feather near the base and draws it through the partly close beak, nibbling as it goes. This distributes the wax and cleans parasites from the feathers. In order to preen its head, the grouse must rub it on other parts of its body. Preening is usually done in a fairly open setting but with a degree of overhead protection, so that the grouse can watch for terrestrial predators while being protected from hawks and owls.

Ruffed grouse preening.

NOVEMBER

Mosses

Mosses are some of the oldest and simplest plants on Earth. They aren't very showy, they don't have flowers, and they are rarely more than a few inches tall, but they are notable—how many other plants exist today in pretty much the same form that they had when dinosaurs roamed the Earth? While other land plants may be more complex, mosses hold their own when it comes to longevity.

Mosses, liverworts, and hornworts are lumped together in a group known as bryophytes. All bryophytes lack true vascular tissue—there are no tubes to transport water and nutrients to all parts of the plant such as trees and flowering plants have. This makes it difficult, if not impossible, for them to retain water for any length of time. Instead of transporting water from the soil, they absorb water from rainfall, dew, and runoff. Because of the lack of lignin, the molecules that bind to cellulose fibers and harden and strengthen the cell walls of vascular tubes, these plants cannot grow very tall. *Dawsonia*, the tallest moss in the world, can grow to a height of 20 inches. In addition, bryophytes do not possess true roots, stems, or leaves, although the plant body is differentiated into leaflike and stem-like parts, and in some species, there are rootlike structures called rhizoids.

Mosses have the greatest species diversity of all the bryophytes—estimates of the number of species range from ten thousand to twenty thousand. Like all land plants, they have a life cycle that consists of alternating generations. In other words, they have a pattern of reproduction that involves regular alternation between two distinct forms, the gametophyte—the leafy, green plant we call moss—and the sporophyte, or spore-producing structure. In lower plants like mosses, the two generations are more obvious than in more complex plants.

Like all bryophytes, mosses can reproduce either sexually or asexually (vegetatively), such as when a piece of stem or leaf breaks off and regenerates to form a new plant. Sexual reproduction through alternation of generations is a bit more complicated than vegetative reproduction. A spore is produced, and under just the right moisture and temperature conditions it develops into a branching, threadlike filament called a protonema, which in turn grows into the green plant we recognize as moss. This is the gametophyte generation, so-called because it produces the gametes, or sex cells—the sperm and egg. If it is a female gametophyte, it produces microscopic flask-shaped structures called archegonia, each of which contains one egg. If it's a male gametophyte, it produces banana-shaped structures called antheridia, each of which contains many sperm. When it rains or dew accumulates, the sperm attempt to swim, by means of two thread-like tails, to the egg inside an archegonium. Once that is achieved, the second generation, or sporophyte, begins to develop. A slender stalk arises from the archegonium, the tip of which enlarges to form a capsule containing anywhere from four to more than a million spores, depending on the species. The hairy cap—the top of the archegonium that was ripped off when the sporophyte started to grow—covering the capsule falls off when the spores are mature, and a tiny lid called an operculum opens. One or two rows of teeth, called the peristome, control the release of the spores. They remain closed during wet

Beaver lodge in marsh.

Haircap moss sporo-
phyte with hood.

Haircap moss sporo-
phyte minus hood.

Haircap moss gametophyte
and sporophyte.

Haircap moss gametophyte.

Haircap moss archegonium.

conditions, preventing the spores from dispersing. In dry conditions they open, increasing
the chance of the spores being dispersed some
distance.

Mosses are not eaten by many animals due
to compounds they contain that make them
unpalatable and indigestible; these same compounds give mosses antibacterial, antifungal, and
antiviral properties. Some mosses have even been
shown to be effective in fighting cancer.

Included in the mosses is the rather common
and widely distributed *Sphagnum*, a genus of more
than three hundred species, most of which have a
remarkable capacity to absorb and retain water—
up to thirty times their dry weight. *Sphagnum* has
the distinction of being the only economically
important bryophyte. Along with other plants

growing among it, *Sphagnum*, also known as peat
moss, becomes compacted into peat which,
in places such as Scandinavia and Ireland, is
dried and used as fuel. Due to its tremendous
water-holding capacity, *Sphagnum* is used in packing live plants for shipment, is added to soil to
improve its water-holding capacity, and has been
employed as absorption material for oil spills.
Because of its absorptive capacity as well as its
antiseptic properties, *Sphagnum* was used for the
manufacture of surgical dressings during World
War I and as a cure for diaper rash by the Inuit.

Mosses have been around for four hundred
million years or more. Even though they are less
specialized than most land plants, they have
managed to survive where other plants often
can't, such as on trees and rocks. Unlike flowering
plants, most of which have seeds that require soil

in order to germinate, mosses only need a source of moisture from which to get their nutrients, and so can be found growing just about anywhere.

Winter Food Supply Preparation by Beavers

Beavers, strict vegetarians, make significant seasonal changes in their diet. In the spring and summer, roughly 90 percent of what they eat consists of herbaceous plants, primarily aquatic. Their preference would be to eat these plants year-round, as they do in the southern part of their range, but in the Northeast that is not an option, so come fall, beavers switch to a largely woody diet, including the bark and cambium, the growing layer of inner bark, of a number of trees, including poplars (aspens), willows, birches, alders, dogwoods, beeches, ashes, and cherry. Poplar bark is the food of choice, and in the United States, the ranges of trembling aspen and the beaver are almost identical.

The woody plants that beavers eat during the winter consist mainly of cellulose, which is indigestible by most mammals. While beavers do not possess enzymes to digest the cellulose, they do possess a caecum; a pouch between the large and small intestine in which colonies of microorganisms reside. These microorganisms digest approximately 30 percent of the cellulose that beavers consume, thereby providing beavers with enough energy to survive the winter. Beavers obtain additional energy by eating their fecal pellets, a practice called coprophagy, thus running them through the digestive process a second time.

The main hurdle that beavers face once winter arrives is that they are locked under the ice. The only food accessible to them throughout the winter—unless a thaw allows them to come up through the ice—is that which is under water. Because food is so limited, conservation of energy is of utmost importance. Beavers have adapted in many ways: little movement, lower body temperature, blood vessel heat exchange,

and constriction in extremities, to name a few. However, the daily food requirement of a beaver is 22–30 ounces of poplar bark, a minimum of six beavers occupy most lodges, and ice usually seals ponds for at least three months, so even with all these energy-saving adaptations, each fall a family of six beavers has to acquire a little over half a ton of branches for its winter food supply.

Because woody plants are available and can be transported, they provide beavers with the sustenance they need in the winter. However, this food supply, in order to be accessible all winter long, requires some forethought on the beavers' part. Come fall, they must scramble to fell an adequate number of trees, cut the branches off, and transport these branches to a location under water near their lodge before their pond freezes over. Once ice forms, the beavers swim out of the lodge to retrieve these branches, the bark of which they consume in the lodge, discarding what remains back into the water, to be used later for construction purposes.

Before they begin to gather their food supply, beavers test the wood by biting into the tree's bark.If the bark is not in the right condition, or if there is still too much sap in the tree, beavers may either bypass it or speed up the drying process by girdling the tree. The condition of the bark is extremely important, because if a branch is stored underwater before it is ready, it will ferment and sour, rendering it unfit for food. It is not unusual for a beaver to girdle a tree and come back a week later to fell it.

Because beavers are so vulnerable to predators on land, and because of the relative ease of transporting the branches a short distance, they usually will harvest trees closest to the water first. Once the branches are cut, the beaver takes one in its teeth, swims out close to the lodge, dives to the bottom of the pond to the food cache, and rams the branch into the mud. Most hardwood trees, particularly poplar and birch, are heavy and have little buoyancy, so it is relatively easy to anchor them in the mud. More branches are

Beaver hauling poplar branch to winter food supply.

Beaver lodge and winter food cache.

Beaver eating poplar leaf.

added, eventually forming a base upon which additional branches are piled. This cache, or winter food supply, is enlarged until it rises above the surface of the water. The top portion of the cache, unreachable from under the ice, often consists of small, leafy branches from trees that are not the beaver's most preferred, which are weighted down by a few heavier branches. The pile of branches can be as much as 40 feet in diameter and 10 feet high. Many people, including Native Americans, used to judge the severity of the coming winter by the size of the local beavers' food cache. To them, a large cache meant a long, cold winter. Truth be told, if anything, the opposite is true. Beavers continue to add to their cache until their pond freezes over. A late-arriving or easy winter allows beavers more time to add to their cache, thereby making it larger.

If you go to an active beaver pond at this time of year, you will see a rather haphazard pile of branches sticking out of the water close to the lodge. This food cache is often mistaken for an unfinished addition to the lodge. In fact, it's at least as, if not more, essential to the family of beavers occupying the lodge than any renovation of their dwelling. It is the product of their labors for the past couple of months and the key to their survival for the coming winter.

Beaver-cut white birch.

Ruffed Grouse: Winter Adaptations

Dispersal, finding food, and survival are three of the main challenges that ruffed grouse (also called partridges) face every fall and winter. The manner in which they confront each of these tasks prove ruffed grouse to be one of the most adaptive species of birds that overwinters in the Northeast.

The challenge of dispersing falls to the young of the year. When they are a little over four months old, grouse begin leaving their brood. Males are usually the first to leave, perhaps because they have a more rigorous search ahead

Ruffed grouse.

Ruffed grouse toe pectinations.

Ruffed grouse nostril feathers.

Gray birch catkins.

of them. It is important that they find a territory before winter, as research indicates that males with established territories are the most successful at attracting females in the spring. Their quest is not a simple one. They must find an area that has not already been claimed by an older male, has plenty of food for winter survival, and is suitable for spring drumming, a courtship ritual that males perform by beating their wings, often while standing on a log. This is a formidable task, and it is not unusual for a young male grouse to return to its brood several times before finding his own territory. Young females also are searching for territories, especially those with good nesting cover. Males tend to travel about 250 yards per day, while females wander roughly 500 yards at a time. Males usually travel 1 to 2 miles before finding an appropriate area, while females have been known to travel up to 10 miles, although it is usually less.

Finding food during the fall usually isn't difficult: acorns, mushrooms, and berries are abundant. But before long, grouse are forced to switch from mostly fruits and nuts, which are either gone or buried by snow, to buds. By October or November, most grouse have returned to trees as their main source of food. Aspen buds and catkins (flower buds) of hazel, alder, and birch sustain them through the winter. Because a grouse stores very little fat, it must eat daily during the colder months. It confines its exposure to predators by rapidly feeding for fifteen to twenty minutes twice a day—usually early in the day and late in the afternoon—storing food in its crop, flying to a place where there is cover, and digesting it there.

Ruffed grouse adapt physically as well as behaviorally for winter. In the fall they grow comblike fringes, or pectinations, on either side of each of their toes, which act as snowshoes and ice-grippers for travel on snow or on icy branches when feeding. Come spring, these structures will disappear. Feathers on their legs grow thicker and closer to their ankles to provide better insulation. Similarly, feathers on their beaks increase and grow over their nostrils, so as to slow the cold air and allow it to warm up in the bird's nostrils before being inhaled.

By diving into deep fluffy snow, which is known as "snow roosting," grouse can escape both frigid night temperatures and predators. If there are 10 or more inches of snow, grouse usually will spend the night in it. They dive in

NOV

head first, leaving only a small hole and little or no scent trail for predators to follow. They then burrow laterally for 5 or 10 feet and hollow out a small cavity where they spend the night. Here they are hidden from owls, foxes, and other predators and are well insulated—it rarely goes below 20 degrees in these cavities, regardless of how cold it is outside. This provides an energy savings of 30 percent or more compared to spending the night in the open. In the morning, grouse explode out of the snow, usually leaving wing prints by the exit hole. A cold winter without snow or a winter with frequent hard crusts promises high mortality for grouse. The ability to survive the rigors of a northeastern winter is no small task for any living creature, much less one that is at the top of so many predators' lists.

NOVEMBER 1

Monarchs Arriving in Mexico

Monarchs from east of the Rocky Mountains are starting to arrive in their overwintering area in the Transvolcanic Mountains of central Mexico. This miraculous flight, which takes a monarch roughly two months, can be up to 3,000 miles long. Using the sun, and most likely the Earth's magnetic field, they head for specific stands of oyamel fir trees, where they will cluster and be protected—unless weather conditions are severe—from extreme temperatures, predators, rain, and snow until next March, when their journey north begins. These butterflies will get only about halfway back to the Northeast, at

Poison Ivy vs. Virginia Creeper

Poison Ivy
3 leaflets
Petiole (stem) on central leaf
Leaf edge has few teeth/serrations
Mature fruit is white
Hairy rootlets, no pads/disks

Virginia Creeper
5 leaflets (usually)
No petiole
Many teeth/serrated leaf edges
Mature fruit is dark blue/black with red stems
Adhesive pads/disks at end of tendrils

Poison ivy.

Virginia creeper.

Monarch.

Black-capped chickadee.

which time they mate and lay eggs. The third or fourth generation of these monarchs will reach their eastern destination.

Woolly Oak Leaf Galls

Of the two thousand kinds of galls found on North American plants, eight hundred different kinds form on oaks. One of these is the woolly oak leaf gall, produced by a tiny cynipid wasp. This gall is usually attached to the mid-vein on the underside of an oak leaf and looks like a ball of wool. It may be as large as three-quarters of an inch and is often bright pink or yellow, fading to brown in the fall. Oak trees have lots of tannic acid, which makes the tree unpalatable to herbivores, and the highest concentration of tannin is found in oak

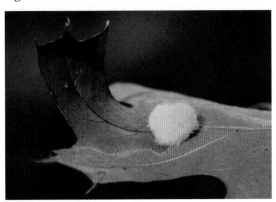
Woolly oak leaf gall.

galls. The bitter taste is where the name "gall" originated. It is possible, since tannins are somewhat antimicrobial, that high-tannin galls such as the woolly oak leaf gall may protect the wasp larvae against fungi and bacteria.

Black-Capped Chickadees Refreshing Brains

Black-capped chickadees refresh their brains once a year. Every autumn, black-capped chickadees allow brain neurons containing old information to die, replacing them with new neurons so they can adapt to changes in their social flocks and environment.

NOVEMBER 2

Cecropia Moths Pupating

Our largest North American native moth, the cecropia moth, spends the winter as a pupa inside a cleverly crafted 3- to 4-inch-long shelter, or cocoon, which it creates and attaches lengthwise to a branch while still in its larval stage. The cecropia caterpillar, using the silk glands near its mouthparts, spins not one, but two silk cases,

Cecropia moth cocoon.

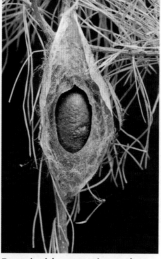

Pupa inside cecropia moth cocoon.

one inside the other. In between the two cases, it spins many loose strands of very soft silk, presumably to enhance the insulating properties of the cocoon. Inside the inner case, the caterpillar splits its skin and transforms into a pupa. Come spring, an adult moth will emerge from the pupal case and exit the cocoon through one end, which is intentionally spun more loosely, allowing the moth to crawl out.

Flying Squirrels Visiting Feeders

Flying squirrel.

Although they can't technically fly, flying squirrels can travel long distances without touching the ground. By gliding, they can travel as far as 295 feet from tree to tree or from tree to ground. These nocturnal rodents stretch their legs out and direct their glide by controlling the position of the flap of skin, called a patagium, that extends from the outside of the wrist on the front leg to the ankle of the hind leg on both sides of their body.

Their broad, flattened tail acts as a parachute, rudder, stabilizer, and brake during the glide. If you train a flashlight on your winter bird feeder after dark, you may be rewarded with the sight of one or more flying squirrels.

Wood Ducks Foraging on Acorns

In eastern North America, about one-third of wood ducks are permanent residents, and the others are migratory. For those that overwinter in the Northeast, seeds, fruits, and other plant material make up roughly 80 percent of their diet. Because waterfowl frequently feed in areas where they are threatened by predators, they often eat quickly and digest their food later, under cover. What enables them to do this is an esophagus that is capable of expanding to accommodate substantial amounts of food. Unlike some birds, waterfowl do not have a true crop.

Acorns are a preferred food for wood ducks, which swallow up to a dozen or so at one time. After being stored in the esophagus, the acorns travel to the proventriculus, a glandular stomach that secretes digestive enzymes that soften food. From there, the softened acorns travel to the ventriculus, or gizzard, a muscular organ that functions as a wood duck's "teeth." The ventriculus often contains sand or small stones which help grind up large food items, such as acorns, before they enter the intestines, where they are digested and nutrients are absorbed.

Male (left) and female (right) wood ducks.

Japanese knotweed fruits.

Fisher scent post.

NOVEMBER 3

Japanese Knotweed Seeds Dispersing

Japanese knotweed reproduces by spreading underground stems called rhizomes as well as by seeds. Seed production, however, is not common, as the plants are unisexual, with male and female flowers on separate plants, and rarely are both found in the same colony. The rhizomes don't need much help, though, as they can survive temperatures of -31 degrees and can extend 23 feet horizontally and up to 10 feet deep. Small wonder that Japanese knotweed, introduced as an ornamental, has thrived and out-competed native plants. Its delicate, three-winged, brown fruits belie the hardiness of this practically indestructible invasive plant.

Fishers Posting Scent

Fishers tend to travel along corridors when they are hunting, and where these corridors intersect each other or other trails, fishers will often delineate their territory by marking a sapling or old stump by urinating, defecating, and/or rubbing themselves on it. They revisit these scent posts on a regular basis, so that signs and scents accumulate over time. In winter, these "bulletin boards" are obvious to humans due to the fisher's tracks, but at this time of year they are much more subtle. Look for scat and hairs caught on stumps and branches.

Red-Tailed Hawks Migrating

The migration of northeastern red-tailed hawks begins in August and continues through early December, peaking during the first week in November. Red-tails generally migrate alone or in small, loosely organized flocks. These raptors usually avoid crossing large bodies of water and concentrate along shorelines, peninsulas, and other topographic features. Red-tails migrate during the day, taking advantage of thermals, soaring and gliding 79 percent of the time. Even in harsh winters with extensive snow cover, however, some northern birds overwinter near their breeding territories.

Red-tailed hawk.

NOVEMBER 4

Red Oak and White Oak Acorns

There are two main groups of acorns—those in the red oak family and those in the white oak family. Acorns from trees in the red oak family generally have higher tannic acid content than those from white oaks, making them more bitter. Given a choice between the two, white-tailed deer will eat the white oak acorns first and turn to red oaks only when the others are gone. There is another reason for quick consumption of white oak acorns, however. White oak acorns germinate in the fall, but red oak acorns do not germinate until spring. Because the energy is funneled into growing, the nutritional value of an acorn drops when it germinates. Thus, deer, turkeys, bear, and rodents do not let white oak acorns sit on the ground for very long.

White oak (left) and red oak (right) acorns.

North American River Otters Active in Ponds and Wetlands

North American river otters are considered semi-aquatic mammals, comfortable on land as well as in water. The bulk of their diet is fish, and they are well adapted for an aquatic environment year-round. They have dense fur with a waterproof

North American river otter.

undercoat, a layer of insulating fat, and a long, streamlined body. Otters also have webbed feet; clear eyelids, or nictitating membranes, which act like goggles; valves in their ears and nose that close automatically when they submerge; and the ability to stay underwater for up to eight minutes.

Surprisingly, young otters are not instant swimmers and must be taught how to swim when they are a couple of months old. The mother pushes them into the water and then stays close, repeatedly pushing them under the water and then up to breathe. When the lesson is over, she grabs each otter by the neck and pulls it out of the water.

Raccoons Fattening Up

In the Northeast, raccoons spend the fall fattening up, for little, if any, food is available during the winter. Acorns, hickory nuts, beechnuts, and hazelnuts are favorite sources of fat. When insects are available, they form a large part of a raccoon's diet. Delicacies include larvae of dug-up yellow jacket and bumble bee nests, honey bees, and the honey the bees have stored for the winter. Injured birds and rabbits, mice, bats, wild grapes, and an occasional crayfish provide raccoons with enough sustenance so that fat makes up almost 50 percent of their weight as they head into winter.

NOV

Raccoon.

On the coldest winter days, raccoons will seek shelter in hollow trees, sometimes holing up for as long as a month. Sometimes they den communally, with up to twenty-three raccoons occupying the same den. Considered deep sleepers, raccoons do not lower their metabolism significantly, and therefore are not considered true hibernators.

NOVEMBER 5

Pellets

Roughly six to sixteen hours after consuming prey, owls, hawks, and many other birds cough up a small pellet that consists of the indigestible bones, fur, nails and teeth of the prey they've eaten. In addition to getting rid of indigestible matter, the casting of pellets is thought to improve the health of a bird by scouring its throat, or gullet. In general, the larger the bird, the larger the pellet. The pellets of most birds of prey are 1 to 2 inches long, and those of pellet-making songbirds measure roughly ½ inch long.

Barred owl pellet.

Lady Fern Spores Dispersing

Lady fern is found on every continent in the northern hemisphere and is one of the Northeast's most common ferns. Its large, bright green, leathery fronds are found in moist woods, meadows, and swamps, as well as along streams. The derivation of its name varies according to what source you consult. Explanations range from its elegant and graceful female form to the way in which its reproductive spore-bearing structures, called sori, are curved and shaped like a lady's eyebrow or, some say, like a buttonhook. These structures are on the back side of the leafy fronds. When the membrane, or indusium, that covers the spores shrivels up, the spores are exposed to the breezes that disperse them.

Lady fern.

Lady fern sori.

NOVEMBER 6

Red-Backed Salamanders Migrating Downward

Eastern red-backed salamanders reside in the leaf litter throughout the Northeast during the summer months. Here they feed on invertebrates, lay their eggs, and scentmark their territories on the forest floor with pheromones and fecal matter in order to convey information

Red-backed salamander.

concerning their body size and gender to other red-backed salamanders. If the temperature soars or the humidity drops, these salamanders do just what they do in the fall—seek deeper, moister, protected areas such as beneath stones, under and within rotting logs and stumps, or underground in animal burrows.

Whereas they migrate downward in summer to avoid the heat and dry air that would impair their ability to breathe through their skin, these salamanders are avoiding the approaching cold when they migrate downward in the fall. Red-backed salamanders are not freeze tolerant, and thus must avoid freezing temperatures. Once ensconced in a freeze-free cavity, they usually remain there until snowmelt.

Bountiful Apple Crop a Double-Edged Sword When It Comes to Porcupines

An outstanding apple crop bodes well for the fecundity of the white-tailed deer, mouse, black bear, raccoon, wild turkey, and porcupine populations the following year. There are other more subtle ramifications of a bountiful soft mast production, however, one of which is an increase in porcupine salt-seeking behavior.

Porcupines are avid consumers of apples. Typically, the supply of apples is depleted by the end of August, when porcupines move on to beechnuts and acorns. However, occasionally the apple crop is so plentiful that apple trees provide sustenance for wildlife well into the winter. High in carbohydrates, apples help porcupines gain the extra weight necessary to help them survive

Apple tree.

through the winter months. Porcupines often leave the cores of apples untouched, avoiding the cyanide-rich apple seeds.

Apples have a relatively low pH, however, and are acidic, some varieties more than others. Porcupines prefer less acidic apples, but even these contain several hundred times more organic acid than other food, such as poplar or basswood leaves, that porcupines consume in the summer. High acid intake impairs sodium resorption in mammalian kidneys, causing porcupines to lose sodium in their urine. Consequently, as a result of a high proportion of apples in their diet, porcupines seek extra sodium. While they find salt in aquatic plants, insects, animal bones, and outer bark, porcupines are also drawn to plywood, car tires, outhouses, sweat-soaked tool handles, and other human-related sources of sodium. When there is an exceptional apple crop, make sure your hammers, hoes, rakes, and shovels are well out of the reach of quill pigs.

Apple chewed by a porcupine.

Black Bear Tracks

This is often the last month until spring in which signs of active black bears can be found. Cold weather and a poor beechnut and acorn crop can hasten their retreat into their dens. A black bear's hind track is fairly distinctive, if only due to its size: 3½ to 6 inches wide by 4 to 9 inches long. Black bears are flat-footed, or planti-grades, and therefore a track usually consists of more than just toe imprints; heel pad inden-tations are often visible, with those of the hind feet being larger than those of the front feet. Black bears have five toes on each foot, but the smallest, inner toe often doesn't register. The long, curved nails on a black bear's front feet used for marking trees and climbing are often visible in their tracks.

Clouded sulphur.

have already mated, laid eggs, and died, but if the weather has been relatively mild, you can still see them in early November.

Dog-Tooth Lichen

Like most lichens, dog-tooth lichen consists of an alga and a fungus living together in a symbiotic relationship. The fungus provides a structure for taking up moisture and nutrients; the alga is capable of photosynthesizing and producing food for both itself and the fungus. The brown structures in the photograph are the fruiting, or spore-producing, bodies of this lichen, and their resemblance to dog teeth gives this lichen its common name. In the Middle Ages, dog-tooth

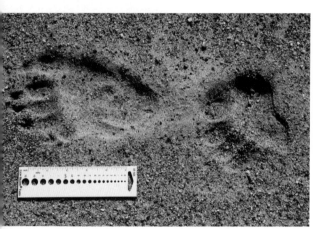

Black bear's hind (left) and front (right) tracks.

Last of The Sulphur Butterflies Flying

The few lingering clover, goldenrod, aster, and dandelion blossoms provide nectar for late-flying butterflies such as the clouded sulphur. Typically, you will find this butterfly in the open, flying very fast and close to the ground. Many

Dog-tooth lichen.

NOV

381

lichen was used to treat rabies. It was felt at the time that this lichen's resemblance to dog teeth indicated that it could cure dog-related ailments.

NOVEMBER 8

Eastern Hophornbeam

As a young tree, eastern hophornbeam, also known as ironwood due to the hardness and heaviness of its wood, has smooth bark, but as it

Eastern hophornbeam bark.

Eastern hophornbeam fruit.

matures, its bark becomes shaggy, making it easy to identify any time of year. It is as though tiny rectangular-shaped bits of bark have been carved out, with many of the ends peeling away from the tree. Equally distinctive is its fruit—clusters of papery bladders, each containing a seed. You often find these on the ground, as they fall off the tree about the same time the leaves do.

Moles Digging Deeper

Moles are well designed for life in dark, narrow tunnels. Adaptations include small, weak eyes; small hips for turning around in tight places; and velvety fur that is reversible, to make backing up easy. Moles construct two kinds of tunnels:

Hairy-tailed mole.

surface tunnels and deep runways. Surface tunnels are used primarily in the summer and are 1 to 4 inches below the surface of the ground. The resulting ridges above ground are quite noticeable. They connect with deeper runways that are used in the winter. These deeper tunnels can be up to 40 inches deep, and they provide protection from the cold and access to overwintering insects.

Mole summer tunnel sign.

NOVEMBER 9

Wintergreen

Wintergreen, also known as checkerberry and eastern teaberry, is an aromatic, evergreen plant that creeps along the ground. Its single, white flowers develop into bright red berries which white-tailed deer and ruffed grouse eat with relish. Not surprisingly, these berries taste like oil of wintergreen, as their name implies. The active ingredient in this oil is synthesized and used as a flavoring in chewing gum, toothpaste, breath

Wintergreen.

fresheners, candy, and medicines. This same ingredient, methyl salicate, is similar to aspirin, which explains why Native Americans chewed and made a tea from the leaves and berries of wintergreen to alleviate pain.

Canine Predation of Birds

The remains of avian prey often subtly offer clues as to the identity of the predator. One such clue is the way in which feathers were removed from the bird by the predator. If feathers have been neatly cut, it is most likely the work of a mammal. Often there are clumps of feathers. If the feathers in a clump have all been sheared off at the same angle, a canine may well be responsible, for dogs, foxes, coyotes, and wolves possess carnassial teeth designed specifically for shearing. Bobcats and lynx have carnassial teeth, but they are not as sharp as those of canines and thus leave a more ragged edge.

Sheared American crow feathers.

Red Fox Kits Dispersing

The playful, carefree red fox kits of this past spring are roughly seven months old, and they are ready to venture out on their own. The males leave earlier than the females and travel farther—as far as 150 miles away, being less tolerated by their father. The young foxes will frequently invade the territories of other established foxes and get chased out. Eventually they will either take over another fox's range or find an unoccupied area of their own. The females usually stay close to their birthplace. In some cases, one or more female kits will remain with their parents for a year. These "helper vixens" assist in the rearing of their younger siblings by capturing prey for them. Kits born this past spring will be fully grown and ready to mate this coming winter.

Maturing red fox kits.

NOVEMBER 10

Moose Chewing Cud

Moose—like cattle, goats, sheep, and deer—are ruminants. They have a four-chambered stomach, which is necessary in order to digest the

Moose chewing cud.

cellulose in the vegetation they consume. Food goes to the rumen, the first of the four chambers, which contains bacteria and other microorganisms that help digest the cellulose. Food is circulated from the rumen back to the moose's mouth by the second chamber, the reticulum, and the moose ruminates, or "chews its cud." The third chamber, or omasum, functions as a pump, sending the food to the final chamber, the abomasum, where the digestion process is completed.

Backswimmers Active under Ice

Backswimmers are true bugs and belong to the order Hemiptera. Most Hemipterans are land dwelling, such as stink bugs and assassin bugs, but there are a few, such as water striders, water boatmen, and backswimmers, that are aquatic. While some backswimmers hibernate at the bottom of ponds in winter, others remain active, sculling through the water with their oar-like hind legs that are covered with fine hairs, preying on all forms of life up to the size of a small fish.

Thanks to bubbles of oxygen that they obtain from pockets of air just under the ice and carry around with them like miniature aqualungs, backswimmers can stay below the surface of the water for several minutes. Like most aquatic insects, backswimmers supercool their bodies—they produce antifreeze compounds called cryprotectants that allow their body fluid to go down to 19 to 26 degrees without freezing. A pond with a thin layer of ice and no snow is a window into the life of these active insects.

Blackberry Psillids Heading for Conifers

Occasionally you see a wild or cultivated blackberry bush with leaves that have stunted growth and are curled up. This malformation is due to the blackberry psyllid, also known as the jumping plant louse. Closely related to aphids and scale insects, psyllids are plant-feeding bugs which typically have one specific host on which they feed and lay their eggs.

Blackberry psyllids, small insects similar to cicadas that hold their wings tentlike over their body, feed only on blackberry, and in so doing, cause this leaf distortion.

Blackberry psyllids have one generation per year. The adults mate and lay up to 200 eggs on blackberry bushes in early summer. The nymphs, small and wingless, also feed on the sap of blackberries. They are often

Blackberry branch with psyllid damage.

found inside the curled leaves during the summer months, where they secrete several types of waxy structures as they feed. In the fall, the nymphs mature and overwinter as adults in conifers, such as pines, spruces, and cedars, prior to returning to blackberry bushes in the spring. If blackberries are a mile or more from conifers, no psyllid damage will be found; those growing within an eighth of a mile of conifers are at the greatest risk of psyllid damage.

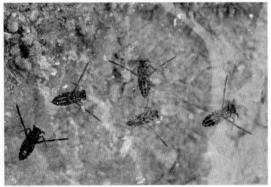

Backswimmers under ice.

NOVEMBER 11

White-Tailed Deer Actively Practicing Rub-Urination

On the inside of the hind legs of all white-tailed deer are glands called tarsal glands. They consist of a tuft of long hair coming from an area of skin from which glands secrete a fatty substance. This fatty substance adheres to the long hairs.

Doe engaged in rub-urination.

When deer urinate, they often assume a crouched posture, causing their urine to run over these hairs, and they often rub their hind legs together. The lipid, or fatty material, on the hairs causes some of the urine that runs over them to remain there. Excess urine is licked off by the deer. The combination of fatty material and urine gives the glands a unique smell—not the typical deer urine smell. During the breeding season, mature bucks urinate on the tarsal gland much more frequently and don't lick off the excess urine, which creates a distinctive rutting odor. This practice is referred to as rub-urination. All deer urinate on these glands throughout the year.

House Sparrow Molt and Pecking Order

After molting in late summer or early fall, male house sparrows have a black breast that is mostly concealed by pale feather tips. By the time their breeding season comes along in the spring, the

Male house sparrow in late fall, post-molt.

Male house sparrow in spring.

pale tips of these feathers have worn off, and the black feathers form a black bib. The size of the bib is correlated with the bird's hierarchy in the flock. Males with larger patches of black tend to be older, and they dominate males with less black. By broadcasting this information for all to see, house sparrows can often avoid fights and thereby save energy.

NOVEMBER 12

Naked Buds

Tree buds are formed in the summer, so if you look at a deciduous tree today, it will have buds in the axils of where the leaves used to be. There are two kinds of buds—leaf buds and flower buds, typically the fatter of the two. Both are usually covered with scales that help protect the bud from drying out during the long, dry winter, when water is frozen and therefore unavailable.

Hobblebush bud.

Different tree species have different types and numbers of bud scales. There are a few trees and shrubs whose buds lack scales completely, and these buds are referred to as naked. Witch hazel, bitternut hickory, and hobblebush all have naked buds. In the photograph, a hobblebush leaf bud is on either side of a flower bud.

Beaver Scat

Beavers are meticulous housekeepers, in that they almost always defecate in the water, rather than in their lodge, and rarely on land. The best place to find beaver scat, should you be so inclined, is where they have been working for an extended period of time, for example, in the water adjacent to their dam. Their scat consists of walnut-size pellets, which, as you might expect, are full of tiny bits of woody fiber. The pellets are essentially little balls of sawdust and disintegrate easily if disturbed, although handling is discouraged due to the presence of giardia. Their light color makes them visible even under water.

Beaver scat.

Tufted Titmice Caching Seeds for Winter Consumption

Tufted titmice and black-capped chickadees are in the same family and share several traits, one of which has to do with storing food. They are both frequent visitors of bird feeders, where they not only take seeds and soon thereafter eat them, but they also collect and cache food throughout their territories for times when food is scarce. Tufted titmice usually store their seeds within 130 feet of the feeder. They take only one seed per trip and usually shell the seeds before hiding them.

NOVEMBER 13

Catbird Nests Exposed

Gray catbird nests are distinctive and relatively easy to identify. Typically, catbirds build their nest in the center of thickets, briars, vines, or a shrub, where it is next to invisible during the breeding season. When leaves have fallen, however, these bulky cup nests are fairly obvious. In addition to being rather large—5 to 6 inches wide and at least 2 inches deep—the walls of the nest are quite thick and incorporate twigs, dried grasses, mud, grapevines, and sometimes pieces of trash. The lining of the nest is of softer material, such as grass, hair, and pine needles, and almost always contains rootlets.

Catbird.

Tufted titmouse.

Catbird nest.

Winterberry fruit.

Eastern chipmunk.

Winterberry Fruits Brightening the Landscape

Winterberry fruits mature in late summer or early fall, but they are much more evident now that most of the leaves have fallen off this deciduous member of the holly family. Because these shrubs are dioecious, meaning male and female flowers appear on separate plants, only the females bear fruit. While winterberry flowers are small and not particularly showy, they produce nectar which attracts honey bees and other pollinators. The bright red berries often persist through the winter and provide cedar waxwings, eastern bluebirds, and American robins with food long after most fruit has disappeared.

Eastern Chipmunks Soon to Encounter Round-the-Clock Darkness and Periodic Torpor

Eastern chipmunks will soon retreat underground to their maze of interconnecting tunnels for the winter. This burrow system usually has one unobstructed entrance with the opening of other tunnels that lead to the surface plugged with leaves. A chipmunk may dig part of the burrow system using its forefeet and cheek pouches to loosen and transport soil, but the renovation of old root channels and existing burrows of other mammals is the primary method of burrow construction. The 2-inch-diameter tunnels are roughly 12 to 30 feet long and typically 18 to 36 inches deep. Off of these tunnels are several food galleries as well as a chamber 6 to 10 inches in diameter which contains a nest of leaves.

Chipmunks reside in their subterranean environs from mid-November until late March or early April, with local snow depth and temperatures influencing the duration. They are not true hibernators and accumulate little body fat prior to winter. Throughout the winter, chipmunks are aroused from their state of torpor every week or two to snack on their underground caches of food—up to five or six thousand nuts per chipmunk, according to one source. During mid-winter thaws, some chipmunks may leave their burrows, even digging through several feet of snow to forage for seeds in nearby areas where the snow has melted, exposing the forest floor.

NOVEMBER 14

Bruce Spanworm Moths Emerging and Mating

Depending on the woods you walk in, you may be greeted by a flurry of inch-long, tan wings belonging to male Bruce spanworm moths. They

NOV

387

Bruce spanworm moth.

are also called winter moths and hunter moths because the adults emerge, mate, and lay eggs from October to December, when hunters are also in the woods. These late-flying moths appear after many of their main predators, birds, have left for the winter. The moths you see flying are males; females cannot fly—they crawl up the trunk or branch of a tree and send out pheromones to attract winged males. After mating, the female lays eggs, which are pale green initially but become bright orange with age. The eggs hatch in the spring, and the larvae feed on a variety of deciduous leaves, favoring trembling aspen, willows, sugar maple, and American beech. Periodic outbreaks of these caterpillars can result in heavy defoliation.

Nannyberry

Nannyberry is a species of *Viburnum*, and as such has opposite branching. It is commonly found growing in moist woodland edges. Nannyberry's branches are pendulous and quite flexible, and when crushed they are said to smell like sheep. The fruit of nannyberry is green at first, then yellow, red, and, finally, bluish black. When ripe, it is slightly sweet, juicy, and edible. Many species of wildlife eat the fruit of nannyberry, including ruffed grouse, brown thrashers, cedar waxwings, red squirrels, and white-tailed deer.

Nannyberry buds and fruit.

NOVEMBER 15

Pink Earth Fruiting

You have probably walked right over this lichen a million times and perhaps even thought it was a fungus. To all appearances, pink earth appears to be colonies of tiny, pink mushrooms, but in fact, these aren't mushrooms. They are the fruiting bodies, or apothecia, of a lichen, that is, a fungus combined with an alga or cyanobacterium. If you look closely at these ⅛-inch bubblegum-colored structures, you'll see that they are at the apex of tiny stalks that grow out of a gray crusty matter, which is the body, or thallus, of the lichen. Look for pink earth growing in disturbed areas such as roadsides.

Pink earth.

Shagbark Hickory Nuts Ripening

Shagbark hickory, a member of the walnut family, is named for the shaggy appearance of the bark on older trees. Shagbark hickory produces nuts which are covered with thick husks. As time goes by, the green husks turn brown and open, exposing the nuts, which fall to the ground—if squirrels haven't managed to eat them while they are still on the tree. It takes about ten years for a shagbark hickory tree to start producing nuts, but large quantities are not produced until it is forty years old. Nut production continues—a good crop every three to five years—for at least one

Shagbark hickory nut tree.

hundred years. Shagbark hickory nuts are sweet and highly nutritious. They were a staple food for the Algonquians, and squirrels, raccoons, chipmunks, mice, bears, foxes, rabbits, wood ducks, and wild turkeys also feed on this excellent source of protein, fats, and carbohydrates.

Porcupines Entering Winter Dens

During the summer, porcupines are almost always found out in the open. Around the first week in November, they den up for the winter in the Northeast, with up to a dozen porcupines sharing the same den. While some adult males will spend days at a time in a conifer, most porcupines seek out rocky crevices in which to spend the day, with a smaller number finding shelter in hollow trees. Porcupines are hardy creatures. Although dens do protect them from heat

Porcupine in hollow tree den.

loss, they contain no insulation, the entrances are open, and porcupines do not huddle together for warmth. In addition, porcupines emerge from their dens to feed at night, when outside temperatures are lowest.

NOVEMBER 16

Barred Owls Catching and Digesting Prey

Owls swallow small prey whole, while larger prey is torn into pieces before being swallowed. Once eaten, prey goes directly into the owl's stomach, as owls have no crop, and thus no ability to store food for later consumption. The glandular first part of its stomach is the proventriculus.

Barred owl proventriculus.

Contents of barred owl proventriculus, left to right: meadow vole, masked shrew, northern short-tailed shrew, northern short-tailed shrew, deer mouse or white-footed mouse.

Barred owl.

Like other birds, owls have a stomach with two chambers—one is the glandular stomach, or proventriculus, which produces enzymes, acids, and mucus and begins the process of digestion. Because these acids are weak, only the soft tissues are digested. The second stomach is the muscular stomach, or gizzard, also called the ventriculus. The gizzard lacks digestive glands, but it serves as a filter, holding back bones, fur, teeth, and feathers that are difficult to digest. The soft parts of the food are ground by the gizzard's muscular contractions and allowed to pass through to the rest of the digestive system.

Several hours after an owl has eaten, the indigestible parts remaining in the gizzard are compressed into a pellet that is the same shape as the gizzard. The pellet travels back to the proventriculus and remains there for up to ten hours before being regurgitated. Because the stored pellet partially blocks the owl's digestive system, often new prey cannot be swallowed until the pellet is ejected. If more than one prey is eaten within several hours, the remains are consolidated into one pellet.

Leafy Liverworts Growing on Trees

Plants that have no conductive (vascular) tissue are referred to as bryophytes. They include mosses, hornworts, and liverworts, all of which reproduce with spores and do not form flowers or seeds. Liverworts are common in the tropics, but certain species are plentiful in the Northeast. They are divided into two groups: flat, leafless thallus liverworts and leafy liverworts, which typically resemble flattened moss. You can easily confuse leafy liverworts with mosses, but there are differences between the two. If you examine them under a microscope, you will find that leafy liverworts have leaves that are arranged in two or three rows, while the leaves in mosses are spirally arranged. Liverworts of the *Frullania* genus are classified as leafy liverworts. They are quite common and typically have a reddish-brown color and attach themselves to a tree or other plant, obtaining moisture and nutrients from the air.

Frullania sp.

Common Mergansers Migrating

Common mergansers are hardy, fish-eating, cavity-nesting ducks that can be found in the Northeast year round, as they winter as far north as open water allows. However, the birds we see in the winter on large bodies of water most likely are not the same birds that breed here, but are breeding birds from the north. All North American populations of common mergansers migrate,

NOV

Hibernating Animals and Where They Spend the Winter

- American bullfrog—On top of mud at bottom of pond
- Northern leopard frog—On top of mud at bottom of lakes, ponds, streams, and marshes
- Gray tree frog—Under leaf litter and tree roots
- Four-toed salamander—In decaying root systems of trees
- Marbled salamander—In deep mammal burrows
- Eastern red-backed salamander—In tunnels, mammal burrows, and ant mounds
- Wood turtle—In streams
- Painted turtle, snapping turtle—In mud at bottom of pond
- Eastern box turtle—Under leaf litter or in dead stumps
- Common garter snake—In rock crevices, anthills, or rotting logs
- Northern water snake—In rocky ledges, in banks of rivers and ponds, or inside muskrat or beaver lodges
- Eastern hognose snake—Under leaf litter or in dead stumps
- Queen bumble bee, bald-faced hornet, yellow jacket—Underground, in rotten tree stumps, or in leaf litter
- Ladybug beetles (adult)—Clustered under tree bark and leaf litter
- Mourning cloak (adult)—Beneath loose bark
- Question mark (adult)—In wood piles, hollow trees, or logs
- Woodchuck—In woodland burrow
- Woodland jumping mouse—In underground burrow
- Little brown bat—In caves

Woodchuck.

Leopard frog.

Common garter snake.

Juvenile common mergansers.

Ring-necked ducks.

generally short to intermediate distances. Populations near the coast move only short distances, while interior birds migrate farther. Heavier birds and adult males seem to tolerate colder winter temperatures and remain farther north than immature birds. They can often be seen on large lakes and rivers, as well as the coast, where they form small groups that may gather into large numbers at favored sites.

Migrating common mergansers tend to leave late in the fall, and this week marks the peak of their fall migration, making them among the last waterfowl migrants to head south. Common mergansers typically migrate over land at night and along seacoasts or major river systems by day. In the spring, adult males return north first, as soon as open water is available, followed by females a few weeks later.

NOVEMBER 18

Ring-Necked Ducks Migrating

Ring-necked ducks winter as far north as southern New England, and breed as far south as northern New England. They are most prevalent in most of the Northeast twice a year, during their migration to and from Canada and Florida. Look for them passing through between October and December. Flocks of migrating ducks circling 500–1,000 feet above a marsh before departing in single file are a common sight in wetlands near sunset at this time of year. During the day they tend to coalesce into larger flocks on fall staging areas to rest and refuel. Adult males precede females and young to wintering areas.

Northern Red Oak Buds

There are approximately six hundred species of oaks in the genus *Quercus*, all of which are in the beech family. This genus has two subgroups, the red oaks and the white oaks. The red oak group is characterized by leaves with sharply pointed, bristly lobes. The leaves of the white oak group have rounded lobes lacking bristles. Although usually there are a few oak leaves on a tree that persist well into the winter, it is helpful to be able to identify a species by its buds alone. Oaks tend to have several terminal buds. Northern red oak's terminal buds are large, pointed, cone-shaped, and covered with reddish-brown, mostly hairless scales that overlap like shingles, with one edge covered and the other edge exposed, while white oak buds are small, blunt, and rounded.

Red oak buds.

NOVEMBER 19

Ancient Lineage of Scouring Rush Traces Back 350 Million Years

Scouring rush belongs to a group of non-flowering, spore-producing plants that are known as horsetails. The group is named for some of the species in it that are branched and were thought to resemble the tails of horses. There are several species of horsetails, including scouring rush, that do not branch. Three hundred and fifty million years ago, horsetail relatives dominated the understory, with some individuals growing as high as 100 feet.

Scouring rush's rough stems terminate in a pointed cone within which spores develop. Their evergreen, hollow stems are jointed, and the stem can be separated into sections easily by pulling at joints. The leaves have been reduced to small sheaths encircling each joint. Scouring rush is often found near streams and ponds and can form large colonies.

The stems of all species of horsetails contain silica. Those of scouring rush, as one might gather from its name, were bundled together and used as a fine abrasive for scouring pans. In addition, they were used for sanding wood and smoothing reeds for woodwind instruments.

Yellow-Bellied Sapsucker Sign

Yellow-bellied sapsuckers have headed south for the winter, but signs of their summer activity remain. Especially on standing birch, apple, and mountain ash, rows of ¼-inch holes that these woodpeckers drilled in order to gain access to nutritious phloem sap can be seen. Once the sap begins to flow, sapsuckers insert their tongues into these holes. Regardless of their name, sapsuckers do not suck sap; they lap it up with the aid of tiny hairlike projections on the edge of their tongue, which hold the sap by capillary action. Each flick of the tongue brings more sap into the woodpecker's mouth.

Because sap is so essential to a tree, wounds are quickly sealed to prevent loss of sap. Scientists still have not determined how sapsuckers overcome a tree's defenses and maintain a continuous flow of sap. One theory is that sapsucker saliva may contain a substance that acts as an anticoagulant, preventing sap from clogging up and sealing over the holes the bird creates.

Patch of scouring rush.

Scouring rush spore-bearing cone, or strobilus.

Yellow-bellied sapsucker tongue.

Yellow-bellied sapsucker holes.

NOVEMBER 20

Nictitating Membranes Provide Moisture and Protection

If you look closely, you'll see that this juvenile bald eagle's eye appears white. This appearance is due to a transparent part of the eye referred to as a third eyelid, or nictitating membrane. Many animals, including some fish, mammals, reptiles, amphibians, and birds, have nictitating membranes. Instead of moving up or down like our upper and lower eyelids, they move horizontally across the eye, much like windshield wipers. These membranes lie under a bird's eyelids. When not in use, they are curled up in the inner corners of a bird's eyes, but can be quickly drawn across the eyes to protect, clean, and moisten them without shutting out the light.

Juvenile bald eagle.

Japanese Barberry Fruiting

Japanese barberry is very much like the shrub burning bush—it turns many shades of red and orange in the fall and thus has had great appeal as an ornamental. Birds, including turkeys, grouse, mockingbirds, and waxwings, find the fruit of both of these woody shrubs irresistible and spread the seeds far and wide—a bit too far and wide, in fact. Like burning bush, Japanese barberry has escaped from cultivation and is

Japanese barberry fruit.

established and reproducing in the wild so successfully that it is classified as invasive. It is a particular threat to open and second-growth forests. An established colony can grow thick enough to crowd out native understory plants, reducing wildlife habitat and forage and thereby increasing pressure on native plants that are eaten by white-tailed deer and other herbivores. Japanese barberry may also act as a nursery for deer ticks, which can transmit a number of diseases.

NOVEMBER 21

Beavers Bumping Ice

The days are numbered when beavers can be out grooming themselves on land or eating freshly cut branches. There is a period of time in the fall, usually when the temperature has yet to drop down to 16 degrees, when the ice on a beaver pond is thin enough to break under the pressure of a beaver's head punching it from below and not quite hard enough to support a beaver's weight. As long as the ice is thin enough to crack by swimming under it and bumping their heads against it, beavers will do so, for soon it will be thick enough to lock them into their pond. The beaver swims up to the undersurface of the ice and bumps its head against it, creating an

audible crack. The beaver then pokes its head up through the hole in the ice, lifts its front feet up onto the edge of the ice in front of it, and lunges forward, breaking a path with its body through the ice. Over and over the beaver may lunge, pausing periodically to catch its breath, until it reaches its destination.

NOVEMBER 22

Pine Grosbeaks Feeding Voraciously

The pine grosbeak is the largest of the winter finches that sometimes appear during the winter in search of food farther south than their normal range. When a fruit-laden tree is found, a flock of pine grosbeaks may descend upon it and not leave until every piece of fruit has been eaten.

Beaver breaking through ice.

Male (top) and female (bottom) pine grosbeaks eating crabapples.

They are relatively messy eaters, and often when feeding have most of the fruit on their beaks. The reason for this is that when pine grosbeaks eat cherries, crabapples, and other fruit, they bite through them and concentrate on crushing and eating the seed, while the fleshy pulp spills out of their beak.

White Ash Bark

White ash bark.

White ash is a member of the olive family and has several distinctive characteristics: narrow, winged seeds; opposite branches; and compound leaves, among others. One of the most noticeable features of white ash is the shape of its trunk and the pattern of its bark. The trunk of a white ash is usually straight, and while the bark on a young white ash is relatively smooth, the bark of a mature tree has interlacing corky ridges that form obvious diamond-shaped fissures. If you find one of these trees now, make a note to revisit it in the spring when you may find edible morel mushrooms growing at its base.

NOVEMBER 23

Canada Geese Switch Diet to Berries and Grains

During migration and throughout the winter, Canada geese are highly gregarious, often gathering and feeding in flocks that consist of over a thousand geese. Almost exclusively herbivorous, they are efficient grazers, having serrations on their stout, flat bills. During summer, they feed primarily on grasses and sedges. Considered a nuisance by many people with large lawns,

Canada geese in corn field.

Canada geese are attracted to these lawns not only because they can digest grass, but also because they have an unobstructed view that allows them to detect approaching predators. During and following migration, berries, especially blueberries, and agricultural grains, including sorghum, corn, and winter wheat, make up most of their diet. When you see them in cornfields, they are feeding on fallen kernels as well as corn still on dry cobs. They are very good at removing the kernels.

Bald-Faced Hornet Nests Being Vacated

A typical bald-faced hornet nest is roughly the size of a football or basketball. The maximum size is between 14 and 18 inches in diameter and up to 29 inches in length. This nest is built over a period of four or five months. It is started by a queen bald-faced hornet that, after emerging from hibernation this past spring, chews some wood fiber, mixes it with her saliva, and creates a few brood cells surrounded by one or more paper envelopes. She lays an egg in each cell and feeds the hornet larvae insects which she first masticates into tiny bits. When the larvae pupate and emerge as adult workers, they assume the duties of nest building, food collection, feeding the larvae, and protecting the nest, while the queen continues laying eggs in horizontal tiers of cells. This ongoing activity produces a colony of anywhere from one hundred to four hundred

Bald-faced hornet nest.

workers by the end of the summer. Shortly before the first hard frost in the fall, the new fertilized queen(s) leave the colony and find a protected spot in which to spend the winter. When freezing temperatures arrive, the workers all die, leaving a nest that will never again be inhabited by bald-faced hornets.

NOVEMBER 24

Thimbleweed

Often thimbleweed, *Anemone virginiana*, is overlooked when its white flowers are blooming during the summer, but its seed head is rarely missed in the fall. When flowering, stamens surround a green cone that elongates into a cylindrical fruit twice as long as it is wide, giving this member of the buttercup family its name. The seeds mature in the fall, and the style, part of the female reproductive structure that remains attached to the developing seed, develops a woolly texture, turning the "thimble" into a ball of fluff. A close look reveals that this fluff consists of many tiny dark seeds, each of which bears a cottony tuft to enhance its dispersal by the wind.

Thimbleweed seeds dispersing.

Thimbleweed produces chemicals which inhibit seed germination and seedling growth in many species of plants, so often the ground is relatively bare around this plant. Mammalian herbivores usually leave thimbleweed alone, because the foliage contains a blistering agent that can irritate the mouth parts and digestive tract.

Slug Scat

Slugs produce lots of mucus. Some covers their whole body and makes it difficult for them to be picked up by a predator, some forms a slime trail that aids them when they are moving, and some envelopes their waste. After eating and digesting a wide variety of plants, fungi, earthworms, carrion, and the scat of other animals, a mucous string of scat leaves through a slug's anus, which is hidden under the leathery patch called a mantle, located just behind the head.

Thimbleweed flower.

Thimbleweed seedhead.

Slug and scat.

The odd position of this opening is a result of slugs' evolutionary descent from snails. In a snail, this opening must be outside the shell and thus is far forward on its body.

NOVEMBER 25

Mice vs. Voles

Mice and voles are commonly lumped together, probably because the differences between them are so slight. Both are small, furry rodents, but mice generally have large eyes, large ears, and long tails that are close to or greater than the length of their bodies. Voles have smaller eyes, smaller ears that are often concealed in their fur, and shorter tails. Voles tend to be active day and night, whereas mice

Southern red-backed meadow vole (top) and white-footed mouse (bottom).

are mainly nocturnal. Meadow voles are commonly referred to as field mice, which tends to add to the confusion. There are five species of mice in the Northeast—white-footed, deer, house, meadow jumping, and woodland jumping—and four species of voles—meadow, southern red-backed, rock, and woodland.

Sweetfern Buds Set

The pungent aroma, reminiscent of turpentine, given off by the crushed leaves and stems of this 3-foot-tall shrub gives sweetfern its common name, and although it resembles a fern, it is not

Sweetfern buds.

one. It is found and can survive in dry, acid, sandy soil, because it fixes nitrogen through a close partnership with bacteria in the genus *Frankia*. It is among the first plants to colonize barren, nutrient-poor soils such as areas disturbed by fire, logging, clear-cutting, or road construction.

The wind-pollinated flowers are small and inconspicuous in the spring, but the buds are quite evident at this time of year. The male staminate flower buds are cylindrical and clustered in groups of three or four on the tip of the previous year's growth.

NOVEMBER 26

Carpenter Ants Overwintering in Galleries

Insects that live in the Northeast have different strategies for surviving the winter. Carpenter ants live in the center of both dead and living trees, in galleries that they have chewed. Although wood is a good insulator, it still freezes during the winter. The ants tend to cluster together and enter a

Carpenter ants.

state of slowed metabolism called diapause. In addition, carpenter ants produce glycerol, a compound that acts as antifreeze, preventing destructive ice crystals from forming in their bodies.

Naming Staghorn Sumac

During the summer, the antlers of male white-tailed deer, commonly referred to as bucks or stags, are covered with fuzzy velvet, a vascular skin that carries blood-supplying oxygen and nutrients to the growing bone. The velvety, rusty hairs that grow on the stems of leaves and the branches of staghorn sumac, as well as the forking pattern of its branches, resemble the antlers of stags to such a degree that it was given this common name.

Staghorn sumac.

NOVEMBER 27

Wattles, Caruncles, and Snoods

Male wild turkeys, or toms, have a number of ways of impressing hens in addition to displays involving their feathers. Among them are wattles, caruncles, and snoods—fleshy protuberances that adorn their throats and beaks. A large wattle, or dewlap, is the flap of skin on the throat of a male turkey. The bulbous, fleshy growths at the bottom of the turkey's throat are major caruncles. Large wattles and caruncles have been shown to correlate with high testosterone levels, good nutrition, and the ability to evade predators, which makes the genes of a tom turkey with a large wattle very desirable to a female. The snood, another fleshy outgrowth, which hangs down over the tom's beak, is normally pale and not very long. When a tom turkey starts strutting and courting a hen, the wattle, caruncles, and snood become engorged with blood, become bigger, and turn bright red or blue. This impresses both male and female turkeys: the males avoid or defer to him and the females'

Male wild turkey.

interest in him is heightened. A longer snood has also been correlated with a lack of internal parasites, making toms with large snoods even more irresistible to hens.

White-Tailed Deer Scat and Diet

White-tailed deer scat varies considerably from season to season, due to the amount of moisture that is in a deer's diet. In the summer, when deer are eating primarily herbaceous green plants, their droppings are fairly loosely formed. In the fall, when they are transitioning from green plants to the buds and twigs of shrubs and trees, their scat often consists of pellets that are squeezed together into clumps. During the winter, their drier diet results in harder, well-defined pellets.

Fall white-tailed deer scat.

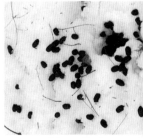

Winter white-tailed deer scat.

Striped Maple Bark and Buds

Striped maple buds.

Striped maple, also known as moosewood and moose maple, can easily be identified in summer or winter by its greenish bark that bears the vertical white stripes that give rise to its common name. This tree's buds are equally notable. Their graceful shape, smooth surface with few bud scales, and pinkish-red coloration distinguish them from all others. These buds and the young branches that bear them are devoured by rabbits and hares, are frequently eaten by porcupines and beavers, and provide browse for deer and moose.

Woodpeckers Bark Sloughing

Several species of woodpeckers search for wood-boring beetle larvae by removing the bark from a tree, in addition to drilling holes. This is referred to as bark sloughing. Some birds, such as nuthatches, remove only scales of bark, not the whole layer, and this is referred to as scaling. After finding or creating an opening, the woodpecker repeatedly slips its pointed beak under loose bark, prying it off of the tree. It then uses its long, barb-tipped tongue to capture the

Woodpecker sloughing.

exposed insects. Different woodpecker species tend to feed on either trunks or branches, and at different heights. Initially the sloughing can resemble the work of porcupines, but close examination may reveal the marks of a beak, which are perpendicular to the trunk or limb, rather than the grooves left by a porcupine's incisors.

Lichens Turning Green After a Rain

You may have noticed that the green pigment in many lichens often becomes more intense after it rains. Lichens are made up of an alga or cyanobacterium, which makes food, and a fungus, which absorbs water and nutrients. A typical lichen has a three-layered structure. A middle layer containing algal cells entwined in threadlike fungus fibers called hyphae is sandwiched between two layers of fungal tissue. Lichens that turn bright green after it rains contain green algae which

Green lichen.

contains chlorophyll, a green pigment. When it rains, the fungus, which surrounds the algae, soaks up water like a sponge, causing the fungus to become more transparent and allowing the green pigment of the algae to be seen more clearly.

Black Bears and Humans

Black bears are opportunistic eaters. Most of their food consists of grasses, roots, berries, and insects. They will also eat fish and mammals—including carrion—and easily develop a taste for human foods and garbage. If winter comes late, and the acorn and beechnut crops are poor, the bears that are still active will soon detect bird

Black bear.

Black bear scat filled with sunflower seed husks.

feeders as a nutritious source of food. These conditions are conducive to conflict between humans and bears.

A close look at bear scat near human dwellings this time of year almost inevitably reveals many sunflower seed husks, along with millet and other bird seed. Black-oiled sunflower seeds are high in fat and protein and are quite irresistible to black bears. The problem with this, other than damaged bird feeders, is that the bears become habituated to this diet and repeatedly return for more. Before long, the bear becomes a nuisance, and because of this it often gets killed. Although biologists use December 1 as the date when feeding birds is safe, because in a typical year, bears have gone into hibernation, it is best to wait to start filling feeders until the weather has been very cold for a substantial amount of time.

NOVEMBER 30

Ribbed Pine Borers Overwintering as Adults

The larva of the ribbed pine borer lives just under the inside of a pine tree's bark. It is a long-horned beetle, and in the fall, when it is ready to pupate,

it creates an oval cell by chewing a relatively flat chamber approximately 1¼ inches long. The ribbed pine borer uses the woody fibers it chewed to form a raised wall surrounding the chamber. It then pupates inside the wall and overwinters in the chamber as an adult beetle, emerging to mate in the spring.

Ribbed pine borer cell.

Red Squirrel's Winter Coat

There is a marked seasonal difference in the red squirrel's appearance due to its two annual molts, in the spring and the fall. In the winter, a broad, rusty red band extends along its back, from the ears to the tip of the tail. The red squirrel's thicker winter coat also includes ear tufts, which no other species of squirrel in the Northeast possesses. Come spring, when the squirrel sheds again, it loses its ear tufts and its new coat is closer to an olive-green color than red.

Red squirrel in winter.

DECEMBER

Overwintering Tree Frogs

Winter's freezing temperatures pose a particular challenge for cold-blooded, or ectothermic, animals in the Northeast. Amphibians, reptiles, fish, insects, and arachnids are incapable of regulating their own body temperature. Their body is roughly the same temperature as the air surrounding them, which means that they are vulnerable when it gets very hot or cold, and in the winter they must either seek out a protected area (hibernaculum) or somehow cope with freezing temperatures.

The strategy that a given frog uses to stay alive through the winter depends largely on the type of habitat in which it resides, as well as its digging ability. Aquatic frogs, such as bullfrogs, green frogs, and northern leopard frogs, remain submerged for over half the year, hibernating at the bottoms of ponds. Because they breathe through their skin during hibernation (they use both lungs and skin the rest of the year), they don't burrow into the mud, as their skin needs to be near oxygen-rich water. Rather, they sit on the bottom of a pond, sometimes with a light layer of debris over them to hide from predators.

Terrestrial frogs typically hibernate on land. Some species of frogs and toads that are good diggers burrow deep in the soil, safely below the frostline. However, tree frogs, such as the spring peeper and gray tree frog, and wood frogs are not capable of digging that deep and are forced to seek out cracks and crevices in logs or rocks or, more typically, to dig into the leaf litter, where the temperature inevitably goes below 32 degrees for weeks or months, at a time. Even so, most of them make it through the winter. The ability of ectothermic tree frogs to endure and survive freezing temperatures has been, and still is, a mystery to scientists and laymen alike.

The largest challenge for the frog is to endure the formation of ice within its body, for ice crystals can puncture small blood vessels and, if they form inside cells, can squeeze and deform the cells to the breaking point. Few, if any, organisms can survive the structural damage that is caused by ice formation inside of cells, so freeze-tolerant animals such as tree frogs typically confine ice formation to the outsides of cells, while using protective measures to keep the water inside their cells from freezing.

Before the first frost, but after the temperature has started to drop, most tree frogs seek out a hibernaculum and bury themselves as far under the leaf litter as they can. Their legs and the lenses on their eyes start to freeze as the daily temperatures drop below 32 degrees. When a tree frog first touches an ice crystal, a survival

Gray tree frog.

process is set in motion. Special proteins in their blood cause the water in their blood to freeze first. This ice, in turn, sucks water out of the frog's cells so that the water freezes outside of the cells, causing much less damage. (Humans lack these proteins, so when our skin freezes, we get frostbite, which sucks all the water out of our cells and causes them to collapse.) The first sign of freezing also stimulates a frog's brain to send a message to its liver, which starts to convert stored glycogen into glucose, a sugar. The glucose circulates through the frog's bloodstream into the cells, where it acts as an antifreeze by lowering the freezing point of water. Inside the cells there's thick, sugary syrup, while outside the cells all the water is frozen. This syrup not only prevents cells from freezing, but it protects them from dehydration, which can destroy them.

Essentially, water pulls away from the center of the body, so the internal organs are wrapped in a puddle of water that then turns into solid ice. The frog's heart stops beating, its brain shuts down, muscles stop moving, and the frog stops breathing. Core organs such as the heart and liver freeze last and thaw first, which means that vital body functions such as circulation and metabolism are maintained for the longest possible time. As much as 65 percent of a tree frog's total body water is converted to ice. If you were

Spring peeper.

to hold a frog in your hand while it was hibernating, and pull your hand away, it would drop like a stone and land with a thud. For several months, the frog is in this state of suspended animation.

An amazing feature of this strategy is that in the spring, when the temperature starts to rise, the glucose is reabsorbed by the liver, and the frog thaws out in a matter of hours. Mating begins immediately for spring peepers and wood frogs. This spontaneous resumption—the ability to survive freezing and thawing—is thought to have its origin in mechanisms that amphibians evolved to deal with water scarcity during warmer months. Due to their water-permeable skins, frogs experience great variations in body water content and can recover from dry spells even after losing half of their total body water.

One day, humans may be able to duplicate the molecular mechanics that allow tree frogs to survive freezing. This would greatly improve the current human organ transplant procedure, as today, doctors have only hours to get a donated organ into a living patient before the organ becomes too damaged; freezing organs isn't an option, as the cells dehydrate.

Wood frog.

Bird Survival in Winter

There are good reasons why many birds leave for a warmer climate in the fall, despite the risks of migration. The food supply is greatly reduced, as insects and other invertebrates which many migrants such as swallows, warblers, and flycatchers depend on all but disappear. The daylight hours, when many species of birds forage for food, are reduced. Shortened days mean longer nights, resulting in fourteen or fifteen hours during which birds aren't feeding. Finally, it is much colder, forcing birds to use more energy to keep warm. Even with these obstacles, some species do remain in the Northeast year-round and have adapted in a variety of ways to these winter challenges.

The structure of feathers is one of the biggest factors that allow birds to stay warm and thereby reduce their need for food in the winter. A typical wing or tail feather consists of a central shaft, with rows of interlocking barbs down either side of the shaft. There are different kinds of feathers, however, designed for different functions. The feathers that cover a bird's body—contour feathers—have interlocking barbs, but only at their tips, where they aren't covered by an overlapping feather. The rest of the barbs on the feather are not connected. They are loose and fluffy, similar to down feathers, and create many air pockets between the bird's skin and its feathers. This layer of air provides excellent insulation, preventing much of the bird's 110- to 112-degree body heat from escaping into the air.

Bird feet and legs are usually featherless and thus are exposed to the cold, but they consist largely of tough tendons, not fleshy muscles that would be susceptible to freezing. Even so, birds take measures to reduce heat loss in their extremities, primarily by reducing the flow of warm blood through the arteries into their legs and feet. Heat loss is reduced by up to 90 percent in a bird's extremities by reducing the diameter of the arteries in their legs and feet and through

Blue jay.

a heat exchange system. The arteries and veins in a bird's legs and feet are adjacent to each other. The heat of the warm, oxygenated blood in the arteries is transferred to the cooler blood in the adjacent vein before the blood reenters the body.

When temperatures drop significantly, resting birds will often shiver for several minutes at a time, as shivering converts muscular energy into heat. They also will tuck their exposed heads into their feathers and sit on their feet.

If it is so cold that a bird cannot maintain its body temperature at its normal high level through shivering or by puffing out its feathers and other behavioral tactics, some may go into a state of torpor for several hours, allowing the body temperature to drop 30 or 40 degrees lower than normal. A few birds, hummingbirds and nighthawks among them, are known to do this. Their metabolism drops dramatically, their heart beat slows down, their breathing rate slows, and their body temperature drops. This change in metabolism conserves energy, often enough to allow the bird to survive a frigid night when otherwise it would expire.

When a bird is in a state of torpor, it is unresponsive to its surroundings, but when the temperature rises, the bird is capable of raising its body temperature back to normal, and it resumes normal activities—unlike humans who

Avian Techniques for Opening Acorns

Common grackle.

Wild turkey.

Wood duck.

- The **common grackle** has a hard keel on the inside of its upper mandible, which is used to saw open acorns and other hard nuts. Typically they score the outside of the narrow end and then bite the acorn open.

- While **blue jays** prefer acorns still on the tree and will struggle to break green acorns from twigs, they will also eat acorns they find on the ground. In the fall, an individual blue jay eats or caches several thousand acorns, beechnuts, chestnuts, hickory nuts, and hazelnuts. It retrieves cached nuts from the ground by digging with its beak.

- **Wild turkeys** have some of the longest intestines of all birds, allowing them to extract nutritional value from even extremely coarse vegetation, such as acorns. Food, including whole acorns, is ingested through the esophagus and stored temporarily in an expandable organ called the crop. It then continues into the gizzard, an impressively strong organ that crushes and grinds the acorns into a digestible pulp.

- Many birds gather food rapidly and digest it after they have left the exposed and vulnerable areas where they feed. **Wood ducks** are among these, deftly picking acorns from trees and the ground with their short, narrow bills. Unlike wild turkeys, wood ducks don't have a crop, but their esophagus is very flexible and able to expand to accommodate large amounts of food. It can hold as many as thirty small or twenty large acorns at a time before they are passed on to the glandular stomach, where digestive enzymes are secreted, and then on to the muscular gizzard, which acts as the duck's teeth to grind the food.

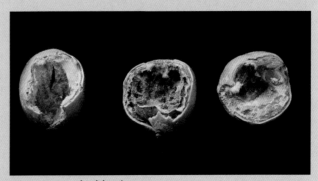

Acorns eaten by blue jays.

White-breasted nuthatch.

Pileated woodpecker tucking head under wings.

experience severe hypothermia. There is one species of bird, the insect-eating common poorwill, which researchers feel is a true hibernator. The same bird was found in a torpid state for weeks at a time, in the same location in California, over a period of four winters. This little-known phenomenon was discovered long ago by native Hopis who referred to this bird as *holchko*, which means "the sleeping one."

Night is the biggest challenge of all, as small birds do not feed at night and have to go many hours without food. Many save body heat by roosting in places where they can get out of the wind. Grosbeaks, cardinals, and crossbills are known to head for the thick branches of conifers, which act as a windbreak. Some birds, mostly cavity-nesting birds such as chickadees, nuthatches, and woodpeckers, roost at night in tree cavities for this same reason. Another strategy employed by certain birds is huddling. As many as twenty-nine white-breasted nuthatches have been found clustered together in a large tree cavity to minimize heat loss. On especially cold nights, grouse will fly headfirst into a soft snowbank, tunneling their way into short, well-insulated burrows.

One last example of the ingenuity of avian winter adaptations is overnight food storage. Evening grosbeaks and some other northern finches are able to store relatively large amounts of seeds in their well-developed crops, and this helps them get through the night. Common and hoary redpolls can survive colder temperatures than any other songbird due to a special storage pouch in their esophagus which they fill with high-calorie seeds (often birch) just before dark; the seeds are then digested throughout the night.

Fluffy feathers next to the skin, sinewy legs and feet, shivering, torpidity, cavity-roosting, huddling, and specialized anatomy that accommodates extra food storage—an impressive array of both physical and behavioral adaptations that allow some birds to withstand the rigors of winter in the Northeast.

Male common redpoll.

Insect Survival in Winter

When you think of something as small as a bark beetle that is one-tenth of an inch long surviving a winter with temperatures that dip well below zero for days on end, it seems miraculous. How does ice not form within its cells, killing it? That beetle and millions of other insects are capable of manipulating their metabolism and biochemistry in order to avoid freezing to death.

All insects are ectothermic, or cold-blooded, and thus assume the temperature of the air around them. Cold weather slows them down, and during the winter they enter a resting stage called diapause, often referred to as hibernation. During diapause their metabolism slows down and normal activities cease. Many insects recognize that it's time to begin preparation for diapause by the decreasing amount of daylight in the fall. In response, they start to migrate downward, where there's more protection from the elements—moving from trees, shrubs, and plants down to the leaf litter, rock crevices, in or under rotting logs, and under rocks. Even in these hideaways, however, more protection is usually necessary to avoid freezing. Two strategies insects use to protect themselves include tolerating freezing (freeze tolerant) and relying on other mechanisms to avoid freezing (freeze avoidant).

Freeze tolerant insects can survive the formation of internal body ice, whereas freeze avoidance insects avoid freezing by keeping their body fluids liquid. In the Northeast, where there are long periods of cold, the main strategy of most insects is freeze avoidance. This can be achieved in several ways. One is to seek out a spot where ice usually doesn't form, such as a very dry location. Another is the creation of some kind of physical barrier, such as a wax coating, that protects against ice forming on the external skeleton. Regardless of such strategies, all freeze avoidant insects that can't tolerate the formation of ice in their body fluids lower the temperature at which their body fluids freeze. A process known as supercooling allows water to cool below its freezing point without changing to a solid. Water needs a particle in order to crystallize, and with no particles, it can cool to -43 degrees without freezing. Freeze avoidant insects that engage in supercooling remove or inactivate all of the food particles, dust, and bacteria in their gut or inside their cells, so the fluid within their bodies can't solidify in the Northeast's winter temperatures. In addition, some insects synthesize substances such as glycerol throughout their head, thorax, and abdomen. This substance acts as antifreeze, reducing the lethal freezing temperature of their bodies.

Fire-colored beetle larva.

Click beetle larva.

Carpenter ants in log.

This state of suspended animation, or diapause, often takes place in or just under the bark of a rotting log. The insects that seek winter shelter here often have the company of other ectothermic creatures, including spiders, snails, and slugs.

DECEMBER 1

Hairy and Downy Woodpecker Bills

Distinguishing hairy woodpeckers from their smaller relatives, downy woodpeckers, can be challenging if you don't have a chance to view both species at the same time. The easiest way to tell them apart is to note the relative size of their bills. The hairy woodpecker's bill is proportionately much larger than the downy woodpecker's—it is almost as long as its head—whereas the downy woodpecker's bill is not nearly as long. Because of this, hairy woodpeckers looking for insects can drill and probe deeper into harder substrates than downy woodpeckers.

Hairy (left) and downy (right) woodpeckers.

Hoar Frost

Frost is to dew as snowflakes are to raindrops. When water vapor condenses into liquid water, you get dew and raindrops. When water vapor condenses directly into ice, you get frost and snowflakes. Snowflakes are not frozen raindrops, and likewise, frost is not frozen dew.

When frost forms as minute ice crystals covering the ground, we call it all frost. But sometimes the frost grains grow larger and are called hoar frost crystals. On clear frosty nights in winter, especially when there is a source of water vapor nearby, such as an unfrozen lake or stream, soft ice crystals might form on vegetation or any object that has been chilled below the freezing point by radiation cooling. These deposits of ice crystals are hoar frost. The interlocking ice crystals become attached to branches of trees and shrubs, as well as vegetation on the ground and any other object below freezing temperature that is exposed to supersaturated air, that is, where the relative humidity is greater than 100 percent. Hoar frost vanishes once the sun has risen and warmed the surface of branches, grasses, and other objects, so it is most easily observed in the early morning.

Hoar frost on black-eyed Susan seedhead.

Scat Revelations

Predators and scavengers of all stripes and colors are reaping the benefits of deer hunting season. A close look at the composition and form of the pictured scat reveals much more than the fact that a coyote dined on a white-tailed deer. Note that the scat consists almost entirely of deer hair. When a predator such as a coyote comes upon a carcass, it tends to eat the internal organs first, which produce black, moist, soft scats with next to no bones or hair in them. As it continues to feed, the coyote's scats contain more and more

409

Eastern coyote scat.

bones and hair, until eventually that is all they consist of.

Not only can we deduce that this coyote was finishing up the tail end of a deer carcass, we can also surmise that if the entire pack consumed the carcass, the coyote that left this scat was not at the top of its pack's hierarchy. The alpha pair usually has first dibs on the internal organs, with lower members of the pack having access to the less choice parts, such as hair and bones.

DECEMBER 2

Some Spiders Still Active

Long-jawed orbweaver spiders have huge, powerful pincers called chelicerae, and a long, slender abdomen. They are active long after most spiders have disappeared. This quarter-inch spider increases its ability to camouflage itself in grass by forming a straight line, with four of its legs stretched forward and four backward. There are twenty-five species in this genus (*Tetragnatha*) in North America, all of which are called stretch spiders, referring to their elongated body form. As their name implies, these spiders are orb weavers, although their webs are relatively open, with few spokes and spirals. They are agile and can navigate on the surface of water very well.

Discerning Eastern Gray Squirrels

In the fall, eastern gray squirrels bury acorns from red and white oaks to sustain themselves through the winter. The acorns of red oaks have delayed germination and can be stored up to six months before they germinate. The acorns of white oaks, however, have no such dormancy and germinate in the fall, soon after they fall from the tree. Once acorns sprout, they are less nutritious, as the seed tissue converts to the indigestible lignins that form the root. Gray squirrels, as a means of long-term cache management, selectively remove the embryos from white oak acorns, but not from red oak acorns, before burying them. Germination is prevented, and the storage viability of the white oak acorns is extended by six months, equaling that of the red oak acorns.

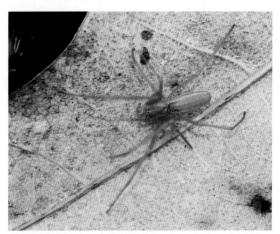
Green long-jawed orbweaver.

Eastern gray squirrel.

DECEMBER 3

Gray Birch Nutlets and Bracts Dispersing

Gray birch produces separate male and female flowers on the same tree, both in the form of cylindrical clusters of flowers called catkins. The

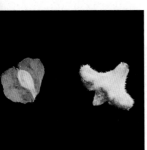

catkins form in the fall and overwinter in a dormant state. In the spring they mature as the leaves develop, becoming pendulous. Male catkins are 2 to 4 inches long, whereas female catkins are usually 1 to 2 inches long, and both lack petals, enhancing wind pollination. After fertilization occurs, the male catkins wither away, while the female catkins droop downward and become conelike. The female catkins consist of tiny winged nutlets that are located behind three-lobed, hardened, modified leaves called bracts and are usually dispersed by the wind during the fall and early winter. Birch bracts are species-specific—different species of birch have differently shaped bracts, allowing one to identify the species of birch that a bract comes from.

Gray birch catkins.

Gray birch nutlet (left) and bract (right).

Salamander Defense Mechanism

Red foxes have a diverse diet: birds, small mammals, snakes, frogs, eggs, insects, fish, earthworms, berries, and fruit. The list is endless, and this diversity is part of the reason that foxes thrive in almost any habitat. However, they appear to

draw the line when it comes to spotted salamanders. The story the red fox tracks below this salamander tell suggests that the fox dropped the salamander after unearthing it from its hibernaculum and carrying it some distance. It is likely that it detected the sticky white toxic liquid that spotted salamanders secrete from poison glands in their skin when they are threatened. Unfortunately, it didn't happen in time to save the salamander's life. Either its

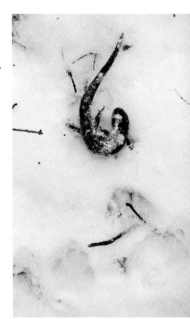

Spotted salamander and red fox tracks.

experience with the fox or the freezing temperatures killed the salamander, preventing it from going back into hibernation.

DECEMBER 4

Black Bear Signs

If the weather has been mild and American beechnuts and acorns are plentiful, bears, especially males, have been known to remain active year-round, although that is a rarity. However, they do den later than usual when there is a good supply of food, and signs of their activity are clearly visible if snow comes before bears den.

TRACKS: Bears are flat footed and walk on the soles of their soft feet, so they often do not leave distinct tracks, but when bear activity and snow overlap, their tracks show details not seen in most other conditions. Bears have five toes on each foot, but the small inner toe does not always register, even in snow. The front feet leave rounder imprints than the hind feet, because

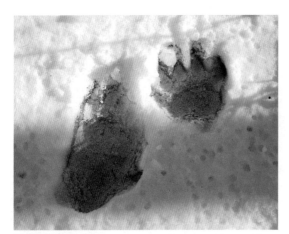

Black bear tracks.

Blackberry Knot Gall

Blackberry is host to numerous gall-making insects, including mites, midges, and gall wasps, and their temporary homes, the galls, are more obvious now that blackberries have lost their leaves. The blackberry knot gall is caused by a cynipid gall wasp.

the heel pad of the front foot does not register. Often bears will place their hind feet just in front of where the front foot was placed, leaving a double track.

Bears often follow deer trails but also make their own trails, which they use year after year, placing their feet in the exact same footsteps. With a sharp eye, you can occasionally find such a trail in the woods even without snow on the ground.

SCAT: Bird seed is available and accessible this time of year, and it is common to see bear scat that is filled with millet and sunflower seed husks. This is no surprise, as by eating one cup of sunflower seeds a bear consumes 818 calories, 72 grams of fat, and 29 grams of protein.

Many galls are inhabited by a solitary insect, but the blackberry knot gall contains many individual chambers, each containing the larva of the tiny gall wasp. A cluster of small, globular, seedlike galls within which the gall wasp larvae live are pressed together in a lump surrounding the cane. Each of these 1/10-inch-diameter chambers bears a spine, and together they create a reddish brown, hairy mass.

Blackberry knot gall.

During the spring and summer months, this little wasp deposits eggs into the ridged stems of blackberry bushes, which stimulates the plant to create abnormal growth along the stem. This particular colonial gall can be 6 inches in length, although 2 or 3 inches is more typical—the more eggs that are laid, the larger the gall. The eggs hatch, and the larvae overwinter inside the gall. Adult

Black bear scat.

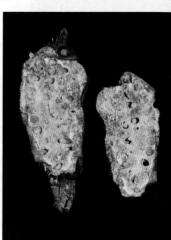

Wasp larvae inside blackberry knot gall.

wasps emerge in the spring and chew their way out of the gall, leaving tiny holes along the gall's lumpy ridges.

Muskrats' Last Few Days above Ice

Muskrat.

Muskrats and beavers are experiencing the last few days that they will spend above the ice for perhaps several months. Fortunately for muskrats, they can hold their breath and remain under water for up to twenty minutes, time enough to get from one unfrozen patch of water to another. Before the ice freezes solidly, muskrats push up vegetation through cracks or holes in the ice, creating "push-ups" or "breathers," which act as resting places and breathing holes.

Throughout the year, muskrats eat the roots and stems of a number of aquatic plants, as well

Muskrat collecting vegetation.

as crayfish, frogs, turtles, snails, mussels, insects, and slow-moving fish. Unlike beavers, muskrats don't store food for the winter, but forage for vegetation. Sometimes muskrats will feed from the winter food supply piles gathered by beavers, and they've been known to use the walls of their own lodge as food.

DECEMBER 6

Coyotes Feeding on Deer Carcasses

Ninety percent of a coyote's diet is animal matter, including creatures as varied as meadow voles, mice, muskrats, raccoons, beetles, and grasshoppers—basically, anything it can outrun. Coyotes have the reputation as major predators of deer. While research confirms that deer and rabbits compose a good portion of a coyote's diet in the Northeast, most of the deer that coyotes consume are scavenged as carrion. Because they cannot move as fast as adult deer, fawns are more vulnerable to coyote predation.

White-tailed deer carcass.

Indigo Bunting Nest Exposed

Without leaves on deciduous trees and shrubs, bird nests are far easier to detect. Look in stands of black raspberries and gray dogwood for indigo bunting nests. The female indigo bunting builds the nest alone—a process that takes up to ten

Indigo bunting nest.

days early in the season and
as little as two days later in
the summer. The male may
watch but does not participate. The nest consists of an
open cup woven of leaves,
grasses, stems, and bark,
and is wrapped with spider
web. The inside of the cup
is lined with slender grasses,
tiny roots, strips of thin bark, thistle down, and
sometimes deer hair. Indigo bunting nests are
often parasitized by brown-headed cowbirds.

Female indigo bunting.

Male indigo bunting

Porcupine Chewing Technique

In the winter, the bulk of a
porcupine's diet is the inner
bark, or cambium, of trees.
The porcupine removes the
outer bark—unless the tree
is young or has thin outer
bark, in which case it eats
the outer bark as well—in
order to reach the cambium
layer, which lies directly
beneath the outer bark. At
this point, the exposed surface is very smooth, more
finely finished than the final
work of a beaver. Then the
porcupine removes the
cambium in small, trian-
gular patches, each patch
composed of five or six
scrapes converging at one
point, like sticks in
a tepee. The point
where the scrapes
meet is where the
upper incisors are
placed and held
fixed against the
tree. The lower inci-
sors scrape, making
a fresh path with
each scrape, as the
lower jaw swivels in
a narrow arc.

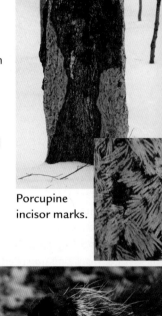

Porcupine
incisor marks.

Porcupine.

Sharp-Shinned Hawk

If the majority of your diet consisted of one type
of food, and that food was concentrated in
certain spots, it would make sense to frequent
those spots. Bird-eating predators, such as the
sharp-shinned hawk, are frequently seen at bird

Sharp-shinned hawk.

feeders for this very reason. Although not very large—roughly the size of a blue jay, with the female being a third again larger than the male—this accipiter is a formidable predator, and one which causes feeder visitors to either disappear or become motionless for a considerable amount of time. The sharp-shinned hawk is the smallest hawk in North America and derives its common name from the sharp-edged "shin" on the lower part of its legs. Its long tail and short wings make it extremely adept at flying through dense woods in search of small birds.

DECEMBER 8

Sedge Seeds Eaten by Wildlife

Longhair, or bottle-brush, sedge.

Over five hundred species of sedges in the genus *Carex* are found in the U.S.—over half of the world's total. The great majority of these perennial, grasslike plants grow in the moist soil of meadows, marshes, and bogs, as well as in high altitudes. The flowers of sedges, each surrounded by a bottle-shaped bract, or modified leaf called a perigynium, are clustered on spikes. The tips of these bracts persist after the seeds have formed, giving the spikes a prickly appearance.

Because of their wide availability, the triangular sedge seeds are eaten by many kinds of wildlife, especially birds. Ducks, rails, wild turkeys, American woodcock, northern cardinals, horned larks, snow buntings, Lapland longspurs, sparrows, redpolls, and finches relish them. *Carex* seeds, along with insects, are the most regular items in the diet of ruffed grouse chicks in the Northeast. Moose also occasionally feed on sedge seeds.

Mourning Dove Diet

Seeds, including cultivated grains, grasses, weeds, and berries, make up 99 percent of a mourning dove's diet. Because they can find enough food to sustain themselves, mourning doves are permanent residents, even in the most northern parts of the Northeast. These birds feed on the ground and in the open, consuming 12 to 20 percent of their body weight per day, or 71 calories on average. Mourning doves swallow the seeds and store them in an enlargement of the esophagus called a crop. Once their crop is filled—the record is 17,200 bluegrass seeds in a single crop—they fly to a protected area where they can safely digest their food. In pigeons and doves, the lining of the crop also secretes crop milk, a semisolid food which is fed to their young.

Mourning dove.

DECEMBER 9

Hooded Mergansers Find Open Water in Winter

Hooded mergansers are short-distance migrants that can be found in eastern North America year-round where ponds and rivers remain open, and slow-moving fish, insects, and crayfish are plentiful. Some individuals migrate south or southwest in winter and most of the Northeast population of hooded mergansers winters off the eastern coast from New Jersey to Florida. At this time of year, hooded mergansers are more plentiful in southern U.S. than in the Northeast. A smaller number migrate north to spend winters on the Great Lakes and in southern Canada—20 percent of the birds banded in northern New England wintered in Ontario and Quebec.

Male hooded merganser.

Eastern Hemlock Seeds Dispersing

It may take 250 to 300 years for an eastern hemlock tree to reach maturity—some live for 800 years or more—but once it is mature, its cone production is massive. Not only is this species of tree one of the most frequent cone producers among eastern conifers, it produces cones for a

Eastern hemlock cone.

long time—one eastern hemlock was still bearing cones at 450 years of age.

Eastern hemlocks are monoecious, producing both male (pollen) cones and female (seed) cones on the same tree. Pollen cones develop near the tips of leafy twigs, while seed cones occur at the very tips. The seed cones are small, the smallest of all the trees in its genus, measuring from ½ to ¾ of an inch long. Wind is the primary agent for pollination in the spring as well as dispersal of the seeds in the winter. The tiny winged seeds of eastern hemlock are eaten by birds such as the black-capped chickadee, red crossbill, white-winged crossbill, and pine siskin, and by mammals including the red squirrel, white-footed mouse, and deer mouse.

DECEMBER 10

Hide and Seek: Voles and Foxes

Unlike wolves, which hunt in packs and often take down prey larger than themselves, red foxes are solitary hunters and as a result usually catch prey much smaller than themselves, such as mice and voles. During the winter, mice and voles become more active during daylight hours because much of their time is spent under the snow, where they remain hidden from view.

Red fox.

Red fox and meadow vole tracks.

seeds, which goldfinches incorporate into their nests and also feed to their young. Female American goldfinches build a very neat nest composed of plant fibers and line it with downy plant materials. The walls are thick, making it quite durable, so it is not unusual to find one in relatively good shape even well into the winter.

DECEMBER 11

Speckled Alder in Winter

Speckled alder is a shrub in the birch family that grows in wetlands. It is named for the speckles on its bark—horizontal lines or lenticels, spongy openings for the transfer of gases. In winter, speckled alder branches are distinctive because they carry two kinds of buds as well as last year's fruit. The male flower buds are in the form of inch-long catkins that appear reddish in winter. They begin to turn yellow in March just before they extend into long, yellow, pollen-bearing flowers. The female flower buds are small and drooping just ahead of the catkins on the branch. They look like miniature unopened versions of the seed-bearing fruit they'll become. Last year's woody fruits, or cones, are also present, having opened and had their seeds dispersed by the wind last fall.

Consequently, in winter you are more likely to see a fox hunting during the day than in the summer.

Whenever it is hunting, night or day, a fox depends heavily on its acute sense of hearing. It is most sensitive to lower noises such as the rustling and gnawing sounds that small animals make as they move through vegetation or feed on seeds, buds, and twigs. Foxes can locate these sounds from several feet away, to within inches of their true location, even under 3 feet of snow. Recent research suggests that they may also use Earth's magnetic field to help them locate prey.

American Goldfinch Nests Exposed

American goldfinches breed later than most North American birds. They wait until June or July when milkweed, thistle, and other plants have produced their wind-dispersed

American goldfinch nest.

female buds (catkins)

male buds (catkins)

last year's fruit

Speckled alder.

Common Garter Snakes Brumating in Hibernacula

Being ectothermic, common garter snakes must seek shelter from freezing temperatures in the winter. They often form large groups—hundreds of snakes in some places—with fellow garter snakes, as well as other snake species, in their hibernacula. Temperatures in a hibernaculum rarely drop below 37 to 39 degrees. Common garter snakes may safely remain in these protected areas for sixteen weeks without serious loss of body weight or harm to their health. Their metabolic processes slow down, and they enter dormancy, or brumation, while sustaining themselves on body fat they accumulated by feeding heavily during the late summer.

Common garter snake.

Spiders Hibernating

Spiders that don't lay eggs and die in the fall have developed several adaptations to survive the cold temperatures and lack of food that winter presents. They seek out microhabitats for protection, increase their resistance to cold, and reduce their metabolic rate.

About 85 percent of spiders that overwinter do so in leaf litter, where they are well insulated against the cold. Most of these spiders assume

Eastern parson spider under silk case.

Eastern parson spider without silk case.

a rigid position, with their legs drawn close to their bodies so that the amount of exposed body surface is kept to a minimum. Leaf litter protects spiders from extreme temperature fluctuations and from desiccation. A heavy snow cover ensures a fairly steady temperature of 32 degrees regardless of the air temperature, even in weather as extreme as 40 degrees below zero.

Many of the remaining overwintering spiders can be found under the loose bark of dead trees. Some have no further protection, while others, such as the eastern parson spider, spin a silk case within which they spend the winter.

Does Bird Feeding Foster Dependency?

Decades ago, birds remaining in the Northeast in the winter survived almost exclusively on weed seeds and insects they gleaned from crevices in tree bark. Today, nearly one-third of Americans provide about a billion pounds of bird seed each year, to say nothing of suet, seed cakes, and the like. Should we be worried about creating a population of food-dependent wintering birds? Studies suggest that this is not the case.

Black-capped chickadee.

Mouse impaled by shrike.

Researchers removed feeders from woodlands where black-capped chickadees had been fed for the previous twenty-five years and compared survival rates with those of chickadees in a nearby woodland where there had been no feeders. They found that the chickadees familiar with feeders were able to switch back immediately to foraging for natural foods and survived the winter as well as chickadees that lived where no feeders had been placed. Not only did the feeder-fed birds retain their ability to find food, but the researchers also showed that food from feeders had made up only 21 percent of the birds' daily energy requirement in the previous two years.

DECEMBER 13

Butcher Birds Overwintering

Northern shrike.

The northern shrike is highly unusual in that it is a predatory songbird. Birds, mammals, and insects are preferred over nectar, nuts, and seeds. This tundra-nesting bird comes as far south as New England in the winter, where it preys mainly on mice, voles, and small birds. The northern shrike often kills more prey than it can eat or feed to its young, and it stores the excess food for later, when living prey may be scarce. The manner in which it stores this extra food is what gives it the nickname "butcher bird." It often impales prey on a thorn, broken branch, or even barbed wire, or it wedges prey into narrow V-shaped forks of branches, where it hangs until reclaimed by the shrike.

White-Tailed Deer Conserving Energy

The diet of white-tailed deer goes from herbaceous plants in the summer to woody plants in the winter. This winter diet is lower in protein and less digestible than the deer's summer diet, requiring more energy to digest and resulting in fewer calories. A deer must conserve its energy in every way possible: heavier coats, congregating and forming "yards" in sheltered spots, and minimizing movement. These adaptations also include taking advantage of trails that already have been made by other animals, such as the porcupine trail in this photograph.

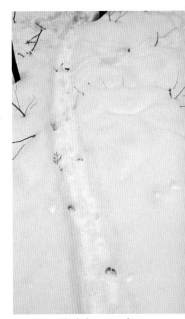

White-tailed deer tracks on porcupine trail.

419

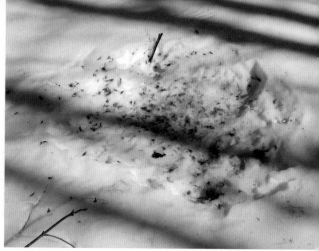
Raptor kill site.

DECEMBER 14

Bark Scaling

There are two main ways that woodpeckers and other birds remove bark in search of insects beneath it. One is bark sloughing, where a bird pries off the entire dead layer of bark on a tree. Another method of finding insect larvae that both woodpeckers and nuthatches employ is the removal of individual scales of bark. This is referred to as bark scaling.

Hairy woodpecker bark scaling eastern hemlock.

Interpreting a Kill Site

When there's snow on the ground and you come upon a site where a predator successfully caught prey, there are usually signs that will help you determine what creatures were involved. In this scene, remnants of red squirrel fur confirm the identity of the prey.

To identify the predator, there are several things to look for. At the top of this photograph, there is a faint wing impression. Although not in this case, both wings of an avian predator often touch the surface of the snow, allowing you to measure the wingspread; this information can help narrow down the potential species of raptors.

A bird of prey often defecates at a kill site. In the lower left corner of the photograph, as well as to the left and right of the packed area where the squirrel was eaten, you can see white (uric

acid) bird droppings. Given that it is a hawk or an owl, knowledge about their respective evacuation habits narrows down the possibilities even further. Owls tend to let their droppings do just that—drop, leaving small deposits on the ground. Hawks, on the other hand, tend to forcefully eject their droppings some distance away. The long, thin streaks at this site were definitely propelled outward, making it likely that the predator was a hawk. Familiarity with the hawks that overwinter in your area can help pinpoint which species it could be.

DECEMBER 15

Teasel

Teasel is an introduced biennial, considered an invasive plant in the U. S. due to its ability to crowd out native species. Nonetheless, the seed head that remains after the 3- to 8-foot plant has flowered is strikingly beautiful. It consists of a cone of spine-tipped, hard bracts, or modified

Teasel seedhead.

leaves. Since the Middle Ages, Europeans have used dried seed heads of the teasel plant to raise the nap on woolen cloth. Teasing wool creates a soft, almost furry texture on one side of the cloth. Baize, the cloth traditionally used to cover pool tables and card tables, is a classic example of wool that has been teased.

Yellow-Rumped Warbler Winter Diet

The yellow-rumped warbler is the only warbler that is able to digest the waxes found in bayberries and wax myrtles. Its ability to use these fruits allows it to winter farther north than other warblers, sometimes as far north as Newfoundland.

Yellow-rumped warbler in winter plumage.

DECEMBER 16

How Beavers Digest Cellulose

Some beavers are still managing to find openings in their ponds that give them access to fresh cambium, the soft layer of wood just under the bark of a tree. Cambium contains a lot of cellulose, in addition to starches and sugars. Like all herbivores, beavers do not possess enzymes that are capable of breaking down the large cellulose molecules, or cellulases. In their place, beavers employ microorganisms, such as bacteria, to break down cellulose.

Beaver.

Tree that has been chewed by a beaver.

These bacteria are situated in a pouch called a caecum, located at the beginning of the large intestine. Colonies of microorganisms in a beaver's intestines digest up to 30 percent of the cellulose from the woody material they eat. More nutrients are recovered in the form of fecal pellets that the beaver will ingest.

Contrary to that which one might think, the faster food passes through the beaver's system, the higher the rate of nutrient absorption. Poplar passes through a beaver's digestive tract in roughly sixteen to eighteen hours, while red maple takes up to eighty-four hours. Because of the limitations on how much of each food can pass through a beaver's digestive system each day, a beaver's energy requirement could never be met if they ate red maple exclusively.

Noctuid Moth Larvae

The striped caterpillar that is occasionally seen crawling along the surface of fresh snow is the larval stage of a noctuid or owlet moth. Noctuids are dull-colored, medium-sized, nocturnal moths that are attracted to lights in the summer. They usually possess a well-developed proboscis, the mouthpart, for sucking nectar.

421

DEC

Winter cutworm.

Pictured is a winter cutworm, also known as the greater yellow underwing moth, a recent immigrant from Europe.

DECEMBER 17

Bitternut Hickory Buds

Habitat, silhouette, bark, and buds can all be helpful when trying to identify a tree in winter. Occasionally, a species has one characteristic that is so distinctive that it serves as a diagnostic feature. The sulfur yellow color of bitternut hickory buds is such a characteristic. Both lateral and terminal buds have a powdery coating, which gives them a bright yellow appearance. Look for bitternut hickory on moist lowlands (hence, its other common name, swamp hickory) and rich uplands. Although humans find the nut of this hickory inedible, the smoke produced by burning its wood produces what is considered the best smoked hams and bacon.

Bitternut hickory bud.

Winter Mouse House

Most songbirds only use their nest once. After their young have fledged, the nest is usually abandoned. In the spring, the material used in old nests is often reused by birds building new nests. Long before this occurs, white-footed mice and deer mice, both of which remain active year-round, often use old nests as larders where they store food for the winter. Occasionally, they renovate a nest in the fall in order to make a snug winter home. They do this by constructing a roof of milkweed or cattail fluff—or, in this case, fiberglass insulation—over the nest, which serves to insulate it.

Bird nest renovated by mice.

DECEMBER 18

Ample Food and Lingering Warm Weather Will Delay Black Bear Hibernation

Typically, cold weather and a scarcity of food trigger a reduction in the metabolism of a black bear, which signals the onset of hibernation. This usually happens sometime in November. However, when there is an ample

Black bear.

supply of acorns, hickory nuts, or beechnuts, and/or the weather is relatively mild, bears forgo hibernation and will remain active and forage into and sometimes through the winter.

DECEMBER 19

Maidenhair Spleenwort Greening Up the Woods

Maidenhair spleenwort.

Five species of spleenworts (genus *Asplenium*) can be found in the Northeast. Most of these small, native, evergreen ferns are found growing among rocks or on cliff faces. The Greeks believed that a species of spleenwort was useful for treating diseases of spleen. The genus *Asplenium* is derived from *splen*, the Greek word for spleen.

Maidenhair spleenwort is divided into two sub-species, one that grows in crevices of acidic rocks and one that grows on more basic, or alkaline, rocks. It grows in clusters and has delicate 3- to 6-inch fronds made up of short, round leaflets paired from the central dark reddish brown stem (stipe and rachis).

Snow Worms

Occasionally worms can be seen crawling on top of the snow. These are not our familiar earth-worms, but skinny and relatively short worms of 1 to 2 inches in length. These snow worms are in the phylum Annelida, which they share with earthworms. Like ice worms, which are found only on glaciers, snow worms are thought to live off of snow algae and are most active at night. These worms are studied by scientists interested in seeing

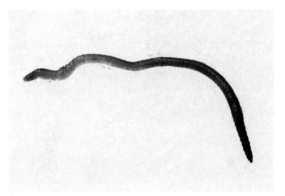

Snow worm.

if their proteins exhibit the right characteristics to be of use in transplant surgeries, where keeping an organ cold but not freezing is key.

DECEMBER 20

Goldenrod Ball Galls Provide Important Source of Winter Food for Downy Woodpeckers

A number of insects cause goldenrod plants to form galls—abnormal growths that house and feed larval insects. The goldenrod ball gall is caused by a fly, *Eurosta solidaginis*. The fly lays an egg on the stem of a goldenrod plant in early spring, the egg hatches, and the larva burrows its way into the stem; the plant reacts by forming a gall around the larva. The larva overwinters inside the gall, pupates in late winter, and emerges in early spring as an adult fly. Prior to pupating, the larva chews an exit tunnel to, but not through, the outermost layer of gall tissue. As an adult fly it will not have chewing mouthparts, so it is nec-essary to do this work while in the larval stage.

Downy woodpeckers and black-capped chickadees have discovered this abundant source of winter food and dine on the larva after chisel-ing a hole into the gall. Downy woodpeckers tend to make a tidy, narrow, conical hole by pecking, while black-capped chickadees tend to make a

Fly larva inside goldenrod ball gall.

Empty goldenrod ball galls.

They are excellent swimmers and can dive as deep as 16 feet. Tracks will run along the frozen sections of a stream and disappear into the water, only to reappear on the ice farther downstream when the mink decides to travel on solid ground again.

DECEMBER 21

Red Squirrel Tracks

This is the common bounding pattern of a red squirrel in snow. When it bounds, or hops, its smaller front feet land first, and then the larger hind feet pass to the outside and around the front feet to land in front of them. In this photograph, the squirrel tracks are headed toward the top. There are many exceptions to the rule, but

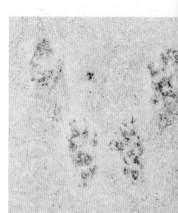

Red squirrel tracks.

often bounding animals that are tree climbers, such as squirrels, place their front feet more or less side by side, whereas animals such as rabbits and hares, which do not climb trees, often place their front feet diagonally, one in front of the other.

messy, large, irregular hole by grabbing bits of the gall with their bill and tugging them free.

While woodpeckers prefer larger galls that are located high on goldenrod plants near wooded areas, these are not the only factors taken into consideration. A woodpecker extracts the fly larva through the tunnel the larva excavates prior to pupating, as this facilitates rapid removal of the larva. Downy woodpeckers can determine whether or not a gall has an exit tunnel, and if it doesn't, they usually abandon the gall without drilling into it. The likelihood of smaller parasitic wasp larvae occupying the gall—and a plump fly larva not being present—is much greater if there is no exit tunnel, and these smaller prey apparently are not always worth the woodpecker's time or energy.

Mink Meanderings

Mink spend a lot of time in the water foraging for fish, frogs, aquatic insects, and crayfish.

Mink tracks.

Living Hollow Trees

Often one comes across a living tree with a portion of its trunk, or even its entire trunk, hollow. How is it possible for a tree to thrive even when its center, or heart, has completely decayed? It comes down to the different kinds of wood that are produced by a tree: sapwood and heartwood.

Sapwood, often light colored, is younger than the dark-colored heartwood which it surrounds. Sapwood's principal function is to conduct water from the roots to the leaves via xylem tissue.

Hollow tree.

Heartwood—so called because of its central position, not because it is essential to the health of the tree—is basically non-functioning xylem tissue that has become blocked with resins, tannins, and oils. Although the dead heartwood can lend stability to a tree, it is no longer part of the transport system, and therefore, not vital to the tree.

Cavities and hollows result from an injury to a tree caused by fire, storms, lightning, insects, or birds. Bacteria and fungi lose no time moving in when a tree is injured, and any wood formed prior to the injury is vulnerable to decay. The cambium limits decay in new tissues, but dead heartwood is vulnerable, and when it rots, it occasionally results in a hollow tree. Because the sapwood, and therefore the transport system, is still intact, the tree lives, despite the loss of its inner heartwood.

DECEMBER 22

Canada Lynx Snowshoes

Bobcats and Canada lynx are in the same genus, and are roughly the same size, averaging 15 to 35 pounds, with bobcats usually weighing a bit more than lynx. The size of their feet, however, is vastly different and not proportional to their weight. A lynx has much larger feet and longer legs than a bobcat. Its range extends farther north, which means it must be well equipped to deal with snow much of the year. A lynx has big, furry paws, and when its feet land, the toes spread way out. Both of these adaptations help a lynx's feet act like snowshoes, enabling it to chase down food in the winter.

Much of the time, this food consists of snowshoe hares—anywhere from 60 to 90 percent of the diet of lynx is made up of hares. The soles of snowshoe hare feet are also well furred, particularly in winter, enabling them to run on soft, deep snow without sinking in very far. Because snowshoe hares are extremely fast and agile, reaching speeds of 30 mph and jumping 12 feet in a single bound, the feet of any serious predator must also be well adapted to traveling on snow.

Lynx (left) and bobcat (right) feet.

Pileated Woodpecker Droppings

Pileated woodpeckers usually defecate frequently during the day at their foraging sites. As they pry off long slivers of wood to expose carpenter ant galleries, the wood chips pile up on the ground. A substantial pile usually indicates that the woodpecker has been working long enough at this site for there to be some droppings in the pile.

Pileated woodpeckers eat ants, primarily carpenter ants, and beetle larvae throughout the year. Fruit and nuts are eaten when available. The primary food shifts seasonally, with fruit mainly in the fall, carpenter ants in the winter, wood-boring beetle larvae in early spring, and a variety of insects in the summer.

Animal Tail Functions

Animals use their tails in many ways, including as a fifth hand, a rudder, an air conditioner, a noisemaker, a blanket, a fly swatter, a weapon, a lure, a motor, and a warning device. Tails are made of feathers, quills, fur, scales, skin, and chitin, and each material lends itself to the function that the tail performs.

- Grasping/holding—Virginia opossum
- Warning—White-tailed deer, striped skunk, eastern milk snake, beaver
- Courtship song—Common snipe
- Courtship display—Ruffed grouse
- Distraction display—Killdeer
- Balance—Squirrel, meadow jumping mouse, birds
- Propulsion—North American river otter, tadpole
- Rudder—Flying squirrel, beaver, muskrat, birds
- Warmth—Red fox, gray fox, eastern coyote
- Weapon—Porcupine, honey bee
- To catch food—Bat
- Predator foil—Four-toed salamander
- Thermoregulation—Beaver
- To assert dominance—American mink

Virginia opossum.

White-tailed deer.

Ruffed grouse.

Common milk snake.

Killdeer.

North American river otter.

Baltimore oriole.

Beaver.

Striped skunk.

Gray squirrel.

Porcupine.

Red fox.

Pileated woodpecker scat.

Pileated woodpecker feeding holes in tree.

Like humans, birds excrete metabolic waste products, mainly nitrogen, which remains after food is broken down. Humans excrete waste nitrogen as urea in urine, which is diluted with water. Birds, needing to be as light as possible for efficient flight, do not have heavy, water-filled bladders. They excrete nitrogen as a chemical called uric acid in a concentrated form with no dilution necessary. The white outer coating of bird droppings is uric acid, while the insides of the droppings are the actual feces, or the indigestible parts of a bird's diet. The insides of a pileated woodpecker's droppings at this time of year consist of bits of carpenter ant exoskeletons and a small amount of wood fiber. Birds simultaneously evacuate uric acid and feces from an opening just under the tail called the cloaca, or vent.

DECEMBER 23

White-Tailed Deer Beds

White-tailed deer frequently travel in small groups and bed down together. By looking at the edges of the indentation left when a deer lies down, you can usually determine which direction the deer was facing—its back leaves a fairly

symmetrical curve in the snow, and its knees often make impressions. In an area where there are several deer beds, close inspection may reveal that each deer is facing a different direction. This is not coincidental. As a result of this behavior, the group may have a 360-degree

White-tailed deer beds.

view of their surroundings, allowing them to spot an approaching predator. The deer that occupied the closest bed in this photograph was facing right, while the farther deer was facing left.

Bobcat Tracks

Because of their shy and elusive nature, bobcats are rarely seen, but in the right habitat, their tracks and sign can be found. Sometimes bobcats direct register, placing their hind foot exactly where their front

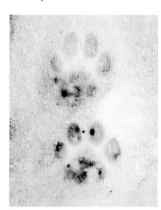

Bobcat hind foot (top) and front foot (bottom) tracks.

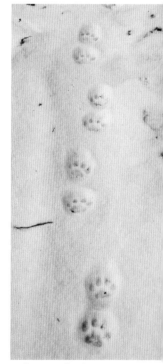

Bobcat trail of tracks.

foot has been. At other times, such as in these photographs, the bobcat's hind foot touches down beyond where the front foot has been, called an overstep. When a bobcat has been walking with an overstep, a close look allows you to see that the bobcat's hind foot track is more elongated and symmetrical than its front foot track. Because bobcat numbers are increasing in the Northeast, your chances of coming upon their tracks are as high as they have been in the past fifty years.

DECEMBER 24

Ice-Coated Tree Buds

At this time of year, a freezing rain can coat trees with ice. Most of the buds on deciduous trees and shrubs in the Northeast are protected by overlapping scales that form a watertight, protective covering for the embryonic leaves and flowers that will emerge in spring. The buds of conifers are covered with protective wax or pitch, giving them extra insulation against winter weather.

When a tree is covered with ice, as long as it is not heavy enough to break branches, it can be an advantage, as it is an added layer of protection for its buds. When water freezes, heat is produced at a rate of 80 calories per gram of water, the heat of fusion. Ice-coated buds remain at approximately 32 degrees and are protected from lower temperatures. Orchardists often take advantage of this fact, spraying their trees with water in the spring when there is an unexpected frost.

Ice-coated sugar maple buds.

Wild Turkeys Foraging on Fertile Fern Fronds

During winters that follow autumns with poor acorn or beechnut crops, wild turkeys are busy foraging for any accessible food, including eastern hemlock buds, burdock seeds, and the fertile fronds of sensitive and ostrich fern that stick up above the snow. These two ferns are in the same family, and their spores are borne on a stalk, referred to as a fertile frond, that is separate from the leafy vegetative fronds that are present all summer and die back in the fall. Fertile fronds persist all winter, sticking up out of the snow as if beckoning to hungry turkeys. Upon finding a clump of these fertile fronds, a turkey will peck repeatedly at them, causing the clusters of sporangia which produce and contain spores to burst and release thousands of spores onto the surface of the snow. It is very apparent—from tracks, scat, and snow darkened with spores— when a turkey has been feeding on ferns.

Sensitive fern spores.

Wild turkey eating sensitive fern spores.

DECEMBER 25

Owl Night Vision

Like humans, birds have a retina in the back of their eyes that absorbs incoming light, senses it, integrates the information in it, and sends this information on to their brain. An avian retina is much thicker than ours and contains more rod cells, for dim light vision, and cone cells, for acuity and color vision.

As most owls are active at night, their eyes must be very efficient at collecting and processing light. Their eyes are proportionately large, enabling them to collect as much light as possible. In addition, the retina of an owl's eye has an abundance of light-sensitive rod cells. Owls have almost a million rods per square millimeter compared to humans, which have only about two hundred thousand. Barn owls can see a mouse at 6 to 7 feet with an illumination of .00000073 foot-candles—the equivalent of humans seeing a

mouse a mile away by the light of a match. Eye size, an abundance of rod cells, and various neural mechanisms provide owls with vision greater than most of their prey.

Since owls have extraordinary night vision, it is often thought that they are blind in strong light. This is not true, because their pupils have a wide range of adjustment, allowing the right amount of light to strike the retina. Some species of owls can see better than humans in bright light.

Fisher Scat and Track

Fishers are constantly marking their territory by rolling on and breaking limbs of conifer saplings as well as urinating and defecating on or near saplings or on prominent, elevated stumps or rocks. In the winter, a fisher can travel up to 10 miles a day in search of prey. Its tracks are quite distinctive, in that, like all members of the weasel family, they have five toes on both front and hind feet. Often all five digits do not register, but in shallow, wet, prime tracking snow you can often see them.

More than other members of the weasel family, fishers can control the amount of scat they deposit, so that there can be a minuscule amount, or

Barn owl.

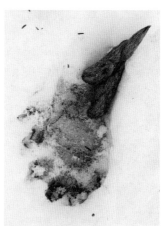

Fisher track with scat.

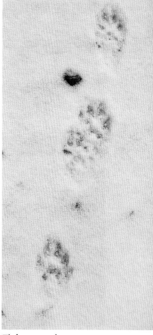

Fisher tracks.

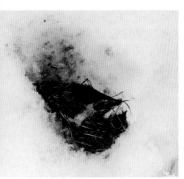

Fisher scat containing porcupine quills.

a full-size scat that is 2 inches to 7 inches long. Perhaps because of their predilection for marking with their scat frequently, they often use this medium sparingly.

Fisher scat is usually twisted, and the color typically ranges from black to a mustard color. Once in a great while, one happens upon bright orange fisher scat, a sure sign that the fisher has lived up to its aquatic name and has dined on crayfish in the recent past. The diet of fishers consists mostly of snowshoe hares, porcupines, ground-nesting birds, and smaller rodents. However, they do frequent streams that remain open in the winter, where they hunt for crayfish and, rarely, fish.

DECEMBER 26

Blueberry Stem Galls

The ¾- to 1¼-inch-long, brown kidney bean–shaped or round structure found on blueberry bushes at this time of year is the summer and winter home for a dozen or so wasp larvae that will pupate and emerge in the spring as very small (less than ⅛ inch) black wasps. This past summer, a female wasp laid her eggs in a tender, developing blueberry shoot. She then climbed to the tip of the shoot and stabbed it repeatedly, causing considerable damage. Within two weeks the eggs hatched, and the larvae began feeding, which, along with the egg-laying, stimulated the formation of the gall. Initially a blueberry stem gall is green and spongy; by fall it turns red, and by late autumn, it is brown and woody. Next summer, look for the holes in these galls that were chewed by the exiting wasps.

Red Fox Tracks

Although the individual characteristics of an animal's track can help greatly with identification, the red fox's foot, in winter, is very furry, and details of the individual pads and nails are very hard to detect.

Instead, a quick glance at the track pattern reveals an animal that direct registers—its hind feet land almost exactly where the front feet were placed, with each impression representing two tracks.

You can tell the pattern of a fox from a small domestic dog by this trait—a domestic dog's hind feet fall next to or partially on top of where its front feet fell.

In addition, a fox's trail is often relatively direct because it is intent on finding prey, unlike the domestic dog, which tends to wander aimlessly here and there, knowing its dinner will be provided.

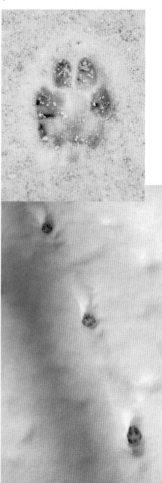

Red fox trail.

Blueberry stem gall.

DECEMBER 27

Eastern Coyotes Making Snow Angels

Has your dog ever flopped down into the snow, rolled over, and wriggled its body back and forth, appearing to rub its back? This behavior is exhibited by other members of the dog family, including coyotes. With a little imagination, you can see the coyote's head print at the left side of this coyote "angel" and its hind feet on the right, both made while it was rolling in the snow.

Black cherry bud.

Young black cherry bark.

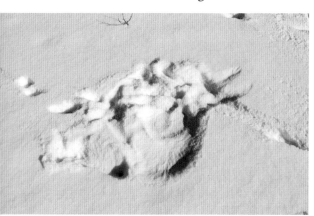

Eastern coyote impression in snow.

Identifying Black Cherry in Winter

Black cherry, more than most tree species, has several identifying features that indicate what tree it is, even after its leaves have fallen to the ground. The buds of black cherry have about ten scales, each of which is brown at the tip and green at the base. The bark of young black cherry trees is typically smooth, reddish in color and covered with grayish, horizontal lines called lenticels—small openings that allow the passage of gases in and out of the tree. The bark on older black cherry trees consists of squarish scales, curved outward at their vertical edges and somewhat resembling burned potato chips. Black cherry is one of several trees on which the fungus *Apiosporina morbosa* causes black knot galls. Lastly, black cherry is the

Black knot gall.

Eastern tent caterpillar egg masses on black cherry tree.

primary host for the eastern tent caterpillar moth. These moths encircle black cherry branches with their egg masses, and the eggs hatch just as black cherry's leaves emerge from their buds, providing food for the young larvae.

DECEMBER 28

Snowshoe Hare Scat

Where there are snowshoe hares, there are many signs of them: runways, tracks, forms, browsed plants, urine, and scat. Usually you find a single pellet of scat, unless the hare has paused in order to feed or rest, in which case there may be several pellets deposited.

Snowshoe hare scat.

The scat of rabbits and hares that we find—little round, brown, fibrous pellets—has been ingested twice. On the first passage of food through the digestive system, bacteria act on it in the large caecum—a pouch near the start of the large intestine, which most herbivorous mammals possess—reducing it to a more easily digestible form and concentrating it, particularly its vitamin B and protein content. The caecum, however, is past the portion of the digestive tract in which most resorption takes place. It is therefore necessary for the animal to eat the resulting pellets, which are soft and green and covered with mucus, to extract as much of the nutrition as possible. These soft pellets are eaten directly from the anus, which is why we do not find them.

Turtlehead Seedhead

Turtlehead is named for the flower's resemblance to the head of a turtle. These wetland flowers are pollinated by bumble bees, which crawl in between vertically paired petals causing them to open, much like a turtle's jaws. Ruby-throated hummingbirds are

Turtlehead seedhead.

also attracted to this flower. After pollination has taken place, the ovary swells and forms capsules which open to release flat, brown seeds. The seed capsules that persist through the winter bear as much or more similarity to this plant's namesake than the flowers.

DECEMBER 29

Wing Shapes Reveal Flight Habits

You can often determine the type of flight that a bird is capable of by looking at the shape of its wings. Long, narrow wings, such as a herring gull has, are excellent for gliding, while the short, rounded wings of a ruffed grouse allow for tight maneuvering in the dense forests where they live. The shape of their wings and their quick-contracting muscles equip grouse for the short bursts of high speed they need for short distances when feeding or evading predators. In this photograph, a ruffed grouse walked a short way and then took flight, beating its wings against the snow twice before it was airborne.

Ruffed grouse wing impression.

Raccoons Denning

Although raccoons are not true hibernators, they do become very lethargic and seek shelter for up to a month, often in hollow trees, during cold

Raccoon.

spells. When the temperature dips way down, or when there is a bad storm, as many as twenty-three raccoons will den together to save energy.

DECEMBER 30

Weasels Hunting in Stone Walls

When looking for signs of weasels in winter, whether long-tailed or ermine (formerly called short-tailed weasel), stone walls are a likely spot to find some. Both of these nocturnal mustelids prey on small rodents such as mice and voles, which frequent the nooks and crannies of stone walls. In winter, weasels cover a lot of ground looking for prey. The home range of an ermine

Weasel tracks along stone wall.

is between 30 and 40 acres, and when food is scarce, they may travel 2 or 3 miles in one night. Often their tracks will run down one side of a stone wall and return along the other side. Intermittent pauses may be made as the ermine stands on its hind feet and stretches its neck out, searching the landscape for both movement and sound.

Christmas Ferns Staying Green

Christmas fern, a native, perennial, evergreen fern, is common throughout the woods of the Northeast. The association with Christmas is an old one, for the evergreen fronds were once harvested by the ton, baled into bundles, and sold to florists for use in making wreaths. One easy way to confirm the identification of this fern is to examine an individual pinna, or leaflet, which bears some resemblance to a Christmas stocking. This year's fronds will die next spring as the new fiddleheads unfurl, revealing the coming year's fronds.

Christmas fern pinna.

Christmas fern.

DECEMBER 31

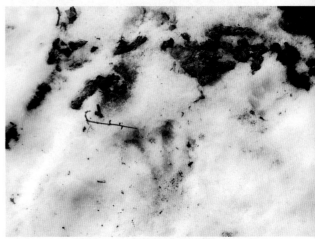

Otter scat and beaver track on beaver lodge.

Overwintering Bald Eagles

Bald eagles will winter as far north as ice-free water permits. Many northeastern eagles migrate south, but some do overwinter here. The majority of wintering eagles are found near open water where they feed on fish and waterfowl, often taking dead, crippled, or otherwise vulnerable animals. Eagles are known to take advantage of ice fishermen, who often are willing to share their catch. White-tailed deer that slip on frozen ponds and cannot get up eventually die and are a significant source of food for overwintering eagles.

between these two animals, meaning one animal benefits while the other is unaffected. The beaver is unaffected: it is an herbivore, so its food supply is not threatened by the presence of meat-eating otters, and though an occasional beaver is eaten by an otter, it is a rare occurrence. The otter, on the other hand, benefits from beaver den sites, both bank dens and lodges, as well as an ample supply of fish due to the impoundment of streams by beavers.

Otters often take over abandoned beaver lodges and occasionally even active lodges. This photograph of fresh otter scat, mostly fish scales and crayfish shells, on top of a beaver lodge and right next to the hind foot print of a beaver, suggests that both an otter and at least one beaver inhabit the lodge. Look for freshly placed sticks on the lodge to confirm that it is occupied by beavers. You may also see an otter's stream of air bubbles as it exits the lodge and pops its head up above the surface of the water.

Bald eagle.

Otter and Beaver Cohabitation

Studies show that there is a strong correlation between beaver habitat and its use by otters. There appears to be a commensal relationship

appendix a

Common and Scientific Names for Species Featured in *Naturally Curious Day by Day*

COMMON NAME	SCIENTIFIC NAME
Plants	
American basswood	*Tilia americana*
American beech	*Fagus grandifolia*
American elm	*Ulmus americana*
American ginseng	*Panax quinquefolius*
American hornbeam	*Carpinus caroliniana*
Balsam fir	*Abies balsamea*
Beaked hazelnut	*Corylus cornuta*
Bear's head tooth fungus	*Hericium americanum*
Bee balm	*Monarda sp.*
Beechdrops	*Epifagus virginiana*
Bigtooth aspen	*Populus grandidentata*
Bitternut hickory	*Carya cordiformis*
Black cherry	*Prunus serotina*
Black walnut	*Juglans nigra*
Bloodroot	*Sanguinaria canadensis*
Blue-eyed grass	*Sisyrinchium angustifolium*
Bog laurel	*Kalmia polifolia*
Bog rosemary	*Andromeda polifolia*
Boneset	*Eupatorium perfoliatum*
Bottle gentian	*Gentiana clausa*
Box elder	*Acer negundo*
Bunchberry	*Cornus canadensis*
Butternut	*Juglans cinerea*
Burning bush	*Euonymus alatus*
Calopogon	*Calopogon tuberosus*
Canada lily	*Lilium canadense*
Cattail	*Typha sp.*
Checkered rattlesnake plantain	*Goodyera tesselata*
Christmas fern	*Polystichum acrostichoides*
Clematis	*Clematis sp.*
Coltsfoot	*Tussilago farfara*
Common burdock	*Arctium minus*
Common clubmoss	*Lycopodium clavatum*
Common cottongrass	*Eriophorum angustifolium*
Common juniper	*Juniperus communis*
Common milkweed	*Asclepias syriaca*
Common polypody	*Polypodium amorphum*
Creeping snowberry	*Gaultheria hispidula*
Cut-leaved grape fern	*Botrychium dissectum*
Cut-leaved toothwort	*Cardamine concatenate*
Dandelion	*Taraxacum officinale*
Dog-tooth lichen	*Peltigera canina*
Dutchman's breeches	*Dicentra cucullaria*
Dwarf ginseng	*Panax trifolius*
Early saxifrage	*Micranthes virginiensis*
Eastern cottonwood	*Populus deltoides*
Eastern hemlock	*Tsuga canadensis*
Eastern hophornbeam	*Ostrya virginiana*
Eastern larch	*Larix laricina*
English plantain	*Plantago lanceolate*
False foxglove	*Aureolaria sp.*
False Solomon's seal	*Maianthemum racemosum*
Field horsetail	*Equisetum arvense*
Foamflower	*Tiarella cordifolia*
Forget-me-not	*Myosotis sp.*
Fringed polygala	*Polygala paucifolia,*
Liverwort	*Frullania*
Giant puffball	*Calvatia gigantean*
Goatsbeard	*Aruncus dioicus*
Goldenrod	*Solidago sp.*
Grass	Family: Gramineae
Grass of Parnassus	*Parnassia glauca*
Gray birch	*Betula populifolia*
Haircap moss	*Polytrichum sp.*
Hairy beardtongue	*Penstemon hirsutus*
Helleborine	*Epipactis helleborine*
Hepatica	*Hepatica nobilis, var. obtusa*
Hobblebush	*Viburnum lantanoides*

Hophornbeam	*Ostrya virginiana*
Indian cucumber root	*Medeola virginiana*
Indian pipe	*Monotropa uniflora*
Jack-in-the-pulpit	*Arisaema triphyllum*
Japanese barberry	*Berberis thunbergii*
Japanese knotweed	*Polygonum cuspidatum*
Jewelweed	*Impatiens sp.*
Joe-pye weed	*Eutrochium sp.*
Labrador tea	*Chamaedaphne calyculata*
Lady fern	*Athyrium filix-femina*
Large cranberry	*Vaccinium macrocarpon*
Large purple fringed orchid	*Platanthera grandiflora*
Leafy liverworts	*Frullania sp.*
Leatherleaf	*Chamaedaphne calyculata*
Liverwort	Division: *Marchantiophyta*
Longhair sedge	*Carex comosa*
Maidenhair fern	*Adiantum sp.*
Maidenhair spleenwort	*Asplenium trichomanes*
Marsh marigold	*Caltha palustris*
Meadowsweet	*Filipendula ulmaria*
Miterwort	*Mitella diphylla*
Morel (true)	*Morchella sp.*
Morrow's honeysuckle	*Lonicera morrowii*
New England aster	*Symphyotrichum novae-angliae*
Nodding ladies' tresses	*Spiranthes cernua*
Northern pitcher plant	*Sarracenia purpurea*
Northern red oak	*Quercus rubra*
Northern tooth fungus	*Climacodon septentrionale*
Old man's beard	*Clematis vitalba*
One-flowered cancerroot	*Orobanche uniflora*
One-flowered pyrola	*Moneses uniflora*
One-flowered wintergreen	*Moneses uniflora*
Ostrich fern	*Matteuccia struthiopteris*
Painted trillium	*Trillium undulatum*
Pine sap	*Monotropa hypopitys*
Pink earth	*Dibaeis baeomyces*
Pink lady's slipper	*Cypripedium acaule*
Pitcher plant	*Sarracenia purpurea*
Plaintain	*Plantago sp.*
Poison ivy	*Toxicodendron radicans*
Pokeweed	*Phytolacca Americana*
Poplar	*Populus sp.*
Prickly ash	*Zanthoxylum americanum*
Ragged robin	*Lychnis flos-cuculi*
Ram's-head lady's slipper	*Cypripedium arietinum*
Red baneberry	*Actaea rubra*
Red maple	*Acer rubrum*
Red trillium	*Trillium erectum*
Red-osier dogwood	*Cornus sericea*
Rhodora	*Rhododendron canadense*
Rock polypody	*Polypodium virginianum*
Roses	*Rosa sp.*
Rose pogonia	*Pogonia ophioglossoides*
Round-lobed hepatica	*Hepatica americana*
Round-leaved sundew	*Drosera rotundifolia*
Running clubmoss	*Lycopodium clavatum*
Saxifrage	*Saxifraga sp.*
Scouring rush	*Equisetum hymale*
Sedges	Family: Cyperaceae
Sensitive fern	*Onoclea sensibilis*
Shadbush	*Amelanchier sp.*
Shagbark hickory	*Carya ovata*
Sheep laurel	*Kalmia angustifolia*
Shinleaf	*Pyrola elliptica*
Showy lady's slipper	*Cypripedium reginae*
Showy orchis	*Galearis spectabili*
Silky dogwood	*Cornus amomum*
Silver maple	*Acer saccharinum*
Skunk cabbage	*Sympocarpus foetidus*
Small cranberry	*Vaccinium oxycoccos*
Small purple fringed orchid	*Platanthera psycodes*
Smartweed/knotweed	*Polygonum sp.*
Snakeroot	*Ageratina altissima*
Solomon's seal	*Polygonatum biflorum*
Speckled alder	*Alnus incana*
Spreading dogbane	*Apocynum androsaemifolium*
Spring beauty	*Claytonia virginica*
Squirrel corn	*Dicentra canadensis*
Staghorn sumac	*Rhus typhina*
Steeplebush	*Spiraea tomentosa*
Striped maple	*Acer pensylvanicum*

Wild columbine	*Aquilegia canadensis*
Wild cucumber	*Echinocystis lobata*
Wild ginger	*Asarum canadense*
Wild leek	*Allium tricoccum*
Wild strawberry	*Fragaria virginiana*
Willows	*Salix sp.*
Winterberry	*Ilex verticilatta*
Wintergreen	*Gaultheria procumbens*
Witch hazel	*Hamamelis virginiana*
Yellow birch	*Betula alleghaniensis*
Yellow lady's slipper	*Cypripedium pubescens*
Yellow morel	*Morchella esculenta*

Fungi

American Caesar's mushroom	*Amanita jacksonii*
Bearded tooth fungus	*Hericium erinaceus*
Bear's head tooth fungus	*Hericium americanum*
Blue-green cup fungus	*Chlorociboria aeruginascens*
Bolete	Order: Boletales
Cauliflower coral	*Ramaria botrytis*
Caesar's mushroom	*Amanita caesarea*
Chicken of the woods	*Laetiporus sulphureus*
Cinnabar polypore	*Pycnoporus cinnabarinus*
Comb tooth	*Hericium coralloides*
Coral fungi	*Clavarioid*
Dead man's fingers	*Xylaria polymorpha*
Destroying angel	*Amanita bisporigera*
Elegant stinkhorn	*Mutinus elegans*
Elfin saddle	Family: Helvellaceae
Giant puffball	*Calvatia gigantea*
Hemlock varnish shelf	*Ganoderma tsugae*
Jelly fungus	Orders: Tremellales, Auriculariales, Dacrymycetales, Sebacinales
Lobster mushroom	*Hypomyces lactifluorum*
Netted stinkhorn	*Dictyophora duplicate*
Oyster mushroom	*Pleurotus sp.*
Ravenel's stinkhorn	*Phallus ravenelii*
Shaggy mane	*Coprinus comatus*
Stinky squid	*Pseudocolus fusiformis*
Turkey tail	*Trametes versicolor*
Velvety fairy fan	*Spathulariopsis velutipes*
Violet coral	*Clavaria zollingeri*

Sugar maple	*Acer saccharum*
Sweet autumn clematis	*Clematis terniflora*
Sweet fern	*Comptonia peregrine*
Teasel	*Dipsacus sp.*
Thimbleweed	*Anemone cylindrical*
Thistle	Family: Asteraceae
Toothwort	*Cardamine diphylla*
Trailing arbutus	*Epigaea repens*
Trembling aspen	*Populus tremuloides*
Turtlehead	*Chelone glabra*
Twinflower	*Linnaea borealis*
Twisted stalk	*Streptopus amplexifolius*
Viper's bugloss	*Echium vulgare,*
Virgin's bower	*Celmatis virginiana*
Virginia creeper	*Parthenocissus quinquefolia*
Walnut	*Juglans sp.*
Watershield	*Brasenia schreberi*
White ash	*Fraxinus americana*
Wild blueberry	*Vaccinium sp.*
Yellow birch	*Betula alleghaniensis*
White ash	*Fraxinus americana*
White baneberry	*Actaea pachypoda*
White birch	*Betula papyrifera*
White pine	*Pinus strobus*
White rot fungus	*Daedalea unicolor*
Wild blueberry	*Vaccinium sp.*

White pine blister rust	*Cronartium ribicola*
White rot fungus	*Daedalea unicolor*
Witches' butter	*Dacrymyces chrysospermus*
Yellow-orange fly agaric	*Amanita muscaria var. formosa*

Slime Mold

Coral slime	*Ceratiomyxa fruticulosa*
Dog vomit slime mold	*Fuligo septica*
Yellow-fuzz cone Slime	*Hemitrichia clavata*

Invertebrates

Mollusks

| Slug | Class: Gastropoda |
| Snail | Class: Gastropoda |

Annelids

Earthworm	Order: Megadrilacea
Millipede	Class: Diplopoda
Snow worm	Phylum: Annelida
Snow flea	*Hypogastrura nivicola*

Nematodes

| Roundworm | *Baylisascaris procyonis* |

Arthropods

Arachnids

Antmimic spiders	Family: Corrinidae
Black and yellow argiope	*Argiope aurantia*
Black-legged (deer) tick	*Ixodes scapularis*
Crab spider	Family: Thomisidae
Eastern parson spider	*Herpyllus ecclesiasticus*
Eriophyid mite	Family: Eriophyidae
Funnel weaving spiders	Family: Agelenidae
Green long-jawed orbweaver	*Tetragnatha viridis*
Harvestman	Order: Opiliones
Jumping spider	Family: Salticidae
Itch mite	*Sarcoptes scabei*
Lyme disease bacterium	*Borrelia burgdorferi*
Mites	Subclass: Acari
Nursery web spider	Family: Pisauridae
Orb weavers	Family: Aranaidae
Red grasshopper mite	*Eutrombidium sp.*
Sac spiders	Family: Clubionidae
Six-spotted fishing spider	*Dolomedes triton*

| Snow spider | *Tetragnatha sp.* |
| Wolf spider | Family: Lycosidae |

Insects

Abbott's sphinx moth	*Sphecodina abbottii*
Alder flea weevil	*Orchestes testaceus*
Ambush bug	Subfamily: Phymatinae
American lady	*Vanessa virginiensis*
Annual cicada	*Okanagana rimosa*
Ants	Family: Formicidae
Antlion	Family: Myrmeleontidae
Assassin bug	Family: Reduviidae
Backswimmer	Family: Notonectidae
Bald-faced hornet	*Dolichovespula maculata*
Baltimore checkerspot	*Euphydryas phaeton*
Banded bullet gall wasp	*Dryocosmus imbricariae*
Banded longhorn beetle	*Typocerus velutinus*
Beaverpond baskettail dragonfly	*Epitheca canis*
Bed bug	Family: Cimicidae
Bee-like robber flies	*Laphria sp.*
Black saddlebags	*Tramea lacerata*
Black swallowtail	*Papilio polyxenes*
Black-tipped darner	*Aeshna tuberculifera*
Black vine weevil	*Otiorhynchus sulcatus*
Black and yellow mud dauber	*Sceliphron caementarium*
Blackberry knot gall wasp	*Diastrophus nebulosus*
Blackberry psyllid	*Trioza tripunctata*
Blackberry seed gall wasp	*Diastrophus cuscutaeformis*
Blinded sphinx moth	*Paonias excaecatus*
Blueberry stem gall wasp	*Hemadas nubilipennis*
Box elder bug	*Boisea trivitatta*
Brachonid wasp	*Cotesia congregate*
Broad-necked root borer	*Prionus laticollis*
Bronze carabid	*Carabus nemoralis*
Bruce spanworm moth	*Operophtera bruceata*
Bumble bee	*Bombus sp.*
Burying beetle	*Nicrophorus sp.*
Caddisflies	Order: Trichoptera
Calico paint	*Cucullia convexipennis*
Camel cricket	Family: Rhaphidophoridae

438

439

Tri-colored bumble bee	*Bombus ternarius*
Twelve-spotted skimmer	*Libellula pulchella*
Twelve-spotted tiger beetle	*Cicendela duodecimguttata*
Unequal cellophane bee	*Colletes inaequalis*
Variegated meadowhawk	*Sympetrum corruptum*
Viceroy	*Limenitis archippus*
Virginia ctenucha	*Ctenucha virginica*
Wandering glider	*Pantala flavescens*
Water boatman	Family: Corixidae
Water scorpion	Family: Nepidae
Weevils	Superfamily: Curculionoidea
Whirligig beetle	Family: Gyrinida
White-marked tussock moth	*Orgyia leucostigma*
White admiral	*Limentis arthemis subspecies arthemis*
Wild cucumber	*Marah sp.*
Willow beaked gall midge	*Rabdophaga rididae*
Willow leaf beetle	*Calligrapha multipunctata*
Winter crane fly	*Trichocera sp.*
Winter firefly	*Ellychnia corrusca*
Winter stonefly	Family: Taeniopterygidae
Witch hazel cone gall aphid	*Hormaphis hamamelidis*
Wool carder bee	*Anthidium manicatum*
Woolly aphid	Family: Aphididae; subfamily: Eriosomatinae
Woolly adelgid	*Adelges tsugae*
Woolly oak leaf gall wasp	*Callirhytis lanata*
Yellow jacket	*Vespula sp., Dolichovespula sp.*
Yellow-shouldered slug	*Lithacodes fasciola*

Vertebrates

Amphibians

American bullfrog	*Lithobates catesbeianus*
American toad	*Anaxyrus americanus*
Spring peeper	*Pseudacris crucifer*
Eastern newt	*Notophthalmus viridescens*
Eastern red-backed salamander	*Plethodon cinereus*
Four-toed salamander	*Hemidactylium scutatum*
Gray tree frog	*Hyla versicolor*
Green frog	*Lithobates clamitans*
Marbled salamander	*Ambystoma opacum*
Mink frog	*Lithobates septentrionalis*
Northern leopard frog	*Lithobates pipiens*
Pickerel frog	*Rana palustris*
Spotted salamander	*Ambystoma maculatum*
Spring peeper	*Pseudacris crucifer*
Wood frog	*Rana sylvatica*

Reptiles

Eastern box turtle	*Terrapene carolina carolina*
Common garter snake	*Thamnophis sirtalis*
Eastern box turtle	*Terrapene carolina carolina*
Eastern hognose snake	*Heterodon platirhinos*
Eastern milk snake	*Lampropeltis triangulum triangulum*
Northern water snake	*Nerodia sipedon*
Painted turtle	*Chrysemys picta*
Redbelly snake	*Storeria occipitomaculata*
Ring-necked snake	*Diadophis punctatus*
Snapping turtle	*Chelydra serpentine*
Wood turtle	*Glyptemys insculpta*

Birds

American bittern	*Botaurus lentiginosus*
American crow	*Corvus brachyrhynchos*
American goldfinch	*Spinus tristis*
American kestrel	*Falco sparverius*
American redstart	*Setophaga ruticilla*
American robin	*Turdus migratorius*
American wigeon	*Anas americana*
American woodcock	*Scolopax minor*
Bald eagle	*Haliaeetus leucocephalus*
Baltimore oriole	*Icterus galbula*
Barn owl	*Tyto alba*
Barred owl	*Strix varia*
Belted kingfisher	*Megaceryle alcyon*
Blackburnian warbler	*Setophaga fusca*
Black-capped chickadee	*Poecile atricapillus*
Black-throated blue warbler	*Setophaga caerulescens*
Black-throated green warbler	*Setophaga virens*

Common name	Scientific name	Common name	Scientific name
Blue jay	*Cyanocitta cristata*	Hooded merganser	*Lophodytes cucullatus*
Blue-headed vireo	*Vireo solitaries*	Horned lark	*Eremophila alpestris*
Bobolink	*Dolichonyx oryzivorus*	House finch	*Haemorhous mexicanus*
Bohemian waxwing	*Bombycilla garrulus*	House sparrow	*Passer domesticus*
Broad-winged hawk	*Buteo platypterus*	Indigo bunting	*Passerina cyanea*
Brown creeper	*Certhia americana*	Killdeer	*Charadrius vociferus*
Brown-headed cowbird	*Molothrus ater*	Lapland longspur	*Calcarius lapponicus*
Canada goose	*Branta canadensis*	Least sandpiper	*Calidris minutilla*
Cape May warbler	*Setophaga tigrina*	Long-eared owl	*Asio otus*
Cedar waxwing	*Bombycilla cedrorum*	Magnolia warbler	*Setophaga magnolia*
Chimney swift	*Chaetura pelagica*	Mallard	*Anas platyrhynchos*
Chipping sparrow	*Spizella passerina*	Mourning dove	*Zenaida macroura*
Cliff swallow	*Petrochelidon pyrrhonota*	Northern bobwhite	*Colinus virginianus*
		Northern cardinal	*Cardinalis cardinalis*
Common goldeneye	*Bucephala clangula*	Northern flicker	*Colaptes auratus*
Common grackle	*Quiscalus quiscula*	Northern harrier	*Circus cyaneus*
Common loon	*Gavia immer*	Northern mockingbird	*Mimus polyglottos*
Common merganser	*Mergus merganser*	Northern saw-whet owl	*Aegolius acadicus*
Common poorwill	*Phalaenoptilus nuttallii*	Northern shrike	*Lanius excubitor*
Common raven	*Corvus corax*	Northern waterthrush	*Parkesia noveboracensis*
Common redpoll	*Carduelis flammea*	Osprey	*Pandion haliaetus*
Common yellowthroat	*Geothlypis trichas*	Ovenbird	*Seiurus aurocapilla*
Cooper's hawk	*Accipiter cooperii*	Pied-billed grebe	*Podilymbus podiceps*
Dark-eyed junco	*Junco hyemalis*	Pileated woodpecker	*Dryocopus pileatus*
Downy woodpecker	*Picoides pubescens*	Pine grosbeak	*Pinicola enucleator*
Eastern bluebird	*Sialia sialis*	Pine siskin	*Carduelis pinus*
Eastern kingbird	*Tyrannus tyrannus*	Pine warbler	*Setophaga pinus*
Eastern meadowlark	*Sturnella magna*	Purple finch	*Haemorhous purpureus*
Eastern phoebe	*Sayornis phoebe*	Red-breasted nuthatch	*Sitta canadensis*
Eastern screech owl	*Megascops asio*	Red crossbill	*Loxia curvirostra*
Eastern towhee	*Pipilo erythrophthalmus*	Red-shouldered hawk	*Buteo lineatus*
European starling	*Sturnus vulgaris*	Red-tailed hawk	*Buteo jamaicensis*
Evening grosbeak	*Coccothraustes vespertinus*	Red-winged blackbird	*Agelaius phoeniceus*
		Ring-necked duck	*Aythya collaris*
Giant egret	*Ardea alba*	Ring-necked pheasant	*Phasianus colchicus*
Golden-crowned kinglet	*Regulus satrapa*	Rose-breasted grosbeak	*Pheucticus ludovicianus*
Gray catbird	*Dumetella carolinensis*	Ruby-crowned kinglet	*Regulus calendula*
Great blue heron	*Ardea herodias*	Ruby-throated hummingbird	*Archilochus colubris*
Great egret	*Ardea alba*	Ruffed grouse	*Bonasa umbellus*
Great horned owl	*Bubo virginianus*	Sharp-shinned hawk	*Accipiter striatus*
Greater yellowlegs	*Tringa melanoleuca*	Short-eared owl	*Asio flammeus*
Green heron	*Butorides virescens*	Snow bunting	*Plectrophenax nivalis*
Hairy woodpecker	*Picoides villosus*	Snow goose	*Chen caerulescens*
Hermit thrush	*Catharus guttatus*	Snowy owl	*Bubo scandiacus*
Herring gull	*Larus argentatus*	Solitary sandpiper	*Tringa solitaria*
Hoary redpoll	*Carduelis hornemanni*	Song sparrow	*Melospiza melodia*

Spotted sandpiper	*Actitis macularius*
Swainson's thrush	*Catharus ustulatus*
Swamp sparrow	*Melospiza georgiana*
Tree swallow	*Tachycineta bicolor*
Tufted titmouse	*Baeolophus bicolor*
Turkey vulture	*Cathartes aura*
Veery	*Catharus fuscescens*
Warbling vireo	*Vireo gilvus*
Whip-poor-will	*Caprimulgus vociferus*
White-breasted nuthatch	*Sitta carolinensis*
White-crowned sparrow	*Zonotrichia leucophrys*
White-throated sparrow	*Zonotrichia albicollis*
White-winged crossbill	*Loxia leucoptera*
Wild turkey	*Meleagris gallopavo*
Wilson's snipe	*Gallinago delicata*
Wood duck	*Aix sponsa*
Yellow warbler	*Setophaga petechial*
Yellow-bellied sapsucker	*Sphyrapicus varius*
Yellow-rumped warbler	*Dendroica coronata*

Mammals

American red squirrel	*Tamiasciurus hudsonicus*
Beaver	*Castor canadensis*
Big brown bat	*Eptesicus fuscus*
Black bear	*Ursus americanus*
Bobcat	*Lynx rufus*
Canada lynx	*Lynx canadensis*
Deer mouse	*Peromyscus maniculatus*
Eastern chipmunk	*Tamias striatus*
Eastern cottontail	*Sylvilagus floridanus*
Eastern coyote	*Canus latrans var*
Eastern gray squirrel	*Sciurus carolinensis*
Eastern mole	*Scalopus aquaticus*
Fisher	*Martes pennant*
Gray fox	*Urocyon cinereoargenteus*
Gray squirrel	*Sciurus carolinensis*
Hairy-tailed mole	*Parascalops breweri*
Little brown bat	*Myotis lucifugus*
Long-tailed weasel	*Mustela frenata*
Meadow jumping mouse	*Zapus hudsonius*
Meadow vole	*Microtus pennsylvanicus*
Mink	*Neovison vison*
Moose	*Alces alces*
Muskrat	*Ondatra zibethicus*

New England cottontail	*Sylvilagus transitionalis*
North American porcupine	*Erethizon dorsatum*
North American river otter	*Lontra canadensis*
Northern flying squirrel	*Glaucomys sabrinus*
Northern short-tailed shrew	*Blarina brevicauda*
Porcupine	*Erethizon dorsatum*
Raccoon	*Procyon lotor*
Rats	*Rattus sp.*
Red fox	*Vulpes vulpes*
Short-tailed weasel/ermine	*Mustela erminea*
Snowshoe hare	*Lepus americanus*
Southern flying squirrel	*Glaucomys volans*
Star-nosed mole	*Condylura cristata*
Striped skunk	*Mephitis mephitis*
Virginia opossum	*Didelphis virginiana*
White-footed mouse	*Peromyscus leucopus*
White-tailed deer	*Odocoileus virginianus*
Woodchuck	*Marmota monax*
Woodland jumping mouse	*Napaeozapus insignis*

appendix b

Recommended Resources for Further Reading

AMPHIBIANS
Books
Bishop, Sherman. *Handbook of Salamanders.* Ithaca and New York: Comstock Publishing Co., Inc. 1943.

Conant, Roger, and Joseph Collins. *A Field Guide to Reptiles and Amphibians, 3rd Edition—Peterson Field Guides.* Boston and New York: Houghton Mifflin, 1998.

Tyning, Tom. *A Guide to Amphibians and Reptiles—Stokes Nature Guides.* Boston, Toronto, London: Little, Brown and Company, 1990.

Audio
Cornell Laboratory of Ornithology. *Voices of the Night: The Calls of the Frogs and Toads of Eastern North America.* (CD). MacAulay Library (www.macaulaylibrary.org).

Elliott, Lang. *The Calls of Frogs and Toads.* (Book & CD) Mechanicsburg, PA: Stackpole Books, 2004.

———. *The Frogs and Toads of North America: A Comprehensive Guide to Their Identification, Behavior, and Calls.* (Book & CD) New York: Mariner Books, 2009.

ANIMAL SIGN
Elbroch, Mark. *Bird Tracks & Sign.* Mechanicsburg, PA: Stackpole Books, 2001.

———. *Mammal Tracks & Sign.* Mechanicsburg, PA: Stackpole Books, 2003.

Rezendes, Paul. *Tracking & the Art of Seeing: How to Read Animal Tracks and Sign.* New York: HarperCollins, 1999.

BEES
Tautz, Jurgen. *The Buzz about Bees: Biology of a Superorganism.* New York: Springer, 2009.

Wilson, Joseph and Olivia Carril. *The Bees In Your Backyard.* Princeton University Press, 2016.

BEETLES
Evans, Arthur V. *Beetles of Eastern North America.* Princeton University Press, 2014.

BIRDS
Field Guides
Brinkley, Edward, and Craig Tufts. *National Wildlife Federation Field Guide to Birds of North America.* New York and London: Sterling Publishing, 2007.

Crossley, Richard. *The Crossley ID Guide: Eastern Birds.* Princeton University Press, 2011.

Dunn, Jon and Jonathan Alderfer. *National Geographic Field Guide to the Birds of North America,* 5th Edition. Washington, D.C.: National Geographic, 2006.

Elbroch, Mark. *Bird Tracks & Sign: A Guide to North American Species.* Mechanicsburg, PA: Stackpole Books, 2001.

Hanson, Thor. *Feathers: The Evolution of a Natural Miracle.* New York: Basic Books, 2012.

Kaufman, Ken. *Kaufman Field Guide to Birds of North America.* New York: Houghton Mifflin, 2000.

O'Brien, Michael, Richard Crossley, and Kevin Karlson. *The Shorebird Guide.* Houghton Mifflin Harcourt, 2006.

Pasquier, Roger. *Watching Birds: An Introduction to Ornithology.* Boston: Houghton Mifflin, 1977.

Peterson, Roger Tory. *A Field Guide to the Birds of Eastern and Central North America, 5th Edition.* New York: Houghton Mifflin, 2002.

Scott, S. David; McFarland, Casey. *Bird Feathers: A Guide to North American Species.* Mechanicsburg, PA: Stackpole Books, 2010.

Sibley, David. *The Sibley Field Guide to Birds of Eastern North America*. New York: Alfred A. Knopf, 2003.

Stephenson, Tom, and Scott Whittle. *The Warbler Guide*. Princeton University Press, 2013.

Terres, John K. *The Audubon Society Encyclopedia of North American Birds*. New York: Alfred A. Knopf, 1980.

Audio Resources

Borror, Donald. *Common Bird Songs*. Mineola, NY: Dover Publications, 2003.

Cornell Laboratory of Ornithology. *Guide to Bird Sounds*. Cornell Laboratory of Ornithology, 1985.

Elliott, Lang. *Music of the Birds—A Celebration of Bird Song*. (Book & CD) Boston & New York: Houghton Mifflin, 1999.

Elliott, Lang, and Marie Read. *Common Birds and Their Songs*. (Book & CD) Boston & New York: Houghton Mifflin, 1998.

Kroodsma, Donald. *The Singing Life of Birds*. (Book & CD) Boston & New York: Houghton Mifflin, 2005.

Lawson, Robert, and Richard Walton. *Birding by Ear: Guide to Bird Song Identification*. (Booklet & CD) Boston & New York: Houghton Mifflin Harcourt, 2002.

———. *More Birding by Ear: Eastern and Central*. (Booklet & CD) Boston & New York: Houghton Mifflin Harcourt, 2000.

Peterson, Roger Tory, ed. *A Field Guide to Bird Songs of Eastern and Central North America*. Boston & New York: Houghton Mifflin Harcourt, 1999.

Stokes, Donald. *Stokes Field Guide to Bird Song (Eastern)*. Hatchet Audio, 1997.

BIRD NESTS

Harrison, Hal. *A Field Guide to Birds' Nests*. (The Peterson Field Guide Series). Boston: Houghton Mifflin, 1975.

Headstrom, Richard. *A Complete Field Guide to Nests in the United States*. New York: Ives Washburn, Inc., 1970.

BUTTERFLIES

Brock, Jim P., and Kenn Kaufman. *Butterflies of North America*. Kaufman Focus Guides. New York: Houghton Mifflin, 2003.

Glassberg, Jeffrey. *Butterflies Through Binoculars*. Oxford University Press, 1993.

CATERPILLARS

Allen, Thomas, Jim Brock, and Jeffrey Glassberg. *Caterpillars in the Field and Garden: A Field Guide to the Butterfly Caterpillars of North America*. Oxford University Press, 2005.

Wagner, David. *Caterpillars of Eastern North America*. Princeton University Press, 2005.

———. *Owlet Caterpillars of Eastern North America*. Princeton University Press, 2011.

DRAGONFLIES AND DAMSELFLIES

Lam, Ed. *Damselflies of the Northeast*. Forest Hills, New York: Biodiversity Books, 2004.

Nikula, Blair, Jennifer Loose, and Matthew Burne. *A Field Guide to the Dragonflies and Damselflies of Massachusetts*. Massachusetts Division of Fisheries & Wildlife, Natural Heritage & Endangered Species Program, 2003.

Paulson, Dennis. *Dragonflies and Damselflies of the East*. Princeton University Press, 2012.

FERNS

Cobb, Boughton, Elizabeth Farnsworth, and Cheryl Lowe. *A Field Guide to Ferns and Their Related Families*. Boston & New York: Houghton Mifflin Harcourt, 2005.

Moran, Robbin C., and Alice F. Tryon. *The Ferns and Allied Plants of New England*. Lincoln, MA: Massachusetts Audubon Society, 1997.

FLIES

Marshall, Stephen. *Flies: The Natural History and Diversity of Diptera*. Richmond Hill, Ontario: Firefly Books, 2012.

FLOWERING PLANTS

Newcomb, Lawrence. *Newcomb's Wildflower Guide*. Boston, New York, Toronto & London: Little, Brown and Co., 1977.

Sanders, Jack. *The Secrets of Wildflowers*. Guilford, CT: Globe Pequot, 2003.

FRESHWATER INVERTEBRATES

Voshell, J. Reese. *A Guide to Common Freshwater Invertebrates of North America*. Blacksburg, VA: The McDonald & Woodward Publishing Company, 2002.

FUNGI

Lincoff, Gary. *National Aububon Society Field Guide to North American Mushrooms*. New York: Alfred A. Knopf, 1981.

Pacioni, Giovanni. *Simon & Schuster's Guide to Mushrooms*. New York, London & Toronto: Simon & Schuster, 1981.

HABITAT

Benyus, Janine. *The Field Guide to Wildlife Habitats of the Eastern United States*. New York & London: Simon & Schuster, 1989.

Thompson, Elizabeth, and Eric Sorenson. *Wetland, Woodland, Wildland—A Guide to the Natural Communities of Vermont*. Vermont Dept. of Fish and Wildlife and The Nature Conservancy, 2000.

INSECTS

Borror, Donald, and Richard White. *A Field Guide to Insects*. Boston & New York: Houghton Mifflin Harcourt, 1998.

Charney, Noha and Charley Eiseman. *Tracks & Sign of Insects and Other Invertebrates*. Mechanicsburg, PA: Stackpole Books, 2010.

Elliott, Lang, and Wil Hershberger. *The Songs of Insects*. Boston & New York: Houghton Mifflin Harcourt, 2007.

Holm, Heather. *Pollinators of Native Plants: Attract, Observe and Identify Pollinators and Beneficial Insects with Native Plants*. Pollination Press, 2014.

Kaufman, Kenn. *Kaufman Field Guide to Insects of North America*. Boston & New York: Houghton Mifflin Harcourt, 2007.

Marshall, Stephen. *Insects—Their Natural History and Diversity*. Buffalo, NY: Firefly Books, 2006

National Audubon Society. *Field Guide to North American Insects and Spiders*. New York: Alfred A. Knopf, 1980.

White, Richard, and Roger Tory Peterson. *Beetles*. (Peterson Field Guides). Boston & New York: Houghton Mifflin Harcourt, 1998.

LICHENS

Brodo, Irwin M. *Lichens of North America*. New Haven, CT: Yale University Press, 2001.

MAMMALS

Elbroch, Mark. *Mammal Tracks & Sign: A Guide to North American Species*. Mechanicsburg, PA: Stackpole Books, 2003.

Feldhamer, George, Bruce Thompson, and Joseph Chapman, eds. *Wild Mammals of North America*. Baltimore & London: The Johns Hopkins University Press, 2003.

Godin, Alfred J. *Wild Mammals of New England*. Baltimore & London: The Johns Hopkins University Press, 1977.

Naughton, Donna. *The Natural History of Canadian Mammals, 2nd Edition*. University of Toronto Press, Scholarly Publishing Division, 2012.

Reid, Fiona. *Peterson Field Guide to Mammals of North America: Fourth Edition* (Peterson Field Guides). Boston: Houghton Mifflin Harcourt, 2006.

Roze, Uldis. *The North American Porcupine, 2nd Edition*. Ithaca & London: Comstock Publishing Associates, Cornell University Press, 2009.

Schwartz, Charles, and Albert Franzmann, eds. *Ecology and Management of the North American Moose* (Zoo and Aquarium Biology and Conservation Series). Washington, D.C.: Smithsonian Books, 1998.

Whitaker, John, and William Hamilton. *Mammals of the Eastern United States*. Ithaca & London: Comstock Publishing Associates, Cornell University Press, 1998.

MOTHS

Covel, Charles. *A Field Guide to Moths of Eastern North America*. Martinville, VA: Virginia Museum of Natural History, 2001.

Himmelman, John. *Discovering Moths: Nighttime Jewels in Your Own Backyard*. Camden, ME: Down East Books, 2002.

NATURAL HISTORY INTERPRETATION

Eastman, John. *Birds of Field and Shore*. Mechanicsburg, PA: Stackpole Books, 2000.

———. *Birds of Forest, Yard, & Thicket*. Mechanicsburg, PA: Stackpole Books, 1997.

———. *Birds of Lake, Pond and Marsh*. Mechanicsburg, PA: Stackpole Books, 1999.

———. *The Book of Field and Roadside*. Mechanicsburg, PA: Stackpole Books, 2003.

———. *The Book of Forest and Thicket*. Mechanicsburg, PA: Stackpole Books, 1992.

———. *The Book of Swamp and Bog*. Mechanicsburg, PA: Stackpole Books, 1995.

Elliott, Lang. *A Guide to Night Songs: The Nighttime Sounds of 60 Mammals, Birds, Amphibians and Insects*. Mechanicsburg, PA: Stackpole Books, 2004.

Haskell, David George. *The Forest Unseen: A Year's Watch in Nature*. Penguin Books, 2013.

Heinrich, Bernd. *Life Everlasting: The Animal Way of Death*. New York: Mariner Books, 2013.

———. *Summer World*. New York: HarperCollins.

———. *Winter World*. New York: HarperCollins.

Nardi, James. *Life in the Soil: A Guide for Naturalists and Gardeners*. University of Chicago Press, 2007.

Wessels, Tom. *Reading the Forested Landscape: A Natural History of New England*. Woodstock, VT: The Countryman Press, 2005.

NEW ENGLAND NATURAL HISTORY

DeGraaf, Richard M., and Mariko Yamasaki. *New England Wildlife: Habitat, Natural History, and Distribution*. Hanover & London: University Press of New England, 2001.

REPTILES

Conant, Roger, and Joseph Collins. *A Field Guide to Reptiles and Amphibians* (Peterson Field Guides). Boston & New York: Houghton Mifflin, 1988.

Klemens, Michael. *Amphibians and Reptiles of Connecticut and Adjacent Regions*. State Geological and Natural History Survey of Connecticut, Bulletin 112.

Krulikowski, Linda. *Snakes of New England*. Old Lyme, CT: LuvLife Publishing, 2004.

SKULLS AND BONES

Elbroch, Mark. *Animal Skulls—A Guide to North American Species*. Mechanicsburg, PA: Stackpole Books, 2006.

Wolniewicz, Richard. *Field Guide to Skulls and Bones of Mammals of the Northeastern United States, Vol. 1 and 2*. Magnolia, MA: Richard Wolniewicz, 2001.

SPIDERS

Foelix, Rainer. *Biology of Spiders*. New York & Oxford: Oxford University Press, 1996.

Ubick, Darrell, Pierre Paquin, Paula E. Cushing, and Vince Roth, eds. *Spiders of North America: An Identification Manual*. American Arachnological Society, 2005.

TREES

Farrar, John Laird. *Trees of the Northern United States and Canada*. Iowa State Press, 1995.

Foster, David. *Hemlock: A Forest Giant on the Edge*. New Haven, CT: Yale University Press, 2014.

Tudge, Colin. *The Tree*. New York: Crown Publishers, 2005.

VERNAL POOLS

Colburn, Elizabeth. *Vernal Pools*. Blacksburg, VA: The McDonald & Woodward Publishing Co., 2004.

Kenney, Leo, and Matthew Burne. *A Field Guide to the Animals of Vernal Pools*. Westborough, MA: Massachusetts Division of Fisheries & Wildlife, Natural Heritage & Endangered Species Program, 2000.

index

The End.